MOTIVATION AND AGENCY

MOTIVATION
and
AGENCY

Alfred R. Mele

OXFORD
UNIVERSITY PRESS

2003

OXFORD
UNIVERSITY PRESS

Oxford   New York
Auckland   Bangkok   Buenos Aires   Cape Town   Chennai
Dar es Salaam   Delhi   Hong Kong   Istanbul   Karachi   Kolkata
Kuala Lumpur   Madrid   Melbourne   Mexico City   Mumbai   Nairobi
São Paulo   Shanghai   Taipei   Tokyo   Toronto

Copyright © 2003 by Oxford University Press, Inc.

Published by Oxford University Press, Inc.
198 Madison Avenue, New York, New York 10016

www.oup.com

Oxford is a registered trademark of Oxford University Press

Library of Congress Cataloging-in-Publication Data
Mele, Alfred R., 1951–
Motivation and agency / Alfred R. Mele.
   p. cm.
Includes bibliographical references
ISBN 0-19-515617-X
1. Agent (Philosophy) 2. Motivation (Psychology) I. Title.
BD450 .M383 2002
128'.4—dc21   2002025751

9 8 7 6 5 4 3 2 1

Printed in the United States of America
on acid-free paper

For my children (in alphabetical order): Al, Angela, and Nick

Preface

Although philosophers of mind and action share a serious interest with moral philosophers in some deep and exciting philosophical topics, the level of cross fertilization is not nearly as high as I think it should be. One such topic is motivation; another is human agency. They are the topics of this book. What I seek are answers to a web of questions about motivation and human agency that take into account important work in the philosophy of mind and action and moral philosophy, as well as some relevant empirical work in such fields as the psychology of motivation, social psychology, physiological psychology, and neurobiology. The questions include the following: Will an acceptable moral theory make warranted conceptual or metaphysical demands (of a kind to be identified) on a theory of human motivation? Where does the motivational power of practical reasoning lie? How are reasons for action related to motivation? What do motivational explanations of different kinds have in common? What is it to decide to do something? What is it for an attitude essentially to encompass motivation to act? What is it for one such attitude to have more motivational force or strength than another? What room will an acceptable view of the connection between motivational strength and intentional action leave for self-controlled agency? Is it likely that a proper account of motivated, goal-directed action will be a causal account? Can a causal perspective on the nature and explanation of action accommodate human agency par excellence? What emerges from my answers is a view of human agency.

Work on this book was supported by a 1999–2000 NEH Fellowship for College Teachers while I was still a member of the faculty of Davidson College, a place whose charms are unforgettable. Some of the work was done while I was a visiting fellow in the Philosophy Program (June through August 1999) in the Research School of Social

Sciences at the Australian National University (ANU). I am grateful to the NEH, the ANU, and Davidson College for their past support and to Florida State University for the support it provides now.

Portions of this book derive from some of my published articles. Parts of the introduction and chapters 1 and 6 first appeared in "Motivation: Essentially Motivation-Constituting Attitudes," *Philosophical Review* 104 (© 1995 Cornell University; material reprinted by permission of the publisher), and part of section 4 of chapter 1 borrows from "Noninstrumental Rationalizing," *Pacific Philosophical Quarterly* 79 (© 1998 University of Southern California and Blackwell Publishers). Chapter 2 is an augmented, refined, and empirically updated version of "Goal-Directed Action: Teleological Explanations, Causal Theories, and Deviance," *Philosophical Perspectives* 14 (2000). Much of section 2 of chapter 3 derives from "Acting for Reasons and Acting Intentionally," *Pacific Philosophical Quarterly* 73 (© 1992 University of Southern California and Blackwell Publishers). Chapter 4 is a distant descendent of "Motivational Internalism: The Powers and Limits of Practical Reasoning," *Philosophia* 19 (1989; material reprinted by permission of Asa Kasher, ed.); some elements of the original article survive in it. Chapter 5 is a beefed-up, refined version of "Internalist Moral Cognitivism and Listlessness," *Ethics* 106 (© 1996 by the University of Chicago Press; all rights reserved). Chapter 7, a thorough revision of "Motivational Strength," *Noûs* 32 (1998), develops important extensions and refinements of the view advanced in the original article. Chapters 8 and 9 are revisions, respectively, of "Strength of Motivation and Being in Control: Learning from Libet," *American Philosophical Quarterly* 34 (1997), and "Deciding to Act," *Philosophical Studies* 100 (© 2000 Kluwer Academic Publishers).

Despite my having borrowed from my published work, my views on certain questions about motivation and agency have evolved much more than I expected. The main cause was my grappling with how to work scattered parts of the picture into a unified whole.

I am indebted to a great many people for comments on parts of this book. Undoubtedly, this list is incomplete: George Ainslie, Jay Atlas, Robert Audi, Bruce Aune, Kurt Baier, Joe Beatty, Helen Beebee, John Bishop, Karin Boxer, David Braddon-Mitchell, Myles Brand, Michael Bratman, Randy Clarke, Jonathan Dancy, Steve Darwall, Doug Ehring, Jim Friedrich, Andre Gallois, Steve Gardiner, Eve Garrard, Josh Gert, Grant Gillett, Irwin Goldstein, Dorothy Grover, John Heil, Mark Heller, Richard Holton, Brad Hooker, Jen Hornsby, Frank Jackson, Karen Jones, Corey Juhl, Jeanette Kennett, Vera Koffman, Rae Langton, Michael Levine, Kirk Ludwig, Jack Lyons, Cindy Macdonald, Graham Macdonald, Mike Martin, Hugh McCann, Matt McGrath, Michael McKenna, David McNaughton, Maria Morales, Paul Moser, Dana Nelkin, Natika Newton, David Owens, Charles Pigden, Piers Rawling, Rainer Reisenzein, Mike Ridge, Dave Robb, Abe Roth, Scott Sehon, Mike Smith, Michael Smith, Peter Smith, Lance Stell, Bob Stern, Rowland Stout, Steve Sverdlik, Bill Talbott, Raimo Tuomela, Art Walker, Bob Ware, George Wilson, Nicole Wyatt, Gideon Yaffe, and Nick Zangwill. Peter Hanowell provided efficient, cheerful assistance with numerous tasks, and Diana Palmieri helped with some research on neurobiology.

Drafts of sections or chapters were presented at the Australian National University, Bielefeld University, Birkbeck College, Ghent University, Monash University, Southern Methodist University, Texas A&M University, the Universidade Nova de Lisboa, Wake Forest University, the World Congress of Philosophy (Boston, 1998), and the Universities of Auckland, Canterbury, Durham, Edinburgh, Florida, Georgia, Glasgow, Helsinki, Idaho, Keele, Manchester, Minnesota-Morris, Otago, Reading, Sheffield, Stirling, Texas at Austin, Western Australia, and Zurich. I am grateful to my audiences for their help.

My children, to whom this book is dedicated, have enriched my life beyond expression. Without that enrichment, I don't know whether I'd be motivated to do much of anything.

Contents

MOTIVATION AND AGENCY

Introduction

Philosophers with very different theoretical concerns seek to understand motivation, a topic of much discussion in the philosophy of mind and action and in moral philosophy. The term "motivation" appears prominently in theories about how purposive behavior is to be explained; in efforts to clarify the nature, structure, and power of practical reasoning; in work on the concept of a reason for action; in debates about the constitution of moral judgments and moral reasons; and in a related controversy over moral realism. In this book, I explore the nature of motivation and its place in explaining not only intentional behavior in general—including behavior in the moral sphere and such nonovert behavior as practical reasoning and decision making—but also the acquisition of such states of mind as desires, intentions, and beliefs. With motivation as my primary focus, I develop a view of human agency.

Here are six popular theses in the philosophical and psychological literature on motivation:

1. Motivation is present in the animal kingdom but does not extend throughout it.[1]
2. Motivated beings have a capacity to represent goals and means to goals.
3. A motivation-encompassing attitude may have either a goal or a means as its object.
4. Motivation varies in strength.
5. The stronger an agent's motivation to A is, in comparison to the agent's motivation for alternative courses of action, the more likely the agent is to A, other things being equal.[2]
6. Whenever agents act intentionally, there is something they are effectively motivated to do.[3]

Divergent conceptions of motivation may be at work in philosophical thought about motivational matters. My concern in this book is a notion of motivation consistent with (among other things) these six claims. Readers who accept all six claims are likely to be more interested in the result than those who do not, but I conjecture that most readers do accept all of these claims, on some reading or other. Also, readers who reject one or more of these theses or who believe that no acceptable conception of motivation is consistent with all of them will be offered good reason to change their minds!

1. Preview

This book divides pretty naturally into four main parts. Part I, "Motivation and Action," comprises chapters 1 and 2. Chapter 1 prepares the way for subsequent chapters by introducing some semitechnical terminology and some important distinctions that facilitate forging ahead with the central project of this book. In chapter 2, I argue for a constraint on a proper theory of motivation—roughly, that proper motivational explanations of goal-directed actions are *causal* explanations.

Chapters 3 through 6 make up part II, "Motivation and Normativity." Some claims that are driven by normative considerations—prominently, some claims about the nature of agents' reasons, about practical reasoning, and about moral agency—are at odds with the position I defend on the place of motivation in human agency. In part II, these claims are criticized in the course of developing my positive view, but I also argue that the view I defend does not exclude nearly as much as it may seem to in normative spheres and that what it does exclude ought to be rejected. Chapters 3, 4, and 5 tackle questions about connections between motivation and normativity. Their central topics are, respectively, the connection between motivation and reasons for action, the motivational power of practical reasoning, and moral motivation. Chapter 6, building partly on results of preceding chapters, offers an analysis of a paradigmatic kind of motivational attitude.

Part III, "Strength and Control," develops an account of the motivational strength of desires of a certain important kind (chapter 7) and explores the place of motivation and motivational strength in the sphere of self-controlled agency (chapter 8). Although it is often taken for granted that desires differ in motivational strength, some philosophers are deeply skeptical of the idea. Careful attention to their main objections will remove obstacles to a broader acceptance of a promising causal approach to understanding human agency and promote a better grasp of the nature and functions of motivation and motivational strength. One worry about the idea that desires vary in strength is that combining it with a causal theory about how actions are to be explained has the consequence that we are at the mercy of whatever desire happens to be strongest when we act. I have argued elsewhere that this worry is unfounded (Mele 1987, ch. 5; 1992e, ch. 4; 1995a, ch. 3; 1996b). Chapter 8, which benefits from some well-known, intriguing experiments by physiologist Benjamin Libet, provides a new route to that conclusion.

Part IV, "Decision, Agency, and Belief," offers an account of decision making (chapter 9), defends my causal conception of human agency in response to an objection against a "standard" causal view (chapter 10), and wraps things up with a discussion of motivationally biased belief and of what motivational explanations of various kinds have in common (chapter 11). Practical decisions are motivated decisions and play a role in generating a range of intentional actions. They also have been regarded as central to a distinctively human form of agency. For these reasons and others, it is important to understand what practical deciding is and how practical decisions may be explained. Reacting to the objection I consider in chapter 10 against "the standard [causal] story of human action" (Velleman 1992, p. 461)—even though I argue that the objection is misguided and does not undermine the standard story—provides me with the opportunity to reinforce the significance of aspects of my own causal conception of human agency that emerge earlier in the book and to show more fully and explicitly how that conception applies to the upper range of human action. The focus of chapter 11 is the bearing of motivationally biased belief on the project of producing an account of motivational explanation.

2. A Perspective on Action

A human agent is a human being who acts. A major part of what a theory of human agency should provide is a framework for explaining intentional human actions. Among our intentional actions, it seems, are rational and irrational actions, morally proper and improper actions, actions in which our involvement as agents is very impressive, and simple, routine actions. There are intentional mental actions—for example, solving chess problems in one's head and deliberating about what to do—and overt intentional actions, actions that essentially involve peripheral bodily motion. A proper theory of human agency will have actions of all of these kinds in its sights. A full-blown theory of human agency will also take a stand on what it is to be a free or autonomous agent and on whether any human agents are free or autonomous. I have already written a book on autonomous agency (Mele 1995a), and I will not directly tackle that topic again now. However, I can say that my position on autonomous agency is consistent with the view of human agency presented here.

The view of human agency developed in this book is a causal one. In chapter 2, I offer a partial defense of a popular causal perspective on intentional action that I defended in a previous book (Mele 1992e). At the heart of this perspective—I dub it "perspective *P*"—are a pair of theses: (1) all intentional actions are *caused* (but not necessarily deterministically so);[4] (2) in the case of any intentional action, a causal explanation framed partly in terms of *mental* items (events or states), including motivation-encompassing attitudes, is in principle available. Given my purposes in this book, I can safely be somewhat relaxed about the interpretation of the second thesis. On one reading, the idea is that the relevant mental items are realized in physical states and events that are important causes of intentional actions, and—owing to the particular relations of the mental items to the realizing physical items, to appropriate counterfactual connections between the mental items and the actions, and to the truth of relevant psychological and psychophysical generalizations—the mental items properly enter into causal explanations of the actions (Mele 1992e, ch. 2; cf. Jackson 2000 and Jackson and Pettit 1988, 1990). Perhaps a more ambitious construal of the thesis will work, one lodging causal powers directly in mental features of physical items; but that is a topic for another time. In this book (except where I indicate otherwise), claims about the causal powers and roles of attitudes should be read, disjunctively, as claims about the causal powers and roles of the physical realizers of the attitudes *or* of the attitudes themselves (qua attitudes). Fortunately, a fruitful philosophical investigation of motivation does not require a resolution of the mind-body problem.

An approach to understanding behavior that features mental items in causal roles is by no means peculiar to philosophers. As psychologist Douglas Mook reports, the leading, "cognitive" approach to motivation in his field investigates "theories about internal *mental* operations as part of the *causation* of behavior" (1987, p. 53; my emphasis). And as Huw Price, a critic of perspective *P*, remarks, this perspective "has enormous application in contemporary thought. It is widely taken for granted by economists and decision theorists, by psychologists and cognitive scientists, and . . . by most philosophers" (1989, p. 119).

Perspective *P* is an alternative to at least three others. In one (*P1*), intentional actions, or some of them (e.g., *free* actions), are not caused and are to be given noncausal explanations partly in terms of mental items (see, e.g., Melden 1961). In another (*P2*), all intentional actions may be caused, but explanations in terms of such things as beliefs and desires (normally) are noncausal explanations (see, e.g., Peters 1958 and Wilson 1989, 1997).[5] In yet another (*P3*), intentional actions are caused, but mental states and events are involved neither in the causation nor in the explanation of intentional actions (see, e.g., Skinner 1953). Obviously, proponents of these perspectives are not egalitarian about them; lively, instructive debates have been staged over their relative merits.

All four perspectives face familiar problems. Perspective *P* is usually embraced as part of a naturalistic stand on agency according to which mental items that play a causal/explanatory role in intentional conduct bear some important relation to physical states and events. Relations that have been explored include identity (both type-type and token-token) and various kinds of supervenience. Each relation faces difficulties, and some philosophers have argued that anything less than type-type identity (which encounters familiar problems) will fail to avert an unacceptable epiphenomenalism.[6] There is a general problem about the causal relevance of the mental in a naturalistic framework. This is not to say, however, that the problem is insoluble.[7]

Theorists attracted to *P1* or *P2* face the difficult task of developing an adequate notion of *noncausal* explanation of action in terms of mental items. Four decades ago, Donald Davidson (1963) issued a challenge to proponents of these perspectives: given that when we act intentionally we act for reasons, provide an account of the reasons *for which* we act that does not treat those reasons as figuring in the causation of the relevant behavior! Depending on how one understands reasons for action, one might instead frame the challenge in terms of havings or apprehensions of reasons. And one who worries about the causal relevance of the mental may frame it disjunctively, in terms of (havings or apprehensions of) reasons *or* neural realizations thereof. In chapter 2, I argue that the most detailed attempts to meet this challenge fail in instructive ways.

A major problem for *P3*, as part of a *behaviorist* perspective, is standard fare in textbooks on motivational psychology. An animal sometimes behaves in very different ways under exactly similar external conditions. This indicates that the link between stimulus and response is mediated by unobserved internal states (Mook 1987, pp. 58–59). Considerable support for the hypothesis that, even in such animals as rats, relevant internal states include mental representations of goals and means may be found in many discussions of animal learning (see, e.g., Toates 1986, chs. 6 and 7). Of course, *P3* is not solely a behaviorist perspective. Old-style epiphenomenalism (i.e., the combination of epiphenomenalism and substance dualism) may also endorse it; but a dangling mental life, one causally and explanatorily inert with respect to overt behavior, is an unattractive prospect.

3. Flexibility: A Mark of Motivation

Although my primary concern with motivation is ontic rather than epistemic, a brief look at a popular criterion in motivational psychology for the warranted attribution of motivation will prove instructive. Attention to the criterion brings out some noteworthy commonalities among motivational psychology, so-called folk psychology, and what sometimes is termed "moral psychology" or "philosophical psychology." Philosophers seeking to understand the nature of motivation can find an anchor of sorts in the psychology of motivation.[8]

The precise manner in which motivation is to be understood is a disputed issue in motivational psychology, but it is widely accepted there that what distinguishes species capable of motivated behavior from other species is flexibility of behavior.[9] For example, rats can learn a variety of alternative strategies for obtaining food (e.g., pressing levers or running mazes in an experimenter's lab) and flies cannot (Toates 1986, pp. 22–23). Feeding behavior in flies, but not in rats, is stimulus-bound. "To infer motivation," Philip Teitelbaum writes, "we must break the fixed reflex connection between stimulus and response" (1977, p. 12). Once the connection is broken and motivation is accorded a place in the explanatory scheme for (some of) an animal's behavior, so is a capacity to identify means to goals. Thus, at least an approximation of belief-desire psychology is postulated.

There is a simple way of viewing the flexibility criterion for warranted attribution of motivation-encompassing attitudes to an entity. If an entity's behavior is not influenced even by the most carefully designed attempts at positive and negative reinforcement, that is evidence that there is nothing the entity wants and that the entity is devoid of motivation. The entity might fly and drink, as a fly does; but not because it *wants* to. Rather, these activities are direct, mindless responses to nonmental stimuli. However, if efforts to reward (positively reinforce) a kind of behavior increase the frequency of behavior of that kind and efforts to punish (negatively reinforce) another kind of behavior decrease its frequency, that is evidence that there is something the entity wants. Using an animal's desires as a lever, we get it to learn strategies for satisfying its desires. Notice that accepting this criterion gives us an easy answer to the question why we should not attribute motivation-encompassing states to present-day chess-playing computers, robots, and the like. Their behavior is not modifiable by reward or punishment.

Imagine a human being, *S*, with no motivational attitudes. Lacking such attitudes, *S*'s behavior will not be modified by positive or negative reinforcement—of either intentionally administered or naturally occurring varieties. *S* might mindlessly twitch and fidget, as a fly does, but in the absence of motivation, *S* will never get beyond that point. Having no motivation, *S* lacks a requirement for learning strategic behavior. Normal human beings plainly meet the flexibility criterion for attribution of motivation. To the extent that the criterion is acceptable, normal human beings may safely be attributed motivation-encompassing attitudes.

Motivation, in the psychological view under consideration, is required specifically for intelligent or learned behavior, not for behavior in general (e.g., the mating behavior of flies). Via positive reinforcement of bar-pressing behavior, rats may learn a strategy for making water available to themselves. Such learning, in the present view, requires motivation. Furthermore, once a rat has learned a strategy of this kind, our evidence that the rat has pressed a bar in order to make water available is evidence that the rat had a relevant desire and a relevant belief—a desire to drink water, we may say, and a belief to the effect that pressing the bar would make water available. Many motivational psychologists are happy to attribute mental representations to rats (see, e.g., Mook 1987, pp. 305–11; Toates 1986, chs. 2, 6, 7).

Imagine that an entity, *S*, has a property, *P*, such that *S*'s possessing *P* is sufficient for *S*'s being subject to behavior modification by means of reward or punishment of its behavior. In the view under consideration, at least some state of *S*, as imagined, is a motivation-encompassing attitude. Motivation is required for the possession of a capacity to learn strategic behavior via reward or punishment. However, not everything required for this is motivation. An entity with no capacity for memory cannot learn. A rat with no memory may be consistently rewarded for pressing a bar, but that will have no effect on the frequency of its bar-pressing behavior. This indicates that it is conceptually possible for there to be a being with motivation-encompassing attitudes that nevertheless does not satisfy the behavioral flexibility criterion for warranted attribution of motivation. However, that does not undermine the criterion. The criterion is not offered as a statement of necessary and sufficient conditions for the presence of motivation in a being; rather, it is a criterion for the warranted *attribution* of motivation-encompassing attitudes to a being.[10] A motivated being may nevertheless be a being we are not warranted in attributing motivation to (as an agent guilty of a crime may be a being we are not warranted in deeming guilty).

Even so, the flexibility criterion is suggestive about the nature of motivation. Motivation is required for a capacity to learn strategic behavior by way of reward and punishment of the being's behavior. Memory is required also, but memory is distinguishable from motivation. Memory enables a being to form and retain an associative link between behavior of a particular kind and its rewarding or punishing consequences. Motivation typically inclines or disposes a being to seek consequences of some kinds and to avoid consequences of other kinds. Inclinational aspects or functions of motivation are a central topic of this book.

Notes

1. For an informative discussion of how the lines are to be drawn, see Toates (1986, ch. 2). For a statement of a popular view in motivational psychology, see Mook (1987, pp. 104–5).

2. John Atkinson elegantly articulates an alleged connection between motivational strength and behavior: "The act which is performed among a set of alternatives is the act for which the resultant motivation is most positive. The magnitude of response and the persistence of behavior are functions of the strength of motivation to perform the act relative to the strength of motivation to perform competing acts" (1957, p. 361). Compare this with a thesis advanced by Donald Davidson: "If an agent wants to do x more than he wants to do y and he believes himself free to do either x or y, then he will intentionally do x if he does either x or y intentionally" (1980, p. 23). For criticism of Davidson's thesis and a defense of an alternative, see (Mele 1992e, ch. 3; also see chapter 7 below).

3. Claim 6 does not assert that every intentional action is a motivated action. It takes no stand, for instance, on whether certain unwanted actional side effects of intentional actions are themselves intentional actions. For example, when I play tennis in my tennis shoes, I knowingly shorten the life of my shoes, while having no desire to do that. Claim 6 is silent on the question whether I *intentionally* shorten the life of my shoes, but it asserts that some relevant intentional action is motivated at this time: for example, my playing tennis.

4. Probabilistic causation is an option.

5. For a variant of this perspective in which reasons, construed as nonmental items of a certain normative kind, take the place of beliefs and desires in *P2*, see Dancy (2000). I discuss this perspective in chapter 3.

6. Heil and Mele (1993) is a useful collection of essays on these themes.

7. For my own attempt at a resolution, see Mele (1992e, ch. 2).

8. For a detailed, fruitful attempt to benefit from motivational psychology in understanding the role of representational states of mind in the production of behavior, see Dretske (1988).

9. See Toates (1986, ch. 2) for discussion and references. See Mook (1987, pp. 104–5) for a statement of the prevailing view.

10. The flexibility criterion discussed here is a criterion for being warranted in classifying an entity as a motivated being. Perhaps someone may, in principle, be warranted in attributing motivational attitudes to an inflexible supernatural being. However, even if the flexibility criterion's application is limited to real inhabitants of the natural order, it is philosophically serviceable. I should also emphasize that the criterion does not address the question what kinds of flexibility would be required for warranted attribution of specific motivation-encompassing attitudes. For my purposes here, the latter—enormously difficult—issue need not be tackled.

I

MOTIVATION AND ACTION

1

Motivation and Desire

"Motivation" is an everyday term that philosophers, psychologists, and other theorists use for theoretical purposes. Ordinary usage of this term and its cognates is pretty loose. Unfortunately, the same is true of much philosophical usage of them. The sophistication of issues debated about roles claimed or rejected for motivation in, for example, intentional human action generally, practical reasoning, and moral conduct is not matched by similarly sophisticated usage. This makes progress unnecessarily difficult. Too often, because they misunderstand their opponents, philosophers who think they are disagreeing about some motivational claim may not be, may not be nearly as far apart on the issue as they think, or may seriously underestimate what is to be said for their opponents' views. My primary aim in this chapter is to make this book's project easier to undertake and assess by laying conceptual and terminological groundwork that will help to make it clear exactly what my central questions—and answers—are. While I am at it, I report on, and in some cases clarify, distinctions that are relatively common in discussions of motivation and of desire.

1. What Is Motivation? What Is the Question?

Compare the questions "What is motivation?" and "What is knowledge?" The latter admits of a reformulation—"What is it for S to know that p?"—that makes the structure of propositional knowledge explicit: Such knowledge involves a subject, an object, and some relationship between them. Is there a similarly revealing reformulation of the question about motivation? Consider the question "What is it for S to be motivated to do x?" Here, there is structure, but there also is ambiguity. Being motivated to

13

do *x* is sometimes understood as requiring a motivated *doing* of *x*: there is a *success* reading of "motivated to do *x*." Alternatively, when we say that someone is (or was) motivated to do *x*, we sometimes mean only that he has (or had) some motivation to do *x*. Consider in this connection such claims as that Ann was motivated to run for office or that Bob was motivated to run to school. Out of context—and sometimes in context, including dry philosophical contexts—one cannot tell whether the speaker means to be saying not only that the agents had some motivation to do these things but also that they did them. In mentioning doing, the question under consideration also seems too narrow as a reformulation of the original question. People desire such things as world peace and financial security, but even though such things are not doings, such desires seem to be motivational states.

One may try to recast the original question as "What is a motivational state?" There is ambiguity here, too. Ann desires to own a car and she believes that she will own one only if she buys one. She buys a car, desiring to do that and being motivated to do precisely that. Is Ann's belief itself a motivational state in virtue of the role it plays in Ann's motivated car purchase? That depends on how "motivational state" is to be read. On a very broad reading, any attitude that plays a major, typical role in producing a motivated action may count as a motivational state.[1] Interpreted more narrowly, motivational states are limited to states that themselves constitute or include motivation. Plainly, Ann's belief that her owning a car hinges on her buying one neither constitutes nor includes motivation to buy a car. Ann's brother, Ed, believes that his owning a car hinges on his buying one, but he has no interest at all in owning a car and no motivation to buy one.

William Alston writes that "the concept of motivation is an abstraction from the concept of a motivational explanation, and the task of specifying the nature of motivation *is* the task of bringing out the salient features of this kind of explanation" (1967, p. 400). There is something to this, but it is not quite right. There is a debate, for example, about whether our judgments that we ought, morally, to *A* essentially encompass motivation to *A* (see chapter 5). The discovery that moral ought-judgments play an important role in some motivational explanations may leave it open whether these judgments themselves encompass motivation. Perhaps instead of encompassing motivation to *A*, or motivation at all, judgments that we ought, morally, to *A* combine with motivation-encompassing attitudes to produce desires or intentions to *A*. The supposition that this is so does not stand in the way of the supposition that first-person moral ought-judgments play an important role in some motivational explanations. They may do so without themselves encompassing motivation. The same is true of instrumental beliefs—for example, Ann's belief that she will not own a car unless she buys one.

Although it is tempting simply to adopt the convention of using the expression "motivational state" in the narrower sense I mentioned, doing so would obscure some points of disagreement in the literature. Refraining from adopting that convention also has costs, but merely stylistic ones. I need a term for attitudes (i.e., for attitudinal states of mind) that themselves are, constitute, or include motivation. The term I have chosen is "motivation-encompassing attitudes." The question "What is a motivation-encompassing attitude?"—or "What is it for an attitude to be motivation encompassing?"—avoids the ambiguities I have mentioned. Unfortunately, there is ambiguity here also.

Philosophers and others use expressions of the form "*x* is motivation to *A*" in a variety of different ways, even when they share the assumption that attitudes are the loci of motivation. If Ann wants to swim today because she wants to exercise today and believes that, on the whole, swimming is the best form of exercise for her today, is it true that her desire to exercise today *is*—that is, *constitutes*—motivation for her to swim, or is it true instead that this desire *provides her with* motivation to swim? Is it correct to say *both* that Ann's desire to exercise today constitutes motivation to swim *and* that it provides such motivation? For some purposes, philosophers need not care much how they use these expressions, and they may comfortably use them without explanation. (Indeed, they might start caring only when arguments against views they favor seem to turn on distinctions framed in such terms.) For my purposes in this book, however, connections between attitudes and motivation do matter. I would like, as far as possible, to avoid arguing about words, but I would also like to avoid a lot of linguistic legislation. So, in a latitudinarian spirit, I distinguish in this section among ways an attitude may be, constitute, or include motivation to *A*, in senses of these terms broad enough to accommodate ordinary uses of expressions of the form "*x* is (or constitutes or includes) motivation to *A*." I draw distinctions in a preliminary way now and fill in details later.

First, in the pertinent broad senses of the terms I mentioned, attitudes can be, constitute, or include motivation to *A* in more and less *direct* ways. Ann's desire to swim today directly is, constitutes, or includes motivation to swim today, and her desire to exercise today less directly is or does so. It is the indirectness in the latter case that inclines some speakers toward a preference for the assertion that her desire to exercise *provides* her with motivation to swim over the assertion that this desire is, constitutes, or includes motivation to swim. I return to the topic of providing motivation in section 3.

Second, a distinction can be drawn between attitudes that *essentially* are, constitute, or include motivation to *A* and attitudes that *contingently* are or do so. Using "encompass" as a term of art to cover the three-part disjunction of terms, the distinction can be formulated as follows: an attitude of an agent *S essentially* encompasses motivation to *A* if and only if it encompasses motivation to *A* not only in *S*'s actual situation but also in all possible scenarios in which *S* has that attitude; and an attitude of an agent *S contingently* encompasses motivation to *A* if and only if although, in *S*'s actual situation, it encompasses motivation to *A*, this is not the case in some possible scenarios in which *S* has that attitude. I return to this distinction in section 4 and again in chapters 5 and 6.

2. Motivation, Desire, and Action-Desire

Richard Peters concludes *The Concept of Motivation* by chiding motivational psychologists for their scientific aspirations and suggesting that "scrutiny of the conceptually illuminating start made by Aristotle" would provide a more promising approach (1958, p. 157). One of the chief faults that Peters finds with motivational psychologists is their commitment to a *causal* approach to explaining behavior. When writing his conclusion, Peters seemingly forgot a striking claim in book 6 of

Aristotle's *Nicomachean Ethics*: "the origin of action—its efficient, not its final cause—is choice, and that of choice is desire and reasoning with a view to an end" (1139a31–32).

The term *orexis*, translated here as "desire," also may be translated as "motivation." One reason that "desire" is more convenient than "motivation" as a standard translation for *orexis* is that it allows more easily for the precise specification of the *object* of a motivation-encompassing attitude—that is, of what is desired. Another is that the noun *orexis* has a cognate verb, *orego*, and both can be translated as "desire," but not, of course, as "motivation." Setting classical Greek aside, related points may be made about philosophical uses of the terms "desire," "want," and "motivation." We can say that someone desires to swim today or, more naturally, that she wants to swim today; and we can say that someone has a desire to swim today or, less naturally, that she has a want to swim today. However, the expressions "is motivated to swim today" and "has motivation to swim today" are not only more awkward than their most elegant counterpart but also less precise. Suppose that Ann wants to swim today because she wants to exercise today (as she does every day) and believes that, given a tendon injury sustained in her daily running, swimming currently is the best form of exercise for her. Then Ann is motivated to swim today, in the sense that she has motivation to swim today, and some speakers find it natural to say that the attitudes motivating her to swim today include both her desire to exercise today and her desire to swim today. The assertions that Ann is motivated to swim today and that she has motivation to swim today do not, at least in some idiolects, distinguish between these two motivation-encompassing attitudes.

Partly for reasons of precision, some philosophers have adopted the convention of using the noun "desire" or "want" as a synonym for "motivation" in some contexts. This practice occasionally troubles aficionados of ordinary usage. "Desire" brings to mind affective tone or appetitive content, and "has a want to *A*" is stilted. These worries can be quelled. As I noted elsewhere (Mele 1992e, p. 47, following Goldman 1970, pp. 53–54), distinctions blurred by this usage can be recaptured by differentiating among types of wants or desires (which terms may be used interchangeably as terms of art). For example, one can distinguish egoistic from altruistic desires, affective from nonaffective desires, and appetitive from nonappetitive desires (compare my desire to drink a pint of Guinness with your desire to continue reading this chapter). However, there are other, more substantive worries, as I explain later.

Consider Ann's desire to exercise today, her desire to swim today, and my desire to shoot pool with Jack tomorrow. These desires are *action-desires*, desires to act in certain ways. Presumably, action-desires are paradigmatic motivational attitudes. What are they motivation for, or motivation to do? At the very least, it seems, desires to *A*, where *A* is a prospective course of action, constitute motivation to *A*. For example, Ann's desire to exercise today constitutes motivation to exercise today, and my desire to shoot pool with Jack tomorrow constitutes motivation to shoot pool with Jack tomorrow. Agents' desires to *A* may also be said to *provide* them with motivation to do other things. Owing partly to relevant beliefs of hers, Ann's desire to exercise today seemingly provides her with motivation to swim today. One of my aims in the ensuing, preliminary discussion of the concept of an action-desire is to set part of the stage for an interpretation, to be developed in the following section, of a desire's providing motivation for A-ing.

Exactly what an agent desires to do often is underdetermined by ordinary attributions of desires. Bob says, correctly, that Cyd wants to play catch with her brother while their father watches. But does she want merely (*W1*) that she and her brother play catch and that their father watch, or does she want, more fully, (*W2*) that she and her brother play catch in such a way as to hold their father's visual attention? Bob's attribution leaves both possibilities open. Now, as I understand the concept of an action-desire, what counts as a desire of this kind depends on what counts as an action. Partly for this reason, it is important to attend to the looseness and incompleteness of ordinary attributions of desires.

To forestall confusion, my way of dealing with a relatively basic, contested issue in the philosophy of action, the individuation of actions, requires brief attention here. Since I do not see how to settle the issue, a neutral framework should be sketched. By the end of the 1970s, a collection of relatively precise alternatives were available: a coarse-grained view, a fine-grained view, and componential views. Consider an example of Donald Davidson's: "I flip the switch, turn on the light, and illuminate the room. Unbeknownst to me I also alert a prowler to the fact that I am home" (1980, p. 4). How many actions does the agent, Don, perform? Davidson's coarse-grained answer is one action "of which four descriptions have been given" (p. 4; cf. Anscombe 1963). A fine-grained alternative treats A and B as different actions if, in performing them, the agent exemplifies different act-properties (Goldman 1970). On this view, Don performs at least four actions since the act-properties at issue are distinct. An agent may exemplify any of these act-properties without exemplifying any of the others. One may even turn on a light in a room without illuminating the room: the light may be painted black. Componential views represent Don's illuminating the room as an action having various components, including his moving his arm, his flipping the switch, and the light's going on (Ginet 1990; Thalberg 1977; Thomson 1977). Where proponents of the coarse-grained and fine-grained theories find, respectively, a single action under different descriptions and a collection of intimately related actions, advocates of the various componential views locate a larger action that has smaller actions among its parts.

In this book, I proceed in a neutral way regarding the leading contending theories of action individuation. Readers may treat my action variable "A" as a variable either for actions themselves (construed componentially or in a more fine-grained way) or for actions under A-descriptions, depending on their preferred mode of action individuation. The same goes for the term "action."

That having been said, I return to action-desires. Playing catch with her brother is something Cyd does, an action. Playing catch with her brother while their father watches is *not* something *else* Cyd does, nor is it an action that includes her playing catch with her brother and something else—namely, their father's watching. If what Cyd wants is *W1* (that she and her brother play catch and that their father watch), two desires seem to be at work—a desire to play catch with her brother and a desire that their father watch. The former is an action-desire; the latter is not. If, however, what Cyd wants is *W2* (that she and her brother play catch in such a way as to hold their father's visual attention), she has a more complicated action-desire. When, in ordinary speech, we say such things as that "Cyd wants to play catch with her brother while their father watches," we may seem to be attributing a single desire to the agent. When we reflect on what we think it is the agent wants, we are sometimes in a position to be more fine-grained, or at least to see distinct, relevant possibilities. Among the possibilities is that what we casually express in a way that suggests a single desire may instead be a combination of an action-desire and a non-action-desire.

I suggested that two desires are at work, if what Cyd wants is *W1*. Why not say instead that Cyd has a single desire for a pair of things constituted by her playing catch with her brother and their father's watching? Suppose that Cyd thinks it very unlikely that their father will watch. Then it is natural to say that she wants to play catch with her brother and *hopes* that their father will watch. This natural assertion certainly suggests two distinct desires, hopes being desires. Now, the distinctness of these two desires—there being the two desires I mentioned rather than a single desire for a pair of things—is not plausibly regarded as contingent on Cyd's subjective probability that her father will watch. If the two desires are, in fact, distinct states of mind, this would be so even if Cyd were to feel certain that her father will watch. The difference is that, under the counterfactual assumption, it is incorrect to say that Cyd *hopes* that their father will watch, if hoping that *p* entails uncertainty whether *p*. In the counterfactual scenario, instead of being paired with a low subjective probability that their father will watch, Cyd's desire that he watch is paired with a very confidently held belief that he will watch.

An agent's action-desires, as I understand them, are desires to *A*, where "*A*" is a variable for prospective courses of action, and if they are satisfiable, they are satisfiable by, and only by, actions the agent performs (and truths, states, or facts for which the satisfying actions are conceptually sufficient; for stylistic reasons, I suppress the parenthetical qualification in the remainder of this chapter).[2] Any desire that is satisfiable in and only in this way is an action-desire. If Ann's desire to swim a mile today is satisfied, it is satisfied by an action of hers today that is her swimming a mile and not by anything other than an action of that kind. My desire to shoot pool with Jack tomorrow may be, more specifically, a desire to shoot at least several games with him tomorrow night. If that desire is satisfied, it is satisfied by my so doing, an action (which may be temporally scattered, with conversations, brief trips to fetch drinks from the bar, and the like separating segments of actual pool shooting), and not by anything other than an action of that kind. These desires, then, are action-desires.

Consider Bob's desire that he do—not merely sometimes, but always—what he is morally required to do. One may try to give that desire the ring of an action-desire: "Bob's desire *to* do—and to do, not merely sometimes, but always—what is morally required of him." Is Bob's desire an action-desire? Suppose that what Bob in fact desires is not simply that there be no time at which he does not do what he is morally required to do—something that is the case if there are no moral requirements at all—and that Bob's desire is such that its satisfaction requires that there be at least one time at which he is morally required to do something and does it. Even so, always doing what one is morally required to do is not an action, even a temporally scattered one. Nor is it a sequence or collection of actions. Suppose it turns out that Bob did what was morally required of him, not just sometimes, but always. What makes this true—and therefore what makes it true that the desire at issue was satisfied—is not just Bob's morally required actions but also the fact that there were no times at which Bob was morally required to do something that he did not do. That fact is neither an action nor a collection of actions; nor is the occurrence of Bob's actions conceptually sufficient for the fact's obtaining. To see that this is so, consider a counterfactual scenario in which, although Bob performed all the actions he in fact performed, each of them being morally required, there was a time at which he did not do what he was morally required to do. A time at which Bob was not in fact morally required to do anything is, in the counterfactual scenario, a time at which Bob was morally required to do something and did not do it. In this scenario, his desire is not satisfied. Hence, actions of Bob's are not themselves sufficient to satisfy the desire, in which case the desire is not an action-desire in my sense.

3. Providing Motivation and Motivational Bases

I turn to a desire's *providing* motivation to act. The *word* "provide" is not of special interest to me; my interest is in two different connections between desires and motivation to A, a direct and a less direct one. My aim is to distinguish these two connections in a preliminary way. I focus here on the "providing" connection and return to the other connection later.

The attitudes that motivate Ann to swim today, as I mentioned, may (at least in some idiolects) include both her desire to exercise today and her desire to swim today. This is not to say that these desires may somehow combine forces. Instead, Ann's desire to exercise today, given her relevant beliefs, contributes to her having a desire to swim today in a way that makes a positive contribution to the strength of the latter desire. In so doing, her desire to exercise today provides Ann with motivation to swim today. However, as I explain shortly, desires may provide agents with motivation to A without contributing to their having a desire to A.

An ambiguity in the assertion that S's desire for x *provides* S with motivation for A-ing must be noted before I proceed. There is a *success* reading, entailing that the desire actually makes a positive contribution to the strength of a motivation-encompassing attitude that is focused on A-ing—for example, a desire to A. And there is a *potentiality* reading. A desire may be said to provide motivation for A-ing in the sense that it has, or has in some circumstances, the potential to play a role of the kind just mentioned. By "provides motivation," I mean *actually* provides—that is, provides in the success sense—unless I indicate otherwise.

Two bits of technical terminology will prove useful. First, to avoid begging certain questions, I need an umbrella term for desires to A and any nondesires that are, in a certain sense, *directly about* A-ing and may be claimed to encompass motivation to A. I call any such attitudes that encompass motivation to A "A-focused motivation-encompassing attitudes," or "MA attitudes," for short. Examples of A-focused attitudes—but not necessarily of A-focused *motivation-encompassing* attitudes—are desires to A, intentions to A, beliefs that we ought to A, and beliefs that we will A. I do not count desires *not* to A, beliefs that we will *not* A, and the like as A-focused. They are focused on *not* A. Nor do I count desires to *try* to A, beliefs that we will *try* to A, and their ilk as *A*-focused. They are focused on *trying to A*. (That these attitudes are not *A*-focused is compatible with their being focused on some other course of action.)

The focus of a motivation-encompassing attitude may be either simple or complex. Judy may desire simply to nod her head now, or she may desire to express approval of Ann's proposal while also signaling Bob to find an excuse to leave the room by nodding her head now. In the former case, the focus of her desire is her nodding her head now. In the latter, it is her expressing approval of Ann's proposal while also signaling Bob to find an excuse to leave the room by nodding her head now.

The second bit of technical terminology I need now, "positive motivational base," I introduced elsewhere (Mele 1987, pp. 67–69) for another purpose. "The positive motivational base" of a particular *MA* attitude (e.g., a desire to *A*) is the collection of all motivation-encompassing attitudes of the agent that (in a sense to be explained) make a positive contribution to the motivational strength or force of the attitude in question. (On motivational strength, see chapter 7.) For example, when Bob ordered a beer a few moments ago, the positive motivational base of his desire to order one included his desire to drink a beer. Other things being equal (e.g., no demons are interfering with the process), the stronger the latter desire, the stronger the former, if Bob believes that ordering a beer is currently the best way to put himself in a position to drink one.

Many *MA* attitudes have both positive and *negative* motivational bases. "The negative motivational base" of an *MA* attitude is the collection of all motivation-encompassing attitudes of the agent that make an analogous negative contribution to the strength of that attitude. Carl's desire to honor his promise to smoke no more than two cigarettes per day is in the negative motivational base of his current desire to smoke another cigarette, if the former desire renders the latter weaker than it would otherwise have been.

The positive and negative motivational bases of an *MA* attitude constitute its "total motivational base." Incidentally, it is unlikely that the total motivational base of an *MA* attitude, even in conjunction with relevant subjective probabilities, always determines the motivational strength of that attitude. An impressive body of experimental data indicates that modes of representation sometimes significantly influence motivational strength. For example, the manner in which one represents a desired object to oneself can have a marked effect on delay of gratification.[3] (In an effort at self-control, one might picture a tempting wedge of chocolate pie as a wedge of chewing tobacco.)

As I understand the notion of a desire's *providing* an agent with motivation to *A*, this is precisely a matter of the desire's entering into the positive motivational base of an *MA* attitude (where the motivation-providing desire and the *MA* attitude are different attitudes).[4] Now, a desire's making a (normal or nondeviant) causal contribution to an agent's acquiring an *MA* attitude (e.g., acquiring a desire to *A*) is neither sufficient nor necessary for its being in the positive motivational base of that attitude. Ann, who desires a promotion, judges that displaying perceptiveness in the course of flattering Bob would help her get one. As a consequence, she desires to do this. Owing to her desire to display perceptiveness in the course of flattering Bob and her judgment that saying complimentary but plausible things about Bob's garden would turn the trick, Ann desires to make such remarks about Bob's garden. By hypothesis, Ann's desire to display perceptiveness in the course of flattering Bob is a cause of her desire to make remarks of the kind just mentioned. However, the former desire need not contribute to the strength or force of the latter. The strength of the latter desire may derive wholly from the strength of Ann's desire for a promotion. It may be a product of the strength of Ann's desire for a promotion and her subjective probability of getting a promotion, given that she makes remarks of the desired kind. Thus, a desire may make a (normal or nondeviant) causal contribution to the acquisition of an *MA* attitude without being in that attitude's positive motivational base.

Conversely, a desire may be in the positive motivational base of an *MA* attitude without making a causal contribution to the acquisition or retention of that attitude. Among the desires that Don has had for some time are a desire to purchase a Jeep Wrangler and a desire to impress his boss, Donna. Today, he discovers that owning a Wrangler would impress her. Don's desire to impress Donna would naturally enter into the positive motivational base of his desire to buy a Wrangler. Not only is Don's desire to impress Donna not a cause of his acquiring a desire to buy a Wrangler, but it also need not causally sustain his desire to buy one. Don's continuing to desire to purchase a Wrangler may be causally independent of his desire to impress his boss.

Attention to Davidson's (1980, chs. 1 and 12) notion of rationalizing will prove helpful in generating a fuller interpretation of a desire's providing motivation to *A*, especially when the motivation-providing desire is a *cause* of an *MA* attitude. I examine Davidson's notion in chapter 3, but his basic idea is roughly this: a reason's rationalizing an action is a matter of its being a cause of that action that helps to explain the action (partly) by revealing something that the agent was aiming at in performing it and, therefore, something "in light of which" the action makes sense (1980, p. 9; cf. p. 233). Davidsonian reasons are complexes of beliefs and desires. As I explain in chapter 3, some philosophers reject the idea that reasons are states of mind. Disputes about the nature of reasons for action can be set aside for present purposes. In this section, "reasons" may be understood as referring, possibly in a misleading or wrong-headed way, to mental states of certain kinds.

Davidson's notion of rationalizing is a broadly instrumental one. In some cases, the belief component of a reason for *A*-ing represents *A*-ing as a *means* to *x*. In others (e.g., the swimming for exercise case), the belief represents *A*-ing as an *instance* of *x*. In yet others, the belief represents *A*-ing as a *constituent* of *x*. For example, a fledgling vegetarian who wants to serve an excellent Thanksgiving meal may think about what would constitute serving such a meal, judge that serving tofurkey would be part of serving such a meal, and want accordingly to serve tofurkey. In each case, one can say, the belief component represents *A*-ing as *conducive* to *x*, conduciveness being understood to include each of the three relations just mentioned.

When an agent *A*-s for a reason *R* that is not simply an intrinsic desire to *A*, what rationalizes his *A*-ing presumably also rationalizes his desiring or intending to *A*.[5] If Sam's flipping the switch is rationalized by his wanting to illuminate the room together with his believing that the best way to do that is to flip the switch, then, presumably, Sam wants or intends to flip the switch and his so wanting or intending is rationalized by the reason that rationalizes the flipping. If it is plausible that the Davidsonian reason identified is a cause of Sam's flipping the switch that helps to explain the action (partly) by revealing something in light of which the action makes sense, it is also plausible that this reason is a cause of Sam's desire or intention to flip the switch that helps to explain the emergence of that *desire* or *intention* (partly) by revealing something in light of which what it is a desire or intention to do makes sense. In many cases, an agent who A-s in order to B, also B-s in order to C, C-s in order to D, and so forth (which is not to suggest, of course, that the chain is ever infinite). Sam might flip the switch in order to illuminate the room, in order to make it easier to find his car keys, in order to improve his chances of getting to work on time. In such cases, the reasons for which an agent wants to do things that are relatively remote from his A-ing in the in-order-to chain may help rationalize both his A-ing and his wanting to A. For example, Sam's desire to get to work on time and his belief that he needs to find his keys if he is to do that may figure in a detailed rationalization both of his flipping the switch and of his desire to flip it.

The rationalizing of an agent's wanting or intending to A by a Davidsonian reason he has for A-ing may be counted as *instrumental* rationalizing. The subjective reasonability of his A-ing (Davidson 1980, p. 9) lies in its believed conduciveness to something the agent wants, something identified in a reason for which he A-s. And the subjective reasonability of one's wanting or intending to A often derives from that of A-ing. Even if the agent does not represent his desiring or intending to A as a means to an end, the desire and intention have as their object something—the agent's A-ing— that is represented in the reasons that rationalize these attitudes as conducive to the achievement of the object of a desire that is a constituent of those reasons, and this helps to explain why those desires or intentions emerge.[6]

The sketch I have just offered of the rationalizing of desires and intentions to A by Davidsonian reasons for A-ing is, in part, a sketch of one way in which desires enter the positive motivational base of *MA* attitudes, providing agents with motivation to A. The relevant motivation-providing desires are, of course, elements of Davidsonian reasons for A-ing. Insofar as these desires make a positive contribution to the strength of the *MA* attitudes that they help to produce, they enter into the positive motivational base of these resultant attitudes.[7]

Not all desires for x provide motivation for the agent to pursue, promote, or protect x. Ann, a Pistons fan, hopes that they won last night's basketball game. Since hoping that p entails desiring that p, Ann desires that the Pistons won.[8] However, she understandably has no motivation to try to bring it about that they won. It does not follow from this, of course, that Ann's desire that the Pistons won does not provide motivation for anything. When Ann checks her morning newspaper to see who won, it is natural to suppose that her desire that the Pistons won plays a role in motivating her to do this, which supposition suggests that her desire that they won provides her with motivation to check the paper for the game's outcome.

How might the desire provide such motivation? If it is a cause of such motivation, it seemingly is more than *just* a cause, for given that Ann desires that the Pistons won and is a relatively normal fan, it makes sense that she would want to know how the game turned out. A noninstrumental analogue of Davidsonian rationalizing merits attention. My immediate question is whether Ann's desire that the Pistons won can be a cause of her desire to learn how the game turned out that helps to explain the latter desire (partly) by revealing something in light of which that desire makes sense. Can the former desire "rationalize" the latter desire in this sense? In rationalizing the latter desire in a way that contributes to its strength, it would *provide* Ann with motivation to learn the game's outcome.

In some cases, discovering whether *p* is true has an obvious instrumental value for a person who hopes that *p*. If Ann had placed a bet on the Pistons, she would need to learn whether they won in order to know what to do: pay up or collect. And if the Pistons' entering the playoffs were contingent on their having won last night, Ann might need to learn whether they won in order to make plans for next week: she might have the conditional plan to attend their home games next week if they continue to play and to take a vacation in Paris otherwise. But, as it happens, last night's game was just an ordinary midseason game, and Ann had no interest in the Pistons' winning beyond the interest a normal fan takes in her favorite team. Even so, other things being equal, Ann's hoping that they won seemingly makes it reasonable for her to want to learn whether they did.

It may be suggested that "to learn whether the Pistons won" is too thin a description of the content of the attitude that motivates Ann's desire or intention to check her newspaper. Loyal fan that she is, Ann presumably hopes to learn *that* the Pistons won and checks the paper with that hope. In this, she would differ from a bookie who wants to learn who won the game simply to know whom to collect from and whom to pay. So perhaps one should say that Ann's hoping that the Pistons won leads her to hope to learn that they won, which in turn, in conjunction with her belief that checking the paper would be the easiest way to learn that they won, if they did win, leads her to want to check the paper. But this raises a variant of an earlier question: can Ann's hope that the Pistons won rationalize her hope to learn that they won?

It cannot plausibly be claimed that hoping that *p* conceptually or causally necessitates hoping to learn that *p*. A man who hopes that his children will flourish for many years after his death may not hope to learn that this will happen, largely because he believes it impossible for the dead to learn things. Even if people can hope for what they are convinced is impossible, this man may not be the sort to have such hopes. To acknowledge this, however, plainly is not to deny that, often, it is natural and reasonable for one who hopes that *p* to hope to learn that *p*—even if one does not need to discover whether *p* in order to plan for the future (as in the betting and playoff cases involving Ann).

An explanation of why this is often natural and reasonable even in cases in which neither *p*'s truth nor the agent's discovery of that truth has planning value for the agent is that, often, when one hopes that *p* in such a case, discovering that *p* is *pleasant*. However much Ann may hope that the Pistons won last night, their winning will please her in a relatively direct way only if she learns of it.[9] And one expects the pleasantness of her discovering that they won to be proportional to the strength of her hope that they won. Normal, pleasure-seeking people evidently are pleased by "good news"—news that current hopes or desires of theirs have been fulfilled. Insofar as such news is pleasant, they find it attractive. In light of this observation, it is unsurprising that normal folks are disposed to want to learn, of what they hope is true, that it is in fact true. Recognizing that people are so disposed and knowing that Ann hopes that the Pistons won last night, one finds her desiring the good news that they won utterly intelligible.[10]

If there are rationalizing causes, Ann's hope that the Pistons won may noninstrumentally rationalize her desire to learn that they won. The hope would rationalize the desire in virtue of making a causal contribution to the occurrence of the desire that helps to explain that occurrence partly by revealing, to echo Davidson, "some feature . . . or aspect" of learning that the Pistons won that is "agreeable" to Ann (1980, p. 4). The relevant feature in the present case is the pleasantness—hence, agreeability—of the news.[11] In light of Ann's hope that the Pistons won, one can see why learning that they won is attractive to her. Hence, in light of the hope, one has a grip on the reasonableness of her *desire* to learn that they won, which grip enables one to make sense of her having that desire, to understand why she has it.

Other things being equal, it is utterly reasonable to hope for pleasant occurrences, including receiving good news. So if rationalizing is a genuine relation, some desires seemingly may be rationalized by other desires in light of which the former attitudes are reasonable, even though the objects of the rationalizing attitudes are states or events that the agents know are beyond their sphere of influence. The human mind apparently has resources for the reasonable production of desires by other desires the satisfaction of which cannot be promoted by the attitudes produced. If appearance matches reality here, a complete philosophy of mind will acknowledge and account for this truth.

My discussion of the noninstrumental rationalizing of Ann's hope to learn that the Pistons won is suggestive of a simple way to formulate an *instrumental* rationalization of this hope. Consider the following instrumentalist suggestion: Ann's hope to learn that the Pistons won is rationalized by a desire for pleasure together with a belief that it would be pleasant to learn that they won. Although her hope is not a constituent of this rationalization, it does play a supporting role; for Ann's hope that the Pistons won is a partial basis for her belief that it would be pleasant to learn that they won. Other things being equal, if she were not to hope that the Pistons won, it would not be pleasant for her to learn that they won and she would not believe that this would be pleasant. (Nor, other things being equal, would she consciously believe this if she were not aware of her hope that they won.)

Should one accept this instrumental rationalization *instead of* the noninstrumental rationalization that I sketched? Perhaps the rationalizations are complementary rather than competing. Ann's hope that the Pistons won might play a dual role in the production of her desire to learn that they won: it might noninstrumentally rationalize that desire *and* contribute to a belief that it would be pleasant to learn that they won that figures in an instrumental rationalization of the desire. If the rationalizations are not complementary, the noninstrumental one arguably more accurately captures psychological reality. It plausibly accords Ann's hope that the Pistons won a featured role in the rationalization of her desire to learn that they won, whereas its instrumental counterpart leaves that hope out of the rationalization entirely and limits the hope's relevant work to the role it plays in producing a constituent of the rationalization, namely, the belief that it would be pleasant to learn that the Pistons won.

If noninstrumental rationalizing of the sort I have described is a genuine phenomenon, it is a process whereby desires *provide* motivation for actions that are not aimed at producing, promoting, or protecting the objects of the motivation-providing desires. These desires provide such motivation by contributing to the strength of pertinent *MA* attitudes (e.g., desires to *A*), a contribution they make in the course of playing a causal role in the production of these attitudes that helps to explain the agent's acquiring these attitudes partly by revealing something attractive to the agent about what the attitudes are focused on.[12]

I have identified two rationalizing ways in which desires *provide* motivation for action, one broadly instrumental and the other noninstrumental. Both ways seemingly involve the motivation-providing desire itself encompassing motivation since the strength of the motivation provided apparently derives from the motivational strength of that desire. I have also identified a way in which desires provide motivation for acting without contributing to the *production* or *persistence* of an *MA* attitude (e.g., an action-desire) whose strength they augment. (Recall that rationalizing desires are *causes* of the *MA* attitudes they rationalize.) Each way of providing motivation for action is a way of entering into the positive motivational base of an *MA* attitude.

I said that whereas Ann's desire to exercise today *provides* her with motivation to swim today, her desire to swim today *constitutes* motivation to swim today. There is an apparent difference. The latter desire by itself, independently of what else is true of Ann, constitutes motivation for her to swim today. (This idea is defended in chapter 6). Her desire to exercise today, in conjunction with a pertinent belief, makes an important contribution to her acquiring a desire to swim today and to the strength of that desire. If there is a sense in which Ann's desire to exercise today *constitutes* motivation for her to swim today, it is not the same sense. If Ann were not to know how to swim (and knew that this is so), she presumably would have no desire to swim today and no motivation to swim today, even though she desires to exercise today. One can say, if one likes, that in Ann's actual circumstances—which include her believing that she can swim and her believing that swimming is a form of exercise—her desire to exercise today constitutes motivation for her to swim today. But then one should distinguish between more and less direct ways of constituting motivation to *A* and between essentially and contingently constituting motivation to *A* (see section 1).

4. Desire and Direction of Fit

Ann's desire for a Pistons' victory undermines some attempts to characterize desire in terms of "direction of fit," an expression around which a cottage industry has grown.[13] On one notion of satisfaction that applies both to beliefs and to desires, a belief that *p* and a desire that *p* have the same satisfaction condition: its being the case that *p*.[14] Whereas many desires are functionally fit to contribute to their own satisfaction, in this sense, relatively few beliefs are. (Potentially self-fulfilling beliefs are the exception, not the norm.) The point is sometimes expressed in terms of "direction of fit": "belief aims at truth" (Williams 1973, p. 151), it aims to fit the world; desire aims at getting the world to fit it. In this connection, Michael Smith writes that "the difference between beliefs and desires in terms of direction of fit comes down to a counterfactual dependence of a belief and a desire that *p*, on a perception that *not p*: roughly, a belief that *p* is a state that tends to go out of existence in the presence of a perception that *not p*, whereas a desire that *p* is a state that tends to endure, disposing the subject in that state to bring it about that *p*" (1987, p. 54; cf. Pettit and Smith 1990, p. 574).

Smith's characterization of desire is unsuccessful. Ann's desire that the Pistons won does not dispose her to bring it about that they won. In a related scenario, standing at the airport, waiting for Angela's plane to arrive, it occurs to me that I should have called from home to see whether her plane departed at the scheduled time. I now desire that Angela's plane departed on time; but this desire in no way disposes me to bring it about that the plane left on time, because it does not dispose me to endeavor to change the past.[15] This failing of Smith's characterization leaves open the possibility, however, that all *action-desires* have a dispositional aspect of the kind he mentions. Perhaps all desires to A dispose the agent to A. On this issue, see chapter 6.

My desire that Angela's plane left on time might provide me with motivation to check a monitor at the airport to reassure myself about this, just as Ann's desire for a Pistons' victory provided her with motivation to check her newspaper. Suppose that it *actually* provides me with motivation to check a monitor—that is, that it provides such motivation in the success sense. Those who understand the idea of a desire's encompassing motivation to A in such a way that a desire's actually providing motivation to A suffices for its encompassing motivation to A will say that the two desires I mentioned encompass, respectively, motivation to check a monitor and motivation to check a newspaper. In section 1, I drew the following distinction: an attitude of an agent S *essentially* encompasses motivation to A if and only if it encompasses motivation to A not only in S's actual situation but also in all possible scenarios in which S has that attitude; and an attitude of an agent S *contingently* encompasses motivation to A if and only if although, in S's actual situation, it encompasses motivation to A, this is not the case in some possible scenarios in which S has that attitude. Are desires imaginable that neither essentially nor contingently encompass motivation to act?[16]

Consider the following case. Connie is a fan of the New York Giants. The Giants are playing their traditional rivals next month and she hopes they will win. Since hoping that p entails desiring that p, Connie desires a Giants' victory in this game. Now, as Connie knows, she has no chance of discovering the game's outcome, for she is about to begin piloting a spaceship to a remote galaxy and she knows that by game time she will be permanently cut off from Earth's sporting news. Robert Audi has claimed that someone who wants p "tends to think (reflect, muse, or the like) or daydream about p at least occasionally, and especially in idle moments" (1973, p. 4). If this is true, one may plausibly suppose that this cognitive behavior is motivated by the want or desire that p. However, Connie is a special person; when she knows that she has no chance of learning how matters of minor to moderate importance to her have turned out, she has no tendency at all to think or daydream about those matters, even though she desires a particular outcome. If Connie's desire for a Giants' victory does not encompass motivation for behavior of these kinds, perhaps it does not encompass motivation for behavior of any kind. If so, her desire for a Giants' victory neither essentially nor contingently encompasses motivation to act. This may be true even when Connie is conscious of the desire, as she may be, for example, when someone asks her which team she wants to win.[17]

The possibility of desires like this is perhaps sufficiently surprising to merit further investigation. It may be suggested that Connie's desire for a Giants' victory *does* actually provide (and therefore contingently is) motivation to fantasize about their winning and the psychological fact about her that I mentioned simply prevents that motivation from being manifested behaviorally. Is that plausible? Consider the related claim that my desire that Angela's plane departed on time actually provides me with motivation to bring it about that her plane departed on time and my conviction that I cannot change the past simply prevents that motivation from being manifested in action aimed at influencing her plane's departure time. This claim has the ring of a desperate move to save a theory. If the claim is false, so is the claim that Connie's desire for a Giants' victory actually provides her with motivation to bring it about that the Giants win and her conviction that she cannot have an effect on the Giants' game prevents that motivation from being manifested in action directed at producing a Giants' victory. If Connie's lacking motivation to bring it about that the Giants win, even though she desires that they win, is ensured by a fact about her psychological condition, one would need a good reason to deny that psychological facts about Connie ensure that her desire for a Giants' victory does not actually provide her with motivation to do anything. Even if it is usually assumed that all desires either essentially or contingently encompass motivation to act, that fact is not such a reason. Reflection often results in the abandonment of relatively unreflective assumptions.

5. Intention and Desire

There is a significant literature on the connection between desiring to A and intending to A. I have contributed to it myself (e.g., in Mele 1992e). A brief discussion of the issue is in order. In this section, I concentrate on the constitution of intentions and an important difference between intention and action-desire. For a sketch of some functions of intention, see chapter 2, section 4.

Intentions, in my view, are executive attitudes toward plans (Mele 1992e, chs. 8–11). Like beliefs and desires, intentions have representational content. The representational content of an intention is an action-plan. Action-plans, as I understand them, have no motivational force. Yesterday, Ann noticed in a magazine a twelve-step plan for improving one's self-esteem. She committed it to memory purely as a mnemonic exercise. The plan in the magazine plainly has no motivational force. Nor does the plan in Ann's memory.[18] Ann has no problems with self-esteem, and she has no motivation to improve her self-esteem.

In the limiting case, the plan component of an intention has a single "node." It is, for example, a prospective representation of one's taking a vacation in Hawaii two summers from now that includes nothing about means to that end nor about specific vacation activities. Often, intention-embedded plans are more complex. The proximal intention to check his e-mail that Bob executed this morning incorporated a plan that included clicking on his e-mail icon, then typing his password in a certain box, then clicking on the "OK" box, and so on. An agent who successfully executes an intention is guided by the intention-embedded plan.[19]

Although the contents of intentions are plans, I follow the standard practice of using such expressions as "Bob's intention to check his e-mail now" and "Ann intends to shoot pool tonight." It should not be inferred from such expressions that the agent's intention-embedded plan has a single node, for example, checking e-mail now or shooting pool tonight. Often, our expressions of an agent's motivation-encompassing attitudes do not identify the full content of the attitude and are not meant to. Bob says, without intending to mislead, "Ann wants to shoot pool tonight," knowing full well that what she wants is to play nine-ball with him at Pockets tonight and to play for $5 a game until the place closes, as is their normal practice.

According to a popular view of representational attitudes—for example, my belief that p, Ann's desire that p, Bob's desire to A, Carl's intention to A—one can distinguish between an attitude's representational content and its psychological orientation (Searle 1983). Orientations include believing, desiring, and intending. On my view, the executive dimension of intentions is intrinsic to the attitudinal orientation *intending*. We can have a variety of attitudes toward plans: for example, we might admire plan x, be disgusted by plan y, and desire to execute plan z. To have the intending attitude toward a plan is to be settled (but not necessarily irrevocably) on executing it.[20] The intending and desiring attitudes toward plans differ in that the former alone entails this settledness. Someone who desires to A, or to execute a certain plan for A-ing—even someone who desires this more strongly than he desires not to A, or not to execute that plan—may still be deliberating about whether to A, or about whether to execute the plan, in which case he is not settled on A-ing, or not settled on executing the plan.[21] Alan wants more strongly to respond in kind to a recent insult than to refrain from doing so, but, owing to moral qualms, he is deliberating about whether to do so. He is unsettled about whether to retaliate despite the relative strength of his desires (see Mele 1992e, ch. 9).

On a standard view of desire, the psychological features of desires to A in virtue of which they contribute to intentional A-ings are their content and their strength. On my view of the contribution of *intentions* to A to intentional A-ings, the settledness feature of intentions is crucial, and it is not capturable in terms of desire strength (and content) or in terms of this plus belief (Mele 1992e, pp. 76–77 and ch. 9). Intentions to A, as I understand them, essentially encompass motivation to A but without being reducible to a combination of desire and belief (Mele 1992e, ch. 8). Part of what it is to be *settled* on A-ing is to have a motivation-encompassing attitude toward A-ing; lacking such an attitude, one lacks an element of a psychological commitment to A-ing that is intrinsic to being settled on A-ing and, therefore, to intending to A. For ease of exposition, one might define a broad sense of "desire" that includes intentions as desires of a special kind. But I will not do that here. If I am right, both intentions to A and desires to A essentially encompass motivation to A (see chapter 6). Whether any attitudes that neither are nor encompass desires or intentions to A essentially encompass motivation to A is one of the issues to be explored in this book (see chapters 5 and 6).

6. Desire's Breadth

In section 2, I claimed that some distinctions blurred by the convention of using the nouns "desire" and "want" as synonyms in some connections for "motivation" can be recaptured by differentiating among types of wants or desires. As I mentioned, I made this claim in earlier work, too. Not everyone has agreed. In his provocative book on desire, G. F. Schueler (1995) evidently takes this convention to yield an unacceptably broad notion of desire. I have said that I will not use "desire" as an umbrella term for all motivation-encompassing attitudes, including, for example, intentions. Even so, an argument of Schueler's merits attention in a discussion of desire's breadth.[22]

Schueler's (1995) primary arguments "are aimed against two commonly held views" (p. 2): that "desires are somehow essential in the rational justification of actions"; and that desires are "essential to the explanation of actions" (p. 4). He argues that both views are false of what he calls "desires proper." Although Schueler does not offer a precise characterization of desires proper, he reports that they "presumably include such things as cravings, urges, wishes, hopes, yens, and the like, as well as at least some motivated desires, but not such things as moral or political beliefs that could appear in practical deliberation as arguing against the dictates of one's urgings, cravings, or wishes" (p. 35).

Schueler (1995) remarks that he himself deliberated about whether to attend a meeting at his son's school, decided to attend it, and acted accordingly—even though he had no desire to attend (pp. 29–34). He claims that "if we are to make sense of the content of my deliberation in the situation described we will have to do so using a sense of 'desire' and 'want' in which it is possible for me to do things I have no desire to do" (p. 33). Now, one can define a sense of "desire" (whether it is a legitimate one or not) in which it is true that people sometimes decide to do, and intentionally do, things that they have no desire to do. For example, one can make it a defining feature of one sense of "desire"—*desire**—that anyone who desires x in that sense experiences a positive affective reaction to the thought of x. Obviously, at least some people who schedule a root canal operation for themselves do not desire, in this sense, to schedule one. However, it does not follow from this that proponents of the thesis that desires are essential to the explanation of intentional action are mistaken; for the sense of "desire" at issue may not be—in fact, it is not (see chapters 6 and 7)—a sense they intend in asserting the thesis.

A proponent of the thesis at issue may claim, for example, that a species of desire— *action-desire*—is "essential to the explanation of" intentional actions, where action-desire is characterized roughly as follows:

> An attitude x is an action-desire if and only if there is some action-type A such that the agent's A-ing is the focus of x, x is neither an intention nor a combination of two or more attitudes of distinct types (as a hope, e.g., is a combination of a desire and a belief), and, necessarily, if x were to function nondeviantly and effectively, x would contribute to its own satisfaction by inducing the agent to make a suitable attempt.[23]

A philosopher who holds that action-desires are essential to the explanation of intentional actions may be willing to grant that when Schueler decides to attend the meeting and intentionally attends it, he does not have what he calls a "desire proper" to attend it (depending on how desires proper are to be understood). But should such a philosopher also hold that Schueler has no *action-desire* to attend the meeting in this case?

Schueler reports, "I did attend the meeting because I believed I had a responsibility to do so, a responsibility mostly to my son but partly to my community" (1995, p. 29). Even before deciding to attend the meeting, did he have an action-desire to discharge this responsibility, to do whatever (he believes) he has a responsibility to do in the circumstances, or to discharge whatever responsibilities (he believes) he has toward his son (or his family) in the circumstances? Perhaps he had no desire proper or desire* to do any of these things. But I cannot find in Schueler's book a convincing reason for holding that he had no such action-desires. If he did have such a desire, it was well suited to enter into the positive motivational base of an action-desire to attend the meeting. I take up a related general issue in chapter 5.

Just as Schueler offers too few options regarding senses of "desire," he offers too few models of "desire/belief explanations" of actions. He discusses three models:

> (1) a blind-forces model . . . which sees desires (and beliefs) as blind causal forces and provides no obvious place for practical deliberation at all; (2) a vector-analysis model . . . which takes desires as causal forces that we are merely given but which allows for at least a form of practical deliberation about how to satisfy these desires; and (3) a deliberative model . . . which takes seriously the idea of acting on the basis of deliberation and which seems not to use a causal account of desire at all. (1995, pp. 184–85)

As becomes increasingly evident in subsequent chapters, causal models of belief-desire explanation are not limited to the "blind-forces" and "vector-analysis" kinds. And for all Schueler has said, a model that accords action-desires a significant causal/explanatory role in deliberative action may prove much more satisfactory than the acausal deliberative model he sketches.

7. Occurrent versus Standing Desires

A traditional distinction between *occurrent* and *standing* desires or wants (Alston 1967, p. 402; Goldman 1970, pp. 86–88) requires attention. Alvin Goldman, acknowledging a debt to Alston, writes, "An occurrent want is a mental event or mental process; it is a 'going on' or 'happening' in consciousness. A standing want . . . is a disposition or propensity to have an occurrent want, a disposition that lasts with the agent for a reasonable length of time" (p. 86). A distinction of this kind is motivated partly by evidence about the ordinary notion of desire provided by widely shared attributions of desires or wants. Consider Sue, a graduate student who is deeply committed to pursuing a career in philosophy. As the verb "want" is standardly used, "Sue wants a career in philosophy" is true even while she is wholly absorbed in a conversation about her brother's marital problems or dreamlessly sleeping. When Sue's thesis supervisor finds himself inclined to tell a prospective employer that she definitely wants a career in philosophy, he need not phone her to see whether she is awake before he can be confident that he will be speaking the truth. The quoted sentence is also true when Sue is working hard on a cover letter for her job applications. In the latter case, but not the former, Goldman would say that Sue has an occurrent want for a career in philosophy.

Goldman's way of drawing the distinction is problematic. Part of what the distinction is supposed to mark is the difference between desires that influence behavior only if they are first "activated" in some way and desires that are already active (Alston 1967, p. 402; Goldman 1970, p. 88). But not all active desires are present to consciousness—at least if common sense and clinicians may be trusted.[24] A boy might have spoken to his girlfriend as he did because he wanted to hurt her feelings, even though he was not conscious at the time of his desire to do that. Goldman implausibly makes being "a 'going on' or 'happening' in consciousness" an essential feature of oc-current wants. Occurrent wants or desires are "active" in the sense that they do not need to be activated or aroused in order to exert an influence on the agent's conduct. It is implausible that this activeness requires that the agent be conscious of the desire. It should also be observed that occurrent desires are not, as the name may suggest, oc-currences or events: they are states.

Even if it is true that all standing desires are dispositions to have corresponding oc-current desires, it is implausible that all dispositions to have occurrent desires are standing desires. It is natural to say that dreamlessly sleeping Sue wants a career in philosophy and that she is disposed to have occurrent desires to this effect. But not every disposition to have desires of the latter sort is plausibly counted as a desire. Sup-pose that a hypnotist implants in Tom a disposition to want occurrently to tap dance upon hearing the name "Fred Astair." That disposition may last, in Goldman's words, "for a reasonable length of time": Tom may have it for twenty days, twenty months, or twenty years. Suppose that he has the disposition that long without its ever being acti-vated. Does Tom have a *desire*—even a standing one—to tap dance or to tap dance upon hearing the name "Fred Astair"? Or does he merely have a disposition to desire this? More precisely, is it conceptually possible that the hypnotist implants the dispo-sition I mentioned and that the disposition lasts "for a reasonable length of time" with-out Tom's ever having the standing desire at issue?

Audi (1994) makes a nice case for distinguishing what might be termed a "standing belief" that p from a mere disposition to acquire an occurrent belief that p. Most of the time, I have a standing belief that Los Angeles is in California; sometimes I believe this occurrently. The standing belief is a disposition to have occurrent beliefs that Los Angeles is in California. But is it plausible that all dispositions to have occurrent be-liefs that p are beliefs—even standing ones—that p? Before reading this sentence, you had a disposition to believe occurrently that a girl who has 127 apples has more fruit than a boy who has 52 oranges. But that disposition is very different from your stand-ing belief that Los Angeles is in California. That Los Angeles is in California is some-thing that you learned, that you occurrently believed at times in the past, and that you remember. Your relation to the fruity fact is of a very different kind. Presumably, you encountered that fact here for the first time.

In any case, if not all dispositions to believe occurrently that p are beliefs that p, one should not be surprised that not all dispositions to desire occurrently that p are desires that p. A year ago, Sam put a house he inherited on the market, wanting to get at least $75,000 for it. He still wants that, and he has rejected all lower offers. Sam is disposed to want occurrently to sell the house for $75,099, is disposed to want occurrently to sell it for $75,108, and so on. If Sam were offered any of these amounts for his house, he would want occurrently to sell it for that amount. But it certainly seems to be stretching things to claim that Sam has correspondingly numerous desires—even standing ones—to sell the house. His relevant standing desire, if he has one, is to sell his house for at least $75,000, and he is disposed to desire occurrently to sell it for at least that much. However, the numerous related dispositions I mentioned are not plau-sibly counted as numerous desires.[25]

The dispositions that allegedly constitute standing desires have no explicit repre-sentational content. They are accorded a content-supplying description in virtue of the content of the occurrent desires in which their activation consists. Having no explicit representational content, standing desires are not explicit attitudes.[26] Rather, they are dispositions to have explicit attitudes of a certain kind. They are, one may say, *implicit* motivational attitudes. (Discussion of motivational attitudes in this book should be presumed to be about occurrent attitudes unless explicitly noted otherwise.)

Are *any* so-called standing desires actually desires? Return to Sue's case. I said that as the verb "want" is standardly used, "Sue wants a career in philosophy" is true even while she is wholly absorbed in a conversation about her brother's marital problems or dreamlessly sleeping. But is the thought that *at this time* Sue has a desire or want for a career in philosophy? Is the thought something that the following fact would suffice to make true: Sue has frequently had occurrent desires for a career in philosophy that were manifestations of a disposition to have such desires, and she still has this disposition? If it is the latter, then, arguably, to say that dreamlessly sleeping Sue wants a career in philosophy is not to say that she has a want or desire at that time and is instead to say something about past occurrent wants and present dispositions that are not themselves wants. In a related vein, one may doubt that so-called implicit motivational attitudes are attitudes at all (see Pigden, n.d.), and one may argue that only attitudes can be desires. Then again, it is arguably the case that the fact I mentioned is sufficient for the possession of something properly called a standing *desire* to have a career in philosophy.

If the criterion for a successful answer to the present question about so-called standing desires were simply fidelity to ordinary usage, the question would not merit much attention. However, larger issues are at stake. T. M. Scanlon writes:

> To say that people have reasons not to mistreat others, or reasons to provide for their own future interests, only if so doing promotes the fulfillment of their present desires has seemed to many people to make the requirements of morality and prudence "escapable" in a way that they clearly are not . . . quite apart from any desire to criticize others or to influence them, reflection on the nature of our *own* reasons should lead us to resist the substantive claim that all reasons for action are based on desires. (1998, pp. 41–42)

In assessing the thesis that "all reasons for action are based on desires," it matters what does and does not count as a desire. At least some proponents of this thesis will not want to hold that the only desires are occurrent ones. They will want to claim, for example, that partly in light of his standing desire for his niece's welfare, an agent currently has a reason to help her with her homework tonight, even though he has no occurrent desires at the moment on which that reason is based.

By the same token, opponents of the thesis that "all reasons for action are based on desires" will be reluctant to grant that just any disposition to desire is itself a desire. Consider someone who holds that some or most reasons are not based in any way on the agent's desires and the apprehension of a non-desire-based reason can nonaccidentally produce an appropriate desire in an agent without the assistance of any existing desire. Such a philosopher will want to challenge Bernard Williams's announcement that the term "'desire' . . . can be used, formally, for all elements in" an agent's "subjective motivational set," including "dispositions of evaluation, patterns of emotional reaction, personal loyalties, and various projects . . . embodying commitments of the agent" (1979, p. 20). An opponent of the thesis that all reasons for action are desire-based may hold, for example, that rational agents are disposed to desire in accordance with any reasons they apprehend—or are disposed to desire to do whatever they believe they have a reason to do—and that this disposition is not a desire.

The connection between reasons and desires and related issues in the philosophy of mind and moral psychology is examined in chapters 3, 4, and 5. Part of my concern now is to avoid a commitment to potentially misleading terminology. I tentatively suggest that the following is *sufficient* for an agent's having a standing desire for *x*: he frequently has had occurrent desires for *x* that manifested an ongoing disposition to have such desires, and he still has that disposition.

In the preceding discussion, I used the expression "*motivational* attitudes." In light of a point about ambiguity made in section 1, this should have raised a red flag in readers' minds. The dispositions in which standing desires consist, as I understand them, are not motivation *encompassing*; but, in suitable circumstances, they do play a role in *producing* motivation, and both the existence and the strength of the occurrent desires that manifest them may be explicable partly in terms of the associated standing desire.[27] One naturally supposes that some of an agent's standing desires are stronger than others. For example, Sue's standing desire for a career in philosophy may be stronger than her standing desire to watch "Seinfeld" reruns on Sundays. One respect in which it may be stronger is linked to the strength of the occurrent desires that manifest the two standing desires. One can say that, other things being equal, an agent's standing desire for *x* is stronger than his standing desire for *y* if the former disposes him to have stronger manifesting desires than the latter does. Of course, that leaves it open what it is about these standing desires that accounts for this dispositional difference and what it is for one manifesting desire to be stronger than another.

8. Intrinsic versus Extrinsic Desires

Brief discussion of another familiar distinction between ways of desiring will prove useful later. When we desire something (e.g., to do *A* or to possess *B*) we may desire it intrinsically or extrinsically. To desire something *intrinsically* is to desire it for its own sake, or as an end.[28] The paradigm case of desiring something *extrinsically* is desiring it as a means. But to desire something as a constituent of something else that one desires or as evidence of the truth of something that one desires to be true also is to desire it extrinsically. Ann intrinsically desires her continuing to be a good tennis player, and she believes that having a good serve is part of being a good tennis player. Accordingly, she desires her continuing to have a good serve. She desires this extrinsically—not for its own sake but as a constituent of her continuing to be a good tennis player. Bob came to my office wanting to hear that he passed my course. He did not want to hear this for the sake of hearing it (nor as a means of passing, of course). Rather he wanted to hear this because hearing it would be evidence that he passed, passing being something that he desired (Harman 1993, p. 140).

Among intrinsic and extrinsic desires, some are wholly intrinsic or wholly extrinsic and others are not. To desire something *wholly intrinsically* is to desire it as an end and not also as a means to, as a constituent of, or as evidence of something else. Bob may desire his happiness wholly intrinsically while also desiring that he continue to be healthy, both as an end and as a constituent of, or a means to, his happiness. To desire something *wholly extrinsically* is to desire it extrinsically and not also intrinsically. Carol desires living courageously only as a means of impressing her father. Her younger sister, Donna, desires living courageously both for its own sake and as a means of impressing Carol.

From an agent's desiring something intrinsically (or extrinsically) but not wholly so, it does not follow that he has *two* desires for it. It is plausible that, in addition to any other desires Donna has, she has a single desire whose object—her living courageously—she desires both for its own sake and as a means of impressing Carol. I call such a desire a *mixed* desire.

Desires of each kind—intrinsic, extrinsic, and mixed—are relevant to our intentional behavior. Having an intrinsic (or mixed) desire for his family's welfare, Ed might acquire a variety of extrinsic desires for actions that he believes would promote it. Less happily, having an intrinsic desire to be rid of her excruciating backache, Fran might acquire an extrinsic desire to take a pain reliever. If all goes well for Ed and Fran, their desires will be satisfied, and the satisfaction of these desires will be due partly to the desires' effects on their behavior.

9. Summary of Some Technical Terms

A summary of some of the less memorable technical terminology introduced in this chapter will prove useful.

1. *Motivation-encompassing attitudes*: attitudes that themselves are, constitute, or include motivation.
2. *Essentially encompassing motivation to* A: an attitude of an agent S essentially encompasses motivation to A if and only if it encompasses motivation to A not only in S's actual situation but also in all possible scenarios in which S has that attitude.
3. *Contingently encompassing motivation to* A: an attitude of an agent S contingently encompasses motivation to A if and only if although, in S's actual situation, it encompasses motivation to A, this is not the case in some possible scenarios in which S has that attitude.
4. *A-focused motivation-encompassing attitudes* (MA *attitudes*): any attitudes directly about A-ing that encompass motivation to A.
5. *Positive motivational base of an* MA *attitude*: the collection of all motivation-encompassing attitudes of the agent that make a positive contribution to the motivational strength of that MA attitude. A common sort of positive contribution is a rationalizing one. By definition, a motivation-encompassing attitude's *rationalizing* an MA attitude requires that it be a cause of the MA attitude. A motivation-encompassing attitude can contribute to the strength of an MA attitude without being a cause of the existence or the persistence of that attitude. The basic idea is that the items in the positive motivational base of an MA attitude are the motivation-encompassing attitudes of the agent from which the strength of the MA attitude at least partially positively derives.[29]
6. *A desire's providing an agent with motivation to* A: the desire's entering into the positive motivational base of an MA attitude (when the motivation-providing desire and the MA attitude are different attitudes).

7. *Standing desire*: I tentatively suggested that the combination of an agent's frequently having had occurrent desires for *x* that manifested an ongoing disposition to have such desires and his still having that disposition is *sufficient* for his having a standing desire for *x*.

Notes

1. For a broad reading of this kind, see Dancy (1993, p. 2).
2. Sometimes agents desire to continue doing something that they are currently doing—for example, they desire to continue running or to continue watching a movie. The desired continuation is a prospective course of action.
3. For references to empirical work on delay of gratification and discussion of its philosophical significance, see Mele (1995a, pp. 45–54).
4. An intrinsic desire to A is at least partially constitutive of its own motivational base (on this point, see Mele 1987, pp. 67–68). Hence the parenthetical clause in the sentence to which this note is appended. On intrinsic desires, see section 8.
5. I have argued elsewhere (Mele 1988; cf. 1992e, ch. 6) that, in some cases, a reason for A-ing (construed as a psychological state) is wholly constituted by an intrinsic desire to A; the reason has no belief component. I return to this issue in chapter 3.
6. Elsewhere, I have argued that there are reasons for intending to A that are not themselves reasons for A-ing and that such reasons can contribute to rational intention formation (Mele 1992b, 1995b). That issue is orthogonal to the one being pursued here. I have also argued (Mele 1992e, ch. 11; see especially pp. 214–15) that agents do not normally represent their desiring or intending to A as a means to an end. For an opposing view about intentions, see Harman (1976; 1986, ch. 8; 1993).
7. Some desires in a rationalizing chain may not themselves contribute to the strength of a desire produced further along in the chain; the strength of the produced desire may not derive at all from that of some of the rationalizing desires. Recall the example of Ann the flatterer.
8. *The American Heritage Dictionary* reports in the usage note on "expect" that "to *hope* is to desire, usually with confidence in the likelihood of gaining what is desired." (I believe that the final clause is too strong.)
9. Even if Ann does not learn of it, the Pistons' winning might please her—but in a less direct way. For example, their winning this game might contribute to their entering the playoffs months later, and Ann might be pleased, months later, by their entering the playoffs.
10. On desires for "good news," see Harman (1993, p. 149).
11. I am not claiming that noninstrumental rationalization must be linked to pleasure.
12. Jeffrey Foss voices a familiar, contrary view: (1) "desires have no explanatory force without associated beliefs" that identify (apparent) means to the desires' satisfaction; (2) this is part of "the very logic of belief-desire explanation" (1997, p. 112). Claim 1 is undermined by the familiar phenomenon of motivationally biased belief (see Mele 2001 and chapter 11, section 2, below).
13. There is a useful discussion of the literature in Humberstone (1992).
14. It is controversial whether a belief and a desire can have the same content. Alvin Goldman (1970, pp. 101–2), for example, takes the contents of beliefs to be declarative propositions and the contents of desires to be optative propositions. For related views, see Castañeda (1975, ch. 10), Hare (1972, ch. 3), and Kenny (1989, pp. 36–41). The point to be made can be reformulated in a way consistent with these views. (I return to this issue about content in chapter 5, section 5.)
15. Smith, responding to the potential objection that "*desire* is not a suitably broad category of mental state to encompass all those states with the appropriate direction of fit," says that

"desire" may be replaced with "pro-attitude" (1987, p. 55). Notice that, standing at the airport, I had a pro-attitude toward the plane's having departed on time, but that pro-attitude in no way disposed me to bring it about that the plane left on time.

16. Whether one accepts or rejects the thesis that some not-doings are actions may bear on how one answers this question. Ann desires not to vote in a certain election. If her not voting is not an action, perhaps there are scenarios in which her desire not to vote does not encompass motivation to do anything at all. On not-doings and desires for them, see chapter 6, section 4.

17. Notice that Connie's answering that she wants the Giants to win is not *motivated* by her desire for a Giants' victory. When a friend asks me whether I want to complete this book by the end of the year, and I truthfully answer yes, it is not my desire to finish the book that motivates my so answering but a desire to speak truthfully (or something of the sort). One may suggest that desires that *p*, being attitudes, are in part thoughts about *p*. But this suggestion would not support the claim that Connie's desire for a Giants' victory *motivates* her "to think . . . or day-dream about" a Giants' victory. Rather, the suggestion is simply that a desire that *p is* a certain kind of thought about *p*.

18. To avoid confusion, two different tendencies in the literature on the connection between plans and intentions should be mentioned. The contrast is nicely illustrated by Myles Brand's claim that "the cognitive component of prospective intention is a plan" (1984, p. 153) and Michael Bratman's assertion that "We form future-directed intentions as *parts* of larger plans . . ." (1987, p. 8; my emphasis). The difference is largely a matter of convention. Although I believe that intentions are sometimes formed with a view to the execution of larger plans (i.e., plans larger than the ones embedded in the intentions at issue), I have not adopted Bratman's convention of using the word "plan" for items that themselves involve "an appropriate sort of commitment to action" (p. 29).

19. The guidance depends on the agent's monitoring progress toward his goal. The information (or misinformation) that Bob has entered his password, for example, figures in the etiology of his continued execution of his plan. On guidance, see chapter 2, section 4.

20. In the case of an intention for a not-doing (e.g., an intention not to vote tomorrow), the agent may instead be settled on not violating the simple plan embedded in it—the plan not to vote. Again, on not-doings and attitudes toward them, see chapter 6, section 4.

21. A critic may claim that in all cases of this kind the agent is settled on a course of action without realizing it and that he is deliberating only because he does not realize what he is settled on doing. For argumentation to the contrary, see Mele (1992e, ch. 9).

22. The remainder of this section derives partly from Mele (1996d).

23. Compare this with the analysis in chapter 6, section 2, of noncompound *A*-focused attitudes that essentially encompass motivation to *A*.

24. For discussion of some relevant empirical work, see Vollmer (1993).

25. It may be claimed that what I have just called "numerous related dispositions" are all aspects of the same disposition, Sam's disposition to want occurrently to sell the house for at least $75,000. Disposition counting is tricky business. Fortunately, developing rigorous accounting practices is not required for my purposes.

26. Gilbert Harman writes that "one believes something explicitly if one's belief in that thing involves an explicit mental representation whose content is the content of that belief"; later, he speaks of something "explicitly represented in one's mind" as "written down in Mentalese as it were, without necessarily being available to consciousness" (1986, pp. 13–14). This is the general picture I mean to evoke with the expression "explicit attitudes," but I neither venture an opinion about *how* the contents of attitudes are explicitly represented nor claim that they are all represented in the same way (e.g., in a language of thought). Incidentally, my subsequent use of "implicit" in "implicit motivational attitudes" does not parallel Harman's use of the term in his expression "implicit beliefs" (p. 13).

27. Notice that I say "producing"—not "providing"—motivation. As I have explicated the latter notion (section 3), only motivation-encompassing attitudes can provide motivation to act.

28. For discussion of various notions of intrinsic motivation and intrinsic behavior in the psychological literature, see Heckhausen (1991, pp. 403–13). Also see Deci and Ryan (1985).

29. The related notions of negative and total motivational bases have only minor roles in this book.

2

Goal-Directed Action

In subsequent chapters, I build on ideas developed in the preceding one. The primary aims of the present chapter are to make a case for the causal perspective on intentional behavior that I sketched in section 2 of the introduction and to elaborate that perspective.

Teleological explanations of human actions feature aims, goals, or purposes of human agents. Standard motivational explanations of intentional actions are teleological, in this sense. According to a familiar *causal* approach to analyzing and explaining human action, human actions are, essentially, events that are suitably caused by appropriate mental items, or neural realizations of those items.[1] Causalists traditionally appeal, in part, to such goal-representing states as desires and intentions (or their neural realizers) in their explanations of human actions, and they take acceptable teleological explanations of human actions to be causal explanations. Some proponents of the view that human actions are explained teleologically resist this causal approach, regarding it as a rival.[2] I dub this position anticausalist teleologism, or *AT*, for short. I favor the causal approach, as I have mentioned, and I have defended it elsewhere (Mele 1992e, 1997a, 1997b). In this chapter, I develop a serious problem for *AT* that strongly suggests that teleologists need causalism. I also rebut a style of objection to the project of providing a causal analysis of acting in pursuit of a goal that has re-surfaced in the literature on teleological explanations of action. It features a kind of causal deviance described in section 3.

1. Davidson's Challenge and Two Unsuccessful Replies

The idea that our actions are to be explained, causally, in terms of mental states or events is at least as old as Aristotle.[3] The first major source of its revival in contemporary action theory was Donald Davidson's (1963) "Actions, Reasons, and Causes." There, in addition to rebutting various arguments against the causal approach, Davidson raised an important challenge to noncausalists about action-explanation. As I mentioned in the introduction, the challenge, broadly construed (and depending on one's position on the nature of reasons), is to provide an account of the reasons *for which* we act that does not treat any of the following as figuring in the causation of the relevant behavior: those reasons, our having them, our apprehending them, and the neural realizations of any of these things. This challenge is particularly acute when an agent has more than one reason for A-ing but A-s only for some of them. Here is an illustration:

> Al has a pair of reasons for mowing his lawn this morning. First, he wants to mow it this week and he believes that this morning is the most convenient time. Second, Al has an urge to repay his neighbor for the rude awakening he suffered recently when she turned on her mower at the crack of dawn and he believes that his mowing his lawn this morning would constitute suitable repayment. As it happens, Al mows his lawn this morning only for one of these reasons. In virtue of what is it true that he mowed his lawn for this reason, and not the other, if not that this reason (or his having it), and not the other, played a suitable causal role in his mowing his lawn? (Mele 1997a, p. 240)

A general version of this question may be framed as follows: in virtue of what is it true that a person acted in pursuit of a particular goal? No proponent of *AT*, as far as I know, has offered a plausible, informative answer to this question. Carl Ginet (1990, ch. 6) defends a position on "reasons explanation" that holds out the promise of answering Davidson's challenge. In the present section, I criticize Ginet's position and a related idea advocated by R. Jay Wallace (1999). In section 2, I criticize another pair of attempts to answer the challenge.

Two ways of evading the challenge should first be mentioned. It may be claimed that whenever agents who A intentionally have two or more reasons for A-ing, (1) they A for all of them, or alternatively (2) there is no fact of the matter about which are the reasons for which they A. Not only are both contentions ad hoc, but also both are undermined by an objection that I raise to Ginet's (1990) position.

Consider a reasons explanation of the form "S V-ed in order (thereby) to U" (Ginet 1990, p. 137).[4] "The only thing *required* for the truth of a reasons explanation of this sort," Ginet writes, "besides the occurrence of the explained action, is that the action have been *accompanied* by an intention with the right sort of content" (p. 138). In particular, it is not required, in his view, that the intention figure in the causation of V or any part of V. "Given that S did V," Ginet contends, it is sufficient "for the truth of 'S V-ed in order to U'" that "concurrently with her action of V-ing, S intended by *that* action to U (S intended *of* that action that by it she would U)." He adds, "If from its inception S intended of her action of opening the window that by performing it she would let in fresh air (from its inception she had the intention that she could express with the sentence 'I am undertaking this opening of the window in order to let in fresh air'), then ipso facto it was her purpose in that action to let in fresh air; she did it in order to let in fresh air."

Ginet writes, "The content of the intention is . . . the proposition 'By this V-ing (of which I am now aware) I shall U'. It is owing to this direct reference that the intention is about, and thus explanatory of, *that particular* action" (1990, p. 139). He asserts that an intention of this kind, being an intention about a particular action, "could not begin before the particular action does" (p. 139). However, he says, the action need not be complete before one can have an intention about it: "It is enough if the particular [action] has begun to exist." So imagine that, for some reason or other, Ann gets up to open a window and then, while opening it, acquires an intention, N, of her opening it, that by so doing she let in fresh air. Would she have opened the window—performed that action—even if she had not acquired N? Perhaps. Maybe she set out to open the window to get a better view of the street, and perhaps she would have opened it (simply for that purpose) if she had not acquired N or any other intention concerning her letting fresh air into the room. Even then—that is, even if the counterfactual is true—N might properly figure in an explanation of Ann's opening the window. For one thing, the completion of that action might be causally overdetermined by N and Ann's intention to get a better view. N would not causally explain the entire action (from the beginning on) since N was not present until the action was already in progress. But it might enter into a causal explanation of the action's being completed.

Just to pump intuitions, I invite the reader to consider a case that would be question begging were it not employed simply for that purpose. Imagine that God, who is omniscient and never lies, tells us that Ann had the following two *de re* intentions while opening the window and that both were present at the time of the completion of that action: Ann had the intention, N, of her opening the window "that by it she would" let in some fresh air; and she had the intention, O, of her opening the window that by it she would gain a better view. Suppose that God also tells us that exactly one of these intentions explains Ann's opening the window while refusing to say which. And suppose that we believe what God says.[5]

Under what conditions would it be true that Ann's opening the window was explained by N or, alternatively, by O? A natural answer is that the intention that explains her opening the window is the one that figures suitably in the etiology of that action or of her completing the action (or the one whose neural realizer does so). If O (or its neural realizer) helps to produce bodily movements involved in Ann's opening the window but N (like its neural realizer) plays no causal role at all in the production of any part of the action, people who believe God would naturally say that O is the explanatory intention and N is just along for the ride.

Remove God from the story and suppose that a neuroscientist, without altering the neural realization of N itself, renders that realization incapable of having any effect on Ann's bodily movements (and any effect on what else Ann intends) while allowing the neural realization of O to figure normally in the production of movements involved in her opening the window. Here, it seems clear, O helps to explain Ann's opening the window and N does not.[6] Indeed, N seems entirely irrelevant to the performance of that action. And if that is right, Ginet is wrong. For, in his view, the *mere presence* in the agent of an intention about her V-ing (where V-ing is an action) is sufficient for that intention's being explanatory of her action.[7]

Can Ginet (1990) plausibly retreat to the following position? If (1) "concurrently with her action of V-ing, [Ann] intended by *that* action to U" and (2) Ann had at the time no other intention or desire that helped to explain, either in whole or in part, her V-ing, then (3) the intention just mentioned is explanatory of her V-ing even if it (like its neural realizer) is, at the time, incapable of playing a causal role in the production of (any part of) that action. This conditional assertion will seem to some readers to be a nonstarter. Even if a *V*-ing is an *unintentional* action, readers may claim, some associated intentional action will have been caused in part by a desire or intention, and the desire or intention will help to explain *V*'s occurrence. For example, if, when opening a window, I unknowingly let in a fly, one might claim that, say, an intention to open the window, partly in virtue of its figuring suitably in a causal explanation of my opening the window, also figures in a causal explanation of my unintentional action of letting in the fly.

Ginet will have none of this, however. He argues that agents sometimes act in the absence of any relevant desire or intention. Some volitions, he claims, are cases in point, as are some associated exertions of the body. For example, he contends that "a voluntary exertion could occur [owing to an associated volition] quite spontaneously, without being preceded or accompanied by any distinct state of desiring or intending even to try . . . to exert, and it would still be an action, a purely spontaneous one" (1990, p. 9). In the case of a *voluntary* exertion of the body, Ginet says, "clearly, a causal connection between the willing and the body's exertion is required" (p. 39). But the volition itself, for Ginet, need not be caused (even in part) by or concurrent with any desire or intention.

So suppose that in Ann, standing within arm's reach of a window, a steady stream of volitions spontaneously springs up (volitions being momentary actions; Ginet 1990, pp. 32–33), as a result of which Ann's body moves in such a way as to come into contact with the window and smoothly open it in a conventional way. Suppose also that all this happens in the absence of any relevant intention or desire. Since the volitions produce the bodily movements that in turn cause the window to open, we have the makings of a causal explanation of all but the volitional element in Ann's opening the window. (The first and spontaneous volition in the stream is the "initial part or stage" of the voluntary exertion and the action; p. 30.) And the volitional element, in Ginet's view, needs no explanation at all.

Augment the scenario by supposing that Ann intends of her opening the window "that by it she" will let in some fresh air, but that this intention, *N* (like its neural realizer), is incapable of contributing causally to the production of the bodily movements or members of the volitional stream. I do not see how *N* can have any more explanatory significance in this case than it did in the Godless two-intention case—that is, none at all. One may think that the intention is explanatory of the action on the grounds that, in the absence of *any* relevant intention or desire, Ann's opening the window—that action—would be incomprehensible. But if Ginet is right, such an action requires no intention or desire at all for its occurrence: a spontaneous stream of volitions can do the work. Moreover, for those who think it bizarre that, in the absence of any relevant intention or desire, a steady stream of volitions of a kind suitable for window-opening bodily movements would occur in an agent, and who therefore want to bring some intention or desire into the explanatory picture, the best candidate, for reasons identified earlier, is an intention that is *causally explanatory* of the supposed causally effective volitions.

I have been writing as though even if no intention is explanatory of *S*'s *V*-ing, Ginet may be entitled to hold that *S*'s *V*-ing is an action. This issue merits attention. Ginet offers the following alleged counterexample to "the view that *S*'s *V*-ing at *t* was an action if and only if it was caused in the right sort of way by desire or intention" (1990, p. 9). Sal, who "is convinced that her arm is paralyzed," tries "to exert her arm just in order to see what it is like to will an action ineffectually," without "intending or wanting any such exertion actually to occur, perhaps even while wanting it very much *not* to occur." And she succeeds in exerting her arm, an action.

One problem is that this alleged counterexample does not preclude Sal's having a relevant desire or intention that does suitably cause her action. The candidates for relevant desires or intentions are not exhausted by the ones Ginet identifies. For example, Sal might want to discover "what it is like to will an action ineffectually," believe that she can do this now if she wills to exert her arm, and consequently intend to will that. This may explain whatever effort Sal makes, thereby helping to explain, in conjunction with "the motor-neural connections to her arm . . . actually [being] in normal working order," her exerting her arm. In the *absence* of such motivation, why *would* Sal, given Ginet's description of the case, try "to exert her arm"? Indeed, this motivation is implicit in the story. After all, Sal tries "to exert her arm . . . *in order to* see what it is like to will an action ineffectually."

Ginet claims, in the next paragraph, that "a voluntary exertion . . . could be caused by external stimulation of the brain" in the absence of any relevant intention or desire. Later, he asserts that someone might cause an agent to *V* voluntarily by sending signals to "the volitional part of her brain" (1990, p. 144). On Ginet's view, the right sort of causal connection between volition and exertion is sufficient for voluntary exertion (pp. 39–44). So if, by signaling Sam's brain, I cause a volition in him, which volition issues appropriately in some exertion of his body, he has exerted his body, and that is a voluntary action of his.

Can I cause a volition in an agent without causing him to have a relevant desire or intention? Ginet says that volitions are not themselves desires or intentions (1990, p. 32). But this itself does not answer the question: something that is not a desire might be inextricably linked to a desire. An informed answer requires additional information about volition. Volition, for Ginet, is trying (pp. 31–32). What Ginet needs is an argument that one can try to *A* without the trying's having any cause of a sort favored by causalists. His example of the agent who thinks her arm is paralyzed is supposed to turn the trick, but the supposition that she lacks certain desires or intentions (e.g., an intention to move her arm) does not entail that no other relevant intention (e.g., an intention to see what it would be like to try to move her arm now) is present and plays a causal role in the production of the trying (and of her moving her arm). Similarly, Ginet has not shown that if I cause an agent to try to *A* by electronically stimulating his brain, that process does not essentially involve my electronically producing a pertinent intention that is a cause of the trying.

Ginet has not successfully answered the Davidsonian challenge. I argue next that R. Jay Wallace's recent attempt also fails. Wallace's response resembles Ginet's in featuring intentions. He contends that agents' intentions "incorporate information about [their] conception of their reasons for acting as they do" (1999, p. 240; cf. McCann 1998, ch. 8). For example, Al, in a scenario I sketched earlier, might intend *to mow his lawn this morning as a way of getting back at his neighbor*, where the italicized words are an expression of the content of his intention.[8] In Wallace's view, the reason for which Al mows his lawn is "reflected in the content of [his] intention," and agents are "guided by their conception of their reasons when that conception is reflected in the content of the intention on which they act" (p. 239). While leaving open the possibility that decisions and intentions are causes of actions, Wallace rejects the idea that intentions and decisions have beliefs and desires as causes (p. 241, n. 35). Thus, that Al mows his lawn for a reason having to do with getting back at his neighbor can be read off from an intention that plays a suitable causal role in producing the relevant bodily motions even though his desire for revenge and his belief that mowing his lawn this morning would serve that purpose (and their neural realizers) play no causal role in the production of the intention or the action.

This proposal pushes the issue back a step. Wallace and I agree that an agent's deciding to A is itself an intentional action (1999, pp. 236–37; see chapter 9 below). So he should see Davidson's challenge as applying straightforwardly to *deciding* for reasons. Again, Al has a pair of reasons for mowing his lawn this morning, one centrally involving revenge (*R1*) and the other convenience (*R2*), but he mows it for one and not the other. Suppose that Al decides to mow his lawn this morning, but leave open the possibility that this description of what he decides is incomplete. If it was for reason *R1*—or reason *R2*—that he made his decision, in virtue of what is that true? Now, it is plausible that in ordinary cases of executing a decision to A or executing the intention to A formed in so deciding, the reasons for which we A are the reasons for which we decided as we did.[9] So the answer to my question, on a view like Wallace's, may be that it is true that Al decided for certain reasons—the same reasons for which he acted, reasons that can be read off from the content of his decision—in virtue of the content of his decision (i.e., the content of the intention he formed in making his decision). For example, if what Al decided was to mow his lawn as a way of getting revenge, then he decided for reason *R1*, and that in virtue of which it is true that he decided for *R1* is precisely that *what he decided* was to mow his lawn as a way of getting revenge.

This answer is problematic. It is implausible that it is a *general truth* about our decisions to A that the reasons for which we so decide—and the reasons for which we act when we execute decisions—are expressed or reflected in the contents of our decisions. We consider many reasons for and against accepting certain job offers, for example, and sometimes we reach the decisions we do in these cases—and accept or reject a job offer—*for* a whole raft of reasons. It is unlikely that large rafts of reasons can be read off from the contents of our decisions in such cases. It would take a very special mind to represent each member of a large collection of reasons in the content of a decision. If, in cases of this kind, people should say (as, in fact, they do say) and believe that what the agent decided was to accept job offer X—and not that what he decided was, for example, to accept X "as a way of" bringing it about that he and his family live in a more attractive part of the world, enabling his children to attend better schools inexpensively, improving his family's job prospects, reducing his teaching load, increasing his salary, and so on—special grounds need to be offered for holding that, even in relatively simple cases, (partial) representations or reflections of each of the reasons for which agents decide and act as they do uniformly enter into the contents of decisions.

There is a related problem. Suppose that Al decided for reason *R1*. On one view, what he decided was to mow his lawn early this morning (to *M*, for short). On Wallace's

(1999) alternative view, what he decided was (at least) to mow his lawn early this morning as a way of getting back at his neighbor (to M^*). If Al decided to M^*, for what reason did he so decide? If the answer is "no reason," then, unless Wallace is prepared to defend the thesis that there are intentional actions that are done for no reason, he should retract his claim that decisions are intentional actions. (The retraction would be a mistake; see chapter 9.) So suppose there was a reason for which Al decided to M^*. On Wallace's view, apparently, that reason is reflected in the content of Al's decision. Now, that mowing his lawn early this morning would be a way of getting revenge on his neighbor—or, on another view of reasons, the combination of Al's desire for revenge and his belief that he can get it by mowing early—is a reason for M-ing and a reason for deciding to M, not a reason for M^*-ing and for deciding to M^*.[10] The answer to my question about Al's reason for deciding to M^* is not found in *this* reason. If a positive answer is forthcoming, the reason identified seemingly needs to be reflected in the content of Al's decision, on Wallace's view. So what I had been describing as Al's decision to M^* is really a decision to M^{**}—say, a decision to mow his lawn early as a way of getting revenge on his neighbor, partly just for the sake of getting revenge but also both in order to show her that he is not the sort to take rude mowing behavior lying down and to honor his tit-for-tat principle. Of course, if it is claimed that this is what Al really decided to do, the question arises, for what reason did he decide to do this? A vicious regress threatens and must somehow be blocked.

Wallace asserts that "we do not for a minute need to think that it is necessarily a simple matter, even for agents themselves, to ascertain what their real intentions in acting are" (1999, p. 240).[11] If the content of an intention like Al's when he mows his lawn were as complex as Wallace is apparently committed to viewing it as being, we should not be at all surprised about agents' difficulties in this connection! Worries about self-deception are another matter entirely. Even if Wallace can block the threatened regress, his view has the consequence that the contents of decisions are implausibly complicated even in mundane scenarios like the present one.

I supposed that Wallace would not want to deny that Al's decision to M^* was made for a reason. However, that supposition is not required for my purposes. In the story as I sketched it, if Al decided to mow his lawn early as a way of getting back at his neighbor, he made this decision for the reasons I identified. If Wallace were to deny that Al's decision to M^* was made for a reason, he would be wrong.

Here is the bottom line on Wallace's (1999) reply to the Davidsonian challenge. Wallace does not answer the challenge as it applies to mental actions of intention formation—that is, decisions. A natural answer on his behalf, given his position on acting for reasons, is unsuccessful. The contents of our decisions and intentions are not equipped to do the required work. Nor can they do the required work regarding overt actions done for complex collections of reasons. In simple cases, one may think that it is true that the reasons for which an agent acted were R in virtue of R's being reflected in the content of his decision, even though one denies that this is true in many cases. But this stance is unstable. Actual psychological constraints on the complexity of the content of a normal human agent's decisions may permit contents that reflect the reasons, R, for which an agent decided and acted in some cases, but that an effective decision had R-reflecting content certainly does not entail that that in virtue of which it is true that the agent decided and acted for R is that the decision had that content. A credible *general* answer to the "in virtue of" question, one that works in all cases of acting (including deciding) for reasons, is what theorists are after.[12] And causalism has resources for providing such an answer. Perhaps in relatively simple cases (e.g., a father's deciding to try to cheer his daughter up, which he intrinsically desires to do, by throwing a party for her), the reason for which the agent decided and acted as he did—reason *R*—can be read off from the content of his decision. This, of course, is entirely consistent with its being true that he decided and acted for *R* in virtue of its being true that *R* (or his having or apprehending it or the neural realization of one of these things) played a distinctive causal role in generating the decision and overt action. The latter truth, in conjunction with the supposition that *R* was reflected in the content of the agent's decision, would account for its being true that the reason reflected there was the reason for which he decided and acted.

2. Two More Unsuccessful Replies

Currently, the most detailed defense of *AT* and reply to the Davidsonian challenge is found in an intriguing book by George Wilson (1989).[13] In the book's final chapter, Wilson offers a statement of his teleological alternative to causalism as illustrated in a discussion of a man who climbs a ladder to fetch his hat:

> The teleological alternative informs us that the man's desire to retrieve his hat is relevant to explaining why he went up the ladder in virtue of the fact that *this* was a desire he went up the ladder in order to satisfy. He went up the ladder for the *conscious* purpose of satisfying his desire to retrieve his hat. But then, this is just the fact that his movements up the ladder were intended to promote the satisfaction of this desire. It is these teleological truths about the man that support the claims that
> > He went up the ladder because he wanted to retrieve his hat
> and
> > He went up the ladder because he (thereby) intended to satisfy his desire to get his hat.
> (pp. 287–88)

As Wilson notes (pp. 215–16), causalists who accept "teleological descriptions" of the sort present in this passage regard them as descriptions of causally relevant items. For example, that the man went up the ladder *in order to* satisfy his desire to get his hat is understood as a matter of that desire's (or a realizer's) playing a suitable causal role.[14] Naturally, Wilson rejects this idea.

An apparent problem for Wilson's (1989) view may be introduced by way of the following variant of his illustration.[15] Suppose that a man, Norm, left not only his hat on the roof but also a toolbox and a basket of bricks. He wants to fetch each, but he knows he cannot get them all at once, and as he starts up the ladder he is undecided about what to retrieve this time. When he is about halfway up the ladder, Norm forms an intention to get the bricks on the current trip and moves the rest of the way up with that intention.

If Norm "went up the ladder [the rest of the way] because he (thereby) intended to satisfy his desire to get" the bricks, in virtue of what is that true? Wilson's (1989) answer in the passage I quoted is that "his movements [the rest of the way] up the ladder were *intended* to promote the satisfaction of this desire." But imagine that although these movements were indeed intended to promote this, Norm's so intending (and its physical realizer) played no causal role in the production of the movements. Imagine that once Norm decided to get the bricks, his body moved as it did only because random Q signals from Mars just then started providing exactly the right input to his muscles, and even so, it seemed to Norm that he was moving himself up the ladder in just the way he had been doing. (The Q signals struck Norm just when bizarre Z rays from Venus prevented events in his brain from causing muscle contractions and the like.) In that event, it is false that Norm *climbed* the rest of the way up the ladder. Although his body continued to move up the ladder as it had been, and although he *intended of his movements* that they "promote the satisfaction of [his] desire," Norm was no longer the agent of the movements.

More important for present purposes, even though there is a reading of "Norm went up the ladder" on which the sentence is true, it is *false* that "he went [the rest of the way] up the ladder because he wanted to retrieve [the bricks]," and false as well that "he went [the rest of the way] up the ladder because he (thereby) intended to satisfy his desire to get [the bricks]."[16] Instead, Norm went the rest of the way up the ladder because the Q signals provided certain input to his muscles.

This scenario admittedly is a strange one. Even so, it lays bare a point that might otherwise be hidden. Our bodily motions might coincide with our desires or intentions, and even result in our getting what we want or what we intend to get (or what we intend our motions to promote), without those motions being *explained* by the desires or intentions. Part of the challenge for Wilson (1989) is to get want-to-behavior and intention-to-behavior explanation into the picture while not relying on want-to-behavior and intention-to-behavior *causation* (or causation by neural realizations of pertinent mental items). The present case apparently shows that he fails to do this in the passage at issue.

One might counter that, since Norm was not the *agent* of the movements or motions in question, they were not *his* movements and hence were not movements of the sort with which Wilson is concerned in the passage. Two observations are in order. First, if the correct diagnosis of Norm's not being the agent of the movements is that a pertinent desire or intention of his (or an associated realizing state) did not play an appropriate causal role in the production of those movements, then causalism is vindicated. Second, Wilson (1989, p. 49) adopts a very broad conception of action according to which the "movements" on the ladder were, indeed, performed by Norm (e.g., "A man performs a convulsive and spasmodic movement when he clutches and cannot loose a live electric wire, and someone undergoing an epileptic seizure may perform a series of wild and wholly uncontrollable movements"). Wilson regards the broadness of his conception of action as a virtue, and the broad conception figures significantly in his attack on causalism, in some examples of causal deviance (see, e.g., pp. 271–73).

Wilson may claim that, in my case, Norm's movements up the ladder were not, in fact, "intended to promote the satisfaction of" his desire to get the bricks (cf. Wilson 1997, pp. 69–70). In a chapter on intention in action, he writes, "If an agent has intended of her behavior b that it A, then not only was that behavior directed at A-ing, but it was *sentiently* and often *consciously* directed at A-ing" (1989, p. 146).[17] He adds that "sentient direction . . . entails that the mechanisms of the agent's bodily control, as exercised in the performance of *b*, were systematically and selectively responsive to the agent's perception of her environment." So, since Norm did not exercise his mechanisms of bodily control in performing the relevant movements, Wilson can say that those movements were not *intended by* Norm to promote the satisfaction of his desire to get the bricks.

In spinning my story, I assume that Norm's intending of his movements up the ladder that they promote the satisfaction of his desire to get the bricks is sufficient for those movements' being intended by him to promote this. But Wilson can reply that this assumption reveals a mistaken conception of intention. I seem to be presupposing that Norm's intention is an *attitude*. And Wilson rejects the idea that intentions are attitudes (1989, p. 229).

If intentions are not attitudes, what are they? Wilson says that "intentions in actions are very special *properties* of the actions that exhibit them" (1989, pp. 222–23) and that "'Being intended to achieve such-and-such' is, if one likes, a 'mentalistic' or 'psychological' property of behavior" (p. 292).[18] He also tells us that "the concept of 'sentient directionality' . . . is the same as the concept of 'intention in action'" (pp. 146–47). Wilson's view, I think, is that an agent's intending movements of his to promote the satisfaction of his desire to get *x* is precisely his sentiently directing those movements at promoting the satisfaction of that desire. He says that the fact that "the man went up the ladder for the *conscious* purpose of satisfying his desire to retrieve his hat" is the same fact as that "his movements up the ladder were *intended* to promote the satisfaction of this desire" (p. 288). And the latter fact, apparently, is supposed to be the same fact as that the man sentiently directed his movements up the ladder at promoting satisfaction of this desire. Now this one fact, described in three different ways, is alleged to "support" the claims that "He went up the ladder because he wanted to retrieve his hat" and "He went up the ladder because he (thereby) intended to satisfy his desire to get his hat" and, therefore, to support the claim that "the man's desire to retrieve his hat is relevant to explaining why he went up the ladder." But why aren't the claims that are supposed to be supported by the fact that is described in three different ways simply further descriptions of the same fact? The answer, I suppose, lies in the occurrence of the word "because" in these claims.

Notice that from the fact that the man "went up the ladder because he wanted to retrieve his hat" one cannot safely infer that he performed an action. In a variant of Norm's case, malicious Martians take control of Norm's body and cause it to move up the ladder by zapping his feet with levitation rays and his hands with comparable motion controllers because they know he wants to get his hat. His wanting to get his hat figures importantly in the causal sequence that results in his going up the ladder; thus, it is true that he went up the ladder *because* he wanted to retrieve his hat. Even so, it is the Martians who control Norm's body, not Norm. The same point could be made about the fact that the man "went up the ladder because he (thereby) intended to satisfy his desire to get his hat," if "he (thereby) intended" were merely to signal the presence of an intending attitude. The real work here is done by the notion of sentient direction that Wilson wants to capture in such expressions as "he (thereby) intended." And, I think, one can fairly read the second "because" claim as follows: "The man went up the ladder because, at the time, he was sentiently directing his movements at satisfying his desire to get his hat."

Causalists will want to interpret an agent's sentiently directing his movements at the satisfaction of a certain desire in a way that accords to the desire (or its neural realizer) a causal role; and I cannot find in Wilson's (1989) book a clear—and clearly—noncausal account of what it is for a movement to be sentiently directed at the satisfaction of a desire. Wilson says that facts of the following kind "about the context of the action, about the agent's perception of that context, and about the agent's sentient relations to his own movements . . . make it true that he intended of those movements that they promote his getting back his hat" (read: make it true that those movements were *sentiently directed* by him at promoting his getting back his hat):

> [1] The man, wondering where his hat is, sees it on the roof, fetches the ladder, and immediately begins his climb. [2] Moreover, the man is aware of performing these movements up the ladder and knows, at least roughly, at each stage what he is about to do next. [3] Also, in performing these movements, he is prepared to adjust or modulate his behavior were it to appear to him that the location of his hat has changed. [4] Again, at each stage of his activity, were the question to arise, the man would judge that he was performing those movements as a means of retrieving his hat. (p. 290)

But is this enough?

Two observations are in order before this question can be properly answered. The first concerns the second sentence of the passage just quoted. What knowledge is attributed to the man there? Not the knowledge that he is about to perform a sentiently directed movement of a certain kind, if sentient direction is a notion that this passage is supposed to explicate. However, this does not block the supposition that the man knows, in some sense, that he is about to perform a movement of his left hand onto the next rung, for example, in Wilson's (1989) broad sense of "perform a movement."

Second, Wilson claims that "to try to [A] is (roughly and for the pertinent range of cases) to perform an action that is intended to [A]" (1989, p. 270). Brief attention to trying will prove useful. If the qualification is suppressed for a moment, Wilson's claim amounts, for him, to the assertion that to try to A is to perform an action that is sentiently directed by the agent at A-ing. Regarding the following plausible proposition, there is no need to worry about limiting the range of cases: (*T1*) if one is doing something that one is sentiently directing at A-ing, then one is trying to A, in an utterly familiar, unexacting sense of "trying." Although people may often reserve attributions of trying for instances in which an agent makes a considerable or special effort, this is a matter of conversational implicature and does not mark a conceptual truth about trying.[19] A blindfolded, anesthetized man who reports that he has raised his arm as requested quite properly responds to the information that his arm is strapped to his side by observing that, in any case, he *tried* to raise it—even though, encountering no felt resistance, he made no *special* effort to raise it.[20] And when, just now, I typed the word "just," I tried to do that even though I easily typed the word. Now, *T1* entails (*T2*) that one who is not trying to A, even in the unexacting sense of "trying" identified, is not sentiently directing one's bodily motions at A-ing. *T2* is very plausible, as is the following, related proposition: (*T3*) one who is not trying to do anything at all, even in the unexacting sense of "trying," is not sentiently directing one's bodily motions at anything.

In the following case, as I explain, although Norm is not, during a certain time, trying to do anything, even in the unexacting sense of "trying" that I identified, he satisfies all four of the conditions in the quotation at issue during that time. The moral is that these conditions are not sufficient for a person's sentiently directing "movements" of his at the time. Their insufficiency follows from the details of the case and the platitude that an agent who is not trying (even in the unexacting sense) to do anything is not sentiently directing his bodily motions at anything.

Norm has learned that on rare occasions, after he embarks on a routine activity (e.g., tying his shoes or climbing a ladder), Martians take control of his body and initiate and sustain the next several movements in the chain while making it seem to him that he is acting normally.[21] He is unsure how they do this, but he has excellent reasons to believe that they are even more skilled at this than he is at moving his own body, as in fact they are. (The Martians have given Norm numerous demonstrations with other people.) The Martians have made a thorough study of Norm's patterns of peripheral bodily motion when he engages in various routine activities. Their aim was to make it seem to him that he is acting while preventing him from even *trying* to act by selectively shutting down portions of his brain. To move his body, they zap him in the belly with M-rays that control the relevant muscles and joints. When they intervene, they wait for Norm to begin a routine activity, read his mind to make sure that he plans to do what they think he is doing (e.g., tie his shoes or climb to the top of a ladder), and then zap him for a while—unless the mind-reading team sees him abandon or modify his plan. When the team notices something of this sort, the Martians stop interfering, and control immediately reverts to Norm.

A while ago, Norm started climbing a ladder to fetch his hat. After he climbed a few rungs, the Martians took over. Although they controlled Norm's next several movements while preventing him from trying to do anything, they would have relinquished control to him if his plan had changed (e.g., in light of a belief that the location of his hat had changed).

Return to facts [1] through [4]. Fact [1] obtains in this case. What about fact [2]? It is no less true that Norm performs his next several movements than that the man who clutches the live electric wire performs convulsive movements. And the *awareness* of performing movements mentioned in fact [2] is no problem. The wire clutcher can be aware of bodily "performances" of his that are caused by the electrical current, and Norm can be aware of bodily "performances" of his that are caused by M-rays. Norm also satisfies a knowledge condition of the sort I identified. If Wilson is right in thinking that an ordinary ladder climber knows, in some sense, that he is about to perform a movement of his left hand onto the next rung, Norm can know this too. What he does not know is whether he will perform the movement on his own or in the alternative way. But that gives him no weaker grounds for knowledge than the ordinary agent has, given that the subject matter is the performance of movements in Wilson's (1989) broad sense and given what Norm knows about the Martians' expertise. Fact [3] also obtains. Norm is prepared to adjust or modulate his behavior, and one may even suppose that he is *able* to do so. Although the Martians in fact initiated and controlled Norm's next several movements up the ladder while preventing him from trying to do anything, they would not have done so if his plans had changed. Fact [4] obtains also. In Wilson's sense of "perform a movement," Norm believes that he is performing his movements "as a means of retrieving his hat." (He does not believe that the Martians are controlling his behavior; after all, he realizes that they very rarely do so.)

Even though these facts obtain, Norm does not sentiently direct his next several movements up the ladder at getting his hat since he is not sentiently directing these movements at all. As I have mentioned, Wilson (1989) maintains that sentiently directing a bodily movement that one performs entails exercising one's mechanisms of bodily control in performing that movement. However, Norm did not exercise these mechanisms in his performance of the movements at issue. Indeed, he did not make even a minimal effort to perform these movements; because of the Martian intervention, he made no effort at all—that is, did not try—to do anything at the time. And it is a platitude that one who did not try to do anything at all during a time t did not sentiently direct his bodily motions during t.

It might be suggested that although Norm did not directly move his body during the time at issue, he sentiently directed his bodily motions in something similar to the way in which his sister Norma sentiently directed motions of her body when she orally guided blindfolded colleagues who were carrying her across an obstacle-filled room as part of a race staged by her law firm to promote teamwork. If Norma succeeded, she may be said to have brought it about that she got across the room, and her bringing this about is an action. Notice, however, that there is something that she was trying to do at the time. For example, she was trying to guide her teammates. By hypothesis, there is nothing that Norm was trying to do at the relevant time, for the Martians blocked brain activity required for trying. And this is a crucial difference between the two cases. The claim that Norma sentiently directed motions of her body at some goal at the time is consistent with $T3$; the comparable claim about Norm is not.[22]

Now, what is it to exercise one's mechanisms of bodily control in performing a movement that is sentiently directed specifically at promoting one's retrieving one's hat? Again, causalists will favor an answer that features a desire or intention to get one's hat, some event of intention formation or intention acquisition, or some realizing state or event as a cause of the exercise. And, again, Wilson (1989) has failed to provide a noncausalist alternative to this sort of answer. He has not answered the question—a crucial one for teleologists—raised in the introduction to this section: in virtue of what is it true that a person acted in pursuit of a particular goal?[23] Thus, he has not successfully met the Davidsonian challenge.[24]

Scott Sehon (1994) attempts to answer this challenge. Under the heading "Defusing the Davidsonian Challenge," he argues that a teleologist can appeal to counterfactuals to "distinguish between reasons an agent acted on and reasons the agent had but did not act on" (p. 67). Sehon invites us to imagine that Heidi "lifts a heavy book up to the top of a bookshelf" while having the following pair of desires: "a desire to put the book where it belongs and a desire to strengthen her biceps." He assumes that only one of these desires "provides the reason why Heidi lifted the book," and he asks which one does so. Sehon reports that this question, "as viewed from the teleological theory, looks roughly like this: toward which outcome did Heidi direct her behavior, that the book was put away or that her biceps were strengthened?" The correct answer, he contends, depends on what counterfactuals of a certain kind are true of Heidi at the time. If the book had belonged on the bottom shelf, would she have put it there, or would she have placed it on the top shelf? If something more suitable for the purposes of exercising her biceps had been present, would she have lifted it, or would she have lifted the book? And so on.

Suppose that the counterfactual test indicates that Heidi's goal was that the book be returned to its proper place. Even so, one will not know in virtue of what it is true that Heidi directed her behavior toward that goal until one knows in virtue of what it is true that Heidi directed her behavior. One can apply Sehon's (1994) counterfactual test to a case in which Martians who wished to deceive Heidi into believing that she was acting manipulated her muscles in order to make her bodily motions fit the intention she had at the time to return the book to its proper place while preventing her from even trying to return it, and one would get the result that Heidi directed her behavior toward the book's being returned there. But, of course, that result would be false since Heidi was not directing her behavior—that is, acting—at all in this case. Rather, the Martians were controlling the motions of her body.

True counterfactuals are true in virtue of something or other. Their truth is grounded in something factual. If Heidi was executing—that is, acting on—an intention to return the book to its proper place, then, other things being equal, one should expect such counterfactuals as the following to be true: if Heidi had believed that the book belonged on the bottom shelf, she would have placed it there; if Heidi had believed that the book's proper place was the middle shelf, she would have put it there. But if these counterfactuals are true for the reasons one expects them to be, their truth is grounded in part in Heidi's *acting* with the intention of putting the book where it belongs; their truth does not explain what it is for Heidi to be acting with this intention.

One moral of the objections I have raised to Wilson's (1989) and Sehon's (1994) attempted answers to the Davidsonian challenge is clear. Unless desires, intentions, or their physical realizers play a causal role in the production of a person's bodily motions, and not simply the causal role of providing information about goals to mischievous Martians, there is the threat (as in my Martian chronicles) that the person is not acting at all, much less acting in pursuit of the goal(s) that the desire or intention specifies. Partly because teleologists have not offered an acceptable account of what it is to *act*, or to "direct" one's bodily motions, they have not offered an acceptable account of what it is to act for the sake of a particular goal.

3. Causalism and Primary Deviance

Causalists claim to have a solution to this problem. They offer a causal account of human action in terms of mental items—such as beliefs, desires, intentions, and associated events (e.g., acquiring an intention to A straightway)—or their physical realizers. If an account of this kind is correct, the stage is set for a causal account of what it is for a human being to act for a particular goal in the same terms. In this section, I introduce an objection featuring causal deviance that some teleologists have raised against the possibility of a successful causal account of acting in pursuit of a particular goal. First, a word about causalism is in order.

As I have explained elsewhere, a familiar causal approach to understanding and explaining action—I call it *CA*—treats actions as analogous to money and sunburns in a noteworthy respect.[25] The piece of paper with which Norm purchased his hat is a genuine U.S. $1 bill partly in virtue of its having been produced (in the right way) by the U.S. Treasury Department. The burn on his back is a sunburn partly in virtue of its having been produced by exposure to the sun's rays. A duplicate bill that Norm produced with plates and paper stolen from the Treasury Department is a counterfeit $1 bill, not a genuine one. And a burn that looks and feels just like the one on his back is not a sunburn if it was produced by exposure to a heat lamp rather than to the sun. Similarly, according to *CA*, a certain event occurring at *t* is Norm's raising his right hand at *t*—an action—partly in virtue of its having been produced "in the right way" by certain mental items (or their neural realizations). An event someone else covertly produces by remote control—one including a visually indistinguishable rising of Norm's right hand not produced by an intention or desire of Norm's or an associated mental event (or, again, pertinent realizations)—is not a raising of Norm's right hand by Norm, even if it feels to Norm as though he is raising his hand.

No plausible version of *CA* identifies actions with *nonactional* events caused in the right way (see Brand 1984, ch. 1).[26] That would be analogous to identifying genuine U.S. $1 bills with pieces of printed paper that are not genuine U.S. $1 bills and are produced in the right way by the U.S. Treasury Department; and so identifying genuine U.S. $1 bills would be absurd. To say that an event *E* is an action partly in virtue of its having been produced in the right way is not to say that *E* is a nonactional event—any more than to say that a piece of printed paper *P* is a genuine U.S. $1 bill partly in virtue of its having been produced in the right way is to say that *P* is not a genuine U.S. $1 bill.

Jonathan Dancy has offered the following "reason for denying that reasons are causes": "there is no possible metaphysical distinction between the action and the reasons for it, for if we subtract the reasons from the action, there is not enough left to be an action at all. We would only have something like a bodily movement, or the initiation of a change" (1995, pp. 17–18). If, as I believe, reasons are not *parts* of actions, reasons cannot be subtracted from actions.[27] However, this leaves open the possibility that particular reasons may be subtracted from situations in which actions occur. The following argument is an analogue of Dancy's: if we subtract the U.S. Treasury Department from the situation in which the genuine U.S. $1 bill in my pocket was produced, what is in my pocket is not a genuine U.S. $1 bill; so, there is no possible metaphysical distinction between the genuine U.S. $1 bill in my pocket and the U.S. Treasury Department, which entails that the Treasury Department played no role in producing that $1 bill. Obviously, something has gone wrong. The piece of paper in my pocket is a genuine U.S. $1 bill partly in virtue of how it was produced. That, qua genuine U.S. $1 bill, it *essentially* has a causal history that involves the U.S. Treasury Department is obviously consistent with that department's playing a role in producing the bill. Similarly, that, qua action, a certain event essentially has a causal history that involves mental states of a certain kind is consistent with particular mental states' playing a role in the production of the action.

I turn to causal deviance. Several distinct kinds of causal deviance relevant to attempted causal analyses of *intentional* action have received attention in the literature.[28] One kind—what I elsewhere termed "primary" deviance (Mele 1992c, p. 209)—has a special relevance for the project of constructing a causal analysis of action itself. Here is a well-known illustration: "A climber might want to rid himself of the weight and danger of holding another man on a rope, and he might know that by loosening his hold on the rope he could rid himself of the weight and danger. This belief and want might so unnerve him as to cause him to loosen his hold [unintention-ally]" (Davidson 1980, p. 79). Given the prominence of intention in the recent causal-ist literature, a reformulation of this example in terms of intention is in order: a climber intends to rid himself of the danger of holding another man on a rope by loos-ening his hold, and this intention so unnerves him that it causes him to loosen his hold unintentionally.

Some causal theorists who have assessed cases of this kind as attempted coun-terexamples to a causal account of what it is for an action to be intentional have dis-missed them on the grounds that they are not cases of action at all (Brand 1984, p. 18; Thalberg 1984). As they see it, the agent's being unnerved consists at least partly in his losing control over his hands, with the result that his grip loosens; he does not perform an action of loosening his grip. If this diagnosis is correct, primary deviance may pose a problem for the project of constructing a causal analysis of action and, hence, for a related project regarding acting for the sake of a particular goal. Consider the follow-ing simple-minded analysis of action: S performed an action A if and only if S in-tended to A, that intention was a cause of X, and X is a bodily motion of a kind involved in some actual or possible A-ing. In the present case, let X be the climber's relevant fin-ger and hand motions. The problem is evident.[29]

In a recent article, appealing to primary causal deviance, Scott Sehon (1997) sug-gested that no amount of refinement will yield an acceptable causal analysis of teleo-logical locutions like "S performed action A in order to B" and that teleological expla-nations of action are "irreducible" to causal explanations. Rather than offer a causal analysis here, I construct a case in which a teleological explanation of a particular ac-tion is an explanation of precisely the kind that causal theorists have offered and then develop a moral about primary causal deviance.

Some background on the nature of that project is in order. In a discussion of pri-mary deviance, Alvin Goldman remarked, "A complete explanation of how wants and beliefs lead to intentional acts would require extensive neurophysiological informa-tion, and I do not think it is fair to demand of a philosophical analysis that it provide this information . . . [A] detailed delineation of the causal process that is characteristic of intentional action is a problem mainly for the special sciences" (1970, p. 62; cf. pp. 166–69). Goldman's remark may strike some readers as evasive (see Bishop 1989, pp. 143–44; McCann 1974, pp. 462–63), but he does have a point. A deviant causal connection between an x and a y is deviant relative to "normal" causal routes from x-s to y-s. Moreover, what counts as *normal* here is perspective-relative. From the point of view of physics, for example, there is nothing abnormal about Davidson's (1980) example of deviance. And, for beings of a particular kind, the normal route from intention to action may be best articulated partly in neurophysiological terms.

One way around the problem posed by our neuroscientific ignorance is to design (in imagination, of course) an agent's motor control system. Knowing the biological being's design in that sphere, we have a partial basis for distinguishing causal chains associated with overt action from deviant motion-producing chains. If we can distin-guish deviant from nondeviant causal chains in agents we design—that is, chains not appropriate to action from action-producing chains—then perhaps we would be able to do the same for normal human beings, if we were to know a lot more than we do about the human body (including the brain, of course).

4. A Myth About Simple Agents

Epimetheus longed for a new kind of agent, something between god and beast. So he created what he called man, some female and some male. They looked very much like young adult human beings today. Man was utterly inactive, and the entire race would soon have become extinct if Epimetheus's brother, Prometheus, had not spied him crying in the midst of his new beings. "What's the problem?" Prometheus asked. "I created these beautiful beings to play with, and now they won't do anything at all," Epimetheus replied. Prometheus gently chided his brother. "Well, of course they won't," he said. "At least they won't do things of the sort you have in mind. You haven't given them any desires; they have nothing to motivate them. They'll need some beliefs too, so that they'll have some idea how to go about satisfying their desires. And intentions would help too." Prometheus then launched into an explanation of the differences among various kinds of behavior, including tropistic behavior of the sort found in marigolds and mosquitoes and intentional behavior, but his brother quickly lost interest. "Fix them for me, Prometheus," Epimetheus pleaded. Prometheus thought that it would be better to let the race die out and then allow evolution to take its course, but he consented nonetheless.

Two points need to be made before the next part of the story is told. The first concerns Prometheus's conception of action. As I mentioned earlier, Wilson adopts a very broad conception of performing a movement—and hence of overt action—according to which "a man performs a convulsive and spasmodic movement when he clutches and cannot loose a live electric wire" (1989, p. 49). Neither Prometheus nor Epimetheus counts this as action. Give a comatose man a strong and lengthy electric shock and his body will jerk about convulsively and spasmodically for some time, but the comatose man is not acting or performing bodily movements. The sustained jolt of electricity, not the comatose man, is moving the man's body. The same is true of the unfortunate man who cannot let go of the live wire. To be sure, there is a sense of "action" in which even acids, waves, and wind act, but this is not the sense that concerns Prometheus and his brother. Nor are they concerned with tropistic "actions": for example, plants bending—or ticks climbing—toward the light.

The second point is that the part of story I am about to tell is metaphysically more complicated than I make it out to be. Prometheus, in thinking about how to turn man into an agent, was guided by a psychological theory and by biological expertise. He had no definite metaphysical opinion about the precise connection among beliefs, intentions, and the like, on the one hand, and the physical states that realize them, on the other hand. To simplify the story, I tell it largely in psychological language, but some readers may prefer to interpret the psychocausal assertions as assertions about the physical realizers of psychological events and states.

Prometheus's initial concern was overt action (i.e., action essentially involving peripheral bodily motion), and he was a bottom-up designer. In his planning, he started with overt action, as he conceived of it, and worked up. He wanted overt actions to be causally initiated by acquisitions of what he called *proximal* intentions—in the basic case, intentions to A straightaway.[30] (Intentions, as he conceived of them, are executive attitudes toward plans, plans being the representational content of intentions.)[31] So Prometheus reconfigured the human brain and body with this end in view. In the newly configured beings, the acquisition of a proximal intention would initiate the sending of a "command" signal to what he called the Promethean motor cortex (*PMC*). The signal would specify the kind of action to be performed straightaway, and it would be transformed in the *PMC* into "motor signals"—specific, fine-grained executive signals to specific muscles and joints, which signals have the function of producing muscular motions. For example, the acquisition of a proximal intention gently to touch the tip of one's nose with the tip of one's right index finger would initiate the sending of an appropriate command signal to the *PMC*, where it would be transformed into specific motor signals to the appropriate muscles and joints. (Like some philosophers of action, Prometheus took overt actions to begin in the brain.)[32] The motor signals would "command" the muscles and joints to move in certain ways. In the case of intentions that are for movements and not also for what Prometheus called "agent-external results" (e.g., raising one's right hand, as opposed to touching a branch—or one's nose—with one's right hand), the signals would command the muscles and joints to move in such ways that the completion of the movement would ensure satisfaction of the intention. In the case of intentions that include agent-external results (e.g., an intention to pick up an apple with one's right hand), the signals would command the relevant muscles and joints to move in ways appropriate to the satisfaction of the intention.

The new design also was such that Promethean agents engage in overt action *only if* the acquisition of a proximal intention plays this initiating role. The neural architecture of Promethean agents was such that the *PMC* would produce motor signals by, and only by, transforming command signals initiated by acquisitions of proximal intentions. In the absence of motor signals produced by the *PMC*, a Promethean agent was in no position to act overtly. The biological design of Promethean agents included no alternative route to overt action.

The clever Prometheus also assigned a causal role to the *persistence*, or continued presence, of a proximal intention. Such persistence would causally sustain the signaling process and, hence, the relevant bodily motions, until the agent came to believe either that achievement of the (final) goal represented in his intention was ensured or that continuing his present course of action was not worth the trouble.[33] An agent's coming to hold the latter belief would extinguish the intention. Prometheus's design also ensured that the dissolution of a proximal intention would put an end to associated action, unless the action had gone too far to be halted.

Prometheus was particularly proud of his use of intentions in the causal *guidance* of human action sustained by a persisting intention.[34] In the case of intentions that incorporate plans with more than a single node, receipt of feedback indicating that one's body is moving according to plan and that one's bodily motions are getting one closer to one's goal would promote the occurrence of motions called for by the next portion of one's plan. Feedback indicating that things are veering off course would foster corrections of bodily motions, the standard for corrections being provided by the plan embedded in the agent's persisting intention.[35] Even in the case of relatively simple actions like unclenching one's right fist, persisting intentions played a guiding role in Promethean agents. Within a few milliseconds of acquiring a proximal intention to unclench his fist, an agent would begin exhibiting motions called for by his intention, and he would stop exhibiting such motions upon receiving feedback indicating that the fist is unclenched. Prometheus designed human agents in such a way that their "directing" their ongoing bodily motions required persisting intentions to play a guiding role. No other way of endowing them with self-direction occurred to him.

A brief discussion of some post-Promethean research will enable me to provide a fuller description of his design as it applies to guidance.[36] Many representational states and events evidently play important roles even in the production of routine intentional behavior, such as an ordinary agent's buttoning his shirt. The activation of (representational) motor schemata, for example, may help to explain the occurrence of particular finger motions involved in the buttoning, and receipt of feedback contributes to the development of the agent's behavior.[37] Both feedback and "low-level" representations of minute "to-be-performed" finger motions and the like (Gallistel 1980, p. 368) require attention.

It is useful to have an idea of how motor schemata might be realized. Charles Gallistel offers an illuminating speculative account of the neural embodiment or realization of a motor schema that might be involved in a certain target-tracking task (1980, pp. 367–73). The account conveys a firmer sense of the location of motor schemata in the etiology of intentional action than do various functional definitions. The task in question is "to keep the tip of a . . . pointer on top of a sinusoidally undulating target, while the experimenter varies the frequency of the undulation." "At higher frequencies of undulation," Gallistel writes, subjects "generated their own sinusoidal movements and adjusted the parameters of their movements so as to match the trajectory of the pointer to the trajectory of the target" (pp. 367–68). He speculates that the schema involved is embodied in a "neural oscillator . . . whose phase, period and amplitude have been adjusted to correspond with the target's." The subjects "represent the trajectory of the target by means of" such an oscillator; and the "neural embodiment" of the stored representation "records the strengths of six signals," including "the strength of the signal required to make the period of the internal oscillator match the period of external oscillation." Gallistel also suggests that "an appropriately adjusted oscillator is not only the last stage of the perceptual process . . . but also the first stage of the motor process" (p. 369). Thus, "the process of perceiving a sinusoidal movement culminates in the creation of precisely those neural signals that are needed to direct a corresponding voluntary movement." An agent who intends to do his best to comply with the experimenter's request may succeed in keeping the pointer on the target owing significantly to guidance provided by a motor schema of the sort just characterized.

Some psychologists take the representational content of motor schemata to run even deeper. Donald MacKay argues that motor schemata involved in handwriting have "lower-level components" that represent "the neuromuscular activity required to achieve" the movement represented by their "higher-level components" (1981, p. 630). Gallistel (1980, pp. 370–71) denies this.

I take no stand on the disagreement between Gallistel and MacKay. The point of the preceding two paragraphs is simply to convey a sense of just how deep motor schemata might run. Feedback and motor schemata, or some functional, representational equivalent of the latter, evidently play proximal causal roles in the guidance of much intentional action. Now, consider the proximal intention of a particular, experienced shirt buttoner to button the shirt that he has just put on. The content of that intention is a plan for buttoning his shirt. In normal cases, that plan is—by default—the agent's normal plan for that activity. Perhaps this agent normally starts with the top button and moves downward, buttoning each successive button in turn; and his so doing in a particular normal case will be explained partly by his intention's incorporating his normal plan. In the process of buttoning, a host of muscle and joint movements are made, and their occurrence may be partially accounted for by low-level representations of, for example, various trajectories of to-be-performed movements of the agent's thumbs and fingers. Information about the agent's progress is provided by sensory feedback.[38]

Prometheus limited the content of agents' intentions to representations that are accessible to consciousness. Supporting low-level motor schemata were housed separately. Some were activated by the acquisition of a proximal intention, others by a combination of the persistence of such an intention and feedback about progress toward the intended goal.[39] A match between representations of this kind and feedback would promote execution of the next step in the intention-imbedded plan. Radical mismatches would sometimes produce serious confusion, but many mismatches would foster useful minor adjustments.

Incidentally, the subtle Prometheus understood a phenomenon that he called "direct ballistic continuation."[40] Consider an ordinary case of snapping one's fingers. An agent embarking on a conventional right-handed finger snapping with his palm facing up presses his thumb and middle finger firmly together and then, maintaining the pressure, simultaneously slides the thumb to the right and the finger downward. After a certain point, the agent is no longer in control of the process. The finger whips downward, thumping into his palm next to his thumb, and the thumb slides off to the right. Here there is direct ballistic continuation of motions that had been guided. Prometheus regarded the ballistic motions I just described as part of the agent's action of snapping his fingers.

Prometheus gave little thought to the question whether any overt actions are properly regarded as continuing beyond the agent's bodily motions. If Meno throws a rock at a rat and hits the rat with that rock, thereby killing it, does his action of killing the rat end when the rock leaves his hand, when the rat dies, or at some other point? Prometheus viewed this question as distinctly philosophical; he took it to lie beyond the expertise of a biological engineer like himself. However, what he called "agents' contributions" to their overt actions ended with the termination of their *guided* bodily motions.

In Prometheus's opinion, intentions are well suited for the causal function of guiding action since they incorporate action-plans. Given the executive nature of intention, the acquisition of proximal intentions, he thought, would also be an ideal causal initiator of action and their continued presence would causally sustain actions nicely. (Naturally, some fine tuning was required.) Prometheus devised some ways for agents to acquire, and even actively to form, intentions on the basis of practical thinking. That part of the story need not be told for present purposes. The same is true, fortunately, of the story of how he instilled free will into human beings.

Predictably, Prometheus's agents were very clumsy at first, but as time passed they learned to do some relatively simple things. Eventually, they learned to do some truly great things. The simpler things are what concern me now.

One day, as part of a test, Prometheus asked a young woman named Daphne whether she could gently move her right hand upward in order to touch, with the tip of her index finger alone, the golden pear that was growing on a branch a few inches over her head. Daphne indicated that she would try, having acquired an intention to do just that. She gently reached up with her right hand until she saw the tip of her index finger come into contact with the pear, and then she stopped. "Excellent," Prometheus exclaimed. He added, "You can put your hand down now. Later, whenever you feel like touching that pear again, just reach up and touch it as you did this time." A few minutes later, Daphne did so. Confident of success on that occasion, Daphne had the bold intention of touching the pear with the tip of her right index finger rather than the more modest intention of *trying* to do this.

The following assertions (among others) about Daphne certainly seem true.

1. Daphne raised her right hand until her index finger came into contact with the pear.
2. Daphne raised her right hand in order to touch the pear.

Now, teleologists allege that "teleological explanations explain by specifying an action's goal or purpose; for example, when we say that Jackie went to the kitchen in order to get a glass of wine, we thereby specify the state of affairs at which her action was directed" (Sehon 1997, p. 195). But in virtue of what is it true that a person acted in pursuit of a particular goal? Ginet, Wallace, Wilson, and Sehon have failed to answer this question successfully, as I have argued. Nor have they given us the wherewithal to answer the following question about Daphne: in virtue of what is it true that Daphne acted in pursuit of the goal of touching the pear?

Can *CA* do any better? According to *CA*, again, actions are, essentially, events that are suitably caused by appropriate mental items (or their physical realizations). Given the way Prometheus designed Daphne as an agent, and suppressing reference to physical realizations, *CA* suggests that Daphne's second action of raising her right hand until the tip of her index finger came into contact with the pear is a certain series of events that was causally initiated by her acquisition of an intention to touch the pear with the tip of her index finger, causally sustained by the continued presence of that intention, and causally guided by that persisting intention.[41] The series includes command signals, bodily motions, and the finger's coming into contact with the pear. *CA* also suggests that, on this occasion, the fact that the action at issue was initiated, sustained, and guided in the way just mentioned is sufficient for the truth of the assertion that Daphne raised her right hand *in order to* touch the pear. Both suggestions apparently contain what teleologists allege to be a teleological explanation of Daphne's action of raising her right hand since the suggestions include a specification of that action's goal or purpose—namely, that she touch the pear with the tip of her right index finger.

5. Handling Primary Deviance

If these suggestions are correct, then there are informative, conceptually sufficient conditions—conditions that are *causal* in nature—both for (1) an event's being an action and for (2) an event's being an action performed in pursuit of a particular goal. If there are such conditions, causalists are in much better shape than anticausalist tele-ologists. For, as I have argued, such teleologists have not provided informative suffi-cient conditions for either (1) or (2). It merits emphasis here that informative, concep-tually sufficient anticausalist conditions for (2) are called for by the Davidsonian challenge summarized in section 1.

Should the causalist suggestions at issue be accepted? According to anticausalist teleologists, the answer is no. Sehon (1997) contends that reflection on causal de-viance of the sort at work in cases like that of Davidson's (1980) climber justifies the rejection of causalism (cf. Wilson 1989, ch. 9). As it happens, this climber is one of Prometheus's agents, a fellow named Clem. Can causalists identify something of a causal nature in virtue of which it is false that Clem performed the action of loosening his grip on the rope and false that he loosened his grip in order to "rid himself of the . . . danger" posed by continuing to hold the rope? Yes, they can, as I explain. Since Davidson's case is sketchy, several versions need to be considered.

Version 1. Clem's acquiring the intention—intention *N*—to rid himself of the dan-ger of holding his climbing partner on his rope by loosening his hold does not result in motor signals being sent. Instead it unnerves Clem, with the result that he loses control over his hands. His grip loosens and the rope slips from his hands.

Here, Clem does not perform the action of loosening his grip; for Promethean agents are designed in such a way that they can perform overt actions only in cases in which the acquisition of a proximal intention results in motor signals being sent to ap-propriate muscles. And, of course, if Clem does not perform this action at all, he does not perform it in pursuit of a goal.

It might be claimed that there is no difference between *motor signals* that initiate bodily motions and *nervousness* that initiates bodily motions. In Promethean agents, this is false. In his creatures, motor signals carry instructions to muscles and joints, whereas nervousness contains no such instructions. Moreover, in his agents, what Prometheus called the motor control system—a biological system constituted by the Promethean motor cortex and associated areas of the central nervous system—plays an indispensable role in the production of overt action, whereas bodily motion directly produced by nervousness is produced independently of this system.[42] In Promethean beings, direct causation of bodily motion by nervousness is quite distinct from direct causation of bodily motion by motor signals.

Version 2. Clem's acquiring intention *N* results in appropriate motor signals being sent, and the intention is quickly extinguished. The motor signals do not reach his muscles or joints. Instead, they unnerve him, with the result that he loses both his grip on the rope and his intention.

Given that Clem is a Promethean agent, he performs the action of loosening his grip on the rope only if a relevant intention of his sustains the pertinent motions of his body. But the relevant intention is extinguished before the pertinent bodily motions occur. So, again, Clem does not perform the action of loosening his grip and therefore does not perform this action in pursuit of a goal.

Version 3. Again, Clem's acquiring intention *N* results in appropriate motor signals being sent, which signals do not reach his muscles or joints. Again, the signals un-nerve Clem, with the result that he loses his grip on the rope. However, intention *N* is not extinguished. In fact, its continued presence causally sustains the nervousness that results in Clem's temporary loss of control over the motions of his hands (cf. Mele 1992e, pp. 202–3).

If Clem is not "directing" his hand motions (to use a teleologist's term), he is not performing the action of loosening his grip on the rope. As a Promethean agent, Clem's directing the motions of his hands requires that a relevant intention of his be playing a guiding role in the production of his hand motions. But no intention of his is playing this role; Clem's nervousness prevents that by temporarily depriving him of control over the motions of his hands. So, once again, Clem is not performing the action of loosening his grip; a fortiori, he is not performing this action in pursuit of a goal.

Version 4. Clem's acquiring intention *N* results in appropriate motor signals being sent. This time, those signals reach their targeted muscles and joints, and he begins to loosen his grip on the rope. His fingers start moving. This unnerves him, with the result that he loses his grip on the rope (cf. Mele 1992e, pp. 202–3; Sehon 1997, pp. 201–2). In beginning to loosen his grip, he does not yet loosen it sufficiently for the rope to unravel from his hand; the nervousness that results in his losing his grip plays an intervening causal role. And the continued presence of intention *N* causally sustains the nervousness that results in Clem's temporary loss of control over the motions of his hands.

Although there was a time at which Clem was beginning to loosen his hold on the rope—and doing this in pursuit of the goal of ridding himself of his dangerous burden—he does not perform the action of dropping his partner nor the action of loosening his hold enough to drop his partner. Nor, a fortiori, does he perform either of these actions in pursuit of a goal. Given his construction as a Promethean agent, Clem is not capable of contributing to the continuation of an overt action of his once his relevant bodily motions are not being guided by an intention of his. This itself does not entail that, after becoming unnerved, Clem is no longer performing the action of loosening his hold; for, in some cases, direct ballistic continuations of motions that had been guided may be parts of actions, as in the finger-snapping example. However, the nervousness-produced motions of Clem's hands are not direct ballistic continuations of his previous motions. After all, they are produced by the nervousness that his beginning to loosen his grip causes. Even if they are, in some sense, continuations of earlier motions, they are not direct ballistic continuations. So, in short, Clem's performance of the action of loosening his hold is terminated too soon for him to have performed the action of dropping his partner or the action of loosening his hold enough to drop his partner.[43]

Now, my Promethean myth is a myth. One feature of the neural architecture of Promethean agents is that the *PMC* produces motor signals only by transforming command signals that are initiated by the acquisition of a proximal intention. My description of these agents leaves open the possibility that this is a somewhat magical feature. One might imagine that there is no way to avoid the possibility that a counterfeit of such a command signal—for example, a counterfeit signal produced by direct electronic stimulation of the brain and not by the acquisition of a proximal intention—is transformed into motor signals. Then again, Promethean agents may be designed in such a way that such intervention shuts down the motor control system. In any case, my crucial claim in this connection is that the design of Promethean agents is such that they can perform overt actions only in cases in which the acquisition of a proximal intention initiates the sending of motor signals to appropriate muscles.[44] The possibility of counterfeit command signals undermines this claim only if there are cases in which such a signal, and not the acquisition of a proximal intention, initiates an overt *action*. Are there such cases?

Imagine that a neuroscientist stimulates a Promethean agent's brain in such a way as to send a command signal to the *PMC*, which is then translated into motor signals that directly cause bodily motions, and he does not produce the command signal by producing an intention. An intuitive reaction is that the being does not act. Rather, he is manipulated in such a way that his body mimics action. The Promethean being is the locus of bodily motion rather than the performer of an action.[45]

Imagine now that a Promethean agent has just acquired a proximal intention to take a pear from a tree, and because of neurological blockage his acquiring the intention does not send a command signal. A well-meaning neuroscientist who happens to be on the scene sends a counterfeit of such a signal, and things proceed as in the preceding case. Here again an intuitive judgment is that the being does not act and his body mimics action. The same intuition, I submit, will emerge in response to any example of either of the two styles at issue.[46]

Suppose that a neuroscientist produces a proximal *intention* in a Promethean agent by direct stimulation of the agent's brain, and the acquisition of this intention leads to appropriate bodily movement in the normal way, which includes the intention's playing the initiating, sustaining, and guiding roles that I described. The agent certainly has been manipulated, but I see no good reason to deny that he has been manipulated into performing an action. There is a difference between (1) Mr. X causing Mr. Y's body to move without causing Y to move Y's body and (2) Mr. X causing Y to move Y's body. The two cases featuring the production of counterfeit command signals are instances of (1), as I have suggested. An intuitive reaction to the case of intention induction is that it is an instance of (2).[47]

Consider a pair of cases. In the first member of the pair, a hypnotist manipulates Daphne in such a way that her hearing the word "duck" will straightaway cause her to acquire a proximal intention to quack like a duck for five seconds. Daphne hears the word, acquires the intention, and executes the intention. The quacking is initiated, sustained, and guided by her intention. It is natural to hold that Daphne performs the action of quacking. Seemingly, she intentionally quacks. (To be sure, Daphne may wonder what has come over her.)

Imagine now a counterpart case in which, in the absence of any relevant intention, Daphne emits quacking sounds because a neuroscientist produced a command signal that was transformed in the *PMC* into motor signals that caused motions that in turn caused the sounds. Apparently, Daphne did not perform the action of quacking. In producing the sounds via a route that does not involve intention, the process at work does not involve Daphne as an agent. Daphne may wonder what has come over her, but such puzzlement is not ensured by the details of the case. Suppose that the quacking sounds were produced in the way just described *and* the hypnotist produced in Daphne a proximal intention to quack, which intention played no role in the production of the sounds, owing to the neuroscientist's manipulation. Daphne may think that she is performing a quacking action, but she is wrong.

There is evidence that when sighted people move their hands toward targets, vision of the hand and arm helps calibrate proprioceptive signals (Ghez et al. 2000, p. 505). "The nervous system must also transform the intended direction and extent [of hand movement] into feedforward control signals distributed to motor neurons and muscles. For the resulting movement trajectory to conform to the one that was intended, feedforward commands need to anticipate the effects of both environmental forces and of forces arising within the musculoskeletal system itself" (pp. 505–6). This is a feature of Promethean agents, too. Obviously, there is, in principle, room for monkey business here—for example, for alien interveners—and in processes for the guidance of action in general. However, Prometheus's design is such that any alien intervention into normal processes of guidance simply shuts down the motor control system. Some alien intervention may be capable of assisting agents in performing goal-directed actions, but Prometheus's design precludes such assistance.

Early in this section, I asked whether causalists can identify something of a causal nature in virtue of which it is false (in versions of the case in which this *is* false) that Clem, a Promethean agent, performed the action of loosening his grip on the rope and false that he loosened his grip in order to rid himself of the danger posed by continuing to hold the rope. The answer certainly seems to be yes. As far as I can tell, my Promethean myth, stripped of its magical feature, is coherent. And even though the story is relatively simple, it provides the basis for a causal diagnosis of ways in which primary causal deviance blocks action in an agent of a certain kind. The mix of causal initiation, sustaining, and guiding that I have been describing seems to do the trick in a Promethean agent.

Anticausalists will wish to develop counterexamples to the claim that the involvement of this mix in the production of bodily motion is conceptually sufficient, in a Promethean agent, for action. I see no way of producing a conclusive proof of this sufficiency, and I welcome attempted counterexamples. If the attempted counterexamples fail or instead motivate useful refinement of the mix, I obviously would regard that as good news. A counterexample that showed that *no* story about how particular motions of a particular Promethean being are caused will provide conceptually sufficient conditions for action would be bad news for causalists, but I doubt that one is forthcoming.

Elsewhere, Paul Moser and I offered a causal analysis of what it is for someone to *A* intentionally, given that his *A*-ing is an action (Mele and Moser 1994). We did not offer an analysis of action, nor do I do that here. That task is complicated by, among other things, the existence of several alternative live options about the individuation of actions; the fact that there are purely mental actions, overt actions with goals that are changes in the external world (e.g., that my car be functioning again by noon), and overt actions with goals that include nothing external to the agent's body (e.g., the goal that one unclench one's right fist); the apparent need for a distinction between basic and nonbasic actions; disputes about the status of so-called negative actions (e.g., Ann's not voting in today's election: see chapter 6, section 4); and tricky issues about the connection between mental events and states, on the one hand, and what realizes them, on the other hand. Most of these issues are beyond the scope of this book.

Equally obviously, most of these issues must also be addressed by anticausalist teleologists in search of an acceptable account of action and of acting in pursuit of a particular goal. I have shown that Ginet, Wallace, Wilson, and Sehon have not offered adequate accounts—or even informative, general, conceptually sufficient conditions—of either of these things, and I have done this in a way that strongly suggests that it will be very difficult to avoid causalism in producing satisfactory accounts or satisfactory general statements of conceptually sufficient conditions. I have shown that, in the case of at least one kind of agent, causalists can handle the problem allegedly posed by representative instances of primary causal deviance for the project of providing a causal analysis of acting in pursuit of a particular goal.[48]

Notes

1. See Bishop (1989), Brand (1984), Davidson (1980), Goldman (1970), Hornsby (1980), Mele (1992e), Thalberg (1977), and Thomson (1977).
2. See, for example, Sehon (1994, 1997), Taylor (1966), and Wilson (1989, 1997).
3. Again, see, for example, *Nicomachean Ethics* 1139a31–32: "The origin of action—its efficient, not its final cause—is choice, and that of choice is desire and reasoning with a view to an end."
4. Most of the discussion in this section of Ginet's position derives from Mele (1992e, pp. 250–55; 1992d).
5. One may object that an omniscient, honest God could not possibly say this since Ann's alleged intentions are actually a single, complex intention—an intention, of her opening the window, that by it she will gain a better view and let in some fresh air. However, it is not conceptually necessary that the two alleged intentions agglomerate, even if such intentions normally do agglomerate; and a conceptual possibility is enough for present purposes.
6. One may object that the human brain is such that the identified effect of the scientist's tinkering would require a change in the neural realization of N itself. Even if this is so, Ginet's analysis of "S V-ed in order (thereby) to U" is a perfectly general conceptual analysis, and it is conceptually possible that an agent has a brain that allows the scientist to accomplish his trick.
7. I said that an objection of mine to Ginet's position would undermine two claims about cases in which agents have two or more reasons for A-ing: the claim that, in all such cases, the agents A for all of these reasons; and the claim that, in all such cases, there is no fact of the matter about which are the reasons for which the agents A. I had the objection just advanced in mind. Ann had at least two reasons for opening the window—reasons that can be inferred from her intentions. If I am right, she opened it for one of those reasons and not the other.
8. In this formulation of the content of Al's alleged intention, I follow Wallace: "A's intention is to provide assistance as a way of doing what is right, while B acts on the different intention of providing assistance as a way of collecting a financial reward" (1999, p. 240).
9. On other cases, see Mele (1992b, 1995b).
10. Discussion of this issue is complicated by my neutrality on action individuation (see chapter 1, section 2). On a fine-grained view, Al's mowing his lawn early (M) and his mowing his lawn early as a way of getting back at his neighbor (M*) are two different actions. Any reason for which Al M*'s encompasses something that explains his acting to get back at his neighbor, but a reason for which he mows his lawn early need not do this. For example, in reporting that a reason for which Al mowed his lawn early (i.e., M-ed) was to get back at his neighbor, one does not explain the "as a way of getting back at his neighbor" aspect of his M*-ing. On a coarse-grained view, M and M* are the same action under different descriptions, and effective reasons are relativized to action-descriptions. Any effective reason for Al's action under description "M*" encompasses something that explains his acting to get revenge on his neighbor,

but an effective reason for his action under description "*M*" need not do so. A componential view of action-individuation yields a similar result.

11. On an alternative view, the claim would be that it is not always easy, even for the agents, to know for what *reason(s)* they are *A*-ing. For example, Al might believe that it was for reasons of convenience that he decided to mow his lawn early this morning and that he is now mowing it for those reasons, whereas, in fact, it was for reasons of vengeance that he decided to mow it and he is mowing it for the latter reasons. Again, on Wallace's view, the reasons for which Al made his decision and for which he mows his lawn can be read off from his intention, an intention that Al has without realizing it. On the alternative view, the pertinent reasons are the ones that played a suitable causal-explanatory role in the production of Al's decision to mow and his mowing, even though Al does not realize that these reasons are the operative ones.

12. Thus, my points about representational limitations, for example, obviously cannot be accommodated by claiming simply that although, in some cases, only *some* of the reasons for which an agent decided to *A* can be read off from the content of his decision, they are reasons for which he so decided in virtue of that. Of course, a general answer can be disjunctive, but a disjunctive general answer will provide all the disjuncts.

13. After summarizing Davidson's challenge, Wilson (1989, pp. 168–70) complains that anticausalists have left us pretty much in the dark about the connection between reasons and actions, and he remarks that "without some more positive identification of the putatively noncausal connection in question, the nature of this linking remains mysterious" (p. 171).

14. See Goldman's treatment of "*in order to* explanations" (1970, pp. 77–78).

15. The following case first appeared in Mele (1992e, pp. 248–49). In my discussion there of Wilson's position, I neglected to consider a significant reply that is open to him. That reply is taken up shortly.

16. In this paragraph and the next two, I borrow from Mele (1992e, pp. 249–50).

17. In Mele (1992e), I failed to treat this assertion and its kind as *definitional* assertions when criticizing Wilson's position. However, as I argue shortly, the assertion does not help Wilson. (Here and elsewhere in this chapter, I substitute my preferred variables for Wilson's.)

18. Notice that this preserves the apparent synonymy of "Norm's movements *M* were intended by him to *N*" and "Norm intended of his movements *M* that they *N*."

19. See Adams and Mele (1992, p. 325), Armstrong (1980, p. 71), McCann (1975, pp. 425–27), and McGinn (1982, pp. 86–87).

20. See James (1981, pp. 1101–3). For discussion of a case of this kind, see Adams and Mele (1992, pp. 324–31).

21. Some of the details of this case were prompted by an objection Helen Beebee raised to an earlier version.

22. Consider a case that may seem to be problematic for *T3*. Helen has agreed to play a sledding game in which, after seating themselves in a circular sled at the top of a snowy slope and grasping straps to hold themselves in place, contestants are spun around several times and given a solid push. Their objective is to guide the sled through the narrow opening between a pair of bright orange poles twenty yards down the hill. When Helen comes out of her spin. She notices that the sled is heading straight toward the opening. She is prepared to alter the course of the sled, if necessary (by leaning), and she keeps her eyes fixed on the poles. As luck would have it, Helen does not need to alter the sled's course. She does nothing more than continue to grasp the straps and keep her eyes on the poles. Amazingly, the ride was so smooth that Helen did not need to move any part of her body, including her head and her eyes. Did Helen sentiently direct the motion of her body down the slope at promoting her sled's traveling between the poles, or was she too passive on this occasion for that to be so? Notice that a parallel question can be asked about trying: did Helen try to get the sled to travel between the poles, or was she too passive for that to be so? Undoubtedly, intuitions will vary. But should it turn out that the judgment

is warranted that Helen's motion down the hill was sentiently directed by her at the pertinent goal, I conjecture that the warranting considerations would count no less strongly in favor of the judgment that Helen *tried* to achieve this goal. Not only is sentiently directing motion at a goal something we do, but it also involves effort—effort directed at achieving the goal. (For discussion of related matters, see chapter 6, section 4.)

23. It might be suggested that Wilson should add an anti-intervention condition to the four conditions he offers. But if the addition of such a condition would contribute to conceptually sufficient conditions for an agent's sentiently directing his movements at a goal because the relevant kinds of intervention prevent the obtaining of normal causal connections between mental items or their neural realizers and bodily motions, to add the condition would be to admit defeat.

24. For other criticisms of Wilson's attempt to meet the Davidsonian challenge, see Roth (1999, pp. 845–53).

25. In the remainder of this paragraph, I borrow from Mele (1997a, p. 232).

26. In this paragraph, I borrow from Mele (1997b, p. 136).

27. Fred Dretske (1988) has argued that actions have reasons as components. For criticism of his arguments, see Mele (1991).

28. For a taxonomy, see Mele (1992c, pp. 208, 210).

29. There are, of course, other problems with the simple-minded analysis. For example, there are purely mental actions, such as adding a collection of numbers in one's head.

30. Proximal intentions also include intentions to *A* beginning straightaway and intentions to continue doing something that one is already doing.

31. See chapter 1, section 5. For elaboration of this view, see Mele (1992e, chs. 8–11).

32. See Adams and Mele (1992), Brand (1984, p. 20), and Mele (1992e, pp. 201–2).

33. On sustaining roles of intentions, see Bishop (1989, pp. 167–71), Brand (1984, p. 175), Mele (1992e, pp. 130–31, 180–84, 192–94), and Thalberg (1984).

34. On the guiding role of intentions, see Bishop (1989, pp. 167–72), Brand (1984, part IV), Mele (1992e, pp. 136–37, 220–23), and Thalberg (1984, pp. 257–59).

35. On differences between error-correcting and predictive kinds of feedback control, see Jordan (1996, pp. 78–87).

36. Much of the material in this and the next three paragraphs derives from Mele (1992e, pp. 220–23).

37. For an instructive discussion of motor schemata, see Brand (1984, ch. 9).

38. See, for example, Rosenbaum and Krist (1996).

39. If action begins in the brain, the functioning of motor schemata in the production of a bodily motion, including schemata proximately activated by the acquisition of a proximal intention, may be a *constituent* of an action.

40. For a useful discussion of ballistic bodily movements, see Sheridan (1984, pp. 50–54).

41. Recall that on the first occasion, Daphne's intention was to *try* to touch the pear with her index finger. On a distinction between intending to *A* and intending to try to *A*, see Mele (1992e, pp. 132–35, 146–50).

42. On the motor cortex, the central nervous system, and motor signals, see Dum and Strick (1996), Georgopoulos (1995), and Porter and Lemon (1993). Of course, I am not claiming that actual human agents function exactly like Promethean agents.

43. Two additional points about nervousness are in order. First, nervousness does not always block action. Indeed, it sometimes contributes to the performance of an action (see Mele 1992e, pp. 243–44). The second point concerns a case in which Clem knows that he frequently loses control over crucial parts of his body when he tries to execute frightening proximal intentions. Wanting to bring about Don's death in a way that will seem accidental, he hits on the following plan. He will invite Don to climb a mountain with him and form the intention at a suitable time to try to let go of the support rope; his forming that intention, he predicts, will initiate an

attempt to let go of the rope that will cause him to lose control over his hands, with the result that Don falls to his death. Clem climbs the mountain with this plan. At a certain time, he forms the intention to try to let go of the rope, and things happen just as he predicted. Did Clem perform the action of letting go of the rope? No, for he lost control over his hands; they were moving, but he was not moving them. However, on the assumption that forming an intention (as opposed to merely acquiring one) is an action (see chapter 9), in executing his master plan Clem did perform the actions of bringing it about that he lost control over his hands, bringing it about that his grip on the rope loosened, bringing it about that the rope fell from his hands, bringing it about that Don fell to his death, and so on. (For discussion of a related case, see chapter 6, section 3.)

44. Setting aside artificial cases, notice that the neural architecture of a particular kind of being may be such that mere desires, say, are not equipped to send command signals, even if there are possible beings in which action is (sometimes) initiated by proximal desire acquisition rather than by proximal intention acquisition.

45. Wilder Penfield writes, "When I have caused a conscious patient to move his hand by applying an electrode to the motor cortex of one hemisphere I have often asked him about it. Invariably his response was: 'I didn't do that. You did.' When I caused him to vocalize, he said, 'I didn't make that sound. You pulled it out of me'" (1975, p. 76). The patient's reactions are natural and plausible.

46. Three points about predictable intuitions should be made. First, if the scientist were to equip a being suffering from neurological blockage with a device that rapidly produces appropriate command signals in response to acquisitions of intentions, intuitions would shift. But notice that in such cases intention acquisition triggers the machinery. Second, a significantly weaker shift in the same direction may or may not occur on the supposition that the scientist regularly stands in for the device: the Promethean being acquires or forms intentions, and the scientist sends appropriate command signals in response. The scientist's himself *acting* in producing the signals complicates matters. A natural reaction is that the Promethean being sets a goal and the scientist has a greater claim to be the person who moves the being's body accordingly than the being himself does. By contrast, in the former case, seemingly, the Promethean being moves his body and his doing so is a process that involves the device. The difference between him and a normal Promethean agent is that the normal agent's moving his body involves only natural, biological machinery. Third, if the neuroscientist were merely to *enable* a being's acquiring an intention to send an appropriate command signal—for example, by removing blockage that is in place at the time—intuitions would strongly favor the being's acting. One way to block various irksome questions would be to stipulate that the design of Promethean agents is such that all alien intervention simply shuts these beings down, but brief attention to such questions is useful.

47. Some readers may worry that my standards for agency are too low. I discuss this issue in chapter 10.

48. For responses to other alleged problems raised by anticausalist teleologists, see Mele (1992e, ch. 13; 1999a).

II

MOTIVATION AND NORMATIVITY

3

Reasons for Action and Action for Reasons

Much of part II of this book is devoted to clarifying connections between motivation and normativity. My concern in this chapter is such connections in the sphere of reasons for action. In chapters 4 and 5, I move on to the spheres of practical reasoning and moral agency. These three chapters also remove apparent obstacles to the account of a paradigmatic kind of motivation-encompassing attitude developed in chapter 6, the final chapter of part II.

Philosophical work on reasons for action tends to be guided by concerns with two distinct but related topics: the *explanation* of intentional actions and the *evaluation* of intentional actions or their agents. In work dominated by the explanatory concern, reasons for action tend to be understood as states of mind. Philosophers concerned primarily with evaluation may be sympathetic or unsympathetic to this construal, depending on their views about standards for evaluating actions or agents. For example, a theorist whose chief evaluative concern is *rational action* and who holds that the pertinent notion of rationality is subjective—in the sense that a proper verdict about the rationality or irrationality of an action is to be made from the perspective of the agent's own desires, beliefs, preferences, principles, and the like, rather than from some external or partly external perspective—may be happy to understand reasons for action as states of mind. A theorist with a more objective conception of rational action or rational agency is likely also to have a more objective conception of reasons for action, given the common assumption that actions are both evaluated and explained in terms of reasons of the same kind. Such a theorist may find it very natural to insist that many or all reasons for action are facts about the agent-external world.

Traditionally, reasons for action are linked to motivation. There is an interesting body of literature on what the link is. The contributors include moral philosophers and philosophers of mind and action (which is not to say that the two groups are mutually exclusive). My aim in this chapter is to build a bridge of a certain kind between work on reasons in these two branches of philosophy that will facilitate discussion in the following two chapters.

I start in section 1 by sketching a popular version of the view that reasons for action are states of mind, Donald Davidson's influential version. In sections 2 and 3, I undermine some criticisms of a broadly Davidsonian view of action explanation. Sections 4 and 5 are devoted more explicitly to bridge building.

1. Davidsonian Reasons for Action

As I mentioned in chapter 2, Davidson's "Actions, Reasons, and Causes" (1963; 1980, ch. 1) played a major role in the revival of a causal approach to action explanation. It did this not only by advancing telling objections to leading anticausalist arguments but also by offering a way of accommodating in a causal framework the idea, favored by many anticausalists and causalists alike, that intentional actions are explicable in terms of agents' reasons. A central notion in the Davidsonian synthesis is *rationalization*, a species of causal explanation designed in part to reveal the point or purpose of the explananda.

Davidson's article opens as follows: "What is the relation between a reason and an action when the reason explains the action by giving the agent's reason for doing what he did? We may call such explanations *rationalizations*, and say that the reason *rationalizes* the action" (1980, p. 3). His thesis is that "rationalization is a species of causal explanation." "The primary reason for an action is its cause"; and "a reason rationalizes an action only if it leads us to see something the agent saw, or thought he saw, in his action—some feature, consequence, or aspect of the action the agent wanted, desired, prized, held dear, thought dutiful, beneficial, obligatory, or agreeable" (p. 4). When a reason is a rationalizing cause of an action, it is a reason *for which* the agent performs that action. In a later article, Davidson remarks, "Two ideas are built into the concept of acting on a reason . . . the idea of cause and the idea of rationality. A reason is a rational cause. One way rationality is built in is transparent: the cause must be a belief and a desire in light of which the action is reasonable" (1980, p. 233; cf. p. 9). In "Actions, Reasons, and Causes," he says, "In order to understand how a reason of any kind rationalizes an action it is necessary and sufficient that we see, at least in essential outline, how to construct a primary reason" (1980, p. 4), where "*R* is a primary reason why an agent performed an action *A* under the description *d* only if *R* consists of a pro attitude of the agent towards actions with a certain property, and a belief of the agent that *A*, under the description *d*, has that property" (p. 5).

Again, I am neutral on the issue of action individuation raised by Davidson's account of a primary reason (chapter 1, section 2). I leave it to readers to treat the action variable "*A*" as a variable either for actions themselves or for actions under *A*-descriptions, depending on their preferred theory of individuation.

That having been said, Davidson's basic idea about rationalization, under one interpretation and with a little refinement, may be expressed as follows: a reason's rationalizing an action is a matter of its being a cause of that action that helps to explain the action (partly) by revealing something that the agent was aiming at in performing it and, therefore, something that makes the action "reasonable" in some sense. Obviously, the rationality associated with rationalization is understood in a thin and subjective way, and the same is true of reasonableness. An agent who pries the lid off a can of paint for a reason constituted by an intrinsic desire to drink the paint (cf. Davidson 1980, p. 4) and a belief that he can put himself in a position to drink it by prying off the lid strikes one as crazy. Even so, this action is rationalized by this reason, and the associated rationality and reasonableness are of a subjective, instrumental kind: from the perspective of the agent's desire and belief, his prying the lid off the paint can makes sense. From that perspective, this action makes sense, even if there is no perspective from which his desire to drink paint makes sense. Does this combination of thinness and subjectivity undermine Davidson's account of reasons for action? Not, I argue, if all one wants out of an account of reasons for action is a notion that is serviceable for the purposes of action explanation.[1]

2. Arational Actions

In this section, I consider a criticism of Davidson's account of reasons for action that several philosophers have voiced (see, e.g., Quinn 1993, pp. 236–52; Scanlon 1998, p. 38). Because Rosalind Hursthouse (1991) offers the most detailed version of this criticism, I concentrate on her formulation of it. My aim is not to defend Davidson's own account of reasons for action; I have argued elsewhere for the need to modify it (Mele 1988; cf. 1992e, ch. 6). Instead, I defend a broadly Davidsonian account against the objection to be considered. I defend the idea that the account is serviceable for the purposes of action explanation, *not* the idea that it is the only viable account of reasons for action. For other purposes, an alternative account may reasonably be preferred. In section 4, I suggest an account of reasons for action that combines broadly Davidsonian reasons with reasons of another kind. In section 5, I describe a related account that strips broadly Davidsonian reasons of the title "reasons."

Wholly intrinsically motivated actions—actions performed only for their own sakes—are problematic for Davidson's account of reasons for action. Consider such intentional actions as displaying one's gratitude to a friend, when this is done only for its own sake, or whistling a tune just because one feels like it. If Al's displaying his gratitude to a friend is motivated by a wholly intrinsic desire to do this, a desire for this solely as an end, there seems to be no room for a belief of the sort that Davidson's account of reasons requires in the reason for which Al so acts. One might suggest that the reason for which Al performs his intrinsically motivated action—displaying his gratitude to his friend Bob, or, in Davidson's (1980) terms, the action under the description "displaying gratitude to Bob"—is constituted by a wholly intrinsic desire to perform an action with the property of being a display of gratitude to Bob and a belief that displaying his gratitude to Bob would have that property.[2] But that belief lacks an evident explanatory function and has the feel of a device whose only function is to save a theory (see Mele 1988 and 1992e, ch. 6). (It might be suggested that Al's relevant belief is, for example, that buying Bob a bottle of Glenlivet would display his gratitude. But although that belief may be part of a reason for buying Bob a bottle of Glenlivet, it is not part of a reason for displaying his gratitude.)

The problem admits of a simple solution. It has been claimed—plausibly, I have argued elsewhere—that although actions of this kind are done for no *further* reason, they are done for a reason.[3] Insofar as it is plausible (except perhaps in very special cases) that intentional actions are done for reasons constituted by psychological states of agents, showing one's gratitude to a friend, when one does this from a wholly intrinsic desire so to act, is plausibly regarded as something done for a reason constituted by an *intrinsic* desire to display one's gratitude to the friend.[4] Similarly, for the purposes of action explanation, feeling like whistling a tune—or, more precisely, an intrinsic desire to do so—may itself plausibly be understood as a reason for whistling a tune. The *general* worry about intrinsically motivated actions has, I believe, been laid to rest elsewhere: one can modify Davidson's account of reasons for action by allowing that intrinsic desires to *A* are themselves reasons for *A*-ing. The modification yields a broadly Davidsonian account in the spirit of the original one.

Even if the general worry about intrinsically motivated actions can be quelled in this way, problems allegedly posed by a certain *species* of intrinsically motivated action merit scrutiny. Hursthouse launches an interesting attack against a "standard account of actions and their explanations" and the thesis that "intentional actions are done because the agent has a certain desire/belief pair that explains the action by rationalizing it" (1991, p. 57). She attempts to show, via an investigation of what she terms "arational actions," intrinsically motivated actions of a certain kind, that the thesis is false and that the associated "standard account" is "fundamentally flawed" (p. 63), rests on a "false semantic theory" (p. 57), and introduces "mysteries" (p. 64).

"Arational action," as Hursthouse defines it, is action satisfying the following three conditions: (1) it is intentional; (2) "the agent did not do it for a reason in the sense that there is a true description of the action of the form '*X* did it (in order) to———' or '*X* was trying to———' which will 'reveal the favorable light in which the agent saw what he did,'[5] and hence involve, or imply, the ascription of a suitable *belief*'; and (3) "the agent would not have done the action if she had not been in the grip of whatever emotion it was, and the mere fact that she was in its grip explains the action as much as anything else does" (1991, p. 59; dashes replace Hursthouse's ellipses).

Hursthouse (1991) adduces numerous examples of arational actions, focusing on actions whose "explanation would, usually, be of the form 'I *A*-ed because I was so frightened (or happy, excited, ashamed . . . so overwhelmed by hatred or affection or . . .) that I just wanted to, or felt I had to'" (p. 58; my variable, Hursthouse's ellipses). She adds that "these actions are explained solely by reference to desire—'I was so angry/delighted, etc., I just wanted to'—not to an appropriate belief" (p. 59). The "only explanation" of arational actions, Hursthouse says, is that "in the grip of the relevant emotion, the agent just felt like doing them" (p. 61); and it is an "obvious fact that in some sense the agent does arational actions '(just) because she wants to,' or 'for their own sake,' prompted by the occurrent desire . . ." (p. 62). Arational action, then, is a species of intrinsically motivated action.

Hursthouse's immediate target is a view Davidson advances in "Actions, Reasons, and Causes" (1980, ch. 1) and develops further elsewhere (1980, chs. 2–5, 14; 1982a;

1987). She produces a number of examples in which, she contends, an intentional action is not done for a Davidsonian reason. What is directly at issue, as she says, "is certain belief ascriptions to agents performing intentional actions" (1991, p. 59)—hence, the belief component of Davidsonian reasons. Hursthouse maintains that if, as she argues, arational actions "resist appropriate belief ascription . . . then the standard account [i.e., Davidson's] is shown to be fundamentally flawed" (p. 63).

I accept Hursthouse's (1991) claim that some intentional actions are not done for reasons having a *belief component* of the sort required by Davidson. I have defended that claim myself, arguing additionally that Davidson's conception of the reasons for which we act should be expanded to include certain desires that are *not* paired with beliefs, *intrinsic* action-desires (Mele 1988; cf. 1992e, ch. 6). Here I attempt to ascertain whether Hursthouse has uncovered a deeper problem that justifies her claim that the entire Davidsonian approach to understanding and explaining intentional action is fundamentally flawed.

Whereas a critic of Davidson's position on the place of belief in effective reasons may call attention to such intrinsically motivated behavior as whistling a tune just because one feels like it or showing one's gratitude to a friend for its own sake, Hursthouse (1991) focuses on such actions as striking inanimate objects in anger, gouging out the eyes in a photograph of a hated person, and licking something furry (when "seized by a sudden desire to lick something furry"). This divergence is significant: differences in the examples reflect differences in critical intent. Some critics (Mele 1988) are concerned to locate cases in which actions that, with minimal encouragement, their readers would gladly say are done for reasons are nevertheless not plausibly regarded as having been done for strictly *Davidsonian* reasons (belief-desire pairs). Hursthouse's objective runs much deeper.

If Hursthouse were to show that arational actions are done for no reason at all, even though they are intentional, that might raise serious problems for Davidson's overall picture. Not only would he lack an account of the conditions under which an action (under a description) is intentional, but he also would lack a basis for a uniform style of psychological explanation of intentional actions. (Alternatively, if the debate were to turn out to be a terminological one, he might be able to grant that arational actions are not done for reasons and hold on to his general picture articulated in other terms.) Now, there is some intuitive plausibility in the suggestion that many strikings of inanimate things in anger and the like are not done for reasons. Crudely put, whistling just because you feel like it seems reasonable enough (at least not unreasonable, in appropriate circumstances), but blasting away at your television out of anger typically does not. And surely there is some interesting connection between (un)reasonableness and reasons? Then again, there is a difference between good and bad reasons; perhaps intentional actions that are unreasonable, in the sense of "unreasonable" in play now, are done for *bad* reasons, as opposed to no reason at all. It is difficult to be certain whether or on what grounds Hursthouse would reject this idea since she does not say what she thinks reasons are. She does say at one point, however, that "actions prompted by odd physical cravings are . . . genuine examples of cases in which 'one in no way values what one desires' and are thereby counterexamples to the standard account of intentional action" (1991, p. 63). So she thinks, at least, that the standard (or Davidsonian) account of intentional action requires that

agents of intentional actions in some way value what they desire and that in some instances of intentional action there is no such valuing.

Return to Davidson's "Actions, Reasons, and Causes." "A man may all his life
have a yen," he writes, "to drink a can of paint, without ever, even at the moment he
yields, believing it would be worth doing" (1980, p. 4). Such behavior is crazy. Imagine that this man, Paul, yielding to his yen, pries the lid off a paint can in order to put
himself in a position to consume its contents. Did he remove the lid for a reason?
Davidsonians should answer yes, even though Paul's reason was bizarre: he wanted to
drink the paint and believed that in order to do that he must remove the lid. What
makes the reason bizarre obviously is not the belief but the desire.

If Paul pries off the lid for a reason, what undermines the claim that he drinks the
paint for a reason too, a reason constituted by a wacky intrinsic desire to drink the
paint? The bizarreness of his drinking the paint does not greatly outstrip the weirdness
of his prying off the lid *for that purpose*. Nor is the paint drinking any less motivated
than the lid prying. Paul is motivated by a yen to drink a can of paint. The yen, one may
feel confident, is not a *good* reason. But in the absence of a well-motivated theory of
reasons for action that precludes Paul's desire being a reason for which he acted, are
there compelling grounds for insisting that it is not a reason? (Hursthouse 1991 does
not offer a theory of reasons, well-motivated or otherwise.)

Davidson's critic may observe that on Davidson's (1980) view, reasons do not
merely cause actions ("the primary reason for an action is its cause") but also "rationalize" them. It may be argued that Paul's yen does not rationalize his paint drinking.
Rationalizing, it may be claimed, depends on an agent's valuing what he desires. Even
if one can see how a wholly intrinsic desire to *A* can contribute *causally* to an *A*-ing,
that may leave it open whether such desires rationalize actions—hence, whether they
count as reasons.

A potential source of distraction must be eliminated before this criticism is addressed. Explanations of actions in terms of the reasons for which they are done are
rarely, if ever, *complete* explanations (cf. Davidson 1999, p. 639). Often, at least,
much more information would be required for something approaching a full understanding of the behavior. One may want to know, for example, why an agent wanted
the *end* he pursued or why he acted for one reason rather than for another reason
he had at the time. Concerning intrinsically motivated actions, a request for information beyond a specification of the desire on which the agent acted is often appropriate. Requests of the following kind are predictable and natural: "OK, he did it for
its own sake; but why did he want to show his gratitude to his friend, what accounted
for his yen to drink the paint, and what caused Elvis's effective urge to shoot a television?" To produce helpful answers, one must work a lot harder in some cases than
in others. (In no case, if the action is done *only* for its own sake, does a proper answer identify a *further* reason for which the agent *A*-ed.) And appeals to emotions of
the sort Hursthouse (1991) mentions are frequently fruitful. But Davidson has never
claimed that identifying the reason(s) for which an agent acted will, in all cases,
make it plain why the agent acted as he did. In fact, he has denied it. In connection
with akratic action, for example, Davidson observes that citing the reason(s) for
which the agent acted leaves much unexplained (1980, ch. 2, especially p. 42; cf.
1982a).

I set Davidson's view aside and ask a pair of questions: does acting for a reason require that the agent "value what [she] desires," to use Hursthouse's (1991) expression? Does a reason's rationalizing an action require this? Hursthouse offers no argument for an affirmative answer to either question, and I see no compelling reason to deny that sometimes the actions we perform for reasons seem to us, even at the time, not to be worth doing at all. (One might suggest that agents deem them worth doing at least qua means to satisfying desires. But suppose that the desires seem to the agents not to be at all worth satisfying, as in the case of Davidson's paint drinker.) In such cases, the reasons for which we act are not, even by our own lights, good ones.[6] They may even be quite perverse. But perverse reasons are reasons. Furthermore, such reasons arguably rationalize actions insofar as, in addition to figuring causally in the production of the actions, they identify what the agent was aiming at—the agent's purpose or goal—and play their causal/explanatory role partly in virtue of their content. In light of the fact that Paul acted on an intrinsic desire to drink paint, we can make some sense of his drinking the paint. He drank it because he wanted, intrinsically, to drink paint; his purpose or goal—a bizarre one—was to drink paint. We can understand Paul's drinking the paint on the model of the happy man's whistling a certain happy tune because he wanted, intrinsically, to whistle it, even if we cannot understand Paul's wanting to drink paint. If we were to believe that he had no desire to drink the paint and no mistaken beliefs about the contents of the can (e.g., that the can contains ulcer medicine or a milkshake), we would be at a loss to make any sense at all of his paint drinking.

Hursthouse (1991) is in no position to object to the idea that intrinsic desires can help to explain behavior that satisfies them. She insists that the idea is correct. What she needs, then, is an argument that such desires do not constitute reasons or that they do not rationalize. She has advanced no such argument. Indeed, her decision to restrict reasons for which actions are done to belief-desire pairs places the issue about the constitution of reasons entirely out of bounds.

In pointing out that some of our intentional actions, including some bizarre and crazy ones, are not done for a *further* reason, Hursthouse (1991) has not uncovered a fundamental flaw, a "false semantic theory," or "mysteries." Rather, she has vividly identified a technical problem with Davidson's (1980) account of the reasons for which we act—a problem about intrinsically motivated actions—that had been identified more sympathetically in the literature (Mele 1988). Hursthouse intends to provoke worries about whether some intentional actions are done for reasons at all, given how bizarre they are, even from the agent's own perspective. But if our reasons can be every bit as bizarre as our actions, there is no special cause for worry.[7]

Given that someone who has "a yen . . . to drink a can of paint, without . . . believing it would be worth doing" may remove the lid from a paint can for a Davidsonian reason having this yen as its desire component, it may be thought that Davidsonian reasons for which agents act have no essential justificatory or normative dimension. This is not how Davidson sees it:

> In the light of a primary reason, an action is revealed as coherent with certain traits, long- or short-termed, characteristic or not, of the agent, and the agent is shown in his role of Rational Animal. Corresponding to the belief and attitude of a primary reason for an

action, we can always construct . . . the premises of a syllogism from which it follows that the action has some (as Anscombe calls it) 'desirability characteristic'. Thus there is a certain irreducible—though somewhat anaemic—sense in which every rationalization justifies: from the agent's point of view there was, when he acted, something to be said for the action. (1980, pp. 8–9)

Obviously, Davidson's claim is not about *on-balance* justification; the claim is not, for example, that there is at least as much justification for any rationalized action, *A*, as there is for refraining from *A*-ing. Instead, he understands justifications of actions as things "to be said for" the actions "from the agent's point of view" at the time of action. In the case at hand, what can be said for Paul's removing the lid is that it would put him in a position to drink the paint, something that he has a yen to do. There also is something to be said, from Paul's point of view when he drinks the paint, for his drinking it—namely, that in drinking it he is doing something that he (intrinsically) wants to do.

Philosophers can argue about whether either of the "things to be said" just mentioned merits the designation "justification." For my purposes, there is no need to take a stand on this issue. Depending on one's standards for justification, in the sense of "something to be said for," two traditional ideas form an unstable conjunction. The ideas are these: all intentional actions are done for reasons; all reasons for action have a justificatory dimension. This instability will become clear soon enough.

3. Scanlon on Reasons and the "Standard Desire Model"

One might object that Davidsonian reasons for action are not really reasons at all. T. M. Scanlon argues that "desires almost never provide reasons for action in the way described by the standard desire model" (1998, p. 43). He writes: "According to this familiar model, desires are not conclusions of practical reasoning but starting points for it. They are states which simply occur or not, and when they do occur they provide the agent with reason to do what will promote their fulfillment" (p. 43). A desire, in the model Scanlon says he is attacking, is "a state which simply occurs and is then a 'given' for subsequent deliberation" (p. 47). On this model, he says, decision making is "a matter of simply asking oneself what one desires, and how strongly" (p. 54).

Scanlon (1998) apparently has only wholly intrinsic desires in mind here. There is no "familiar model" according to which *instrumental* desires typically "simply occur." On a Davidsonian model, for example, instrumental desires (at least normally) are products of beliefs and desires that rationalize them (see chapter 1, section 2). It should also be noted that endorsing a position on acting for reasons according to which, whenever we act intentionally, the reasons for which we act include psychological states does not commit one to holding that intrinsic desires, including wholly intrinsic desires, simply occur. One who endorses such a position on acting for reasons—I dub it the *psychological reasons* position—may hold that the acquisition of intrinsic desires is causally explicable (Scanlon does not claim otherwise), and even that what explains an agent's having a particular intrinsic desire may help to justify the desire.[8] A proponent of the psychological reasons position may think that some things are intrinsically good; that the fact that something, x, is intrinsically good is a reason to desire and pursue it; and that apprehension of a fact of that kind may help to explain the presence in an agent of an intrinsic desire for x. A proponent of the psychological reasons position need not hold that *all* reasons for action are psychological states, as I explain in more detail in section 4.

Nor need a proponent of this position hold that decision making is "a matter of simply asking oneself what one desires, and how strongly" (Scanlon 1998, p. 54). A position on akratic action that I have defended elsewhere (Mele 1987) is certainly consistent with what I am calling the "psychological reasons" position on acting for reasons, and it features the idea that a distinction between the motivational strength of a desire and the agent's assessment of the value of the "object" of that desire (i.e., of what is desired) is important for a proper understanding of the occurrence of akratic actions. It is consistent with my position that these assessments are sometimes based on apprehensions of *strictly external reasons*, reasons that neither are nor encompass attitudes (desires, beliefs, etc.) of the agent and are not facts, propositions, or the like about actual attitudes of the agent.

A comment on this use of the expression "strictly external reasons" is in order. Bernard Williams, who argues that "external reasons statements . . . are false, or incoherent, or really something else misleadingly expressed" (1979, p. 26), says, "The whole point of external reasons statements is that they can be true independently of the agent's motivations" (p. 22). In my sense of "strictly external reason" here, if R is a strictly external reason for S to A, R is not an attitude of S; does not have an attitude of S as a constituent; and is not, even in part, a fact, truth, proposition, or the like about any actual attitude of S.

Scanlon (1998) asks his readers to imagine an agent—I call him Tim—who has "a desire to have a new computer" but judges that he has "no reason to buy a new machine, since [he believes] that the features of the newer models would be of no real benefit to [him]" (p. 43). He contends that the fact that Tim has this desire "gives [him] no reason to buy a new computer (aside, perhaps, from the indirect one that it would put an end, for a time, to [his] being nagged by the desire and wasting time reading computer advertisements)" (pp. 43–44). Now, the desire to have a new computer is not itself a Davidsonian reason to buy a computer. However the combination in Tim of this desire and a belief that he can bring it about that he has a new computer by buying one would be a Davidsonian reason for buying one. Might an agent who judges that he has "no reason to buy a new machine, since [he believes] that the features of the newer models would be of no real benefit to [him]," nevertheless buy a new machine? I should think so. Notice that the agent may be mistaken in thinking that he has no reason to buy one, and he may act for a reason that he himself—perhaps owing partly to his theory of reasons—believes is not a reason. (Incidentally, the agent in Scanlon's example is Scanlon himself.) If Tim intentionally buys a new computer, it is plausible that he buys it for a reason. One obvious candidate for the reason for which he buys it is a combination of his desire to "have" a new computer and his belief that he can ensure that he has one by buying one. And that desire may well be rationalizable even if Tim believes that "the features of the newer models would be of no real benefit to him." He may desire enjoyment of the kind that fiddling with his new computers usually brings him and realize that the opportunity for such enjoyment depends on his owning a new computer—even if he himself (perhaps owing partly to his personal theory of reasons) judges that this desire and realization do not constitute a reason for owning a new computer.

Scanlon's (1998) attack on what he calls "the standard desire model" is framed partly in terms of his own account of "what is usually called desire." He contends that something's seeming to an agent to be a reason for A-ing is "the central element in what is usually called [a] desire" to A (p. 65). Seemings of this kind do important motivational work, according to Scanlon. He claims that in a thirsty man with a desire to drink, "the motivational work seems to be done by" the agent's taking "the pleasure to be obtained by drinking . . . to count in favor of drinking" (p. 38).

Scanlon's (1998) account of what is usually called a desire is overly intellectualized. It is generally granted that toddlers and pretoddlers desire to do things—for example, to drink some juice or to hug a teddy bear. This common thought is not that although these little agents desire to do things, they lack "what is usually called a desire." The thought is that they have desires in a normal, "usual" sense of the term. But because it is unlikely that toddlers have the concept of a reason for action (or of something's counting in favor of a course of action), it is unlikely that things seem to them to be reasons for action (or to count in favor of actions). There is considerable evidence that younger three-year-olds tend not to have the concept, or a proper concept, of belief and that, although the concept of desire emerges earlier, it does not emerge until around the age of two (see Gopnik 1993 for a useful review). Presumably, even if the concept of a reason for action were to have no conceptual ties to the concepts of belief and desire, it would be sufficiently sophisticated to be out of reach of children too young to have proper concepts of belief and desire. Even so, such children act intentionally and for reasons. So, at least, it is commonly and plausibly thought. (They also have desires and beliefs, on the assumption that having such attitudes does not require possessing proper concepts of these attitudes.)[9] In the case of a thirsty toddler or pretoddler, a desire to drink—rather than any taking of "the pleasure to be obtained by drinking" to be a reason for drinking—seems to do the work of motivating drinking.

To be attracted by the prospect of drinking is one thing; to take an anticipated consequence of drinking to be a reason for (or "count in favor of") drinking is another. Thirsty toddlers are attracted by cups of juice, and not in the way moths are attracted by light. Toddlers are flexible in their approach to getting drinks: they try alternative means. Moths behave tropistically. Even though it is unlikely that thirsty toddlers have the conceptual wherewithal to take features, including anticipated consequences, of drinking to be reasons for (or count in favor of) drinking, they are attracted by cups of juice in a way characteristic of desiring agents. Being attracted to cups of juice because of a sensitivity to certain of their features is distinguishable from being attracted to cups of juice because of the agent's taking these features to be reasons. An agent's behavior may be sensitive to attractive features of things without the agent's taking those features to be reasons. If this were not so, a radically new theory of animal behavior would be required, one entailing either that only members of the most conceptually sophisticated species perform actions (perhaps just human beings) or that many nonhuman species are much more conceptually sophisticated than anyone has thought.

When ordinary, thirsty adults drink (intentionally and in ordinary scenarios), they presumably are motivated at least partly by a desire to drink. The strength of the desire may sometimes be explained partly by their believing that drinking would be pleasant or, more fully, by that belief together with a desire for pleasure. A toddler's desire to drink water and an adult's desire to drink water may admit of the same analysis. Just as something's seeming to be a reason for drinking is not a constituent of the toddler's desire, it may not be a constituent of the adult's desire either. If a seeming of this kind sometimes is at work in thirsty adults, it may function as a partial cause of the desire's strength or of the desire itself.

4. Motivational and Normative Reasons for Action

The term "rational" is opposed not only to "irrational" but also to "nonrational." Plants, pants, and paramecia are nonrational but not irrational. Irrational beings are imperfectly rational. A being wholly devoid of rationality is nonrational and therefore exempt from the charge of irrationality. Even if acting for a reason requires or entails some rationality, it may be irrational of us to do some of the things we do for reasons. Paul, the paint drinker, may be subjectively irrational in drinking the paint. Indeed, he himself may rationally judge, from the perspective of his own desires, beliefs, and the like, that it would be far better to resist his desire to drink paint. Suppose, however, that Paul has no desires that would be frustrated by drinking the paint and that, from the perspective strictly of his own desires, beliefs, and so on, he is not criticizable for drinking it. Might he be criticizable nonetheless? If he has no Davidsonian reasons for refraining from drinking, might there nevertheless be reasons for refraining?

One answer is that the fact that drinking the paint would make him very sick is a reason for Paul not to drink it and that this is so even if (very strangely) he has no desires that would be frustrated by his being very sick. The fact that drinking the paint would make him sick is a strictly external reason. One can argue about whether "the concept of reasons for action" allows there to be strictly external reasons in my sense (see section 3). But, in one view of things, a deeper issue is whether the rationality of actions—or the rationality of agents for their actions—is assessable from a perspective that extends beyond the agent's own psychological states. If some philosophers say that the answer is yes, one can at least understand what they may mean in claiming that the external fact I mentioned is a reason for Paul to refrain from drinking the paint. The idea may be, at least in part, that this fact supports the claim that it would be rational of Paul to refrain from drinking the paint.

I believe that alternative notions of rationality have a place in the grand theoretical scheme of things, but I have no wish to pursue the point here. Important issues about motivation sometimes get entangled in worries about "the concept" of a reason for action in a way that obscures the motivational issues. I want to find a way to keep the motivational issues salient for a readership with a range of competing views about reasons for action and rationality.

Consider the following idea: at least some reasons for action are attitudes that encompass motivation, or, alternatively, there is a sense of "reason for action" in which at least some reasons for action are attitudes that encompass motivation. I dub such reasons *motivation-encompassing reasons*. Davidsonian reasons for action are reasons of this kind.

There is a familiar, albeit controversial, distinction between *motivational* and *normative* or justificatory reasons for action.[10] One may wish to identify motivational reasons with motivation-encompassing ones; but some theorists would resist this, holding out for a more inclusive sense of "motivational reason" according to which, although any motivation-encompassing reason is a motivational reason, it is sufficient for a reason to be motivational that it play an important role in giving rise to relevant motivation—motivation need not be built right into the reason. For present purposes, the broader notion of motivational reason is fine. Normative reasons for an agent's taking a particular course of action may be understood as items that count in favor of his taking it (Dancy 2000, p. 144; Scanlon 1998, pp. 17–22).[11] This leaves open the possibility that motivational and normative reasons overlap. For example, if the combination of my desire to finish this book by the end of the year and my belief that I will not do so unless I work hard on it counts in favor of my working hard on it, and if that Davidsonian reason is a reason, then some normative reasons are motivation-*encompassing* reasons.

How might normative and motivational reasons be related? Consider the following two claims:

1. Normative reasons for action "must be capable of also being" motivational reasons. (Dancy 1995, p. 13; cf. Dancy 2000, p. 101; Williams 1979, p. 18)
2. Normative reasons for action "must be capable of motivating rational persons." (Korsgaard 1986, p. 11)

The following more precise versions of these claims also merit consideration:

1a. Necessarily, a normative reason for an agent S's A-ing is "capable of also being" a reason for which S A-s.
2a. Necessarily, if S is rational, any normative reason for S's A-ing is "capable of motivating" S to A.[12]

In chapter 2, I defended a causal account of acting in pursuit of a goal. Motivation-encompassing reasons mesh with that account, but what about strictly external reasons? For example, what about the fact that drinking paint would make Paul very ill?

One way for a proponent of external normative reasons to proceed is to claim that such reasons may, in the following sense, be capable of being motivational reasons, of motivating rational agents, or of being reasons for which (rational) agents act: a normative reason may play a role in *producing* motivation in an agent, including effective motivation. If, for example, external normative reasons are facts—for instance, the fact that drinking paint would make one very ill "or the fact that something is pleasant, or exciting, or required by duty or by loyalty to a friend" (Scanlon 1998, p. 69)—it may be claimed that those facts can causally contribute to the agent's apprehending them, which in turn causally contributes to the agent's acquiring a relevant motivation-encompassing attitude. One can say that the fact—the external normative reason—is a motivational reason insofar as it makes a contribution of this kind. Of course, these normative reasons are not *motivation-encompassing* reasons since agents' reasons of the latter kind are restricted to their attitudes. But that is consistent with its being possible that sometimes external normative reasons contribute to an agent's acquiring a motivation-encompassing reason. It may be claimed that the fact that my calling my father tonight would cheer him up can contribute causally to my acquiring the belief that this is so. The combination of that belief and my desire to cheer him up is a motivation-encompassing reason for calling him. Furthermore, a philosopher may hold that some things are intrinsically good, that the fact that something is intrinsically good is a reason to desire and pursue it, and that the fact that x is intrinsically good may contribute causally to an agent's acquiring an intrinsic desire for x. Some motivation-encompassing reasons for action have intrinsic desires as constituents; others *are* intrinsic desires for action, or so I suggested in section 2.

A proponent of external normative reasons may have metaphysical worries about claiming that facts of the kind at issue play causal roles (Scanlon 1998, pp. 62–64). The worries can perhaps be avoided by the suggestion that the claims in question are to be rewritten as claims about agents' *apprehensions* of normative reasons. Candidates include the following:

1b. Necessarily, normative reasons for action are such that agents' apprehensions of them are "capable of . . . being motivational reasons."
2b. Necessarily, apprehensions of normative reasons for action are "capable of motivating rational persons."

Related claims about specifically *moral* normative reasons for action also require attention—for example:

3. Normative moral reasons for action depend for their "authority" on their being such that an agent's belief that he has such a reason for action is motivation constituting. (See McNaughton 1988, pp. 48–49).

Claims such as these are evaluated in the following two chapters.

Michael Woods has remarked that "the concept of a reason for action stands at the point of intersection . . . between the theory of the explanation of actions and the theory of their justification" (1972, p. 189). It may be that intentional actions are to be relatively directly explained at least partially in terms of motivation-encompassing reasons and that, when external normative reasons contribute to explanations of intentional actions, they do so less directly, by way of making a causal contribution to the acquisition of motivation-encompassing reasons or by way of a causal contribution made by an agent's apprehending an external normative reason.

5. External and Broadly Davidsonian Reasons for Action

In chapter 2, I argued that its being true that an agent acted overtly in pursuit of a particular goal depends on its being true that some relevant desire or intention, or a physical realizer of such a desire or intention, played a causal role in the production of relevant bodily motions. External reasons for such actions are *screened off* from the actions by these causes in the following sense: if external reasons make a contribution to actions performed in pursuit of a goal, they do so only by way of making a contribution to these causes. One can argue about whether the screening causes include psychological states or events, qua psychological, or instead are only internal physical states or events that realize the psychological items. As I said in the introduction (section 2), I will not argue about that here.

It is open to a believer in external reasons to contend that even if the effects of external reasons on intentional actions are mediated by such psychological states as beliefs, desires, and "broadly Davidsonian reasons," such states, in fact, are neither reasons nor constituents of reasons. One apparent problem for that contention is raised by utterly ordinary cases in which an agent performs an intentional action that is not accounted for by any external reason. Nick, who wants to visit Angela and believes that she is home, intentionally drives to her house. In fact, Angela is not home. So, on at least some construals of external reasons, there is no external reason for which Nick drove to her house. Of course, an external reasons theorist can make the jarring claim that although Nick intentionally drove to Angela's house, he did not drive there for a reason.[13] Theorists can agree to talk in this jarring way. They can also agree to explain Nick's driving to Angela's house in terms of the desire and belief I mentioned while saying that the explanation of this intentional action is not an explanation in terms of any reason Nick had for driving there. It is difficult to see how producing such agreement about how the word "reason" will be used would be a substantive accomplishment. The same is true of agreement to restrict the expression "reasons for action" to broadly Davidsonian reasons and to call "external reasons for action" something else—say, "external facts that provide some justification for (actual and hypothetical) courses of action."

Jonathan Dancy distinguishes between desires that "are held for reasons" and desires that are not (2000, p. 39). He contends that the former "cannot add" to an agent's reasons and that the latter cannot "create" reasons "to do what would subserve" them (p. 39). This contention is an element in an argument that leads Dancy to the view that "motivating reasons do not standardly include psychological states of the agent" (p. 128).

A currently cheerful person's wholly intrinsic desire to sing a certain cheerful tune may be a desire that is not "held for reasons." I suggested that such a desire is a reason for singing that tune. The suggestion derives support from the following collection of considerations: setting aside strange scenarios, singings motivated by such desires are intentional actions; it is standardly held that intentional actions are done for reasons;[14] this wholly intrinsic desire is the best available candidate for a relevant reason; the desire plays a central role in explaining the action; and the role is very similar to that played by typical Davidsonian reasons. If a theory of reasons for action were to entail that this cheerful person's desire is not a reason for singing, and if the result were that the man sang intentionally but did not sing for a reason, one should at least pause to wonder whether the theory at issue is in the business of contributing to a theory of the explanation of overt intentional actions. If the theory is in that business and it merits acceptance, one may have to settle for the view that some commonplace, overt intentional actions are not done for reasons.

There is a reason for thinking that Dancy's (2000) theory of reasons is not in the business just mentioned. In reply to the challenge of Davidson's that I discussed in chapter 2, Dancy (a noncausalist) contends that the truth that the agent acted for one reason rather than another is "a *bare* truth; for causalists, this truth holds in virtue of another truth, while for non-causalists it does not" (p. 162). Essentially the same line of argument that I used in chapter 2 can be used to defend the thesis that an agent performed an overt action for a particular reason only if some desire or intention (or physical realizer thereof) relevantly associated with that reason played a causal role in the production of pertinent bodily motions. If the argument is persuasive, one must reject the claim that the truth that S acted overtly for reason R is a *bare* truth. Whether S acted overtly for R depends on there having been a suitable causal connection between some desire or intention (or physical realizer) relevantly associated with R and pertinent bodily motions.[15] One may be tempted to conclude from this that any theory of reasons for action according to which truths of the sort at issue are bare truths is not in the business of contributing to a theory of the explanation of overt intentional actions. But that conclusion may be too hasty. The claim about bare truths may be an inessential part of the theory, and items of the kind the theory counts as reasons may be—or be such that apprehensions of them are—capable of making suitable causal contributions to relevant bodily motions.

Philosophers' intuitions about which items are reasons for action and which are not tend to vary in ways that are predictable given whether the philosophers are more concerned with the explanation of actions or with the evaluation of actions (or agents). For brevity, the former group may be called "explainers" and the latter "evaluators." Rachel Cohon writes, "A Christian will not say, 'My longing for vengeance is *one* reason to strike this person, but on the other hand it's outweighed by the reason I have to turn the other cheek'" (2000, p. 63).[16] However, a Davidsonian Christian with this longing and a pertinent "connecting" belief will say, "My desire for vengeance and my belief that striking this person would gain me vengeance is a reason to strike him, but I have a better reason to turn the other cheek." Suppose that either hypothetical Christian akratically strikes the offender. Did he strike him for no reason at all?

The worry behind this question has surfaced several times in this chapter. Evaluators tend to focus more intensely on the justificatory than on the motivational dimension of ordinary thought and talk about reasons for actions. Depending on their individual views, theorists with that focus would, if asked, claim that one or more of the following intentional actions are not done for a reason: my happy man's wholly intrinsically motivated whistling of a happy tune; Paul's prying the lid off a paint can; Nick's driving to Angela's house; either akratic Christian's striking someone. Explainers, who tend to have a reversed priority of focus in the sphere identified, find these claims very counterintuitive. By the same token, evaluators find it counterintuitive that something that does not come anywhere close to satisfying their standards for being justificatory can count as a reason. These competing intuitions suggest that two notions of *reason for action* may be in play.

Suppose that someone were to produce knockdown arguments for the following two theses.

1. Necessarily, only strictly external facts provide justification for actions.
2. Necessarily, reasons for action are restricted to items that provide justification for actions.

Then one would have to grant that "broadly Davidsonian reasons for action" are not actually reasons for action. This would undermine my statement of the hypothesis with which I concluded the preceding section, but the hypothesis may be reformulated. I define "reasons* for action" as belief-desire complexes and wholly intrinsic desires of the sort I have been discussing in this chapter—that is, as what I have been calling broadly Davidsonian reasons for action. With that definition in place, the hypothesis at issue may be reformulated as follows: intentional actions are to be relatively directly explained at least partially in terms of motivation-encompassing reasons* for action, and when normative reasons (all of which are strictly external facts) contribute to explanations of intentional actions, they do so less directly, by way of making a causal contribution to the acquisition of motivation-encompassing reasons* or by way of a causal contribution made by an agent's apprehending a normative reason.[17]

Can a philosopher who has embraced a theory of action explanation according to which reasons* for action (or their physical realizers) play an important role in producing intentional actions while being agnostic about whether there are external reasons for action hold on to his or her view of the role played by reasons* (or their physical realizers) in the production of actions and assimilate external reasons for action into his or her story of the explanation of action? I believe that the answer is yes, that the hitherto neutral philosopher can now add a layer on top of what was already in place without modifying what falls beneath the new layer. However, a confident assertion of that answer is not yet appropriate. Central issues in the following two chapters are directly relevant.

Notes

1. It is noteworthy in this connection that in "Actions, Reasons, and Causes," Davidson expresses some attraction to the idea that an intentional action may be defined as "one done for a reason" (1980, p. 6). In a subsequent article, he claims that "it is (logically) impossible to perform an intentional action without some appropriate reason" (p. 264).

2. Compare this with Davidson's remark (1980, p. 232) that when " 'He just wanted to' [is] given in explanation of why Sam played the piano at midnight, it implies that he wanted to make true a certain proposition, that Sam play the piano at midnight, and he believed that by acting as he did, he would make it true." Incidentally, one may distinguish between theses S (for "stronger") and W (for "weaker") below and attempt to protect Davidson from the worry under consideration by claiming that he endorses only the weaker of them:

> (S) If there is a description, D, of x under which x is an intentional action, x is done for a reason under D.
> (W) If there is a description of x under which x is an intentional action, there is a description of x under which x is done for a reason.

However, the passage just quoted is evidence that his is the stronger and more interesting thesis.

3. See Locke (1974, p. 172). My argument is advanced in Mele (1988; cf. 1992e, ch. 6). Aristotle deemed it a necessary condition of being virtuous that an agent perform virtuous actions "for the sake of the acts themselves" (*Nicomachean Ethics* 1144a18–20; cf. 1105a28–33).

4. In an article on Gregory Kavka's (1983) toxin puzzle, I argue that there are very special cases in which an agent intentionally A-s but does not A for a reason (Mele 1992b). Some philosophers hold that, in some cases of double effect, agents intentionally A without A-ing for a reason. I disagree (see Mele and Sverdlik 1996), but that issue is orthogonal to present concerns.

5. This embedded quotation is from McDowell (1982).

6. On acting for a bad reason, see Audi (2001, p. 118).

7. Davidson contends that "the looniest action has its reason" (1980, p. 267).

8. On assessing and justifying intrinsic desires, see Audi (2001, pp. 88–89).

9. Davidson (1982b) has argued that having beliefs requires possession of the concept of belief. For an instructive reply, see Jeffrey (1985).

10. See Hutcheson's (1897, pp. 403ff.) and Frankena's (1958, p. 44) distinction between "exciting" and "justifying" reasons. See also Audi (2001, pp. 119–22), Brink (1989, pp. 38–40), Dancy (2000, chs. 1 and 5), Mele (1989, pp. 432–34), Parfit (1997), and Smith (1994, pp. 94–98, ch. 5). For criticism of Frankena and Hutcheson on exciting and justifying reasons, see Dancy (2000, pp. 20–25).

11. For what may be understood as a distinction between counting in favor of one's being rationally required to A and counting in favor of its being rationally permissible for one to A, see Gert (2000).

12. Thesis 2a is ambiguous in the way 2 is. "Motivating" here may or may not be intended in its success sense.

13. Dancy would say that Nick "acted for a reason that is no reason" (2000, p. 144; see pp. 141–45).

14. Again, I have argued that there are highly unusual scenarios in which this is false (Mele 1992b).

15. Ann apprehends two different external reasons for withdrawing all but a few dollars from her bank account today, a Friday, and she intentionally withdraws funds. One reason concerns paying a debt to Bob Monday morning, and the other concerns making a purchase at an auction on Sunday. Ann knows that she lacks sufficient funds to do both. A scientist has rendered one of the apprehensions (or its neural realization) incapable of making a causal contribution to intention acquisition. One justifiably infers that Ann did not withdraw the money for the reason that is the object of that apprehension.

16. Cf. Scanlon (1998, p. 44): "I would not say, 'Well, I do have some reason to buy the computer, since it would satisfy my desire, but on balance it is not worth it.'"

17. If external reasons cannot contribute to action explanation in "false belief" cases like Nick's, so be it.

4

The Motivational Power of Practical Reasoning

It is commonly supposed that when we act on the basis of practical reasoning, the reasoning plays a role in the action's production. But what role does it play? And how is it, more specifically, that reasoning issuing in a judgment in favor of A-ing produces motivation-encompassing attitudes toward A-ing? In particular, does practical reasoning's producing such attitudes depend in some interesting way on motivation that is already present in the agent before these attitudes appear on the scene? My primary aim in this chapter is to develop a plausible answer to this last question. To set the stage, I tell another Promethean tale.

1. Another Promethean Tale

Prometheus continued tinkering with his agents. His concern now was to make them efficient practical thinkers. A variety of possible designs occurred to him. In Prometheus's mind, they fell into two groups. A simple method for imbuing reasoning with practicality, he thought, was to arrange for it to be driven by a suitable desire or desires. Practical reasoning might be theoretical reasoning that is motivated in a certain manner, as a sunburn is a burn that is caused in a certain manner. The other method, he believed, was to build practical reasoning out of intrinsically practical inferences. To get a sense of the latter method, imagine that Ann's desire to entertain an old friend from another country next weekend and her acquisition of a belief that playing golf at a fine local course would be an excellent source of entertainment were jointly and directly to give rise, in a way governed by a rule of practical inference, to her desiring to play golf with her friend next weekend. That would be an instance of an intrinsically practical inference. The process is inferential insofar as it is governed by a rule of inference. The inference is practical because the desire that constitutes its conclusion is a state of mind of a kind suitable for motivating action; it has the right "direction of fit." And the inference is *intrinsically* practical in that it does not derive its practicality from anything external to it.

It occurred to Prometheus that it might be useful to build capacities for both kinds of practical reasoning into his agents, but he preferred the first kind and started with it. The initial grounds for his preference are easy to state. First, he wanted his beings eventually to have a robust capacity for theoretical reasoning anyway, and efficiency suggested employing that very capacity in practical reasoning rather than having to invent another inferential capacity. Second, insofar as practical reasoning is an intentional activity, it is motivated. Consequently, efficiency also suggested ascertaining whether what would naturally motivate intentional practical reasoning would also render it practical.

Often, Prometheus realized, practical reasoners would face the relatively simple task of figuring out how to attain specific, very modest goals—for example, how to get a pear from a tree. Even in many simple cases of this sort, he recognized, his agents would notice alternative means. Judging that his agents would need some mechanism for evaluating means, he decided to give them a capacity for practical *evaluative* reasoning.

It is a truism that practical reasoning is reasoning about what to do. One might say that it is reasoning conducted with a view to answering the question "What shall I do?" (That question must be distinguished from "What will I do?" The former calls for a decision, or at least the acquisition of an intention. The latter calls for a prediction.) How should people go about answering this question, Prometheus wondered? His first thought was that they should settle on what to do by ascertaining what it would be best to do in the circumstances—best by their own lights. (He was disinclined to give his agents a specific conception of the good.) But it occurred to him that agents who always resolve their practical questions by making judgments about what it would be best to do will spend too much time reasoning and not enough time acting (overtly, that is). Too many of them will be eaten by predators while absorbed in thought about the *best* means of escape. Although he thought that it would be fine for some practical reasoning to take the form of deliberation about what it would be best to do, he judged that other practical reasoning should take the form of reasoning about what it would be *good enough* to do. For example, an agent with the goal of getting a pear from the top of a tree might benefit from reasoning about how to do this in a way that he would find acceptable, or good enough.

Both kinds of reasoning just described include evaluative judgments, and both, Prometheus thought, would be motivated by a desire or intention to settle on what to do in response to a practical question. Practical evaluative reasoning, as Prometheus designed it, is an inferential process, involving evaluative premises, driven at least partly by motivation to settle on what to do (cf. Mele 1992e, ch. 12; 1995a, ch. 2). This settling motivation naturally disposes agents to intend in accordance with the reasoning's evaluative conclusion if, as I have said (chapter 1, section 5), agents become settled on a course of action in forming or acquiring an intention. Their being so disposed supports the primary point of practical evaluative reasoning, which is to lead to a satisfactory *resolution* of one's practical problem. An agent who judges it best to *A* but is still unsettled about whether to *A* has not resolved his practical problem.

It did not occur to Prometheus that there might be a kind of practical reasoning that produces motivation that does not derive, even partly, from motivation already present in the agent. As he saw it, an agent whose current practical reasoning takes the form of reasoning about what it is best to do has a desire to do whatever is best in the circumstances that plays a role in explaining why the agent is reasoning about what it is best to do. The motivational force or strength of such a desire, Prometheus thought, would be a partial source of the motivational strength of relevant resultant desires and intentions—that is, desires and intentions for the specific courses of action judged best in practical reasoning. Prometheus also thought that, in the case of practical reasoning about what it would be good enough to do, the strength of a desire for an acceptable course of action would similarly be a partial source of the strength of relevant, resultant motivation-encompassing attitudes. This is not to say, of course, that he took the relevant generic desires to be the only sources of the strength of these resultant attitudes. But I want to avoid getting ahead of the story. The foregoing helps set the stage for this chapter's central issue.

Prometheus gave his creatures a disposition to desire to settle on what to do upon encountering a significant practical question. The design was *not* such that resulting "settling desires" always led to reasoning. For example, agents who acquire a desire to settle a practical question sometimes have a much stronger desire to proceed with a more pressing task instead and act at the time on the latter desire rather than the former. Prometheus also equipped his creatures with a disposition to acquire either of two generic desires upon acquiring a settling desire, depending on such things as how much the agent takes to be at stake and how complicated he takes the issue to be: a desire to do whatever is best in the circumstances and a desire for an acceptable course of action. These desires, when effective, motivate (in the "success" sense) episodes of practical reasoning, and they do so in conjunction with a desire to settle on what to do. In some cases, partly because he has the latter desire and partly because he learned that matters were much more complicated than he had thought, an agent who was reasoning about what it is best to do changes tactics and reasons about what it would be good enough to do.

Prometheus's thinking about practical reasoning was influenced by his thinking about motivation in general. A phenomenon that he called "motivational spread" struck this biological engineer as potentially very handy. He believed that with the benefit of a robust capacity for learning, an agent with dispositions to have desires of a handful of basic kinds can acquire an impressively broad array of useful desires. Prometheus regarded dispositions to desire pleasant experiences and to desire to avoid painful ones as especially promising in this connection. He knew, for example, that pleasure can be derived not only from activities that his beings share with animals but also from deeply intellectual or aesthetic activities and from doing what one believes one morally ought. (He himself found pleasure in such activities.) Prometheus hoped to design beings whose earliest motivation to pursue pleasant activities and to avoid painful ones would eventually spread to the intellectual, aesthetic, and moral domains. Regarding morality, he did not have the aim of building beings who would desire to do what is right for the sake of the pleasure involved. Rather, his thought was that his beings would learn to take advantage of the pair of dispositions at issue in developing systems of moral education and that such education would eventually foster morally appropriate desires for moral conduct. Children who initially are motivated to do what they believe to be morally right by desires for the pleasure of rewards for so acting and by desires to avoid painful consequences of acting otherwise, he hoped, would eventually be motivated to perform the actions they believe to be morally right by, perhaps among other things, intrinsic desires for the well-being of others. He decided to wait and see whether desires for one's own well-being would figure in the production of desires for the well-being of those closest to one and whether both kinds of desire might contribute to the production of desires for the well-being of others.[1] But he was prepared to introduce in subsequent generations, if need be, a (perhaps finely tuned) disposition to have altruistic desires.

2. The Antecedent Motivation Theory

What I call "the antecedent motivation theory" (*AMT*) is a Promethean position on practical evaluative reasoning. It asserts that, in actual human beings, all motivation nonaccidentally produced by practical reasoning issuing in a belief favoring a course of action derives at least partly from motivation-encompassing attitudes already present in the agent before he acquires the belief—what I term "antecedent motivation-encompassing attitudes," or "antecedent motivation," for short.[2] What I call "the cognitive engine theory" (*CET*) is a non-Promethean position. It asserts that, in actual human beings, some instances of practical evaluative reasoning, in or by issuing in a belief favoring a course of action, nonaccidentally produce motivation that does not derive at all from antecedent motivation. Both theories, on the interpretations germane to the purposes of this chapter, understand evaluative beliefs in a *cognitivist* way. They hold that evaluative beliefs are attitudes with truth-valued content and that not all evaluative beliefs are doomed to be false, as they would be if an "error theory" about them were true.[3] Since both theories can take a variety of forms, these formulations are rough sketches at best. They serve only as a point of departure.

The antecedent motivation theory has an impressive pedigree. Both Aristotle and Hume propound versions of it when they claim, respectively, that "intellect itself . . . moves nothing, but only the intellect which aims at an end and is practical" and that "reason is . . . the slave of the passions, and can never pretend to any other office than to serve and obey them."[4] They are not speaking about moral motivation exclusively but about motivation in general. In this chapter, I articulate and defend a version of *AMT*. The simplest version is a crude instrumentalism, according to which reasoning generates motivation in us only by identifying means to antecedently desired ends. The view advanced here is much less restrictive.

The antecedent motivation theory must be distinguished from a seemingly related view—what I dub "the motivationally grounded reasons view," or *MGRV*. The *AMT* is a theory about the motivational capacities of our practical reasoning. The *MGRV* is a view about the conditions under which such normative claims as the following are warranted: "There is *reason* for S to A"; "A is the *rational* thing for S to do." The *MGRV* asserts, in Bernard Williams's words, that the truth of sentences such as these "implies very roughly, that [S] has some motive which will be served or furthered by his [A]-ing . . ." (1979, p. 17). Whereas *MGRV* is a thesis about a normative issue, *AMT* is concerned instead with a *causal* question—roughly, whether in actual human beings, reasoning that purports to show that there is some reason for an agent to *A* sometimes nonaccidentally generates motivation to *A* without the assistance of antecedent motivation.

As I explain in more detail in section 5, the distinction just made has some ties to the familiar distinction between *motivational* and *normative* reasons for action that I mentioned in chapter 3. The *MGRV* seemingly asserts that alleged normative reasons for action are actually *reasons* for action only if they are suitably grounded in motives the agent has. The proponent of *AMT*, as I show (section 5), is not committed to this assertion.

The literature does not uniformly treat either of these two views—that is, *AMT* or *MGRV*—as logically prior to the other. Williams (1979) attempts to motivate *MGRV* by means of an argument for a version of *AMT*. Christine Korsgaard (1986) investigates arguments *from MGRV* to something like *AMT*. I offer an independent argument for *AMT* and argue that the theory does not entail *MGRV*.

The antecedence of "antecedent motivation," again, is *temporal*. On the antecedent motivation view, the production of new motivation by reasoning involves motivation that is already in place before the agent reaches his cognitive conclusion—motivation present in what might be called, following Williams, the agent's antecedent "motivational set." Williams claims, without explanation, that "'desire' . . . can be used, formally, for all elements in [the set]," including "dispositions of evaluation, patterns of emotional reaction, personal loyalties, and various projects . . . embodying commitments of the agent" (1979, p. 20). His use of "desire" here is obviously very broad. In this chapter, the broad sense of "desire" that I articulated in chapter 1 is operative in my development of *AMT*; in my critical discussion of Williams's article, his own broader sense of "desire" is operative. A "motivational set," as I use the expression in the former connection, is composed *only* of motivation-encompassing attitudes.

In chapter 1 (section 3), I rejected the idea that the total motivational base of a motivation-encompassing attitude always determines the attitude's motivational strength since there is weighty evidence that modes of representation have a significant influence on motivational strength. A plausible formulation of *AMT* must accommodate this point about modes of representation.[5] Another requirement on a plausible *AMT* is that it not entail that antecedent motivation *must*, on conceptual grounds, be involved in the generation of motivation by reasoning. Perhaps, in some possible worlds, other things occasionally do the work of antecedent motivation—for example, divine intervention. Rather, the idea is this:

> *AMT**. Actual human beings and the real world are such that the capacity of justificatory reasoning to generate in a human being, *S*, a motivation-encompassing attitude whose object is *S*'s *A*-ing and to do this in virtue of that reasoning's providing *S* with what he takes to be justification for *A*-ing is contingent on *S*'s having antecedent motivation capable of being at least a partial positive motivational base for the generated motivation-encompassing attitude; and whenever such reasoning does generate a motivation-encompassing attitude of this kind in us in the way identified, antecedent motivation is in the positive motivational base of the generated attitude.

As a convenient bit of shorthand, I use the expression "*nonaccidentally* to produce in *S* motivation to *A*" for the clause between "reasoning" and "is contingent" in *AMT**.

It can be agreed on all sides that intentional action is motivated. Antecedent motivation theorists and cognitive engine theorists are distinguished by their respective claims about how practical reasoning generates motivation in actual human beings.

3. Some Unsuccessful Arguments for the Antecedent Motivation Theory

This section examines some unsuccessful arguments for *AMT**. My aim, in part, is to clarify the position by eliminating from contention familiar but specious or tendentious grounds for accepting it. In section 4, I argue that the plausibility of *AMT** rests on the role it plays in a general theory of action explanation.

The arguments to be examined here are introduced by way of a single claim of Bernard Williams (1979) in a much-discussed article.[6] One item of background is in order: for Williams, an "external reasons statement" is a statement of an (alleged) reason for action that is in no way grounded in the agent's antecedent motivational set (p. 22). Williams attributes the following position to cognitive engine theorists: in some cases, (1) an agent acquires motivation because, on the basis of correct deliberation, he comes to believe a certain external reasons statement, and (2) this motivation is acquired independently of any antecedent motivation (p. 24). He rejects this view on the grounds that "*ex hypothesi*, there is no motivation for the agent to deliberate *from*, to reach his new motivation" (p. 24).

It will prove instructive to consider various strategies for supporting what I dub Williams's (1979) *central negative thesis*:

> WT. In the absence of motivation for agents to deliberate from, they cannot acquire the new motivation at issue—that is, motivation resulting from their believing, on the basis of correct deliberation, a certain external reasons statement.

Aristotle held that deliberation is, *essentially*, reasoning with a view to the achievement of a desired end, and Williams may be following him in this.[7] Or he may have in mind a more complex line about deliberation—perhaps that the nature of deliberation (as opposed to, say, purely theoretical reasoning) is such that deliberation cannot provide justification for an agent's *A*-ing independently of his having some motivation that both prompts his deliberation and speaks in favor of his *A*-ing.

Very plausibly, all intentional activities, including intentional reasoning, are motivated. Thus, it is very plausible that all instances of intentional reasoning are prompted by motivation-encompassing attitudes. Suppose, for the sake of argument, that something stronger than this is true: necessarily, any instance of intentional reasoning is motivated by a desire. This supposition alone does not entail that motivation generated by a bit of intentional reasoning must derive, in the pertinent sense, from the desire that prompted the reasoning. A student for whom morality is a purely academic matter, who does not care at all whether his behavior is morally proper, may be motivated to reason about what it would be morally best to do in a particular situation by a desire to write an acceptable paper on the topic. Cognitive engine theorists may claim that this reasoning can nonaccidentally result in motivation to do the action deemed best, and they will properly deny that motivation to perform this action has the student's desire *to write a good paper* in its positive motivational base.

If it is replied that the student's reasoning is theoretical and not practical or deliberative, on the grounds that it is addressed to a theoretical and not a practical question, a straightforward response is available to cognitive engine theorists: theoretical reasoning about the right or the good can generate motivation that is not derivative from antecedent motivation. To show that they are wrong about this, some distinct argument is needed. Of course, Williams (1979) attributes to his opponents the view that *deliberation* generates the new motivation. But they may be operating with a less restrictive notion that includes theoretical reasoning about moral matters, or they may just make Williams a present of the *word*.

Can *WT* be defended on the basis of considerations about justification that do not rest on a particular conception of deliberation? Williams may be thinking that no (hypothetical) intentional action is to any degree *justified* (or rational) unless it is supported by the agent's antecedent motivational set—a *normative* thesis. From this it would follow that *no* reasoning, deliberative or otherwise, can produce justification for the performance of an action that is not supported by antecedent motivation.

A salient problem with this line of argument is that cognitive engine theorists can grant that any (hypothetical or prospective) action depends for its being justified (or rational) on supporting motivation antecedent to the *performance of the action*. They can simply contend that in some cases the required motivation is produced by justificatory reasoning whose conclusion does not derive any of its motivational force from—or depend for its motivation-producing effect on—motivation that was already present in the agent. I should also point out that Williams's (1979) argument for the *normative* thesis identified in the preceding paragraph rests on the alleged truth of the antecedent motivation view (pp. 26–27). So he cannot, without vicious circularity, use the normative thesis to establish the truth of this view. Furthermore, Williams would need to overcome arguments for the legitimacy of relevant agent-external conceptions of rationality and reasons for action. This last issue is discussed in section 5.

One may want to argue, in support of *WT* and partly on the basis of an alleged connection between an agent's being justified (or rational) in *A*-ing and his having motivation to *A*, that the *production* of motivation by justificatory reasoning depends on the existence in the agent of motivation to which the reasoning can appeal. But such an argument, if successful, would support *AMT** directly: no detour through *WT* is required. In any event, in the absence of a compelling argument for Williams's (1979) *normative* thesis, antecedent motivation theorists should leave it open that *A* may be the rational thing for an agent to do even in the absence of antecedent motivation that supports his *A*-ing, and they should focus their critical efforts on the idea that in such cases practical reasoning sometimes nonaccidentally generates motivation to *A*.

4. Antecedent Motivation versus the Cognitive Engine

Antecedent motivation theorists are in a position to offer a relatively straightforward account of the generation of motivation by reasoning. The strength of their view lies here. This strength and the corresponding weakness of the cognitive engine theory (*CET*) ought to be emphasized in a defense of *AMT**. A simple antecedent motivation model is a purely instrumentalist one: reasoning generates motivation by identifying means to a desired end or by locating something that the reasoner wants, with the result that antecedent motivation is channeled toward a certain (sort of) action or object (cf. Hume's *Treatise*, p. 459). This model, as I explain, is *too* simple, but necessary revisions can be made.

The channeling image is not particularly apt. Angela, who is spending a week in Canberra, wants to see kangaroos at Tidbinbilla. She had been hoping to take a bus there with her parents, but she discovered that that is not feasible. She judges that what would make the most sense is to ask her parents to rent a car for the trip, and she wants to make that request. It is not as though motivational force or power flows out of Angela's desire to see the kangaroos and into a desire to make the request. The former desire may be just as strong as ever. Part of what does happen, on a plausible version of *AMT*, is that the combination of Angela's desire to see the kangaroos and her making the judgment I mentioned plays a role in producing her desire to make her request, a desire whose strength is partly accounted for by the strength of her desire to see the kangaroos. This is not to suggest that the channeling image is the only problem with the simple view nor the most significant problem with it. The simple instrumentalism is also problematic, as I explain in section 5.

As I explained in section 1, a desire that helps drive all practical evaluative reasoning, on one view of such reasoning—namely, a desire to settle on what to do—disposes agents to intend in accordance with the evaluative conclusions of such reasoning. Whether this reasoning-driving desire sometimes or often enters into the positive motivational base of an intention formed or acquired on the basis of practical evaluative reasoning is an open question. However, it is a good bet that an agent whose current practical reasoning takes the form of reasoning about what it is best to do is reasoning about *this* because, in part, he has a desire to do whatever is best in his circumstances, and a desire of this kind is an obvious candidate for an element in the positive motivational base of an intention or desire for the course of action, *A*, recommended by the agent's evaluative conclusion. In an agent who has an antecedent desire to do whatever is best in his circumstances, one should expect that an intention to *A* formed or acquired on the basis of a deliberative judgment that it would be best to *A* derives at least part of its motivational force from that antecedent desire. A parallel point may be made about an agent engaged in practical reasoning that has the form of reasoning about what it would be good enough to do. Again, this is not to say that the antecedent desires at issue exhaust the positive motivational bases of the agents' desires to *A*. Presumably, an antecedent motivation theorist would hold that such bases often include at least some desires associated with considerations on the basis of which the agent deliberatively judges it best, or good enough, to *A*.

Although much remains to be said about the connection between a desire's strength and its positive motivational base, the foregoing is enough for immediate purposes. It is not at all mysterious how a desire to *A* would derive some of its force from a relevant antecedent desire—for example, an antecedent desire for an end to which the agent regards his *A*-ing as a means or an antecedent desire to do whatever it would be best to do in the circumstances in an agent who desires to *A* (partly) on the basis of a deliberative judgment that it would be best to A. Is there also no mystery about how a nonaccidental motivational upshot of practical reasoning would have a motivational force that is wholly nonderivative from antecedent motivation?

Cognitive engine theorists owe their readers some explanation of the manner in which reasoning generates motivation—especially when reasoning is alleged to do so nonaccidentally and without the generated motivation's having derived any of its force from antecedent motivation. If they are unable to provide a plausible explanation or even a sketch of one, their opponents have won a major battle. The cognitive engine theory's contribution to this battle is the focus of the present section.

In assessing *CET*, one must distinguish between two claims:

1. In actual human agents, either (a) justificatory reasoning sometimes nonaccidentally generates a motivation-encompassing belief that p without any of the agent's antecedent motivations entering into the justification offered for p in the reasoning or (b) justificatory reasoning sometimes nonaccidentally generates a motivation-causing belief that p without any of the agent's antecedent motivations entering into the justification offered for p in the reasoning, which belief straightaway and nonaccidentally issues in corresponding motivation.
2. In actual human agents, either (a) justificatory reasoning sometimes nonaccidentally generates a motivation-encompassing belief that p without any of the agent's antecedent motivations playing a role in the production of the motivation in that belief or (b) justificatory reasoning sometimes nonaccidentally generates a motivation-causing (but not motivation-encompassing) belief, which belief straightaway and nonaccidentally issues in corresponding motivation without the assistance of antecedent motivation.

The (a) and (b) disjuncts in 1 and 2 represent two different forms that *CET* can take. The present point of focus, however, is the difference between 1 and 2. The question whether a cognitivist notion of motivation-encompassing belief is coherent is discussed in chapter 5. I assume for now that the notion is coherent and forge ahead.

The following case illustrates a crucial difference between 1 and 2. Suppose that Sarah reasons as follows and her concluding belief either encompasses motivation to pursue x or straightaway and nonaccidentally issues in such motivation.

A. The great majority of people believe that x is good.
B. Whatever the great majority of people believe is probably true.
So C. X is probably good.

Perhaps Sarah's belief that C can encompass motivation even though her belief that A and her belief that B do not. Perhaps although Sarah's beliefs that the majority take x to be good and that majority opinion establishes probable truth are not at all motivation encompassing, once she comes to believe that x is probably good she has, in that belief, motivation to pursue x. If so, Sarah confirms 1. But she may confirm 1 without confirming 2; for although none of Sarah's antecedent motivations enters into the justification offered for the conclusion, her concluding belief might still derive some or all of its motivational force from antecedent motivation of hers. It may happen, for example, that Sarah's concluding belief derives some or all of its motivational force from an antecedent generic desire for good things. Similarly, if her belief that x is probably good issues straightaway and nonaccidentally in motivation to pursue *x*, it may do so in conjunction with this generic desire.

Here is a second illustration. This time the setting is explicitly practical. Sam was offered an attractive job in another state. He wants to do whatever it would be best to do about this, and he seeks the advice of several knowledgeable, trustworthy friends on the question whether it would be better to accept the new job or keep his present one. After considerable consultation, he reasons as follows:

A. The many knowledgeable, trustworthy people I consulted agree that it would be best to take the job.
B. Such agreement is powerful evidence, and there is little contrary evidence.
So C. It probably would be best to take the job.

Sam, like Sarah, may confirm 1. But given his desire to do whatever it would be best to do about the job offer, it is very difficult to believe that he confirms 2. On the hypothesis that Sam's belief that C is motivation encompassing, it is very likely that the belief derives at least some of its motivational force from this generic desire, not to mention various desires of Sam's that he believes would be satisfied as a result of his taking the job. And on the hypothesis that the belief is motivation causing but not motivation encompassing, it is very likely that the generic desire (along with desires of the other kind to which I just alluded) is in the positive motivational base of the desire in which the belief issues—the desire to take the job.

Proponents of the version of the antecedent motivation theory that I am advocating (*AMT**) can grant 1; for they do not claim that some appeal to antecedent motivation is always involved in assent to the *premises* of justificatory, motivation-producing reasoning, but instead that whenever justificatory reasoning nonaccidentally generates motivation (in actual human beings), antecedent motivation is in the positive motivational base of the generated motivation. The fact that the motivational force of the conclusion of a particular bit of reasoning is not derivative from motivation associated with the premises of that reasoning is compatible with its being derivative from *other* antecedent motivation. Similarly, the fact that a concluding belief issued straightaway and nonaccidentally in corresponding motivation, without the assistance of any motivation associated with the premises of the reasoning that produced the belief, is compatible with the resulting desire's having at least a partial positive motivational base in antecedent motivation. Claim 2 is the central point of contention. Cognitive engine theorists owe their audience some explanation of its (alleged) truth.

It is not easy to see what form this explanation should take. Suppose that, on the basis of justificatory reasoning, Ann, an actual human being, believes that *A* is *B* (e.g., that *A* is good, or morally right, or likely to contribute to Fred's well-being). Supposing that this belief has a motivational character (i.e., is either motivation encompassing or directly motivation producing), what can account for Ann's acquiring a belief with this character if she does not already have some motivation that does or can incline her toward *B*? If Ann has no antecedent motivation that does or can incline her to promote or protect Fred's well-being, how can her belief that her *A*-ing would help Fred encompass or directly produce motivation to *A*?

Some answers are beside the point. Perhaps acquiring a belief on the basis of justificatory reasoning can trigger a posthypnotic suggestion to desire in accordance with one's acceptance of the conclusion of the first apparently convincing practical argument offered to one by Bob on Tuesday (cf. Cohon 1986, p. 549). Perhaps, in some possible world, an internal biological or psychological mechanism occasionally or routinely brings it about, entirely independently of the agent's antecedent motivations, that he desires to perform an action of type A when he comes to believe that A is B on the basis of reasoning. Or, one might suppose, there is a chance that the juxtaposition of thoughts of A and B in an agent's consciousness will, because of a bizarre neural occurrence, directly result in his desiring to A even though he has no antecedent motivation concerning either of A and B. But these possibilities are not enough for cognitive engine theorists. Their concern is not with highly artificial cases or mere possibilities but rather with cases in which, *in ordinary circumstances*, justificatory reasoning produces motivation in actual human agents independently of antecedent motivation. What cognitive engine theorists should explain or shed light on, given the empirical nature of their thesis, is how it happens, in cases of this sort, that agents acquire motivation precisely in virtue of their coming to see the truth of an external reasons statement.[8]

More can be said about the preceding hypotheses, but it should be kept brief. On the hypnosis and juxtaposition hypotheses, it is not in virtue of the apprehension of truth that the agent acquires motivation to A. Rather, it is the hypnosis or the juxtaposition of thoughts of A and B that turns the trick. And given that *CET* (like *AMT*) is an empirical thesis, proponents of this view cannot take much comfort in the mere possibility of the above-mentioned mechanism.

One may suggest that, in the case of a motivation-encompassing or directly motivation-producing belief that A is B, motivation for B need not be present before the agent acquires the belief, and the motivation may itself be nonaccidentally generated, independently of antecedent motivation, by the justificatory reasoning that prompted the belief. But this simply pushes the original question up another level. How is the motivation for B generated by the reasoning?[9]

Now, because of a significant similarity between B and C, one who has no antecedent motivational interest in B might nevertheless acquire motivation to pursue B as a partial result of acquiring the belief that A is B. Suppose that Al tries to convince Ann to A by demonstrating to her that her A-ing would help Fred, and suppose that she has no antecedent motivational interest in helping Fred in particular or people in general. Suppose, however, that in showing her how her A-ing would help Fred (which is part of his demonstrating to her that her A-ing would help Fred), Al causes Ann to see Fred's plight as significantly like that of her beloved brother, Ed, with the result that Ann's belief that her A-ing would help Fred produces in her a desire to A. The strength of Ann's desire to A might not derive at all from an antecedent desire to help Fred: it may be supposed that she has no desire to help him before she acquires the belief that A-ing would help. But, of course, the cognitive engine theorist cannot infer from this that the strength of Ann's desire to A is wholly nonderivative from antecedent motivation. It may be that this desire has a positive motivational base in some desires Ann has concerning her brother, Ed.

Some embellishment will prove useful. Ed is very shy and awkward with women. This causes him considerable distress. Out of compassion for Ed, Ann has often tried to help him improve in this sphere. Fred, a colleague of Ann, is painfully timid and awkward when dealing with his superiors, female and male, at work. When Ann makes the connection between Fred and Ed, and owing significantly to her making it, she finds herself desiring to help Fred with his problem. In the present case, such claims as the following are plausible:

1. Other things being equal, it is likely that if Ann had not desired to help Ed, she would not have desired to help Fred.
2. Other things being equal, it is likely that if Ann had not made a relevant connection between Fred and Ed, she would not have desired to help Fred.
3. Other things being equal, it is likely that if Ann had been less (or more) strongly motivated to help Ed with his problem, she would have been less (or more) strongly motivated to help Fred with his.
4. Other things being equal, it is likely that if Ann had made a looser (or tighter) connection between Fred and Ed, she would have been less (or more) strongly motivated to help Fred.
5. Other things being equal, it is likely that if Ann had desired less (or more) strongly that Ed improve in the relevant respect, she would have desired less (or more) strongly that Fred improve in the relevant respect.

This suggests that a theorist should take seriously the idea that Ann's desire to help Fred has at least a partial motivational base in some desire or desires of hers regarding Ed.

A cognitive engine theorist may make the following maneuver. Granted, a person cannot (under normal conditions) be motivated by a particular episode of justificatory reasoning unless he has the *capacity to be motivated* by it. But this capacity (sometimes) does not involve motivation-encompassing attitudes of the agent at the time. Consequently, motivation produced (under normal conditions) by practical reasoning (sometimes) does not derive, even partly, from antecedent motivation. I dub this *the capacity argument.*

In what might the alleged capacity consist in a particular case if it does not involve items in the agent's motivational set? Stephen Darwall maintains that "a person's motivational capacities, in the broadest sense, are not constituted simply by his desires but also by capacities of imagination, sensitivity, and so on" (1983, p. 39). However, cognitive engine theorists can effectively use the capacity argument only if they can at least *sketch* a plausible account of how it is that justificatory reasoning, with the assistance of certain capacities, nonaccidentally generates motivational items that are wholly nonderivative from antecedent motivation. Moreover, they owe their readers (and themselves) an account of the capacities in question that is detailed enough to support the claim that they do not involve antecedent motivation.

Although the example that Darwall offers of the generation of motivation by an allegedly desire-independent process features perceptual experience rather than justificatory reasoning, consideration of the example will prove helpful. Darwall's heroine, Roberta, first "sees a film that vividly presents the plight of textile workers in the southern United States" and then attends a discussion about how the situation might be ameliorated (1983, pp. 39–40). Even though she had no prior general desire to relieve suffering, she is "shocked and dismayed by the suffering she sees," and she "decides"—and desires—to help these unfortunate people by promoting a boycott.

Darwall (1983) contends that Roberta "may have had no desire prior to viewing the film that explains her decision to join the boycott." But is it plausible that she had no prior desire that even *helps* to explain her decision? Suppose that Roberta never had a desire to relieve any suffering whatever—either her own or that of loved ones. What would explain her being "*shocked* and *dismayed* by the suffering she sees"? How could she have the feelings about suffering, or the appreciation of it, necessary for a depiction of suffering to be shocking and dismaying to her? Roberta's having a proper sense of the suffering depicted in the film would seem to depend partly on her having experienced suffering, and normal experiences of suffering encompass or are accompanied by an awareness of one's associated emotions and desires. Darwall may appreciate the force of this point, for he mentions the possibility of Roberta's having been moved in the past by the suffering of family, friends, and pets, and he says only that Roberta has no *general desire* to relieve suffering—that is, no desire to relieve suffering in general. This is consonant with the very likely hypothesis that the film helped Roberta to feel about the suffering of the textile workers and their families something akin to what she already has felt and is disposed to feel about her own occasional suffering or the occasional suffering of loved ones and friends. This is not to say that she desires to aid the textile workers as a means to satisfying some more general desire of hers concerning suffering. Rather, the point toward which I am heading is that a very plausible etiology of her desire to help these people does include a pertinent antecedent motivation of hers—and in such a way as to locate the antecedent motivation in the positive motivational base of the desire.

Obviously, desires that Roberta had in the past about her own suffering or the suffering of family and friends, if these desires are wholly in the past, cannot be in the positive motivational base of a desire that she acquires now. If dispositions of hers to have desires of certain kinds about her own suffering or that of family and friends are not themselves motivation *encompassing*, they cannot (by definition) be in the positive motivational base of a desire either (see chapter 1, section 3). Even so, such dispositions do play a role in a psychologically very likely story about Roberta's case. It is likely, in light of her relevant dispositions, that the desires prompted in Roberta by the film include such desires as that she herself never suffer like the textile workers, that her younger sister never have to go through anything like the little girl in the film who watched her mother die from emphysema, that her own mother not suffer like that woman, and so on. Skilled filmmakers are adept at evoking such desires. Desires of this kind can contribute to Roberta's acquisition of, and the strength of, her desire to help the struggling textile workers. Imagine that Roberta were devoid of all such desires for herself and her family at the time. Would she be the sort of person who, barring divine intervention, random neural occurrences, and the like, acquires a desire to help the textile workers? What would account for that desire to help and for its strength?

I have strayed from this chapter's central issue, a question about *practical reasoning*. Is there good reason to believe that, in actual human beings, practical reasoning that issues in a belief favoring a particular course of action sometimes nonaccidentally produces motivation that is not even partly derivative from antecedent motivation? It may be claimed that the nature of moral agency entails an affirmative answer to this question, that a conceptual requirement for being a moral agent is that one's practical moral reasoning sometimes nonaccidentally produces such nonderivative motivation. I take up a related issue in the following chapter and argue that this conception of moral agency should be abandoned. Another tack that a proponent of the cognitive engine theory might take should be considered here.

In section 1, I told, in effect, a tale about the psychological architecture of human agents that is in line with the antecedent motivation theory. I have been encouraging proponents of the cognitive engine theory to do the same for their own theory and to argue that the grounds for acceptance of *CET* are at least as strong as those for acceptance of *AMT*. Again, it is very plausible that all practical reasoning is motivated, and at least some of the desires that motivate such reasoning are plausibly located in the positive motivational base of desires nonaccidentally produced by practical reasoning. It is plausible, for example, that practical reasoning motivated partly by a generic desire to do whatever is best in the circumstances is such that a desire to *A* associated with one's conclusion that it would be best to *A* has a partial motivational base in the generic desire. Now, proponents of *CET* can try to construct an agent whose psychological architecture is such that although a generic desire of this kind plays an important role in motivating some of his practical reasoning, it makes no contribution to the strength of the pertinent desire in which the reasoning issues—a desire built into the agent's belief that he should *A* or a desire to *A* that is straightaway produced by that belief. And they can imagine that their agent also is such that in these cases, or some of them, the strength of that desire is wholly nonderivative from antecedent motivation of any kind, including any motivation associated with considerations that the agent regards as supporting his conclusion. But, again, how likely is it that any actual human agents are like that? And what is it about the psychological architecture of these hypothetical agents that accounts for the alleged production of motivation?

The possibility of a mechanism that takes, for example, beliefs that it would be best (or good enough) to *A* as input and yields desires to *A* as output is one thing. The possibility of a mechanism that does this with beliefs produced by processes of practical reasoning that are motivated partly by a desire to do whatever is best (or a desire for an acceptable course of action), and does it without in any way drawing on the motivational force of those desires or any desires associated with considerations that the agent regards as supporting his concluding belief, is another. A mechanism of the latter sort is conceivable; but if there are any empirical considerations that support the claim that a mechanism of this kind is at work in human beings, I have not encountered them. The idea that rather than producing desires independently of antecedent motivation, beliefs in which processes of practical reasoning conclude *encompass* desires or motivation certainly does not lie on firmer ground in this connection. (Again, discussion of the idea that there are motivation-encompassing cognitivist beliefs is reserved for chapter 5.) By contrast, *AMT* is consonant with a familiar empirical approach to the explanation of motivated behavior that has proved fruitful, an approach according to which (setting aside wholly intrinsic desires for action) motivation for specific courses of action is produced by combinations of antecedent motivation and beliefs.

It may be claimed that, in a *rational* agent, the deliberative judgment that a fact of any kind is a reason for *A*-ing is sufficient to provide the agent with a motivation-encompassing attitude that has his *A*-ing as its object. The combination of this judgment and the agent's being rational, it may be claimed, is causally or conceptually sufficient for this.[10] Now, if a motivation-encompassing attitude of this kind—call it a desire to A—comes into being, it presumably was caused to do so. The uncaused coming into being of attitudes of this kind would be mysterious. The judgment that fact F is a reason for one's A-ing may be a candidate for making a causal contribution to the agent's acquiring a desire to A. Is the same true of the agent's being rational? Perhaps. But one would like to know how an agent's being rational contributes causally to his coming to desire to A upon judging that a fact is a reason for his A-ing.

Perhaps it will be said that rationality, or practical rationality, is partly constituted by an indefeasible disposition to desire to A upon coming to believe that one has a reason for A-ing. Some philosophers would count such a disposition as a standing desire, but I forego appeals to standing desires here. If the disposition at issue is a feature of actual rational human agents, what is its psychological basis? Perhaps actual rational human beings are psychologically so constituted that their entertaining questions about what to do, or about what they have reasons to do, activates a disposition to desire to act for good reasons, and the manifesting desire may be part of what disposes rational human agents to think rationally about what to do and about reasons for action and to desire to A upon coming to believe that they have a reason to A. But, then, the alleged fact that rational human agents have an indefeasible disposition to desire to A upon coming to believe that they have a reason for A-ing is quite compatible with its being the case that their coming to have a belief of this kind issues in a relevant desire only with the assistance of another desire—a desire to act for good reasons—and, in fact, a desire that is part of the positive motivational base of the generated desire.[11]

The structure of my argument thus far for *AMT** as against cognitive engine competitors is simple. *AMT** is part of a general theory of the etiology of intentional behavior that also provides a straightforward account of the nonaccidental production of motivation by practical reasoning. The basic psychological architecture that it presupposes in human beings is the architecture of the more general theory. Conversely, it is far from clear that the psychological architecture of actual human agents is capable of sustaining processes in which, under ordinary circumstances and independently of appropriate antecedent motivation, human beings nonaccidentally acquire motivation to A simply in virtue of acquiring a belief that A is B on the basis of practical reasoning.

One may think that, psychologically questionable or not, *CET* is something that philosophers must learn to live with. Some theorists may see no alternative, if they want, with Nagel, "some guarantee that reasons will provide a motive" (1970, p. 28), and are convinced that there are what Williams (1979) calls "external reasons." I return to these matters in section 5.

I conclude this section with a comment on an objection to the line that I have been pursuing. Thomas Reid contends that Hume's view of the relationship of reason to motivation can be defended only "by a gross and palpable abuse of words" (1788, p. 212). Reid's claim is that Hume helps himself to a victory by inventing a distinction between passion and reason that, contrary to ordinary usage, entails that everything motivational falls on the side of passion and passion alone. One may want to charge me with having done the same. However, I leave open the possibility that sense can be given to the idea that reason has its own reservoir of motivation (see section 5). Moreover, *AMT** does not commit one to insisting that reasoning can nonaccidentally generate motivation only if it benefits from the current existence of some motivation-encompassing attitudes that are not justifiable by reason. That is, *AMT** does not specify the *sort* of motivation that justificatory reasoning relies on when it nonaccidentally generates motivation by producing a belief. It claims only that, in human beings as they actually are, there is *some* antecedent motivational base for the generated motivation.

5. Implications of the Antecedent Motivation Theory?

It is time to inquire about implications of the version *AMT* that I have been sketching. In this section, I ask, first, to what extent my position limits the powers of practical reasoning. In particular, does *AMT** warrant Hume's (*Treatise*, p. 415) bold contention that "reason is, and ought to be, the slave of the passions, and can never pretend to any other office than to serve and obey them"? Later in the section, I take up the question whether *AMT** entails the *normative* thesis that the truth of such sentences as "There is reason for *S* to *A*" and "*A* is the rational thing for *S* to do" depends on *S*'s having "some motive which will be served or furthered by his [*A*]-ing" (Williams 1979, p. 17). My aim is to undercut familiar objections to *AMT* that are based on normative considerations by showing that the theory does not have normative implications often claimed for it.

Not all practical reasoning is concerned with identifying means to ends (cf. Williams 1979, p. 20). For example, an agent may engage in practical reasoning about what would *constitute* his achieving a certain desired end. A man who wants to have the most impressive garden in his neighborhood may need to reason not only about means to this end but also about the qualities that his garden must have if it is to be the best in the neighborhood. This point is compatible with Hume's master/slave metaphor only if the metaphor can be so interpreted as to allow reason(ing), on some occasions, to decide what its master is commanding (when, e.g., it commands that one have the most impressive garden in the area).

Moreover, the metaphor must be so interpreted that it permits reason(ing) to make some decisions without having to appeal to a higher master. Consider the following example. Theresa, a young woman who is about to graduate from high school, has a burning desire to do something important with her life. She wants this, not as a means to a further goal, but simply as an end. However, because she is unclear about what would constitute her goal, Theresa's desire gives her little direction. Undaunted, she sets out to determine what it would be to live an important life. She starts by examining the sorts of life that, in her opinion, many people think to be important. Some of the life types, she decides, are not all they are cracked up to be. For example, any life dominated by an intrinsic concern to become wealthy is, she thinks, irrational since money has no intrinsic value. On the basis of various items in her motivational set, she eliminates several other candidates: she will commit herself to no type of life that is incompatible with her being honest, bearing and raising at least one child, and so on. But she is left with a number of candidates and a crucial question: if these lives are important, what makes them so? She decides that she had wrongly been thinking that a necessary condition of doing something important with one's life is that one is widely

regarded as an important person, and she gradually comes to believe that truly important lives have at least the following in common: they are led by loving, unselfish, autonomous individuals who are dedicated to the achievement of a lofty goal or goals
and possessed of strong moral character and who, in pursuing their goals, make a significant contribution to the amelioration of the human condition. *This* is the kind of
person she now wants to be; these are the traits she wants to exhibit. After further reflection, she decides that, given her various talents, *she* can best live an "important
life" in the political realm.

Theresa's reflection and conclusions were influenced by items in her antecedent
motivational set, but the process by which she reached her conclusions was not one of
discovering some item in this set. Rather, through reflection, she developed a new,
more detailed conception of a certain goal; and the newly acquired goal—living an
important life, under the developed conception—supplanted the old one. (Since the
content of what I have called the new goal is very different from that of Theresa's former desire to live an important life, it is properly counted as a new goal.)

I note in passing that the case of Theresa gives some sense to the idea, embraced
by Reid (1788) and others, of a motivational reservoir possessed by reason.[12]
Whereas reason may have no special claim to *instrumental* desires that reasoning
helps to generate, there may be some point in distinguishing reasoned from unrea-
soned desires for *ends*.

In any case, Hume's slave metaphor (whatever his own substantive position may
have been) cannot accommodate the observations made in the last few paragraphs.
Slaves who are free to reject one master in favor of another and to fashion their own
masters are not true slaves at all (provided that they retain this freedom even after the
"master" is chosen or fashioned). The version of *AMT* that I have been defending does
not relegate reason (nor reason*ing*) to a slave's role in producing an agent's behavior.

My concern thus far has been a nonnormative question: what sense is properly
given to the claim that reasoning never generates motivation independently of antecedent motivation? On what interpretation(s) of the claim is it most plausible? However, this question is sometimes thought to have an important bearing on such normative questions as whether it can be *rational* for an agent to A if he has no antecedent
motivation that supports his A-ing and whether there can be *good reason* for an agent
to A if nothing in his motivational set supports his A-ing (Williams 1979, pp. 26–27).

The purpose of the remainder of this section is to show that the version of *AMT* that
I have been developing does not, by itself, entail a negative answer to these normative
questions. My version, again, reads as follows:

> *AMT**. Actual human beings and the real world are such that the capacity of justificatory
> reasoning to generate in a human being, *S*, a motivation-encompassing attitude whose
> object is *S*'s A-ing and to do this in virtue of that reasoning's providing *S* with what he
> takes to be justification for A-ing is contingent on *S*'s having antecedent motivation ca-
> pable of being at least a partial positive motivational base for the generated motivation-
> encompassing attitude; and whenever such reasoning does generate a motivation-
> encompassing attitude of this kind in us in the way identified, antecedent motivation is in
> the positive motivational base of the generated attitude,

It does not follow from this thesis, at least directly, that

N. There is good reason for *S* to *A* (or it is rational for *S* to *A*) only if some member of *S*'s antecedent motivational set would be served or furthered by his *A*-ing.

The following thesis goes some of the way toward filling the gap:

R. There is good reason for *S* to *A* (or it is rational for *S* to *A*) only if justificatory reasoning in support of his *A*-ing can, given *S*'s antecedent motivational set, produce in him motivation to *A* in virtue of its providing him with what he takes to be justification for *A*-ing.[13]

But *R*'s advocates must come to grips with what is, at least prima facie, an important distinction—namely, the distinction introduced earlier (chapter 3, section 4) between motivational and normative reasons for action.

The relevance of this distinction is plain. *R* postulates a tight connection between what there is good reason for an agent to do and the agent's antecedent motivational set. However, the distinction between motivational and normative reasons points the way to a kind of reason-for-*S*-to-*A* that is in no way grounded in *S*'s antecedent motivational set. The alleged existence of such reasons—"external reasons," in one sense of the expression—lies at the heart of a familiar dispute between internalists and externalists (Darwall 1983, p. 51). Suppose that there are such reasons and that, in some cases, the rational course of action is dictated by such reasons. Then there may be cases in which there is good reason for *S* to *A*, even though *S*'s antecedent motivational set is such that justificatory reasoning in support of his *A*-ing cannot do what *R* requires it to do. The crucial point, for present purposes, is that antecedent motivation theorists need not take a stand on these matters. *AMT** is neutral on the question of the existence of external reasons. Believers in external reasons who accept *AMT** may direct their attack at *R*.

Rachel Cohon suggests that the task of "the defender of external reasons" is to find "some rational way in which an agent can come to be moved to act on an external reason" (1986, p. 556). Her claim here is that an external reasons theorist must identify a way in which an agent can be rationally moved to act on (or for) a reason that is not part of *S*'s antecedent motivational set and derives none of its motivational force from that set. A few lines later, intending to make the same point, she says that "external reasons theorists . . . must find considerations that can obtain regardless of the agent's desires, aims, or sentiments that would move the agent to action if she were well informed and thinking rationally."

Part of what I have just been suggesting, in effect, is that the task described in the latter passage is not the one described in the former. Even if *no* human agent's believing an external reasons statement can move him in the way—whatever it may be— that cognitive engine theorists want to claim such beliefs sometimes move human agents, it does not follow that *there are no* external reasons.[14] Nor does it follow that defenders of external reasons cannot find considerations of roughly the sort that, in the second passage, Cohon (1986) says they must find. It is open to such theorists to argue that, precisely because certain human agents lack certain antecedent motivations (e.g., a desire to be fair), they are psychologically incapable of reasoning rationally at the time about some matters. Perhaps, because of the subject matter, rational reasoning about certain questions must be *impartial* reasoning; and some agents may be psychologically incapable of reasoning impartially about certain issues in the absence of a desire to be fair. Its being true that there is no "rational way in which [any] agent can come to be moved" à la *CET* "to act on an external reason" is compatible with its also being true that reflection on considerations *C*, which considerations, as it happens, in no way rest on a particular agent's antecedent motivational set, would contribute to the agent's being moved "to action if she were well informed and thinking rationally." For it may be that rational thinking about the matter at hand depends on one's having antecedent motivation of a certain sort and that reflection on *C* can combine with motivation of that sort (nonaccidentally) to produce an appropriate action-desire. Thus, it may be true that if an agent were well informed and thinking rationally, reflection on *C* would help to produce relevant motivation—even though currently, given his antecedent motivational set, he is psychologically incapable of being nonaccidentally moved by such reflection.[15]

It is sometimes held that if something is to be a reason for *A*-ing relative to a particular agent, it must be capable of being a reason *for which* that agent *A*-s.[16] I have just offered grounds for suspicion about a more precise version of that claim: namely, the claim that if at *t* there is a reason, *x*, for *S* to *A*, then at *t* *S* is psychologically capable of acting for *x*. External reasons theorists should beware of punning on "reason"; I return to this point in chapter 5 (section 4).[17]

Do *moral* reasons have a special motivational status? Must they be motivational because, say, morality is essentially practical, or *action-guiding*? Would a morality be less than practical if it were occasionally to offer reasons for a particular agent to *A* that, given his antecedent motivational set, have no chance of being motivational? In the following chapter, I argue that the answer is no. The prescription of an essentially practical morality for such an agent may be moral education (or antidepressants). And, of course, moral education is not accomplished only, or even primarily, through justificatory reasoning. An agent's motivational set can be modified and enriched in other ways (e.g., through operant conditioning).

I do not wish to champion the existence of external reasons. Rather, my point in the last few paragraphs is that if *AMT** does support *N*, it does so only in conjunction with something like *R*—a controversial principle that is not itself entailed by *AMT**. Those who reject the existence of external reasons cannot demonstrate that the rejection is warranted simply by appealing to *AMT**. There is more to be done, and what remains does not promise to be easy. By the same token, defenders of external reasons need not seek to preserve their view by attacking *AMT**. Again, they can focus their attack on *R* and its ilk.

In chapter 3, I suggested that some philosophers of mind and action who have not taken an official stand on whether there are external reasons for action have offered an account of the relatively proximal springs of intentional actions that is compatible both with there being such reasons and with there being no such reasons. If there are external reasons for action, I suggested, such philosophers can accommodate them by adding a layer on top of the theory of action explanation already in place without modifying what falls beneath the new layer. Part of what I have argued in the present chapter is that a theory of the nonaccidental generation of motivation by practical reasoning that is consonant with the popular, causal approach to action explanation described in the preceding chapters (and fleshed out further in subsequent chapters) is similarly compatible both with the existence and with the nonexistence of external reasons for action. Some confirmation for this is provided in the following chapter.

My primary purpose in this chapter has been to explain what sense ought to be given to the contention that reasoning never generates motivation independently of antecedent motivation and to make a case for a version of the antecedent motivation theory on the basis of its strengths and the cognitive engine theory's weaknesses. The underlying idea, I have argued, is very plausible. I also have argued that, properly interpreted, that idea does not (by itself) have certain normative implications that are sometimes claimed for it and does not commit one to understanding practical reason(ing) as a mere instrument, or slave, of the passions.

Notes

1. For interesting speculation about motivational spread in this connection, see Audi (2001, ch. 6 and pp. 218–19).

2. Thus, *AMT* asserts some version of what R. Jay Wallace calls "the 'desire-out, desire-in' principle" (1990, p. 370).

3. On the error theory, see Mackie (1977, ch. 1).

4. Aristotle, *Nicomachean Ethics* 1139a35f.; Hume, *Treatise*, p. 415. For a defense of the suggested reading of Aristotle, see Mele (1984a).

5. Standing desires (chapter 1, section 7) may also contribute to the strength of occurrent desires that manifest them. Sue's standing desire to have a career in philosophy—that disposition to have occurrent desires for a philosophical career—may be activated, for example, by her receiving an invitation to interview for a position in philosophy, and the strength of the manifesting desire may be accounted for partly by the strength of the disposition. However, because standing desires are motivation producing rather than motivation encompassing (chapter 1, section 7), they are not in what I have called the positive motivational base of the desires that manifest them.

6. Critical discussions of Williams's arguments against the existence of external reasons include Cohon (1986), Hampton (1998, ch. 2), Hollis (1987, ch. 6), Hooker (1987), Korsgaard (1986), McDowell (1995), Millgram (1996), Parfit (1997), Robertson (1986), Scanlon (1998, pp. 363–73), Searle (2001, pp. 214–18), and Smith (1992). The criticisms advanced here derive from Mele (1989).

7. See, for example, *Nicomachean Ethics* 3.3. and 6.2. On Williams's Aristotelianism about related topics, see Korsgaard (1996, pp. 50–51, 77–78).

8. Cf. Williams's (1979, p. 24) description of externalism.

9. E. J. Bond claims that *S*'s desiring *x* is a necessary causal consequence of *S*'s acquiring a true belief that *x* is a value; and, for Bond, "all value is *necessarily* objective, in the sense that it is never a function of desire" (1983, pp. 69, 84). However, as Jan Narveson (1984, p. 329) observes in his review of Bond (1983), Bond offers no explanation of the motivation-independent generation of a desire by the belief that something is good.

10. For a related idea, see Scanlon (1998, pp. 33–35, 62, 77).

11. On a desire to act for good reasons, see chapter 10.

12. Reid (1788, Essay 3, ch. 2). The idea is at least as old as Plato. See, for example, *Phaedrus* 237d9–238a2. Aristotle's notion of wish (*boulesis*), the only form of desire located in the "rational part of the soul" (e.g., *De Anima* 432b5), is well suited to the case of Theresa. On this last point, see Mele (1984b).

13. Williams is plainly attracted to *R*, or something very similar. He contends at one point that an "external reasons statement itself might be taken as roughly equivalent to, or at least as entailing, the claim that if the agent rationally deliberated, then, whatever motivations he originally had, he would come to be motivated to *X*" (1979, p. 24); and he asks a bit later (pp. 24–25), "*What* is it that one comes to believe when he comes to believe that there is reason for him to *X*, if it is not the proposition, or something that entails the proposition, that if he deliberated rationally, he would be motivated to act appropriately?"

14. The same is true if external reasons themselves, construed as facts (see Garrard and McNaughton 1998), are substituted for the agent's believing an external reasons statement in the sentence to which this note is appended.

15. Derek Parfit writes, "To be substantively rational, we must care about certain things, such as our own well-being. . . . To be procedurally rational, we must deliberate in certain ways, but we are not required to have any particular desires or aims, such as concern about our own well-being" (1997, p. 101). In Parfit's terms, it is "substantive rationality" that I am discussing here.

16. See Dancy (1995, p. 13) and Garrard and McNaughton (1998, pp. 47–48), following Korsgaard (1986, p. 10). See also Dancy (2000, p. 101) and Searle (2001, p. 138).

17. John Searle appeals to desire-independent, external reasons in a criticism of what he calls "the Classical Model of Rationality" (2001, p. 5). Searle says that this model insists on generic desires in its account of how desire-independent reasons generate motivation and action and that "this must be . . . wrong, because it implies that in cases where the agent does not have [such] desires, he has no reason at all to speak the truth, to carry out his obligations, or to keep his promises" (p. 124). However, it is a live theoretical option to hold that the agent does have a reason to do these things in these cases—a desire-independent, external reason—and that, in the absence of pertinent antecedent desires, generic or otherwise, actual human beings will have no motivation to do them and will not do them. Searle does nothing to eliminate this option.

5

Moral Motivation and Moral Ought-Beliefs

Internalism versus Externalism

Morally right conduct, insofar as it is intentional, is presumably motivated. My guiding question in this chapter is whether an acceptable moral theory will make warranted conceptual or metaphysical demands of a certain kind on a theory of human motivation. A pair of theses about our beliefs that we ought, morally, to A entails that there are A-focused truth-seeking attitudes that essentially encompass motivation to A. The first thesis is *cognitivism* about such beliefs—again, the thesis that such beliefs are attitudes with truth-valued content and that not all such beliefs are doomed to be false.[1] The second thesis is a robust *internalism* about first-person moral ought-beliefs—the thesis that, necessarily, any belief that one (oneself) ought, morally, to A encompasses motivation to A. Again, an attitude of an agent S *essentially* encompasses motivation to A if and only if it encompasses motivation to A not only in S's actual situation but also in all possible scenarios in which S has that attitude (chapter 1, section 1).

A central thesis of this chapter is that our first-person cognitivist moral ought-beliefs do not essentially encompass motivation to act accordingly. My claim is not that moral ought-beliefs that essentially encompass such motivation are impossible. Rather, mine is the more modest claim that the grounds for holding that we have such beliefs are much weaker than the grounds for denying that we do. Along the way, I argue that the combination of moral cognitivism and this robust internalism places our moral agency at serious risk, and I extend the argument to a less demanding brand of internalist moral cognitivism.[2] I do not challenge moral cognitivism here. Granting internalist moral cognitivists their cognitivism, my target is their internalism.

Although the topic of the present chapter is related to the topic of the preceding one, the connection is not as tight as one might think. For example, the conjunction of cognitivism and the robust internalism that I just described does not entail the falsity of the antecedent motivation theory. A theorist who claims that deliberation some-times produces cognitivist moral ought-beliefs that essentially encompass motivation to act may consistently hold that antecedent motivation figures importantly in the de-liberative production of these beliefs. Also, a proponent of the cognitive engine theory can hold that the evaluative beliefs or judgments in which practical reasoning con-cludes sometimes *produce* motivation independently of antecedent motivation but never *encompass* motivation.

1. Internalism

Various distinct theses have been labeled "internalism" in the literature in moral phi-losophy. As Rachel Cohon remarks, "recent writers define the term 'internalism', and its partner, 'externalism', in . . . a variety of overlapping yet incompatible ways" (1993, p. 266; cf. Darwall 1992, p. 155).[3] My primary concern in much of this chapter is the robust internalism I identified about first-person moral ought-beliefs, or beliefs that one is (oneself) morally required to *A*.

Thomas Nagel's discussion of internalism in *The Possibility of Altruism* is the point of departure of much recent work on the topic. Attention to two internalist strands in the following passage from that discussion will prove instructive:

> Internalism is the view that the presence of a motivation for acting morally is guaranteed by the truth of ethical propositions themselves. On this view the motivation must be so tied to the truth, or meaning, of ethical statements that when in a particular case someone is (or perhaps merely believes that he is) morally required to do something, it follows that he has a motivation for doing it. Externalism holds, on the other hand, that the necessary motivation is not supplied by ethical principles and judgments themselves, and that an additional psychological sanction is required to motivate our compliance. Externalism is compatible with a variety of views about the motivation for being moral. It is even com-patible with the view that such a motivation is always present—so long as its presence is not guaranteed by moral judgments themselves, but by something external to ethics. (1970, p. 7)

At least two distinct internalistic theses about motivation are discernible here:[4]

1. *Requirement internalism.* "When in a particular case someone is . . . morally required to do something, it follows that he has a motivation for doing it." The presence of this motivation is "guaranteed" by the moral requirement.
2. *Belief internalism.* "When in a particular case someone . . . believes that he is . . . morally required to do something, it follows that he has a motivation for doing it." The presence of this motivation is "guaranteed" by the belief.

If we assume that to have "a motivation" is to be in a motivational *state of mind*, thesis 1 may stand a chance of being true if it expresses the view that having a motiva-tion for *A*-ing is a prerequisite of being morally required to *A*. However, this view is problematic for moral cognitivists (cf. Nagel 1970, p. 13). Presumably, on a cogni-tivist view, Hitler may have been morally required to release his political prisoners even if he never had "a motivation," in the identified sense, to do so. Thesis 2, on the same reading of "has a motivation," plainly avoids this problem. This thesis does not imply that Hitler's lacking motivation to release his prisoners is inconsistent with his being morally required to release them.[5] I set thesis 1 aside and pursue thesis 2.

I take the term "guaranteed" in both theses to indicate that the companion claim about motivation is to be regarded as a *necessary* truth. Nagel evidently favors *metaphysical* necessity here: "Human motivation possesses features which are susceptible to metaphysical investigation and which carry some kind of necessity" (1970, pp. 5–6). Thesis 2, as I understand it, asserts that, necessarily, anyone who believes himself to be morally required to *A* simultaneously "has a motivation" for *A*-ing. This alleged truth rests on the nature of *belief* itself and on the *content* of the belief that one is (oneself) morally required to *A*. An agent who has an attitude other than *belief* toward the content "my *A*-ing is morally required" may have no motivation to *A*; for example, someone who *doubts* that his *A*-ing is morally required may be devoid of motivation to *A*. And someone may have a belief with comparable, but nonmoral, content without having corresponding motivation; for instance, one may believe that one's *A*-ing is *legally* required without having "a motivation" for *A*-ing. In the case of believing that one is (oneself) morally required to *A*, it is the combination of *believing* and of *what is believed* that is supposed to be necessarily sufficient for having "a motivation" for *A*-ing. The alleged "guarantee" derives from the nature of morality and the nature of belief.

This alleged sufficiency does not *obviously* entail robust internalism about believing that one's *A*-ing is morally required—that is, the view that, necessarily, such beliefs *encompass* motivation to *A*. Suppose that, in all possible worlds, any agent who believes that he is morally required to *A* has motivation to *A*. But imagine (if you can, and just for illustrative purposes) that this modal truth is partly explained by the fact that God necessarily exists and has necessarily successfully decreed that no beliefs encompass motivation and that whatever produces in an agent a belief that he ought, morally, to *A* simultaneously produces in the agent another, distinct attitude—a desire to *A*. In this scenario, to use an expression of William Frankena (1958) in a seminal discussion of internalism, our beliefs that we ought to *A* lack "built-in" motivation to *A*. Robust internalism is internalist in two senses: first, believing oneself to be morally required to *A* *metaphysically* or *conceptually* (hence internally, in a formal sense) "guarantees" that one "has a motivation" for *A*-ing; second, what is guaranteed, more precisely, is that motivation to *A* is *built into* any belief that one is (oneself) morally required to *A* and is internal to belief of that kind in this sense.[6]

The imprecision of thesis 2 as a statement of robust internalism (or, at least, of the internalistic thesis that primarily concerns me) is avoided by the following proposition:

2i. Necessarily, any belief that one is (oneself) morally required to *A* *encompasses* motivation to *A*.[7]

Thesis 2i is my primary concern here. I dub the robust view it expresses *strong internalism*. Soon, I develop a difficulty for the conjunction of strong internalism and moral cognitivism. First, another distinction is in order, one linked to a distinction between motivational and normative reasons that I discussed in chapters 3 and 4.

There may be a difference between having "a motivation" for *A*-ing and having a *reason* for *A*-ing (cf. Brink 1989, pp. 38–40; Hampton 1998, pp. 79–82; Mele 1989, pp. 432–34). It may be held that insofar as genocide is morally wrong, anyone who has embarked on a campaign for genocide has a moral reason for canceling the campaign. It may be claimed, accordingly, that Hitler had a reason for canceling his campaigns for genocide, even if he had no motivation to do so. On this view, having a reason for A-ing does not "guarantee" having "a motivation" for A-ing. Although a moral cognitivist should find acceptance of thesis 1 awkward, on the grounds identified earlier, the same awkwardness does not apply to a variant of this thesis that substitutes "reason" for "motivation"—provided that reason-having is understood along the lines just sketched.[8] There is a comparable counterpart of 2i—"*reason* internalism" about beliefs that one is morally required to A.[9] That counterpart is *not* my concern in the present chapter. My concern is "*motivation* internalism" about these beliefs—primarily, strong internalism.

2. Present Concerns

If we were to discover that moral ought-beliefs never help to explain actions, we would have little reason to hold that they are motivational in any sense. A plausible presupposition of the issue under investigation here is that sometimes agents act at least partly on the basis of their moral ought-beliefs. Consider Al, a morally decent fellow who is not a candidate for moral sainthood. A week ago, he agreed to help his aunt paint her apartment tomorrow afternoon. Today, he is offered a free ticket to his favorite team's game tomorrow afternoon. Al knows that his aunt has taken great pains to get her apartment ready for painting. He deliberates about whether it is morally permissible to back out of the agreement, intending to back out should he determine that it is. However, Al decides that he ought, morally, to help his aunt paint tomorrow afternoon, as he agreed to do, and he acts accordingly. Al's helping his aunt rather than going to the game may well be explained partly by his feelings for her, but, plausibly, it is also explained in significant part by his belief that he ought to help her. Given the kind of person Al is, it is very likely that, holding the relevant considerations fixed, if he had not come to believe that he ought to help her paint tomorrow he would not have done so. In the absence of that belief, he probably would have explained his situation to his aunt, asked to be let off the hook, and offered to help next weekend instead. It is plausible that the belief at issue is part of the basis on which Al decides to help his aunt tomorrow, as he agreed to do, and that that decision results in suitable action. In utterly mundane cases of this kind, first-person moral ought-beliefs do seem to help to explain intentional actions. They seem to play their *most direct* role in the production of action, the role they play when agents act at least partly *on the basis of* such beliefs. I dub this their *action-basing* role. (Of course, Al's belief that he ought to help his aunt tomorrow has a psychological basis, too; that basis presumably plays a less direct role in the action's production.)

If we assume moral cognitivism, what is wrong with a moderately strong *externalism* about moral ought-beliefs? What is wrong, for example, with the thesis that no such A-focused belief encompasses motivation to A? From a certain explanatory perspective, it may seem that nothing is wrong with this. Even if Al's belief that he is morally required to help his aunt paint tomorrow does not itself encompass motivation to do this, it may help to generate motivation so to act in conjunction with, for example, a desire of Al's to do whatever he is morally required to do in the circumstances. And the resulting motivation may help to produce the action Al believes he is morally required to perform. So, at least, it may seem.

A theorist might argue that the externalist thesis I identified is false, not on metaphysical or conceptual grounds, but as a matter of contingent fact. The claim may be that, as a matter of contingent fact, some beliefs that one is oneself morally required to A encompass motivation to A. On what grounds can this claim be defended? What would count as evidence that a pertinent belief encompasses motivation to A as opposed to helping to generate such motivation? Perhaps it can be imagined that certain neurophysiological tests might provide relevant evidence. But I have found no arguments from neurophysiology in the internalist moral cognitivist literature. Nor does this literature feature appeals to research in social psychology (where beliefs and desires are alive and well). Philosophical psychologizing is an option. It may be argued, for example, that setting aside putative metaphysical or conceptual truths about morality, moral agency, (moral) reasons for action, and the like, the best theory of human behavior and human experience will postulate motivation-encompassing moral ought-beliefs. I have something to say about this later, but my primary concern (given the assumption of moral cognitivism) is certain alleged *necessary* internalistic truths, beginning with strong internalism.

If our moral ought-beliefs help to explain some of our intentional conduct, theorists should want to understand the most direct explanatory role they play—the role they play when we act at least partly on their basis, their *action-basing* role. Strong internalism locates that role in the alleged essentially motivation-encompassing character of these beliefs. Is that plausible?

3. Introducing Listlessness

Some apparent problems for the combination of moral cognitivism and strong internalism have been explored in detail by opponents and proponents of internalist moral cognitivism. The problems of the amoralist and the wicked person are cases in point.[10] Neither side in the debate is particularly impressed by the opposition's treatment of these deviations from moral health. However, another apparent difficulty has not received the attention it deserves. I have dubbed it "the problem of listlessness" (Mele 1996a).[11]

Consider an unfortunate person—someone who is neither amoral nor wicked—who is suffering from clinical depression because of the recent tragic deaths of her husband and children in a plane crash. *Seemingly*, we can imagine that she retains some of her beliefs that she is morally required to do certain things—some of her "*MR* beliefs," for short—while being utterly devoid of motivation to act accordingly, or what I term "*MR* motivation." She has aided her ailing uncle for years, believing herself to be morally required to do so. Perhaps she continues to believe this but now is utterly unmotivated to assist him. If we can imagine this (more precisely, if it is possible), then both belief internalism (i.e., thesis 2 in section 1) and strong internalism are false: agents may believe that they are morally required to A and yet have no motivation to A.

If we assume moral cognitivism, *MR* beliefs aim, at least partly, at *truth*. This is a point that I intend to exploit in my discussion of listlessness. Noncognitivists reject this thesis about *MR* beliefs, and noncognitivist internalism is not a target of criticism in this chapter.[12]

Again, the internalist thesis at issue—strong internalism—is an alleged *necessary* truth. It is a claim about all (metaphysically or logically) possible agents who believe themselves to be morally required to do something. Assuming moral cognitivism, I test strong internalism, initially, on planet Alpha. Bear in mind that Alpha is a *fictional* planet; the question whether the following description of its inhabitants is *coherent* is addressed in subsequent sections.

Alpha is much like Earth. Numerous languages are spoken there, one of which is at least superficially indistinguishable from English. The inhabitants of Alpha have a variety of legal systems much like ours, and they employ well-developed moral vocabularies. Most people there take themselves to have moral duties and obligations, bestow moral praise and blame on others for their deeds, and experience moral guilt on some occasions and moral satisfaction on others. In the "English"-speaking countries, people say such things as "I am morally required to assist my uncle" and "Ann's robbing the bank was morally wrong."

The great majority of adult Alphans have a disposition to desire to do whatever they are morally required to do.[13] The content of the desires that manifest this disposition is expressible as "I do whatever is morally required of me in this situation." For stylistic reasons, the disposition should have a name, say, "the Alphic disposition." The disposition-manifesting desires may be termed "Alphic desires." The Alphic disposition is a feature of the psychological constitution of Alphans. Another feature is that whenever Alphans act *on the basis of* a belief that they are morally required to do something (as opposed, for example, to doing something that they believe themselves to be morally required to do but not at all *because* they believe this), they are motivated by an Alphic desire. Indeed, Alphans are psychologically so constituted that the presence in them of a desire of this kind is *causally necessary* for their acting on an *MR* belief. Alphic desires vary in strength, and the Alphic disposition is stronger in some Alphans than in others and typically varies in an individual Alphan over time.

The Alphic disposition tends to be activated by the acquisition of a belief to the effect that one's present situation has a significant moral dimension. The activation of this disposition consists in the acquisition of a desire to do whatever one is morally required to do in one's circumstances. Desires of this kind have a role to play, not only in motivating actions performed on the basis of an *MR* belief, but also in influencing Alphans' reasoning about what to do. Owing to desires to do whatever they are morally required to do in their circumstances, they reason about what they are morally required to do.

Sometimes, in the absence of any prior belief that their present circumstances have a moral dimension, it simply strikes Alphans that they are morally required to *A*. In such cases, the belief that they are morally required to *A* tends to activate the Alphic disposition. When that happens, they acquire a desire to do whatever they are morally required to do. Typically, that desire combines with their belief that they are morally required to *A* to generate a desire to *A*. Alphan psychology need not have been this way. For example, it might have happened that when it simply strikes Alphans that they are morally required to A, their disposition to desire to do whatever they are morally required to do is manifested directly in a desire to A. However, as it turns out, the desires that manifest the Alphic disposition are always generic. (This psychological fact about Alphans has the fortunate consequence of simplifying exposition.)

Alphan psychologists have long recognized a problem known in the "English"-speaking countries as *listlessness* or *accidie*. The former label derives from their Middle "English" term *list* ("desire"); the latter's roots are in their classical "Greek"—ultimately, the conjunction of the alpha privative ("not") and *kedos* ("care"). In its most severe forms, Alphan listlessness consists in the total absence of motivation to engage in many activities of kinds that formerly were matters of deep personal concern. The phenomenon has been linked in Alphan research to clinical depression; it is investigated by their clinicians and motivational psychologists. Listlessness is a very real problem on Alpha. For present purposes, a point about *moral* motivation is especially relevant: decent people sometimes suffer a loss of moral motivation; some agents suffering from listlessness believe that they are morally required to do certain things while completely lacking motivation to do them.

In a recent case, because of the deaths of her husband and children in a plane crash, a woman, Eve, lost all motivation to continue aiding her ailing uncle, even though she continued to believe that she was morally required to help him. Eventually, Eve received treatment for her depression. Standard medical procedure on Alpha in such cases requires that agents take an electronic lie detector test and then answer questions under the influence of a truth serum. Both tests indicated that Eve believed herself to be morally required to assist her uncle. Another "belief-test" was administered—a test for a neural realization of the pertinent belief. That test, too, indicated that Eve believed herself to be morally required to assist him. Expert Alphan psychologists, testing what Alphan neuroscientists regard as the motivational centers of Alphan brains, concluded that there was a low level of activity in these areas of Eve's brain and that no activity in these areas was associated with Eve's reflection on her moral obligations to her uncle. The psychologists concluded that Eve suffered from a severe case of listlessness. Their conclusion was correct: although Eve continued to believe that she was morally required to aid her uncle, she had no motivation to do so.

4. Testing

Is the scenario just described a possible one? Does it involve a contradiction or violate a metaphysical law? In this scenario, a roughly Humean psychology is true of certain agents, including Eve—a psychology in which belief and desire divide the action-producing labor, with desire shouldering the specifically *motivational* burden. Humean psychology has come under attack, of course, but, usually, not on the grounds that its being true of agents is *metaphysically* or *conceptually impossible*. (Whether Humean psychology is necessarily false of *moral* agents is another question.) I concentrate on the specific question whether it is conceptually and metaphysically possible for Eve to continue to believe that she is morally required to aid her uncle while being utterly unmotivated to aid him—that is, while having no *MR* motivation.

If we assume moral cognitivism, Eve's alleged belief may safely be understood as an alleged attitude having at least the following two features: its representational content is either true or false, and should the content be false, that would suffice for the attitude's being mistaken. So understood, the alleged attitude shares a target with nonevaluative beliefs—namely, truth. Is it conceptually and metaphysically possible (assuming moral cognitivism) that Eve has an attitude of this sort whose content is "I am morally required to assist my uncle," even though she is utterly unmotivated to assist him? During her examination, Eve is asked whether she is morally required to help her uncle. She may entertain this question, recall her earlier belief on the matter, and judge (perhaps erroneously) that no change in her circumstances has rendered her earlier belief false. She may conclude that the moral requirement continues to exist, and she may have an occurrent attitude with the content "I am morally required to assist my uncle" that is either true or false and such that the content's being false would suffice for the attitude's being mistaken. Whether her having such an attitude is incompatible with her having no *MR* motivation remains to be seen. But even if the answer is no, a related question looms large.

If Eve has an attitude of this kind while being entirely unmotivated to aid her uncle, must the attitude fall short of a *belief* that she is morally required to assist him? A cognitivist internalist can answer affirmatively, on the grounds that any belief with this content necessarily encompasses *MR* motivation. But, of course, that simply begs the question at issue. *Perhaps*, as Donald Davidson (1980, p. 27) has claimed, there is a "tendency to say that if someone really (sincerely) believes he ought, then his belief must show itself in his behaviour (and hence, of course, in his inclination to act, or his desire)." However, if the tendency stems from myopic attention to garden-variety instances of believing that one ought, its existence cuts little philosophical ice. Perhaps people normally try to do what they believe they ought to do (and hence are inclined or motivated so to act). But in normal cases, people do not suffer from clinical depression or listlessness.

On a traditional, Humean, division-of-labor view, motivation is present only in desires and intentions (and states partially constituted by desires or intentions), and never in beliefs (Lewis 1988; Smith 1987). On this view, whether an agent who believes that he ought, morally, to *A* has motivation to *A* is contingent on features of his motivational condition (e.g., whether he suffers from listlessness of the kind at issue) that are conceptually and metaphysically independent of his so believing. Again, as Huw Price remarks in an article critical of some recent defenses of the Humean view, "the view has enormous application in contemporary thought. It is widely taken for granted by economists and decision theorists, by psychologists and cognitive scientists, and . . . by most philosophers" (1989, p. 119). So I conjecture that most readers will find Eve's story utterly coherent. However, I have no wish to rest my case on an appeal to the crowd. Cognitivist strong internalists are advancing a reformative conception of cognitivist belief and an alternative to a Humean theory of motivation. Their arguments require attention.

One moral cognitivist argument for internalism proceeds from the alleged nature of the experience of being morally required to *A*. I call it *the argument from moral experience*. It is claimed (*c*1) that part of what it is to have the (veridical) experience of being morally required to *A* is to apprehend a *reason* to *A*; and, on the assumption (*c*2) that all reasons for action are motivation encompassing, it is concluded ($c3$) that having MR motivation is internal to the experience of being morally required to A (McNaughton 1988, pp. 47–50; cf. p. 23).

Assume that $c1$ is true. Then it may be supposed that, in having the experience of being morally required to aid her uncle, Eve apprehends a reason to do so. The reason may simply be that she is morally required to help him, or the reason may be constituted by the considerations on the basis of which she apprehends this moral requirement.[14] But part of what is at issue, on the assumption that $c1$ is true, is precisely whether Eve's apprehending the pertinent reason suffices for her having motivation to help her uncle. Why cannot her clinical depression be such that although she apprehends a reason to continue helping him, she is utterly unmotivated to do so? What strong internalists need here is an argument for the thesis that apprehending a reason for A-ing—in precisely the sense of "apprehending a reason" in which it allegedly follows from one's having an experience of being morally required to A that one apprehends a reason for A-ing—suffices for having motivation to A. No argument for this thesis is presented in the argument from moral experience. Even if some analyses of reasons for action treat motivation as an essential constituent of such reasons, this does not provide grounds for confidence that readings of "reason" on which $c1$ is true are readings on which $c2$ is true. For example, Eve believes on some grounds or other that she ought to help her uncle; simply calling those grounds "reasons" to help him cannot make it the case that they encompass motivation to help him, or any motivation at all.

It may be objected that "in the absence of an account of the nature of motivation which shows that it is independent of judging that one has reason to act," what I have just said "looks like a case of *petitio principii*" (Garrard and McNaughton 1998, p. 49). However, there are excellent grounds for believing that toddlers and many nonhuman animals have motivation-encompassing attitudes, and, again, it is unlikely that all such agents are capable of judging that they have "reason to act" (see chapter 3, section 3). Presumably, such judging requires having a concept of reason for action.

Of course, if reasons for action are analyzed as complexes of desires for goals and beliefs about means, then in apprehending a reason to help her uncle Eve apprehends, among other things, a relevant desire of hers—and, hence, *has* such a desire. But this Humean conception of reasons for action is eschewed by internalist moral cognitivists (McDowell 1978; McNaughton 1988; Nagel 1970), who view it as leading either to noncognitivism or (in cognitivists) to externalism. The combination of moral cognitivism and strong internalism entails that the apprehension of a moral requirement on oneself itself, necessarily, encompasses motivation to act accordingly; it does not depend for its motivational character on the apprehension of a reason that is partially constituted by a desire.

A popular argument for strong internalism is that its truth is required by the practical, action-guiding nature of morality. Judgments that one is morally required to A, or that one ought, morally, to A, are practical judgments—judgments about what to do. As R. M. Hare has put it, "moral judgments, in their central use, have it as their function to guide conduct" (1963, p. 70). It is alleged that to reject strong internalism is to drive a wedge between moral judgments and intentional conduct, thus taking the essentially practical bite out of morality. I call this *the argument from toothlessness*.

(Although Hare himself defends internalism but not cognitivism, the argument from toothlessness is available to noncognitivists and cognitivists alike.)

Some versions of this argument would have less clout on Alpha than in some other places. The great majority of Alphans, having the Alphic disposition (again, a disposition to desire to do whatever they are morally required to do), seemingly have a practical, action-guiding morality. Except in rare cases, they desire to perform those actions that they apparently take themselves to be morally required to perform. Typically, then, their ostensible *MR* beliefs (again, beliefs that they are morally required to *A*) have practical clout.

The Alphans' ostensible *MR* beliefs may have no weaker a grip on their behavior than ours have on our behavior. Presumably, like Alphans, we do not always act as we believe we morally ought. We occasionally exhibit moral weakness, it seems; and we may do so even if our own moral beliefs are uniformly motivation encompassing. A pair of internalist theses should be distinguished: the thesis that *A*-focused *MR* beliefs encompass motivation to *A*, and the stronger thesis that, not only is this so, but also the motivation built into such beliefs is stronger than any competing motivation. The weaker thesis allows for akratic behavior against an *MR* belief: it allows that an agent who believes himself to be morally required to *A* may have stronger motivation to perform some competing action, *B*, and akratically act on the stronger motivation.[15] In any case, on Alpha, the practical effectiveness of (apparent) moral judgments does not hinge on a metaphysical or conceptual "guarantee" that believing oneself to be morally required to *A* suffices for having motivation to *A*.

In a related vein, no actual human being is *essentially* immune to clinical depression, even in its most severe forms. And if some possible (i.e., for us) instances of clinical depression or listlessness are such that people who believe that they ought, morally, to *A* are devoid of motivation to *A*, then moral ought-beliefs do not essentially encompass *MR* motivation in actual human beings. No matter what we believe we are morally required to do, we would be devoid of *MR* motivation were we to suffer from listlessness of the kind at issue while holding the belief.

Cognitivist strong internalists may respond that their internalism is required if a belief alleged to have the content "I am *morally* required to *A*" is actually to have this content. The claim is partly about the essential nature of morality and its bearing on beliefs with the putative content at issue. An agent who takes himself to believe that he is morally required to *A*, but who lacks a *motivation-encompassing* belief that he is so required, does not have a sufficient grasp of morality to believe what he takes himself to believe. If he were to understand morality well enough to have beliefs with this content, then, *necessarily*, those beliefs would encompass *MR* motivation. In the case of *true MR* beliefs, the very *apprehension* of this truth is a motivation-encompassing state of mind. And when the beliefs are false, the grasp of morality that their presence requires ensures that they are motivation encompassing. So the response runs: I dub it *the proper grasp response*.

One way of filling out this response would be risky for cognitivist strong internalists. Suppose it were claimed that achieving a proper grasp of morality is possible only for beings who already have grasp-promoting desires (e.g., a desire for the well-being of other people) and that this helps to explain why, necessarily, anyone who believes that he is morally required to *A* has motivation to *A*. This claim leaves open the possibility that beliefs that one is morally required to A do not *encompass* motivation to A: such motivation may be wholly external to such beliefs, and strong internalism asserts that it is "built into" them. Advocates of the proper grasp response to attempted counterexamples to strong internalism must endeavor to establish that, *necessarily*, no agent with a proper grasp of morality is, even temporarily, a Humean agent with respect to moral motivation—an agent whose *MR* beliefs do *not* encompass *MR* motivation and whose *MR* motivation derives from relevant desires. That is a tall order. I return to it shortly.

5. Belief, Belief*, and *SP*-Belief

Obviously, the most effective way to undermine strong internalism would be to show that it is necessarily false. One may try to do this by showing that, necessarily, no belief of any sort is motivation encompassing. It may be argued that belief, by its very nature, has truth as its target, that the essential nature of belief calls for it to "fit" what is true, and that no state with this direction of fit can also have a motivational direction of fit (Smith 1987). However, even if a common conception of belief does not permit beliefs to be motivation encompassing, moral cognitivists who reject externalism may seek to develop an alternative, coherent conception of belief that does permit this (McNaughton 1988, pp. 108–10).

In this section, I develop a listlessness-precluding notion of belief in the internalist moral cognitivist spirit and then tease out a moral. I set the stage with the following nonstarter: by definition, at *t*, *S* believes* himself to be morally required to A if and only if (1) at *t*, *S* believes that he is morally required to A—in any standard sense of "believes," according to which, as Bernard Williams (1973, p. 151) puts it, "belief aims at truth"—and (2) at *t*, *S* has motivation to A. Any instance of believing* that *p* is an instance of having a belief* that *p*. Now, any *MR* belief* (i.e., any belief* that one is oneself morally required to A) encompasses *MR* motivation. By definition, such motivation is built right into such beliefs*. However, strong internalists will not be impressed by belief*; for, given the definition offered, a simple combination of an externalist belief that one is morally required to A and a desire to A would constitute an *MR* belief*. Strong internalists insist that *all MR* beliefs encompass *MR* motivation—indeed, necessarily so. They cannot be satisfied with a species of *MR* belief—*MR* belief*—that can coexist with *MR* beliefs that do not encompass such motivation. Cognitivist strong internalists do not want a notion of *MR* belief according to which such beliefs may be composed of distinct attitudes, one "aiming" at truth and another at action. Rather, they want a noncompound attitude that—at once and essentially—*is receptive to a species of moral truth* and *encompasses MR motivation*.

On a familiar view, attitudes are at least partially constituted by a psychological *orientation* toward a representational *content*. The view has developed along two divergent lines, which I dub *content constancy* and *orientation constancy*.[16] According to the former line, attitudes of all sorts have representational content of the same general kind and attitude types are individuated by their differing intrinsic orientation toward content.[17] For example, agents desire that *p*, believe that *p*, fear that *p*, and hope that *p*, the content having the same form in each case; what distinguishes attitudes of these different types from one another are the differences in psychological orientation constituted by desiring, believing, fearing, and hoping. On the orientation constancy line, in contrast, the psychological orientation is the same across attitudes of different types—it is something that may be termed "acceptance," "assent," or "endorsement"—and attitudes of different types are distinguished from one another by distinct types of representational content.[18] For example, the contents of beliefs may be declarative propositions, whereas those of desires may be optative propositions (e.g., "Let it be the case that p"); and in both cases the psychological orientation is *assent* (see Goldman 1970, ch. 4).

The orientation constancy line may seem well suited to the concerns of internalist moral cognitivists. Using "endorsement" as the name for the uniform psychological orientation, such theorists may attempt to defend the claim that the endorsed *content*, "I am morally required to A," signals the presence of a very special attitude—an attitude that differs both from nonnormative belief and from desire but also resembles attitudes of these types in important ways. The proffered resemblances are (1) that, like nonnormative belief, this special attitude—*attitude TM*—is truth seeking and (2) that, like desire, it is motivation encompassing. The alleged difference is that attitude *TM* is two-dimensional in this way, whereas desire and nonnormative belief are each one-dimensional—desire not being truth seeking and nonnormative belief not being motivation encompassing. Attitude *TM* is not a composite of other attitudes, as belief* is. Rather, it is a noncompound attitude that is, nevertheless, two-dimensional.

In being noncompound, attitude *TM* differs from familiar two-dimensional attitudes: for example, hope and disappointment. Plausibly, a hope for x encompasses both a desire for x and a belief that x might not obtain or occur, in which case "hope for x" is a *compound* attitude—that is, an attitude that encompasses at least a pair of attitudes.[19] Similarly, being disappointed about x is plausibly regarded as encompassing a belief and a desire or wish (e.g., the belief that x occurred and the desire or wish that x not have occurred).

An alternative route to attitude *TM* starts from a content constancy view of the attitudes. Given this view, whether an attitude is truth seeking or motivation encompassing is determined by its psychological orientation. For example, the believing *orientation* toward representational content constitutes belief as truth seeking, and the desiring orientation toward content constitutes desire as motivation encompassing. (Such psychological orientations as hope and disappointment are naturally regarded as mixed on the content constancy view and as having their two-dimensionality in virtue of encompassing pairs of one-dimensional orientations—one member truth seeking and the other motivation encompassing.)

Against this background, a strong internalist may explore the possibility that some psychological *orientations* are individuated *partly by content*. For example, a theorist may consider the possibility that the psychological orientation operative in such beliefs as that cats drink milk and that squares have four sides is not identical with the orientation operative in *MR* beliefs, beliefs that one is (oneself) *morally required* to A. Possibly, the content of beliefs of the latter kind signals the presence of a special psychological orientation. For reasons I have mentioned, strong internalists should eschew the idea that *MR* beliefs are composite attitudes; but this leaves open to them the idea that *MR* belief is a species of belief whose psychological orientation is something more than *mere* belief.[20] This special orientation, *SP*, may be imagined to be such that particular states of mind having that orientation are, at once, truth seeking and motivation encompassing. Furthermore, mental states having orientation *SP*—unlike hopes, for example—will not be composites of other states: beliefs and desires, for instance. Rather, *SP* states are noncompound, truth-seeking, motivation-encompassing representational attitudes. I call them *SP-beliefs*. *SP*-beliefs that one is (oneself) morally required to *A* are instances of attitude *TM*. These special beliefs are, essentially, both truth seeking and motivation encompassing. They essentially encompass motivation to *A*.

It may even be said that in light of the essential truth-seeking and motivation-encompassing nature of these beliefs, they have compound satisfaction conditions. It may be claimed that an *SP*-belief that one is (oneself) morally required to *A* is *satisfied* if and only if one is morally required to *A* and one *A*-s. On this view, what would satisfy the *SP*-belief is the conjunction of what would satisfy a belief that one is (oneself) morally required to *A*, on a less demanding conception of such beliefs, and what would satisfy a desire or intention to *A*.

If a detailed, coherent conception of *SP*-belief were to be developed, internalist moral cognitivists would have available to them a noncompound, truth-seeking, motivation-encompassing species of moral belief that precludes listlessness. However, one should pause to ask whether, necessarily, all psychological endorsements of the content "I am morally required to *A*" are two-dimensional attitudes of this kind. The proper grasp line could be used in arguing that a proper understanding of morality—specifically, an understanding required for endorsing contents of the form "I am *morally* required to *A*"—metaphysically or conceptually ensures that any endorsement of such content has both dimensions. But should one think that morality metaphysically or conceptually requires this, that is, that the nature of morality places a demand of this kind on the psychological architecture of beings capable of making judgments that they are morally required to act in certain ways and of acting in accordance with those judgments?

Now, assuming that one's theory of morality has a bearing on one's account of the constitution of moral beliefs and that moral beliefs tend to influence the conduct of agents who have them, one's theory of morality may be expected to bear on one's theory of action explanation. Theorists who hold that the nature of morality (and of belief, on some construal) is such that any *MR* belief encompasses *MR* motivation may be expected to differ from theorists who deny this in their explanations of intentional actions performed at least partly on the basis of *MR* beliefs. Theorists of the latter sort may opt for a familiar division-of-labor picture according to which, to put it simply, when a belief that one is morally required to *A* issues normally in an intentional *A*-ing, it does so in tandem with, for example, a separate desire to do whatever is morally required of one in the circumstances. Perhaps the belief and desire issue in an intentional *A*-ing by issuing in an intention to *A* that the agent proceeds to execute. (The belief and desire may do this in conjunction with other beliefs and desires, e.g., the belief that *A*-ing would help one's aunt and the desire to help her.) Strong internalists, on the other hand, will embrace an alternative picture, accommodating the alleged motivation-encompassing character of the relevant belief. However, perhaps the action-explaining mix can, in principle, be carved up in different ways with no change in explanatory power regarding intentional conduct. Perhaps the pertinent motivational ingredient is capable of doing its motivational work whether it is lodged inside a belief or, instead, is external to beliefs. Of course, the character of the motivational ingredient may be sensitive to its location. In the division-of-labor picture that I described, the motivational ingredient is generic in nature: it is a desire to do *whatever* one is morally required to do in the situation. In an internalist picture, the belief-encompassed motivational ingredient may be a desire specifically to A.[21] But perhaps both pictures can be developed to provide putative explanations of moral behavior in terms of agents' attitudes.

If so, theorists face two questions: which picture is more faithful to the psychological constitution of real human agents? And does morality conceptually or metaphysically require that *MR* beliefs encompass *MR* motivation? One moral that may safely be drawn from centuries of disagreement about the nature of morality is that it is hard to be certain just what morality is and difficult to know whether morality entails or presupposes that any cognitivist belief that one is (oneself) morally required to A encompasses motivation to A. If we assume *psychological* realism, it is also difficult to be certain that any actual agents in fact have *SP*-beliefs—noncompound, truth-seeking, motivation-encompassing attitudes. So, unless and until either of these matters is settled, cognitivists seeking a verdict about strong internalism will do so under conditions of double uncertainty.

The least happy candidate for a result, to my mind, is (1) that morality does conceptually or metaphysically require that moral agents have *SP*-beliefs but (2) that, as a matter of fact, no one has ever had such a belief. The upshot would be that no one has ever been a moral agent and none of our conduct has been moral conduct. We would have been wrong all along about a matter of deep importance to us. In light of this, it should prove fruitful to ask how we would be likely to respond to the news that (2) is true, should we somehow discover its truth (say, via unequivocal divine revelation). How would we react should we discover that although human beings are blessed with truth-seeking attitudes and with motivation-encompassing attitudes, in fact no human being has ever had a noncompound attitude that is at once truth seeking and motivation encompassing?

I suspect that the intellectual position of some cognitivist strong internalists is comparable to that of some incompatibilist believers in free will (i.e., some libertarians). At least one libertarian has said that if determinism were shown to be true, he would abandon his incompatibilism, not his belief in freedom (van Inwagen 1983, p. 223). Similarly, I suggest, some cognitivist strong internalists, if the nonexistence of noncompound, truth-seeking, motivation-encompassing attitudes were to be established, would abandon their claim that morality requires internalism, not their belief in the existence of moral agents or in the truth of moral cognitivism. If there are no such attitudes, "moral beliefs" lack the kind of practical clout that cognitivist strong internalists would like to find in them; but, for some, that theoretical preference would be easier to shed than the belief in moral cognitivism and in corresponding moral judgments and moral conduct. Just as some libertarians would settle for what they would view as a metaphysically less robust freedom if the truth of determinism were to be demonstrated, I suspect that some internalist moral cognitivists would settle for what they would regard as a less toothy morality if the nonexistence of *SP*-beliefs were established. I encourage theorists sympathetic to cognitivist strong internalism to conduct the following personal thought experiment. Imagine that you were to learn that there are no motivation-encompassing beliefs. Would you infer that *you* have never believed that you were morally required to do something? Or would you continue to believe that you have had such beliefs and conclude that a theoretical proposition about moral beliefs that you once endorsed is false?

A related question also requires attention. If we were to discover that human beings have always been devoid of *SP*-beliefs, would the "morality" for which we might settle necessarily have less practical bite than a cognitivist strong internalist's morality? Move to a world where a tiny fraction of the adult human population, a few philosopher-kings or Aristotelian *phronimoi*, have *SP*-beliefs, and even these people rarely muster the penetrating cognitive vision required for the presence of such beliefs. A cognitivist strong internalist's morality has bite only for those few individuals; everyone else is left outside the fold of moral agents. Perhaps this morality is toothy for a few, but the beast in whose jaws the teeth are lodged has a very limited range. In that world, too, people who were to discover the distribution of *SP*-beliefs might understandably seek an alternative conception of morality in order to preserve an understanding of cognitivist morality as something having an *extensive* bite.

6. Listlessness Again

In a relevant case of listlessness, one locates a morally good agent, complete with a host of true beliefs about what he is morally required to do, and imagines that a psychologically devastating tragedy befalls him, quashing his motivation to conduct himself in certain ways. In particular, among the things of which he has long been convinced is that he is morally required to *A*, and he loses all motivation to *A*. To the extent that it is an empirical question whether his "moral vision"—his cognitive apprehension of the relevant moral requirement—must be eliminated in the process (the "must" being nomological rather than logical or metaphysical), it can only be answered by means of careful attention to the human psyche. And it is far from obvious, on empirical grounds, that it is *psychologically impossible* for a human victim of clinical depression to retain a belief that he is morally required to *A* without having, any longer, motivation to *A*.

Recognizing this, theorists attracted both to robust internalism and to moral cognitivism may see the question as wholly conceptual or metaphysical—as a question about the essential nature of morality and about what that nature requires concerning the apprehension or vision of a moral requirement. However, once again, they run the very real risk in so doing of committing themselves to a conception of morality that does not mesh with the psychology of real human beings, a conception that is inconsistent with any actual human being's being a moral agent. A cognitivist strong internalist who runs this risk ought to have something approaching a knockdown argument for the thesis that morality conceptually or metaphysically requires that moral agents are equipped with noncompound, truth-seeking, motivation-encompassing mental states. I am aware of no such argument. The arguments from moral experience and from toothlessness and the proper grasp response are less than compelling, as I have indicated, and I know of nothing more persuasive in the literature.

It is, to be sure, an intriguing idea that, from putative conceptual or metaphysical truths about the nature of morality (namely, that morality entails or presupposes strong internalism and is essentially cognitivist) and the premise that some human beings believe themselves to be morally required to do certain things, one can deduce the substantive psychological truth that among the mental states of human beings are some noncompound, truth-seeking, motivation-encompassing attitudes. This idea is comparable to one sometimes found in discussions of free will: namely, that from a conceptual or metaphysical truth about the nature of free will and the premise that we experience our own freedom, we can deduce that determinism is false (or, in another argument of this form, that determinism is *true*). These arguments for theses about psychological and physical reality are not likely to convince psychologists and physicists. But some philosophers will not be daunted by this; and they may observe, of course, that the second premise (the one affirming the existence of *MR* beliefs or of veridical experiences of free will) is an empirical one—the arguments are not completely a priori. This reinforces my point that cognitivist proponents of robust internalism put the existence of *MR* beliefs at serious risk. If, as these cognitivists claim, the nature of morality is such that no belief is an *MR* belief unless it is a noncompound, truth-seeking, motivation-encompassing attitude, there is a very real chance that we have never believed ourselves to be morally required to do anything. If the constraints that morality places on the psychology of moral beings are less stringent, we are more likely to be—as we believe ourselves to be—moral agents.

If morality is essentially practical and if human beings are devoid of truth-seeking, motivation-encompassing beliefs (*SP*-beliefs), but some of us are moral agents even so, then, I believe, morality advises moral agents to cultivate in human nonmoral agents (e.g., our young children) a concern for moral matters. Agents with this concern who believe themselves to be morally required to *A* have, in that concern, motivation well suited for a place in the positive motivational base of a desire to *A* (see chapter 1, section 3). Morality, for them, is not toothless. Once this is recognized, moral cognitivists have little incentive to allow our status as moral beings to hinge on the hope that among our states of mind are *SP*-beliefs. Evidence that we have such beliefs is, at best, feeble. The thesis that moral beings can get along nicely without special attitudes of this kind is a source of theoretical and practical comfort. The population of planet Alpha certainly seems to include moral agents, even if Alphans have no *SP*-beliefs. In the absence of a telling argument for rejecting this impression, it ought to be taken seriously.

I have not directly attacked strong internalism on *noncognitivist* readings.[22] Nor have I argued that strong internalism is *incompatible* with moral cognitivism. However, I should emphasize that strong internalism, being a putative necessary truth, places a considerably heavier burden on its proponents than on its opponents. In the absence of powerful arguments even for the truth of *p* itself, it is wise to eschew endorsing the claim that *p* is *necessarily* true; and moral cognitivists can get along nicely without strong internalism. If the falsity of strong internalism were to entail the toothlessness of morality, moralists would have a powerful incentive to defend this internalist thesis. Fortunately for moral cognitivists, this worry is illusory.

I have not made the empirical claim that, in actual human beings, depression sometimes works in the way imagined in Eve's case. *Perhaps* all actual depressed human beings who believe that they ought, morally, to A do have some motivation to A. Perhaps, when they do not even try to A, that motivation is overridden by stronger motivation that is explained by, or partly constitutes, their depression (e.g., a desire not to exert oneself); or their depression might block the formation or acquisition of intentions that accord with this moral motivation. But even if depression does work in some such way in actual human beings, that plainly is compatible with the idea that actual human beings are not *essentially* immune to depression or listlessness of the kind imagined in Eve's case—hence, with the idea that *MR* beliefs do not *essentially* encompass *MR* motivation in actual human beings. If the actual mechanics of depression in actual human beings leaves no room for cases like Eve's, part of what I have argued, in effect, is that this is a *contingent* fact; more specifically, this supposed truth about the mechanics of depression is not grounded in any essential motivational properties of cognitivist moral ought-beliefs or in any essential psychological features of human beings. Should depression work in an acquaintance of mine in the way I have imagined it works in Eve's case, that is compatible with my acquaintance's being a human being; and, I have urged, it is compatible with anything that we have good reason to believe about moral ought-beliefs.

In attempting to understand and explain intentional behavior, we standardly advert to a host of attitudes, including desires and cognitivist beliefs. Traditional conceptions of this battery of attitudes undoubtedly fall short of perfection; but if there is no defect in these conceptions that would be remedied by altering the battery to include the pertinent reformative notion of cognitivist belief, then there is little to recommend the revision. I see no theoretical need, in moral philosophy or the philosophy of mind, for a conception of cognitivist moral ought-belief that would render Eve's story incoherent.

7. An Alleged Problem with Generic Moral Desires

Michael Smith (1994, pp. 74–76; 1996, pp. 181–83) has argued that a generic desire to do whatever one morally ought to do has no place in a morally perfect agent. He writes, "if what makes a morally perfect person's act right is the fact that it serves the well-being of their family and friends, then we normally assume that what moves them is that very fact: that is, the fact that their act serves the well-being of their family and friends. This is part of what makes them morally perfect: morally perfect people are moved by right-making features" (1996, p. 182). He claims as well that people whose "primary source of moral motivation is a desire to do the right thing" have only "an instrumental desire" to look after "the well-being of their family and friends" because that desire "must have been derived from their non-instrumental desire to do the right thing together with their . . . means-end belief that they can do the right thing by looking after the well-being of their family and friends" (1996, p. 182). "Commonsense tells us," Smith contends, that people motivated by this generic desire have "a fetish or moral vice" (1994, p. 75; cf. p. 76; 1996, p. 183). Morally good people, unlike alleged moral fetishists, "have direct concern" for the particular things that they believe to be morally right (1994, p. 76).

Does Smith's argument show that people who sometimes are motivated by Alphic desires—generic desires to do whatever is morally required of them in specific situations—are moral fetishists? Two preparatory points need to be made. First, a philosopher who accepts something like the general spirit of Smith's distinction between moral fetishists and nonfetishists may be excused for rejecting his formulation. The suggestion that someone was moved by the fact that a certain course of action would serve the well-being of his family and friends will be regarded by some philosophers as shorthand for the idea that the agent's *recognition* of this fact moved him (or for the idea that the fact moved him indirectly by helping to account for the recognition that more directly moved him). After all, presumably, if he had not recognized this fact, he would not have been moved to do what he did. Second, from a certain perspective on action explanation, such recognition does not itself move agents either. Suppose it were the case that our agent did not care about the well-being of his family and friends, either intrinsically or extrinsically. Then, other things being equal, he would not have done what he did. What accounts for the agent's action, it may be claimed, includes his desire for the well-being of his family and friends and his belief that an action of a certain kind would promote this.

It is consistent with an Alphan's having the Alphic disposition and Alphic desires that he has a variety of intrinsic desires, for example, intrinsic desires for the well-being of family and friends, for the success of his favorite sports teams, and for his own pleasure. In Alphans, Alphic desires function in tandem with ought-beliefs when they act wholly or partly on the basis of these beliefs. There is no suggestion that Alphic desires play a role in *all* their intentional actions. When an Alphan, motivated partly by an intrinsic desire for pleasure, attends a play, with no thought that he is morally required to attend, any Alphic desire that he may have at the time is on the sidelines. When an Alphan helps his children with their homework, an Alphic desire of his may again be on the sidelines—even if he happens to believe that he is morally required to help them—for in helping them, he may not be acting either wholly or partly *on the basis of* that belief. He may be moved instead by his intrinsic desire for his children's well-being.

This indicates that an externalist can accept a less tendentious formulation of Smith's (1994, 1996) point about moral fetishists and nonfetishists while consistently embracing externalism. Suppose that, in ordinary circumstances, the morally perfect person—or even an ordinary morally decent person—performs actions that benefit his family and friends out of love or friendship, for the sake of the people he benefits, and not out of a generic concern to do the right thing. The kind of agent at issue may be doing the morally right thing in helping his family and friends, and as it happens, he may *believe* both that he is morally required to help them and that he is morally required to perform helping actions of the kinds he performs. However, by hypothesis, he is not acting even partly *on the basis of* these beliefs. Rather, he is acting solely out of love, friendship, or the like. This is entirely consistent with the externalistic picture that I have sketched since it is a picture about how first-person moral ought-beliefs might help to produce corresponding actions when agents act wholly or partly on the basis of these beliefs.[23]

What should be said about cases in which agents do act (at least partly) on the basis of beliefs of the kind at issue? Would a significant role for Alphic desires in the production of these actions suffice for the agents' being moral fetishists? Return to my story about the man, Al, who helped his aunt paint her apartment at least partly on the basis of his belief that he was morally required to do so. He did not help her simply out of a concern for her happiness, as a morally perfect agent perhaps would have done; this motive was insufficient to turn the trick. That, as Al saw it, he was morally required to help her was, for him, a significant addition to the mix. If the combination of his moral ought-belief and an Alphic desire played a role in explaining his helping his aunt paint, is Al therefore a moral fetishist? I do not see why. Rather, he is someone who, in some cases, will fail to do what he morally ought to do unless he believes that he ought to do it and acts at least partly *on the basis of* that belief. And Al may be psychologically so constituted that his acting on the basis of a first-person moral ought-belief depends on his having a desire to do whatever he morally ought to do in his situation. Al may be an Alphan.

If Smith (1994, 1996) is right, it at least sometimes happens that an agent who believes that he morally ought to *A A*-s intentionally without that belief's playing an action-basing role, and moreover, that is as it should be. Perhaps, in some cases, it would be morally perverse for an agent to do what, as he recognizes, he ought to do for the reason that he ought to do it. Perhaps he should instead do it out of love, friendship, or the like. When should our moral ought-beliefs play a basing role in producing actions that we believe we ought to perform, and when should they not do so? This is a tantalizing question, but I will not try to answer it. My concern in this chapter is with what it is about first-person moral ought-beliefs in virtue of which they do sometimes play their action-basing role, the role they play when we act at least partly *on their basis*. I have argued that these beliefs need not essentially encompass motivation in order to play this role.

Readers will have noticed that I have not said whether Alphic desires are wholly intrinsic, wholly extrinsic, or mixed (see chapter 1, section 8, for the distinction). Seemingly, a desire to do whatever one is morally required to do in one's circumstances might, in principle, be of any of these three kinds. It might be a desire exclusively for an *end* describable as doing whatever one is morally required to do in one's circumstances.[24] It might be a wholly extrinsic desire. One might desire doing whatever one is morally required to do in one's circumstances solely as a means of impressing the people around one, for example. And it might be a mixed desire. For example, one might desire doing whatever one is morally required to do in one's circumstances both as an end and as a means of providing a good example for one's children. Whatever interpretation best fits moral agency is the one that should be adopted in a more precise specification of what I have been calling Alphic desires.

8. Modest Cognitivist Internalism: Problems

My primary claim about listlessness, as it applies to actual human beings, is that there is at least a hypothetical species of this malady to which human beings are not essentially immune, such that a human being suffering from it may believe, in a cognitivist sense, that he ought morally to A without, in so believing, having motivation to A. The upshot is that our first-person cognitivist moral ought-beliefs do not *essentially* encompass motivation to A. Among readers who agree, some may be willing to countenance *contingently* motivation-encompassing cognitivist moral ought-beliefs and others may see this as mistaken. The claim that first-person cognitivist moral ought-beliefs do not *essentially* encompass *MR* motivation is consistent with the anti-Humean thesis that beliefs of this kind *normally contingently* encompass such motivation and even with the stronger thesis that *all actual* beliefs of this kind in fact contingently encompass such motivation. (Of course, our not being essentially immune to listlessness of the sort featured in Eve's case is compatible with our never actually suffering from it.) Although, for my purposes in this chapter, there is no theoretical need to reject the idea that there are cognitivist moral ought-beliefs that contingently encompass *MR* motivation, I find it implausible that our moral agency depends on our having such beliefs. In this section, I explain why.

Strong internalism and the competing thesis that Nagel calls "externalism" are not jointly exhaustive. Strong internalism is the thesis that, necessarily, any belief that one is (oneself) morally required to A encompasses motivation to A. What Nagel calls "externalism" asserts that "motivation [to A] is not supplied by ethical [A-favoring] judgments themselves, and that an additional psychological sanction is required to motivate our compliance" (1970, p. 7). One can reject strong internalism without endorsing this externalist thesis. A theorist who rejects strong internalism can hold, for example, that most (or all or some) beliefs that one is (oneself) morally required to A encompass motivation to A. Jonathan Dancy has advanced a position of this kind (1993; cf. Dreier 1990).[25] Although Dancy himself understands internalism along the lines of strong internalism and therefore denies that his view is internalist (p. 25), his view may be construed as a (modest) species of internalism if it is committed to the existence of beliefs with (in Frankena's 1958 expression) "built-in" motivation to act accordingly.

Again, attitudes that essentially encompass motivation to A are distinguishable as follows from attitudes that contingently do so: an attitude of an agent S *essentially* encompasses motivation to A if and only if it encompasses motivation to A not only in S's actual situation but also in all possible scenarios in which S has that attitude and *contingently* encompasses motivation to A if and only if although, in S's actual situation, it encompasses motivation to A this is not the case in some possible scenarios in which S has that attitude (chapter 1, section 1). Dancy (1993) grants that pertinent cases of listlessness are possible and falsify the claim that moral ought-beliefs essentially encompass motivation to act accordingly (pp. 6, 23–26). In conceding this, he parts company with strong internalists. However, he contends that some cognitive states are "intrinsically motivating."[26] These states satisfy the internalistic idea that some beliefs have built-in motivation (on a natural reading of "intrinsically motivating")[27] but not the stronger internalist thesis that some beliefs are *essentially* motivation encompassing. Dancy contends that "the overall moral judgement 'This is what I ought to do' . . . has a normal motivational force," a "default" force, even though in some cases it is "deprived of" that force by such things as listlessness (p. 26). A belief possessed of its "normal motivational force" is *intrinsically* motivating—it has built-in motivation—without being essentially motivating.

One may reasonably claim (1) that, normally, people who believe that they morally ought to A have motivation to A and, further, (2) that having motivation to A is associated *by default* with so believing. But it is a long way from these claims to the further claim that some beliefs that one morally ought to A are intrinsically motivating (i.e., motivation encompassing).[28] Claim (2) calls for speculation about the nature of the alleged default connection. If it turns out that people who judge that they morally ought to A typically have a desire to do whatever they morally ought in the situation and this fact helps to explain why people normally acquire a desire to A upon judging that they morally ought to A, Dancy's (1993) suggestion is eminently disputable. For then the possibility is left open that the judgments themselves do not encompass motivation— that the relevant motivation is found instead in something external to these judgments, namely, in the generic desire I mentioned.

We want to know in virtue of what, in the absence of a desire of the relevant sort, an agent who judges at t that he ought, morally, to A is supposed to acquire (or *simultaneously* acquire) motivation to A. Guardian angels and the like may do the work, but then the judgment is not *intrinsically* motivating. An intrinsically motivating attitude is such that, *in* forming or acquiring it, one acquires motivation. So it may be claimed that the explanation of the motivation's emergence is provided by an explanation of the attitude's emergence. Dancy's contention that in scenarios in which listlessness, for example, deprives a moral judgment "of its normal motivational force, [it] still has a normal motivational force to be deprived of" is tendentious in a way that bears directly on this move (1993, p. 26). In at least some (perhaps merely hypothetical) instances of listlessness, it is *not* the case that an agent's moral judgment that he ought to A initially has motivational force directed at A-ing and then loses it; rather, at the time at which the judgment is made (and while the judgment is held), the agent is utterly devoid of motivation to A. In such instances, to explain the occurrence of an A-favoring judgment is not to explain the emergence of motivation to A, for no such motivation emerges.

Here is an illustration. Eve's aunt, Mary, had always been utterly self-sufficient, and Eve had never believed that she ought to help Mary. However, shortly after the plane crash that killed Eve's family, Mary became seriously ill and required assistance. To make a long story short, Eve saw no morally significant difference between her aunt and her uncle in the relevant connection and she judged that she ought to help her aunt—just as she believed that she ought to help her uncle. Unfortunately, owing to severe depression, Eve was devoid of motivation to help Mary. If my story about Eve and her uncle is coherent, so is the story about Eve and her aunt. It may require less work to render resistant readers receptive to the idea that one may *retain* a cognitivist belief that one ought, morally, to A without having, any longer, motivation to A; but once that is accomplished, it is a small step to the suggestion that one may *acquire* a cognitivist belief that one ought, morally, to A without acquiring (and without already having) motivation to A.

A theorist might claim that in those cases in which an agent believes that he ought, morally, to A and does have motivation to A, the motivation is built into the belief.[29] An alternative hypothesis is that, in these cases, such beliefs help to generate motivation to A and that, in cases of listlessness involving motivationally inert beliefs that one ought to A, something is missing such that, were the ought-belief to occur in its presence, motivation to A would result. An obvious candidate for what is missing is something like the Alphic desire. Such a desire, in conjunction with the belief that one morally ought to A, can give rise to a desire to A. And the former desire, not the belief, would be in the positive motivational base of the desire to A.

A theorist might make one or both of the following claims in reply:

> C1. An agent who would have no motivation to A even in the absence of a relevant trauma or pathology (and even if A-ing had absolutely no cost to him) does not *believe* that he ought, morally, to A.
>
> C2. An agent who is rational at t and, at t, has no motivation to A does not, at t, *believe* that he ought, morally, to A.[30]

The same theorist might urge that these claims support the view that cognitivist moral ought-beliefs *encompass MR* motivation when abnormal factors are absent or when the person is rational. Suppose that *C1* and *C2* are granted for the sake of argument. Still, to wield this argument successfully, one must show that the concurrent presence of a cognitivist belief that one morally ought to A and of motivation to A, when abnormal factors are absent or when the person is rational, is better explained on the hypothesis that the ought-belief itself encompasses motivation to A than on the alternative hypothesis that the ought-belief is not motivation encompassing and the motivational source of the motivation specifically to A lies in some factor that would be absent were the abnormal factors present or were the agent nonrational at the time. The pertinent factor may be or include something like the Alphic desire. That desire, together with the belief that one ought, morally, to A, may generate a desire to A rather than the belief's encompassing motivation to A. And, on the assumption that *C2* is true, some pertinent desire (e.g., a desire to act for good reasons) may be a constituent of a kind of time-slice rationality that is incompatible with severe listlessness of the sort I have described.

Derek Parfit distinguishes "substantive" from "procedural" rationality. "To be substantively rational, we must care about certain things, such as our own well-being" (1997, p. 101). "To be procedurally rational, we must deliberate in certain ways, but we are not required to have any particular desires or aims, such as concern about our own well-being." *C2* may be false when the occurrence of "rational" in it is read as "procedurally rational" and true when it is read as "substantively rational." Substantive rationality at a time may well be inconsistent with suffering at the time from listlessness of the kind I have described.

It is not as though pretheoretical intuition favors the hypothesis that some cognitivist moral ought-beliefs *encompass MR* motivation over the alternative "generation" hypothesis I expressed. Indeed, to the extent that an enormously popular Humean view of the mind—a view according to which (cognitivist) belief and desire differ essentially in their respective directions of fit—is reflective of pretheoretical intuition, such intuition speaks against the "encompassing" hypothesis. The primary attraction of that hypothesis lies in the fear that, unless it is true, morality does not have the practical clout that it is properly regarded as having.[31] I have argued that this fear should not grip us. And if there are pretheoretical intuitions about the two competing hypotheses, the popularity of the Humean view suggests that its way of carving up the mind is more strongly supported by them than is the way advocated by proponents of the encompassing hypothesis. Proponents of this anti-Humean thesis are urging a *re-formative* conception of cognitivist belief.

An intrinsically motivating ought-belief, on a cognitivist construal of belief, is both truth seeking and motivation encompassing. Now, assuming a realistic under-standing of the attitudes, the claim that we have such beliefs is at least disputable. Sup-pose that, as a matter of fact, such beliefs are not among the psychological repertoire of human beings and that somehow this fact were discovered by us. Would we con-clude that morality is a myth and that it is never the case that we ought, morally, to do certain things and to eschew doing others? I doubt it. If, as it turns out, no moral ought-beliefs encompass *MR* motivation, such beliefs may still contribute to action in con-junction with something like Alphic desires, and moral ought-beliefs will have practi-cal clout for agents with such desires. Allegiance to a certain conception of morality may naturally lead some theorists to hope that we have motivation-encompassing be-liefs. But should that hope be dashed, their allegiance would predictably shift to a modified conception of morality rather than to nihilism. This is an indication that morality does not *conceptually* or *metaphysically* require that moral ought-beliefs of the kind at issue be in the psychological repertoire of moral agents and that morality leaves open the possibility that moral ought-beliefs generate moral conduct in con-junction with generic moral desires.

Suppose that *C1* and *C2* are *conceptual* truths about first-person moral ought-beliefs. What I have argued, in effect, is that even then, it is an open question whether, in the absence of trauma, pathology, and so on or in the presence of rationality, (1) the *belief* encompasses motivation to *A*, or, instead, (2) motivation specifically to *A* is de-rived from a generic desire of a kind that is present whenever the relevant traumas and pathologies are absent—or whenever rationality is present—in an agent who believes that he is morally required to *A*. [I am not claiming that (1) and (2) *exhaust* the possi-bilities.] The supposed conceptual truths are *silent* on this question; and the supposi-tion that *C1* and *C2* are conceptual truths and that either (1) or (2) is true does not entail that the true alternative is itself a conceptual truth. Our concept of moral ought-belief may determine the truth of *C1* and *C2* without determining the particular man-ner in which these truths are realized.

I have neither the desire nor the authority to rule out of philosophical court concep-tions of belief that allow for *intrinsically motivating* cognitivist beliefs. Thus, I am in no position to prove that there are no such beliefs. Nor can any wholly nonempirical argument show that there *are* such beliefs. Furthermore, there is no way to tell by in-trospection whether certain of our cognitivist beliefs include built-in motivation to act accordingly or, instead, are accompanied by pertinent motivation-encompassing atti-tudes. However, I have argued that we have good reason to reject the idea that our being moral agents requires that we have cognitivist beliefs that essentially encom-pass motivation to act accordingly (as moral cognitivism conjoined with strong inter-nalism would have it) or intrinsically motivating beliefs. Given the state of our evidence for the existence of such beliefs, that should be a comforting thought for cog-nitivist believers in moral agency.

A theorist may claim that, *as a matter of contingent fact*, in actual human beings, all (or most or many) moral ought-beliefs do encompass motivation to act accordingly. I dub this *contingent internalism*. Versions of the arguments from moral experience and from toothlessness and a variant of the proper grasp response (see section 3) may be advanced to support this more modest anti-Humean claim. However, arguments of these three kinds face difficult problems even when marshaled in support of the more modest claim. Any version of the argument from moral experience will encounter the problem identified for it in section 4. And concerning the universal version of contingent internalism (i.e., the claim minus the parenthetical clause), what evidence does moral experience provide that no agent who fits Eve's description is an actual human being, one of us? Regarding the argument from toothlessness, why should we think that our existence as moral agents is, in fact, underpinned by the truth of contingent internalism rather than by the truth of the thesis that although *MR* beliefs do not *encompass* motivation, they nevertheless are well-suited for the task of generating corresponding moral conduct in conjunction with relevant desires (e.g., something like Alphic desires)? In the case of the proper grasp response, what is the evidence that people who understand morality well enough to harbor moral ought-beliefs have, *in* their moral ought-beliefs, motivation to act accordingly? Why is this more likely to be true than the alternative thesis that these beliefs do not encompass such motivation but that when agents of this kind act on the basis of these beliefs, the beliefs produce motivation in tandem with relevant desires?

My concern here has been another question—whether an acceptable moral theory will make legitimate *metaphysical* or *conceptual* demands of a certain kind on a proper theory of human motivation—and, more specifically, whether, assuming moral cognitivism, a plausible moral theory will require that moral ought-beliefs essentially encompass motivation to act accordingly or even, more modestly, that some of them are "intrinsically motivating." My answer is no. This answer should be a source of comfort to theorists attracted to moral cognitivism, for if our having cognitivist ought-beliefs of either sort were required for our being moral agents, the door would be wide open to skepticism about human moral agency.

Notes

1. Here I follow David Wiggins (1991, p. 62), from whom I borrow the expression "moral cognitivism." For reservations about affixing the label "moral realist" to this thesis, see Wiggins (pp. 62–64).

2. Brink (1989, p. 43) cites the following as examples of works combining moral cognitivism (or realism) and internalism: Falk (1948), Foot (1978, essays 7 and 8), McDowell (1978, 1979, 1985), Nagel (1970), and R. Price (1969). McNaughton (1988) and Garrard and McNaughton (1998) are more recent examples. Dancy advocates moral cognitivism while rejecting both internalism and externalism, as he construes them; he views his position as approximating internalism (1993, p. 25; cf. Simpson 1999). Brink, an externalist cognitivist, treats externalism as the denial of internalism (p. 42); obviously, Dancy does not regard internalism and externalism as jointly exhaustive.

3. Korsgaard writes that "there is at present so much disagreement in the literature about what internalism is, which of its characteristics are definitive, and what it implies that introducing the issue has become almost a guaranteed way of introducing confusion" (1996, p. 82, n. 63).

4. Cf. Darwall's distinction between "existence" and "judgment" internalism (1983, p. 54; 1992, p. 155).

5. Suppose that being morally required to *A* entails being able to *A* intentionally. Suppose also that one *A*-s intentionally only if one has motivation to *A*. It does not follow from the latter supposition that, for example, a Hitler who has no motivation to release prisoners is unable intentionally to release prisoners. Nothing precludes the possibility that a Hitler of this kind may acquire motivation to release prisoners and may act, intentionally, on the basis of the acquired motivation. Compare my Hitler with Adolf, who has just eaten a large meal and now has no motivation to eat ten minutes hence. From this fact about Adolf's motivational condition, it does not follow that he is *unable* to eat (intentionally) in ten minutes. If someone (now or a little later) were to offer Adolf a significant incentive to eat ten minutes hence, he would eat then—motivated by a desire for the reward.

6. Proponents of this thesis who equate motivation with *desire* are committed to the idea that some beliefs are identical with desires or, at least, encompass desires. Such alleged beliefs have been discussed under the label "besire." The term first appears in Altham (1986, pp. 284–85). Literature on the topic includes Collins (1988), Lewis (1988), Pettit (1987), Pettit and Price (1989), H. Price (1989), and Smith (1987, 1988, 1994). McNaughton (1988, pp. 106–10) explicitly represents first-person moral ought-beliefs as being at once cognitivist beliefs that one ought, morally, to *A and* desires to *A*. McDowell (1978) advances a similar view, with "conceptions" of "how things are" standing in for moral ought-beliefs. Also, see Wiggins (1991, p. 83): "The full moral thought, if you like, is not just a belief. But it is not just a valuation either. The valuation itself can *be* the belief." McDowell (pp. 15–17) attributes a view of this kind to Nagel (1970). Dancy (1993, pp. 8–9) offers an alternative reading of Nagel.

7. I have no objection to substituting "judgment" for "belief." See Nagel (1970, pp. 64–65).

8. I am merely *reporting* this view of reason-having. For present purposes, I have no need either to endorse or to reject it.

9. Here is a counterpart: necessarily, any belief that one is (oneself) morally required to *A* constitutes a reason to *A*. If one can have a reason to *A* without having motivation to *A*, this thesis may be true even if strong internalism is false.

10. See McNaughton (1988, ch. 9) and Milo (1984, chs. 6 and 7). Cf. Brink (1989, pp. 46–50, 59–60, 83–86) and Dancy (1993, pp. 3–6). Stocker (1979) is a seminal critique of internalism.

11. For discussion, see, for example, Dancy (1993, pp. 23–26), Smith (1994, pp. 120–24, 135, 154–55), and Stocker (1979, pp. 744–46).

12. Notice that if an *MR* belief is *nothing but* a certain kind of motivational attitude, with no truth-valued content, then in lacking motivation to help her uncle, the woman lacks a belief that she is morally required to help him.

13. In Mele (1996a), I gave Alphans a *standing desire* to do whatever they are morally required to do.

14. Garrard and McNaughton (1998, pp. 53–54) favor the second construal of "reason."

15. I defend (Mele 1987) the reality of full-blown akratic action.

16. Cf. the discussion of "object-assimilationism" and "attitude-assimilationism" in Brand (1984, ch. 4).

17. For a lucid presentation and defense of this popular line, see Searle (1983).

18. See, for example, Castañeda (1975, ch. 10), Goldman (1970, ch. 4), Hare (1972, ch. 3), and Kenny (1989, pp. 36–41).

19. As I pointed out in chapter 1, note 8, *The American Heritage Dictionary*, in its usage note on "expect," reports that "to *hope* is to desire, usually with confidence in the likelihood of gaining what is desired." (Again, I believe that the latter clause is too strong.)

20. Cf. the quotation from Wiggins (1991) in note 6 above.

21. Readers should bear in mind the ambiguity of "motivation to A." I have left open the possibility, for example, that Ann's desire to swim today and her desire to exercise today both count as (encompassing) motivation to A. See chapter 1, sections 1 and 3.

22. I have attacked some arguments for strong internalism that may be advanced by cognitivists and noncognitivists alike, but that is another matter, of course. Plainly, noncognitivism neither entails nor presupposes the existence of noncompound, *truth-seeking*, motivation-encompassing attitudes. It is worth noting, incidentally, that noncognitivists have a powerful incentive for embracing strong internalism that cognitivists lack. If it were the case both that noncognitivism is true and that *MR* beliefs are not essentially motivation encompassing, in what would *MR* beliefs consist? What would it be like to have a belief that one is (oneself) morally required to A that is neither truth seeking nor motivation encompassing?

23. Notice that an agent who A-s might not A on the basis—even in part—of his belief that he is morally required to A, even if he would not have A-ed if he had lacked that belief. Imagine that if Sam had lacked the belief that he was morally required to help his son with his homework, he would have believed that he was morally required *not* to help him (rather than having no belief on the matter or believing that helping him was morally permissible), and he would have acted on the basis of his belief that he is morally required not to help. Even so, Sam may be helping his son solely out of love. That his love would not have turned the trick if Sam had believed that he was morally required not to help his son, and that Sam would have believed this if he had not believed that he was morally required to help him, does not entail that Sam acted wholly or partly on the basis of the latter belief. Consider the following analogy. This morning, as Sally was setting out to walk to work, as she normally does, her young son asked whether she thought a dragon would eat her on her way to the office. Sally acquired an occurrent belief that no dragon would eat her. In her circumstances, given the question her son raised, if she had not occurrently believed that no dragon would eat her, she would have occurrently believed that a dragon might eat her, in which case she would not have walked to work. However, walking to work this morning is not something Sally does wholly or partly on the basis of that belief. She walks to work this morning for her normal reasons, and the basis for her walking is her normal basis.

24. Smith treats the generic desire to do the right thing as a wholly intrinsic desire when he claims that people whose "primary source of moral motivation is a desire to do the right thing" have only "an instrumental desire" to look after "the well-being of their family and friends" because that desire "must have been derived from their non-instrumental desire to do the right thing together with their . . . means-end belief that they can do the right thing by looking after the well-being of their family and friends" (1996, p. 182). It is worth noting that a desire *D1* that derives from the combination of an intrinsic (or "non-instrumental") desire *D2* and a pertinent belief may itself be an intrinsic (or "non-instrumental") desire. For example, Ann's intrinsic desire always to repay in kind people who have intentionally angered her together with her belief about the intent behind a nasty anonymous letter she recently received may issue in an intrinsic desire to get back at whoever sent the letter. And if, subsequently, through shrewd detective work, she discovers the person's identity, the intrinsic desire last mentioned and her belief that Bob sent the offensive letter may jointly give rise to an intrinsic desire to get back at Bob.

25. He leaves this position behind in Dancy (2000).

26. Dancy (1993, p. 24). Dancy characterizes "essentially motivating" states as states "that cannot be present without motivating" (p. 2) and distinguishes them from "intrinsically motivating states," which "can be present without motivating but which when they do motivate do so in their own right" (p. 24). Because Dancy takes Humean desires to be essentially motivating states, he holds that intrinsically motivating states are not "Humean desires" (p. 24). If it is to be at all plausible that desires are essentially motivating states, Dancy cannot be using "motivating" here in its *success* sense. Some desires to A plainly do not motivate an agent to A in a sense

of "*X* motivates *S* to *A*" that implies "*S A*-s." However, these same desires might motivate *S* to *A* in the sense that they *encompass motivation* to *A*. Given Dancy's understanding of Humean desires as essentially motivating states, his characterizations of essentially and intrinsically motivating states are best read as employing the weaker sense of "motivating."

27. I take Dancy's claim that these states motivate "in their own right" (1993, p. 24) to indicate that they are motivation encompassing, even if Dancy does not explicitly present his view in these terms (see note 26). On another possible interpretation, the claim is that they *produce* motivation "in their own right." The criticisms to be advanced also apply, with minor adjustments, to this claim (also, see chapter 6 for a critical response to a claim of this kind). In any case, on the interpretation that I adopt, Dancy has articulated a qualified version of cognitivist internalism that retains a commitment to motivation-*encompassing* cognitivist beliefs, and the qualified thesis merits attention.

28. The same is true of the further claim that they *produce* motivation "in their own right," independently of desires the agent already has (see note 27).

29. A version of Dancy's position would augment this with the claim that having motivation to *A* is the *default* condition of believing that one ought, morally, to *A*, while rejecting Dancy's contention that in scenarios in which listlessness, for example, deprives a moral judgment "of its normal motivational force, [it] still has a normal motivational force to be deprived of" (1993, p. 26).

30. For an influential brand of internalism that emphasizes rationality, see Korsgaard (1986). For instructive criticism of a version of strong internalism that is geared specifically to rational agents, see Audi (1997, ch. 10).

31. Of course, this is consistent with there being other attractions.

6

Attitudes That Essentially Encompass Motivation to Act

In chapter 1, I distinguished between attitudes that essentially encompass motivation to *A* and attitudes that contingently do so ("*A*" being an action variable). I offered the following definitions. An attitude of an agent *S essentially* encompasses motivation to *A* if and only if it encompasses motivation to *A* not only in *S*'s actual situation but also in all possible scenarios in which *S* has that attitude, and it *contingently* encompasses motivation to *A* if and only if although, in *S*'s actual situation, it encompasses motivation to *A* this is not the case in some possible scenarios in which *S* has that attitude. I used "encompass motivation" as an umbrella term for being, constituting, or including motivation to *A*, and I continue to do so.

I introduced the distinction (chapter 1, section 1) partly to avoid a terminological dispute about whether a desire's *providing* motivation to *A*—as Ann's desire to exercise today may (actually or potentially) provide her with motivation to swim today—may be said to be a way of constituting (or being) motivation to *A*. Some people may find it natural to say that, in its context, Ann's desire to exercise today constitutes (or is) motivation to swim today and that this is so even if she has no desire to swim today. I observed that if there is a sense in which Ann's desire to exercise today constitutes motivation to swim today, it is not the same sense as that in which her desire to swim today does so, and I introduced the distinction at issue partly to mark that difference.

My aim in the present chapter is to develop an account of *A*-focused attitudes that essentially encompass motivation to *A*. *A*-focused attitudes are attitudes that are "directly about" (prospective or actual) *A*-ings in a sense discussed in chapter 1 (section 3). Ann's desire to *A*, Bob's belief that he will *A*, Cyd's belief that she *A*-ed yesterday, Don's intention to *A*, Eve's belief that she ought to *A*, and Fred's fear that he *A*-ed last month are all *A*-focused attitudes. My concern is a subset of such attitudes.

There are many twists and turns in this chapter. Among other things, a host of worries—some of them intricate—about the account being developed here must be formulated and dissolved. I believe that the payoff—a detailed understanding of the nature of paradigmatic motivational attitudes—is well worth the trouble.

1. A Preliminary Thesis

Only some of our desires are what I have called action-desires. As I explained in chapter 1 (section 2), action-desires, in my sense, are agents' desires to A, where "A" is a variable for prospective courses of action, and if they are satisfiable, they are satisfiable by, and only by, actions (and truths, states, or facts for which the satisfying actions are conceptually sufficient; again, for stylistic reasons, I omit the parenthetical qualification in what follows).[1] These remarks are not offered as an analysis of action-desire; much more remains to be said.

The present section makes a case for the following thesis:

T1. All intentions to A and all desires to A essentially encompass motivation to A.

I start with intentions. In chapter 1 (section 5), I suggested that to intend to A is, at least in part, to be settled (but not necessarily irrevocably) on A-ing. I also suggested that part of what it is to be settled on A-ing is to have a motivation-encompassing attitude toward A-ing: an agent who lacks such an attitude lacks an element of a psychological commitment to A-ing that is essential to being settled on A-ing. I defended a position on the nature and functions of intention in a previous book (Mele 1992e), and I intend to avoid significant repetition here. Fortunately, it is relatively uncontroversial that intentions to A encompass motivation to A. According to the once popular idea that intentions are reducible to combinations of beliefs and desires (i.e., action-desires), intentions are every bit as motivational as the desires that partially constitute them. That idea has encountered powerful objections that I regard as persuasive.[2] But nonreductionists about intentions also take them to be motivational (Brand 1984; Bratman 1987; Castañeda 1975; Mele 1992e). Their quarrel is with the idea that there is nothing more to an intention than what is ensured by the presence of a collection of desires and beliefs, not with the idea that intentions encompass motivation to act and are no less motivational than action-desires.

I turn to action-desires. If desiring to A were not to preclude the presence of certain cognitive states, one might desire to A while having no motivation to A. For example, if an agent could desire to A while being convinced that he cannot A, he could desire to A while having no motivation at all to A. However, desiring to A precludes the presence of cognitive states of this kind.[3] If I am convinced that I cannot travel faster than the speed of light, change the past, or defeat the current heavyweight champion of the world in a fair fight, then although I might wish that I could do these things, I do not *desire to do* them. Achieving the represented objects of their action-desires is doxastically open for agents: if they do not explicitly believe that they can A, at least they are not convinced that they cannot A.[4] Any agent's desire to A, given the very nature of action-desire, is an inclination of the agent—sometimes only a very weak inclination—to A. This is part of what it is to be an action-desire.[5] In being an inclination of the kind it is, a kind to be fleshed out in this chapter, an action-desire constitutes motivation to act. Of course, as desires are commonly conceived, someone who desires to A may also desire to B and recognize that he cannot do *both*.[6] But having an inclination to A is compatible with also having an inclination to B, recognizing that one cannot both A and B.

Desiring to A, if I am right, precludes being convinced that one cannot A. A counterpart constraint on what I term "state-desires" (i.e., all desires that are not action-desires, including desires for others to act) merits mention: desiring x precludes being convinced that x is impossible. Carl's conviction that backward time travel is conceptually impossible precludes his desiring that aliens take his wife back to eighteenth-century France. He may wish that aliens *could* do this, but that is another matter. Donna's conviction that traveling faster than the speed of light is physically impossible precludes her desiring that aliens whisk her husband from Earth to Pluto in one second. Of course, she may wish that aliens were able to do this. Were Carl or Donna to lose the pertinent conviction, matters would be different.

In chapter 5, I sought to undermine the primary sources of alleged support for the idea that in actual human beings cognitivist moral ought-beliefs—specifically, agents' beliefs that they ought, morally, to A—essentially encompass motivation to A. Someone may contend that action-desires are on no firmer ground in this respect. It may be claimed, for example, that a jogger may desire to run another lap but be too tired even to try, so that his desire does not constitute motivation to run. Again, an agent who takes his A-ing to be physically impossible may hope or wish that he could A, but he does not *desire* to A. However, someone may believe that he can A and desire to A although, in fact, even an *attempt* to A is beyond his power. We can desire to do what, unbeknown to us, we are unable to do and even to try to do. (To take an extreme case, although Sam desires to A, an irresistible demon will not permit some prerequisite of Sam's trying to A: e.g., his acquiring some suitable intention.) But this possibility, rather than entailing the possibility of action-desires that do not constitute motivation to act, illustrates the possibility of attitudes that constitute motivation to act, although in the circumstances they cannot motivate, in the success sense, even a corresponding attempt. This last possibility differs markedly from the one highlighted in my discussion of listlessness in chapter 5. If my story about Eve is coherent, it is not as though she has a motivation-encompassing belief on which, owing to her listlessness, she is unable to act. Rather, her listlessness consists partly in the absence of motivation to help her uncle (or, alternatively, deprives her of all such motivation), even though she believes that she ought to help him. If Eve believes, as she presumably does, that she has a reason to help her uncle, the point also applies to that belief.

In chapter 2 (section 1), I discussed a scenario in which a neuroscientist, without altering the neural realization of an intention N, renders that realization incapable of having any effect on the agent's bodily movements (and on what else the agent intends) while allowing the realization of another intention to figure normally in that agent in the production of an overt action. The picture of N is of an intention that is, as it were, surgically cut off from the agent's motor control system. Imagine a related case. Ned has a desire to raise his right arm now. Without altering the neural realization of that desire itself, the scientist tinkers with Ned's brain in such a way that the desire's neural realization cannot contribute to Ned's trying to raise his arm. Although Ned desires to raise his right arm now, he is incapable of even trying to act accordingly.

Does Ned's desire constitute motivation to raise his arm now? And is Ned inclined to raise his right arm now? In one sense, he is inclined to do this. His desire to raise his arm is an inclination to raise it. This is entailed by the folk concept of action-desire, and this result does not need to be abandoned. Ned is inclined to raise his right arm, in the sense that he has an inclination to raise it. In a stronger sense—one requiring his having an inclination and more—he is not inclined to raise it, for his desiring to raise his right arm makes no contribution to a nonzero probability that he will raise it. The probability would be no lower in the absence of the desire. By analogy, consider a sugar cube encased in a water-insoluble substance. Is the sugar cube disposed to dissolve in water? In one sense it is. Insofar as it is sugar, it has a disposition to dissolve in water. In that sense, it is disposed to dissolve in water. In a stronger sense, it is not so disposed. Other things being equal, placing the encased cube in water makes no contribution to a nonzero probability that it dissolves. Consider an analogous claim about Eve's belief that she ought, morally, to help her uncle—the claim that, insofar as this belief is a first-person moral ought-belief, it is a motivation-encompassing inclination to help her uncle, even though, given her circumstances, her having the belief does not increase the probability that she will help him. My primary criticisms of cognitivist internalism in chapter 5 apply straightforwardly to this claim.

In being an inclination of the kind it is, Ned's desire to raise his arm constitutes motivation to raise it. This is another case in which, owing to unusual circumstances, an attitude that constitutes motivation to A cannot motivate (in the success sense) an A-ing. The grounds I have offered for this claim can also be offered for the claim that Ned's *intention* to raise his right arm encompasses motivation to raise the arm in a scenario in which that intention has been surgically cut off from his motor control system.

In chapter 1 (section 4), I discussed a spaceship scenario in which an agent has a state-desire that, under normal circumstances, would provide motivation to act but, because of exceptional external circumstances and some psychological facts about the agent, seemingly provides no such motivation. Is it inconsistent to hold that although Connie, the spaceship pilot, is not provided motivation to act by her desire for a Giants' victory, Ned's desire to raise his right arm constitutes motivation to raise it? No. Ned's desire is itself motivation to act, and Connie's desire is not itself motivation to act. The sorts of circumstances that can prevent state-desires from *producing* motivation to act cannot prevent action-desires from *being* motivation to act. Nothing can prevent the latter. Preventing something from making a causal contribution to something else is common. Preventing something from being what it is is impossible.

Another worry requires attention. Consider the following case. Dex is psychologically so constituted that he has no inclination to A unless he is convinced that he would A should he try to A. Might an agent like Dex undermine my claim that any agent's desire to A is an inclination of the agent to A? Suppose that Dex would like to A but does not believe that, should he try to A, the attempt would succeed. Then, given the kind of person Dex is, he has no inclination to A. If, nevertheless, he desires to A, my claim is false.

The fact that someone would like to A does not entail that he desires to A. I would like to sink the winning basket in an NBA championship game and to hit a home run in a World Series game; doing these things would be exciting, and I sometimes day-dream about doing them. But I fully recognize that, at my age and with my athletic tal-ents, these heroic deeds will never be open to me. It would be a misuse of language to say that I *desire* or *want* to do them (or even *wish* to do them; wishing that I *could* do these things is another matter). However, if I thought that I could do them, I would de-sire to do them. Similarly, whereas Dex would desire to A if he were to believe that he would A should he try to A, in the case as it stands he lacks a desire to A, although he would *like* to A. Dex and I differ in that I occasionally have desires to do things I be-lieve I probably will not succeed in doing (e.g., sink a basket from midcourt or throw a dart into the bull's-eye), and he never does. When he lacks the belief that he would A should he try, his attitude toward A-ing is comparable to my attitude toward hitting a home run in a World Series game; he no more desires to do the former than I desire to do the latter, although each of us would like to do these things.

2. Action-Desires and a Hypothesis

I have supported the claim that intentions to A and desires to A essentially encompass motivation to A. It is plausible that human beings have attitudes of these kinds. Is it also plausible that we have A-focused attitudes other than intentions to A, desires to A, and attitudes that incorporate them that essentially encompass motivation to A? Is the following thesis true?

> T2. In human beings as they actually are, any A-focused attitude that essentially encom-passes motivation to A is or encompasses an intention to A or a desire to A.

One way to defend T2 is by elimination. One might search among human attitudes for potential falsifiers and argue either that they do not essentially encompass motivation to A or that they are or encompass desires or intentions to A. In chapter 5, I sought to undermine apparent support for the idea that our beliefs that we ought, morally, to A, on a cognitivist construal, essentially encompass motivation to A. The argument there can be used as part of an argument by elimination for T2 by someone inclined to de-fend T2 by elimination.[7]

Ascertaining whether T2 is true is less important to me than understanding the na-ture of A-focused attitudes that essentially encompass motivation to A. That is partly because a dispute about T2 can easily degenerate into a dispute about the meaning of the word "desire" and partly because it would be useful to understand attitudes of the kind at issue in their own right, independently of the kind of agent who has them. Ac-tually, what I want to understand is more fine-grained than I have indicated. If a hope to A is essentially constituted by a desire to A and, say, a belief to the effect that one has a chance of A-ing, then, if T1 is true, hopes to A essentially encompass motivation to A. But they do so in virtue of having as a component an attitude that essentially en-compasses motivation to A. Attitudes composed of two or more attitudes are *com-pound* attitudes. What I want to understand is the nature of *noncompound* A-focused attitudes that essentially encompass motivation to A—or *EMA* attitudes, for short. Noncompound attitudes are attitudes that do not have distinct attitudes as parts (see chapter 5, section 5).[8]

Now, why have I highlighted the nature of *EMA* attitudes rather than the nature of what they essentially encompass, motivation to *A*? The answer is relatively straightforward. There are many uses of the term "motivation" in the philosophical literature, and some are too broad to permit, for example, a distinction between a desire's providing motivation to *A* and a desire's being or constituting motivation to *A*. If there is a sense of "motivation to *A*" in which Ann's desire that the Pistons won, her desire to collect a bet on the game should they have won, her desire to know whether they won, and her desire to look in the newspaper for the score all count as motivation to look in the newspaper for the score, motivation to *A* in that sense is more general than what concerns me now. In this broad sense of "motivation to *A*" (and even in some less broad senses), my concern is noncompound attitudes that *essentially* encompass motivation to *A* and, specifically, *A*-focused attitudes that do so. I concentrate on *A*-focused attitudes that do so partly because the leading candidates in the literature for attitudes that essentially constitute motivation to *A* without either being or encompassing desires or intentions to *A* are *A*-focused beliefs—for example, my belief that I ought to *A* or my belief that *A*-ing is something I have a good reason to do. My concentrating on such attitudes is also partly explained by a desire to skirt a complicated technical issue that requires a discussion that, I fear, many readers would find extremely tedious, an issue about motivation for actional parts of relatively routine larger actions—for example, motivation to run the thirteenth forty-seven-yard segment of a mile in an ordinary agent who desires to run a mile now.

Attention to action-desires will help generate a hypothesis about *EMA* attitudes. Although the *word* "desire" is of no special interest to me, a certain functional role associated with action-desires is a pressing concern. I stipulatively define "effectiveness" of an action-desire as follows: for a desire to *A* to be effective is for it to be a cause of the agent's *A*-ing. The *A*-ing satisfies the desire, so an effective action-desire is a cause of its own satisfaction. The same is true of effective intentions. In chapter 2 (section 4), I told a story about how proximal intentions might figure causally in producing their own satisfaction.

Consideration of the following case will shed light on how action-desires that contribute to their own satisfaction normally do so. Judy's desire to gain the attention of her fidgeting college students so distracts her that she unintentionally places a piece of chalk between her lips while scrawling on the blackboard with her cigarette. Even though these antics gain the full attention of her students, the desire contributes *deviantly* to its satisfaction. Our seeing this as an instance of deviant causation indicates that we accord action-desires a more precise function than merely contributing to their own satisfaction. We view desires to *A* as having, more fully, a function of contributing to their own satisfaction by way of their contribution to *intentional* conduct of the agent that is *directed toward A*-ing. (The same is true of intentions to *A*.) Trying is essentially intentional, and any instance of trying to *A* or trying to bring it about that one *A*-s is directed toward *A*-ing.[9] So one way to attempt to capture this fuller function is in terms of trying.[10] That is the tack I now take.

As I have already explained (chapter 2, section 2), *trying*, as I understand it, requires no *special* effort. When I intentionally type the word "type," I am trying to do that even if I encounter no special resistance. It should also be observed that trying to *A* is distinguishable from trying to bring it about that one *A*-s. Ed, who wants to exercise daily but fears that he will succumb to laziness, tries to bring it about that he exercises daily by telling his friends and loved ones that he intends to do so. He tries to bring it about that he exercises daily by increasing his motivation to do so. As Ed sees it, once he makes the announcement, failing to exercise daily would carry an extra cost—his friends and loved ones would think less of him for backing out. In making the announcement, he is not trying to exercise daily; but in making the announcement, he is trying to bring it about that he exercises daily. To some ears, "trying to *A*" may sound like a species of—specifically, a *direct* way of—trying to bring it about that one *A*-s. Distinguishing the notions in the way I do is consistent with keeping an open mind about this.

Sometimes agents desire to *try* to do something. Ann believes that it will be difficult to defeat her tennis opponent, and she desires to *try* hard to win the match. She realizes that sometimes, although she wants to win a match, she does not exert herself fully to win. This time, she wants to make an unrelenting effort to achieve that goal. Now, a desire to try to win the match *might* induce Ann to try to bring it about that she tries to win it; it might induce a *second-order* trying. Wanting to try to win the match, she might, for example, try to talk herself into trying to win it. However, Ann's desire to try to win the match might instead have a more direct effect on her: wanting to try to win, she might try to win without trying to bring it about that she tries to win. A desire to try to *A* need not contribute to a second-order trying in order to function nondeviantly and effectively.

In some cases, we try to *A* without trying to get ourselves to try to *A*. If, concerning everything we try to do, we first had to try to bring it about that we try to do it, there would be an impossible regress of tryings. There are, as I put it, some *basic tryings* to *A*—tryings to *A* that do not proceed from tryings to bring it about that we try to *A*. If every desire of ours to try to do something were such that its functioning nondeviantly and effectively depends on its contributing to its own satisfaction by inducing us to try to bring it about that we try to do that thing, then no desire to try to do something would be functionally geared to the production of a basic trying. That would be an unfortunate result, one to be avoided in an account of noncompound *A*-focused attitudes that essentially encompass motivation to *A* (*EMA* attitudes).

Properly speaking, desires to try to *A* and desires to try to bring it about that one *A*-s are satisfied, respectively, by one's trying to *A* and by one's trying to bring it about that one *A*-s. This is so even though, normally, agents who desire to try to *A* or desire to try to bring it about that they *A* so desire partly because they desire to *A*, as in the case of Ann's desire to try to win the match. (On special cases in which an agent tries to *A* while being indifferent about *A*-ing, see Mele 1994.)

In the account of *EMA* attitudes to be offered, I use "*A*," in the expression "*A*-focused attitude," as a placeholder for all (prospective) courses of action, including those that are the focus of, for example, desires or intentions to *try* to do something or to try to bring it about that one does something. To avoid confusion, I adopt the convention, in cases of the latter two kinds, that "*A*" holds the place of "try to *B*" or of "try to bring it about that one *B*-s."

So much for trying. The account to be offered of *EMA* attitudes also features subjunctive conditionals. Now, subjunctive conditionals with impossible antecedents are naturally read as counterfactuals. David Lewis says that he is "fairly content to let counterfactuals with impossible antecedents be vacuously true" (1973, p. 25). So am I, and in the account to be offered, I need to avoid associated pitfalls.

I have said that attention to action-desire would help to generate a hypothesis about *EMA* attitudes, noncompound *A*-focused attitudes that essentially encompass motivation to *A*. Here is a hypothesis:

> *T3.* A non-compound *A*-focused attitude *x* of an agent *S* essentially encompasses motivation in *S* to *A* if and only if
> (1) necessarily, if *x* were to function nondeviantly and effectively, *x* would be a cause of its own satisfaction, and not merely of some part of its satisfaction, and it would contribute to its own satisfaction (a) by inducing *S* to try to *A* or to try to bring it about that he *A*-s or (b) by inducing *S* to try to *B* or to try to bring it about that he *B*-s, where trying to *B* or trying to bring it about that he *B*-s is the focus of *x* (i.e., in this instance, the focus of *x*, *A*, is *trying* to do something—specifically, trying to *B*, or trying to bring it about that one *B*-s), and
> (2) either (a) there is some possible scenario in which *x* functions nondeviantly and effectively in *S* or (b) there is not such a possible scenario and the only relevant differences between *x* and attitudes that satisfy conditions (1) and (2a) are that *x*'s focus is or includes an impossible course of action and any differences entailed by this.

This hypothesis accords a certain direction of fit to *EMA* attitudes (see chapter 1, section 4). When they function nondeviantly and effectively, they *get things to fit them* by inducing the agent to make a suitable attempt.

Four notions at work in *T3* require brief comment. First, I understand *contributing* and *inducing*, in this context, as causal notions; I have not abandoned the causal perspective on action defended in chapter 2. Second, I do not understand either notion to entail causal sufficiency. For example, I do not take the claim that *y* induced *S* to *A* to entail that *y* was causally sufficient for *S*'s *A*-ing. Something that *induces* an agent to make an attempt plays a significant causal role in the production of that attempt. Third, satisfied attitudes should not be confused with satisfied agents. An *EMA* attitude is satisfied by the agent's *A*-ing, but the agent himself may find his *A*-ing unsatisfying. Fourth, some attitudes can be satisfied partly or fully. If Ann, who has a desire to eat dinner and then shoot pool, eats dinner but does not shoot pool, that desire is partly but not fully satisfied.

Condition (2) also requires some commentary. Suppose there is a belief of such a kind that it is *conceptually impossible* for it to function nondeviantly and effectively. Imagine that someone shows that on a correct account of the effectiveness or nondeviant functioning of beliefs, a conceptually necessary condition of a belief's functioning nondeviantly and effectively is that it be at least possibly true. Then Fred's belief that he will demonstrate that a person's having begun to exist at *t* is consistent with his having begun to exist at *t* minus a thousand years—Fred is thinking about time travel—cannot possibly, in the pertinent sense of "possibly," function nondeviantly and effectively. So if counterfactuals with impossible antecedents are true, a version of *T3* that does not go beyond condition (1) yields the unwelcome result that Fred's belief essentially encompasses motivation to demonstrate the thesis about existence.

Although this explains my inclusion of (2a), it leaves (2b) unexplained. I have included the latter disjunct because I believe both that desires for impossible courses of action are possible and that they constitute motivation to act—indeed, essentially so. People have tried to square the circle with a ruler and a compass, to find the highest prime number, to show that there is a way in which a person's having begun to exist at *t* is consistent with his having begun to exist at *t* minus a thousand years (some years ago, a student of mine tried very hard to demonstrate this), and so on. They tried to do these things because, in part, they wanted to do them, and their desires to do them constituted motivation to do them. Of course, given that their desires were for impossible courses of action, these desires could not possibly have contributed to their own satisfaction. If the only relevant differences between desires of this kind and attitudes that satisfy conditions (1) and (2a) are that the objects of these desires are impossible courses of action and any differences entailed by this, condition (2b) allows them— unlike necessarily ineffective beliefs of the kind described—to be *EMA* attitudes.

It may be objected that even if I am right that desires for impossible *A*-ings constitute motivation to *A*, this is true by accident on *T3*, which is unsatisfying. The thought, perhaps, is that since in the case of desires for impossible *A*-ings instances of condition (1) are true because their antecedents are necessarily false, *T3* sheds no light on the (alleged) truth that these desires essentially encompass motivation to act. The worry is misguided. Condition (1) does not do all the work. Condition (2) points to features that desires for impossible *A*-ings share with *A*-focused attitudes that nonvacuously satisfy condition (1); for example, in both cases, the *A*-ings are *doxastically* open for the agent. In any case, I am not claiming that *T3* tells us everything we want to know about *EMA* attitudes. There is more to be said, both in this chapter and in the next.

3. The Hypothesis Tested

Is *T3* true? This amounts, of course, to the question whether the following two claims are true:

> *T3a*. If a noncompound *A*-focused attitude *x* of an agent *S* satisfies conditions (1) and (2) of *T3*, then *x* is an *EMA* attitude.
> *T3b*. If a noncompound *A*-focused attitude *x* of an agent *S* is an *EMA* attitude, then *x* satisfies conditions (1) and (2) of *T3*.

T3a has intuitive grip. A noncompound *A*-focused attitude with the function of contributing to its own satisfaction by inducing the agent to try something appropriate to an *A*-ing certainly seems to be a prime candidate for a state of mind that essentially encompasses motivation to *A*. All tryings are motivated, and attitudes having this functional relationship to trying seem fit to play a motivational role in the production of an attempt. Furthermore, a relevant attitude of which the subjunctive conditional is *necessarily* true seems well suited to encompass motivation to *A* *essentially*. However, appearances sometimes mislead. Potential objections require attention. Are there attitudes that falsify *T3a*?

If counterexamples to *T3a* are to be found, one place to look is the sphere of beliefs. Some action-regarding cognitivist beliefs may help bring about their own truth—

hence, their own satisfaction. They merit consideration. Are there *A*-focused beliefs that satisfy conditions (1) and (2) of *T3* but are not *EMA* attitudes?

Kirk is a placekicker. His coach has informed him that, regarding any field goal he attempts, believing that he will make (i.e., successfully kick) the field goal increases his chance of making it. Kirk, who has heard of the power of positive thinking, decides to augment his preparation for each kick with an attempt to get himself to believe that the kick will succeed. Eventually, he regularly gets himself to believe this, and his confidence in the success of his kicks significantly boosts his success rate. Kirk's beliefs that he will make particular field goals are satisfied by his making them, and his believing that he will make them causally contributes to his making them. Is Kirk's belief that he will make his next field goal such that, necessarily, if the belief were to function nondeviantly and effectively, it would contribute to its own satisfaction by inducing Kirk to make an attempt of one of the kinds specified in *T3*. If so, *T3a* seemingly is false, for this belief seemingly does not encompass motivation.

It is not clear what it would mean to say, in general, that a belief functions effectively and nondeviantly. If "belief aims at truth" (Williams 1973, p. 151) and truth alone, one might propose that there is nothing more to a belief's being effective than its being true. However, it may be said that a belief's effectiveness is a matter of what sort of contribution it makes to the believer's life and that not all true beliefs are equally effective in this regard. In its context, Kirk's belief that he will make his next kick has a special function—to increase the chance that he will make that kick. It can be said that that belief's effectiveness is a matter of the contribution it makes to the success of that kick. But notice that the pertinent belief does not contribute to its own satisfaction by inducing Kirk to *try* to bring it about that he makes the field goal, or to try to make it. Kirk is settled on trying to make the field goal *before* he acquires the belief that he will make it. His having the belief increases his chance of making a successful kick, given that he is settled on trying to do so. But the belief is irrelevant to whether Kirk tries to make the kick. If Kirk's belief's playing the role it played is sufficient for its functioning nondeviantly and effectively in its context, condition (1) is false of this belief.

Consider a case designed to avoid this response. An exceptionally risk-averse person, Rex, is particularly averse to making unsuccessful attempts. He will not attempt anything unless he believes that, if he makes an attempt, the attempt will succeed. Rex is confident about his chance of *A*-ing, something he would like very much to do. He believes that he will *A* if he tries to *A*. Believing this, he also believes that he will *A*, for possessing the conditional belief and realizing that he would like very much to *A*, Rex believes that he will try to *A*. If Rex were to lack the belief that he will *A*, his lacking it would be explained by his lacking the conditional belief—in which case, he would not even attempt to *A* and would not *A*. Rex's making an attempt to *A* is thus contingent on his believing that he will *A*; were he to lack the belief, he would not try to *A*. Does this belief satisfy condition (1)?

Given Rex's peculiar form of risk aversiveness, his trying to *A* is contingent on his believing that he will *A*. But Rex's belief that he will *A* does not induce him to try to *A*. It is true that if he were to lack this belief, he would not try to *A* and would not *A*. But although the attitudes that contribute causally to his trying to *A* include attitudes that partly constitute the basis for this belief, they do not include this belief itself. Rex's belief that he will *A* is epiphenomenal with respect to his trying to *A*. The same is true of Rex's belief that he will try to *A*. If Rex's belief's functioning as it did is sufficient for its functioning nondeviantly and effectively in its context, condition (1) is false of this belief.

Consider a third case. Sally, a Stoic, is disposed to want to perform any action that she believes she will perform. She believes that happiness is found (partly) in discovering what fate has in store for one and in *desiring* to act as one believes oneself to be fated to act, and she wants to be happy. Sally now believes that she will phone her mother by the end of the month. As a consequence, she desires to phone her mother by the end of the month, which desire issues in a successful and timely attempt to phone her mother. Does Sally's belief satisfy condition (1)?

Insofar as Sally's belief plays a role in the production of a desire that issues in a successful attempt to phone her mother, the belief can be said to contribute to its own satisfaction by inducing her to try to phone her mother. However, the *necessity* asserted in *T3* is absent in this case. Perhaps, given that Sally is a Stoic, a belief of hers that she will *A* can be said to be such that it functions nondeviantly and effectively only if it plays a role of the kind just mentioned. But there is no necessity about Sally's being a Stoic. If she were not a Stoic—more precisely, if she were not a person with the relevant sort of psychological constitution—nondeviant and effective functioning of beliefs of hers that she will *A* would not be linked to their contributing to their own satisfaction by inducing an appropriate attempt.[11]

Are there *nondoxastic* attitudes that satisfy the antecedent of *T3a* without essentially encompassing motivation to *A*? One might suppose that such attitudes can be found somewhere in the animal world, if not in us. Consider the following:

> The wasp *Sphex* builds a burrow . . . and seeks out a cricket which she stings in such a way as to paralyze but not kill it. She drags the cricket into the burrow, lays her eggs alongside, closes the burrow, then flies away. . . . In due course, the eggs hatch and the wasp grubs feed off the paralyzed cricket. . . . To the human mind, such an elaborately organized and seemingly purposeful routine conveys a convincing flavor of logic and thoughtfulness—until more details are examined. For example, the wasp's routine is to bring the paralyzed cricket to the burrow, leave it on the threshold, go inside to see that all is well, emerge, and then drag the cricket in. If the cricket is moved a few inches away while the wasp is inside making her preliminary inspection, the wasp, on emerging from the burrow, will bring the cricket back to the threshold, but not inside, and will then repeat the preparatory procedure of entering the burrow to see that everything is all right. If again the cricket is removed a few inches while the wasp is inside, once again she will move the cricket up to the threshold and re-enter the burrow for a final check. The wasp never thinks of pulling the cricket straight in. On one occasion, this procedure was repeated forty times, always with the same result. (Wooldridge 1963, pp. 82–83)

It might be suggested that the wasp has an attitude such that, necessarily, if it were to function nondeviantly and effectively, it would contribute to its own satisfaction by inducing the wasp to try to check the burrow. It might be claimed, further, that this attitude is not motivation encompassing; the wasp's "checking" behavior has all the marks of an unmotivated execution of a fixed subroutine.

Grant the plausible claim that the wasp has no motivation-encompassing attitude with the relevant object. Is this scenario a counterexample to *T3a*? The same considerations that support the claim that the wasp has no motivation-encompassing attitude toward checking its burrow also support the claim that it is not *trying* to check its burrow. Its behavior does not include burrow checking at all. Rather, what might look initially like behavior aimed at checking to "see that all is well" is simply the mindless unfolding of a fixed routine. The wasp, in entering its burrow, is no more trying to check it for safety or for (continued) suitability for egg-laying than a plant, in turning toward the light, is trying to gain energy. Consequently, however the wasp's motions are produced, a proper account of their production does not include an attitude such that, necessarily, if it were to function nondeviantly and effectively, it would contribute to its own satisfaction by inducing the wasp to try to check its burrow.

There is a general moral here. Trying to *A* is, essentially, intentional behavior; and, it is generally agreed, intentional behavior is found only among motivated beings. Beings that lack motivation will not *try* to do anything, and beings that lack motivation to *A* (and motivation to try to *A*) will not try to *A*.[12]

I turn to *T3b*. Cases in which an agent wants to *A* *unintentionally* may seem to undermine that thesis. Ann is promised $10,000 for offending Bob unintentionally, and she knows that there is no reward for intentionally offending him. Wanting the money, Ann desires to offend Bob unintentionally. A straightforward, successful attempt to offend him will not gain her the money, as she realizes: such an attempt would amount to intentionally offending Bob. Does this imply that Ann has an *EMA* attitude of which condition (1) is false?

Two possibilities need attention. First, Ann's desire to offend Bob unintentionally may not have a prospective *action* as its focus. Ann realizes that people sometimes take offense at things she says or does even when she has no desire to offend them. (Sometimes she learns only weeks later that they have been offended by her words or deeds.) Ann might hope—and, again, hope encompasses desire—merely that this sort of thing will *happen* in Bob's case; what she desires may be a mere *happening* rather than a prospective action. Ann's attitude toward her unintentionally offending Bob may be of the same kind as certain of her state-desires: for example, her desire to live to be 100 years old and her desire to sleep peacefully tonight. *T3b* is a thesis about *EMA* attitudes. If Ann's desire to offend Bob unintentionally has a prospective nonaction of hers as its focus, her story fails as a counterexample to *T3b*.

Second, Ann's desire to offend Bob unintentionally may be a genuine action-desire. In one relevant scenario, she knows that she tends to offend Bob unintentionally when she is extremely busy; when she is preoccupied with her work, for example, she tends, without then realizing it, to speak more tersely than she ordinarily does to people who phone her at the office, and when Bob calls her terse speech tends to offend him. Knowing this, Ann may undertake an engrossing project—say, writing a paper on motivation—with the hope that her involvement in it will render her telephone conversation at the office sufficiently terse that, should Bob call (as he frequently does), she will unintentionally offend him. In pursuing this strategy, Ann is trying to bring it about that she offends Bob unintentionally. This is a coherent attempt; in particular, it is not intrinsically self-defeating. An *action-desire* of Ann's to offend Bob unintentionally may contribute to its own satisfaction by inducing her to try to bring it about that she offends him unintentionally. Must her action-desire have functioned deviantly in contributing to its own satisfaction? Again, what counts as a deviant causal connection is context-relative (see chapter 2, section 3). If things go according to plan and Ann reaches her goal, her desire to offend Bob unintentionally functions nondeviantly. Action-desires like Ann's are peculiar; what counts as their functioning in a nondeviant way is sensitive to their peculiarity.

4. Further Testing: Negative Actions

Trying plays an important role in *T3*. It may be claimed that precisely because trying has no place in *negative* actions, the account fails. The thought is that although a desire or intention for a negative action, *A*, essentially encompasses motivation to *A*, nondeviant, effective functioning of such a desire does not involve its inducing the agent to *try* to do anything since there is nothing—including trying to *A* and trying anything else—that the agent *does* in *A*-ing. Alleged examples of negative actions include such things as not moving one's body and not voting in an election, when it is intentional on one's part that one does not do these things or when it is "for a reason" that one does not do them.[13] Insofar as "intentional" and "for a reason" apply in this way to a not-doing, *N*, it is claimed, *N* is an action, a negative one. In this section, I rebut the objection from negative actions to *T3*. I argue that some alleged negative actions are successful tryings (in which case they are not negative in the way that is supposed to be problematic for *T3*) and that alleged desired or intended negative actions that do not involve trying are not actions.

Preparatory comments on two topics are in order. The first is the contents of seemingly negative *desires*. The correctness of the claim that a person "has a desire not to *A*" leaves it open whether the desire being described is an action-desire. Perhaps the person's desire, more fully described, is to bring it about that he does not *A* or to prevent himself from *A*-ing, and perhaps it is instead merely a state-desire. An October conversation with Arlo about their hectic work routine last December elicits in Andy a desire not to work on Christmas this year. His elicited desire, more fully described, is to see to it that he does not work on Christmas. On a yet fuller description, his desire is to arrange things in advance so that he will be free not to work on Christmas this year and will take the day off. Arlo also desires not to work on Christmas this year, but his desire is no more fully articulated than that. At this point, he may simply desire that it not happen that he works on Christmas. Later, owing significantly to that desire, he may acquire a desire like Andy's, an action-desire.

The second topic is descriptions of putative negative actions. In chapter 1 (section 2), I said I would remain neutral on leading theories of action individuation. This makes discussion of the present topic delicate. On a coarse-grained view, if "Arlo's not working on Christmas" is an action description, it may be a description of a collection of actions also describable as "Arlo's watching several football games, eating periodically, drinking a case of beer, and so on, on Christmas." (Suppose that his beer drinking causes Arlo to fall asleep several times during the day. He is not working while he is asleep. Is his not working at these times an action of his, or part of a larger action of not working on Christmas? More on this later.) According to a fine-grained view, an action is "the exemplifying of an act-property by an agent at a particular time" (Goldman 1970, p. 10), and *A* and *B* are different actions if, in performing them, the agent exemplifies different act-properties. If not working is an act-property—Goldman says that "any property which has an *act*-token as one of its instances is an *act*-property" (p. 17)—then, since that act-property plainly is not identical with the act-properties to which I alluded in my description of Arlo's "positive" actions on Christmas or with some combination of those properties, Arlo's not working on Christmas cannot be identified with his positive actions on Christmas even if his not working is an action. On a componential view, if Arlo's not working on Christmas is an action, it may perhaps have "positive" actions as components.

Again, readers are free to use their preferred method of action individuation. The various methods leave it open whether, for example, Arlo's not working on Christmas is an action and whether "not doings" that are alleged to be actions involve pertinent trying. I sometimes write in terms of *descriptions*, such as "Arlo's not working on Christmas." But this is not to presuppose a coarse-grained view. On a fine-grained view, as on the alternative views, one can ask whether that description is of an *action* of Arlo's or, instead, of a nonaction.[14]

Consider the following case. Ann wants to do her part in a passive resistance protest. She wants to remain utterly limp as the police drag her away from the court-house doorway where she had been lying, even though the dragging is painful. As she is being dragged, Ann works hard to master urges to move her body in ways that would minimize pain; she works hard to see to it that she does not move her body. Ann actively uses cognitive control techniques that, as she knows, send signals to muscles to remain relaxed, and she succeeds in keeping her body limp. "Tries" can be smoothly substituted for "works" here. Ann tries hard to see to it that she does not move her body; she tries to do this by using certain mental self-control techniques.

The *fact* that Ann does not move her body is not an action. Fact and action are distinct categories. To the extent that "Ann's not moving her body" describes an action of hers (an action perhaps more fully described as "Ann's seeing to it that she does not move her body" or "Ann's seeing to it that her body remains limp"), it is plausible that it describes her successful attempt to keep her body limp. In this, Ann's seemingly "negative" action is comparable to her "positive" action of stretching her limbs after she is released. That action is a successful attempt to stretch her limbs (see Adams and Mele 1992).

Wittgenstein (1953, p. 621) asked, "What is left over if I subtract the fact that my arm goes up from the fact that I raise my arm?" Frederick Adams and I (Adams and Mele 1992) have argued that the answer is the agent's trying to raise it. Consider a similar question: what is left over if the fact that Ann's body remains limp is subtracted from the fact that she sees to it that her body remains limp? A plausible answer is her trying to keep her body limp.

If Ann's seemingly negative action is comparable, in the ways just mentioned, to the positive actions of her stretching her limbs and Wittgenstein's raising his arm, it is nicely accommodated by a causal theory of what actions are (see chapter 2). Ann has a reason for seeing to it that she does not move her body. She wants to do her part in the protest and believes that this requires her to keep herself from moving her body while she is being dragged. It is natural to say that it is *for this reason* that she sees to it that she does not move her body. Suppose that the reason (or its neural realizer) figures nondeviantly in the production of an intention to see to it that she does not move her body by exercising certain self-control techniques, and the intention (or its neural realizer) plays a normal causal role in the production of the successful effort Ann makes to keep her body limp (see chapter 2). If "Ann's not moving her body" describes an action of hers, namely, her successful attempt to keep her body limp, a causal approach to analyzing action is nicely suited to it.

I suggested that Ann's allegedly negative action is actually a positive one—a successful trying to keep her body limp. *How* does the trying succeed? By hypothesis, the techniques that Ann employs work by sending signals to muscles to remain relaxed. The signals are causal sustainers of the muscles' relaxation; they keep the muscles relaxed. It is not as though the normal condition of muscles is relaxation. Imagine how many muscles are normally at work when normal people sit calmly at their desks while thinking.[15] People with stress problems are taught how to relax muscles. They are taught as well how to maintain, or sustain, relaxation of muscles once relaxation has been achieved. Given that Ann is being dragged across pavement, she needs to try a lot harder to relax than a normal person seated in a normal chair.

Again, the problem that negative actions may be thought to pose for *T3* is that although a desire or intention for a negative course of action, *A*, essentially encompasses motivation to *A*, nondeviant, effective functioning of such a desire does not involve its inducing the agent to *try* anything relevant. However, Ann's case does not raise this problem: trying plays an important role in her successful, desired "passive" resistance, and, on the assumption that her not moving her body is an action, her trying is motivated by a desire to act in that way.

Given the point just made, to explore whether "Ann's not moving her body" is properly treated as describing an action would be to digress from the main project of this section. If it does describe an action, the etiology of the action described, as I have just argued, is consistent with *T3*. And if it does not describe an action, there is little reason to regard Ann's corresponding desire—her desire not to move her body—as an *action*-focused attitude. If the desire is not action focused, it does not pose a problem for *T3*—a thesis about conditions under which noncompound *action*-focused attitudes essentially encompass motivation to perform pertinent actions—and her relevant action-desire would be a desire to see to it that she does not move her body or to bring it about that she does not move her body or something of the sort. Notice that such an action-desire may be rationalized by a state-desire not to move her body together with an appropriate linking belief—for example, the belief that she will not move her body only if she sees to it that she does not.

Digressions are not always bad things, however, especially when they are brief. My brief digression features a quintet of twists on Ann's scenario. In the first, Al, Ann's protesting companion, wants not to move his body should he be dragged away. Because he doubts that he has enough willpower to use techniques like Ann's, he is carrying an instant-unconsciousness pill. The pill, Al knows, will induce complete unconsciousness for ten minutes. When Al sees the police draw near, he pops the pill into his mouth. Unconsciousness instantly sets in. His body goes limp and remains that way while he is being dragged away, as he planned. Al does not move his body, and he successfully tries to bring it about that he does not move it. However, his attempt, unlike Ann's, ends before the police take hold of him, and "his not moving his body" plainly does not describe an action of his. Instead, it describes an intended nonactional consequence of an action of his, namely, his pill-taking action. While he is unconscious, Al has no control at all over his body, and agents who have no control over their bodies at a time are not performing bodily actions at that time.

Here is a second twist. This time, the pill is an instant-paralysis pill. When Al takes it, complete paralysis instantly sets in for ten minutes; his body goes limp and remains that way while the police drag him away. Here again, it seems, "Al's not moving his body" does not describe an action of his and instead describes a desired consequence of an action. As in the preceding case, Al has no control over his body while he is being dragged away. By taking the pill, Al brings it about that he does not move his body. "Al's taking the pill" and "Al's bringing it about that he does not move his body" do describe actions of his.

In a third twist, Al has learned a mental trick for self-paralysis. The paralysis works for only thirty seconds at a time. Al thinks a magic word and the effect is immediate and complete paralysis for thirty seconds. As he is being dragged away, Al thinks the word every twenty-five seconds or so; he does not want to take any chances. He brings it about that his body remains limp, and every twenty-five seconds or so he makes a contribution to its remaining limp. Does "Al's not moving his body while he is being dragged away" describe an action of his, or does it instead describe a nonactional consequence of a series of mental actions? Seemingly, the latter. Al brings it about that he does not move his body over the interval at issue, and his bringing this about is an action composed of a series of effective mental actions. The mental actions keep him paralyzed, and his paralysis ensures that he does not move his body. But his not moving his body is not an action—so, at least, I claim. It is not an action because the entire time he is not moving it he is completely paralyzed, and completely paralyzed agents lack the bodily control required for bodily actions.

Critics may resist on the grounds that it is intentional on Al's part that he does not move his body and it is for a reason that he does not move it. These matters are discussed shortly. But it is worth pointing out now that the "intentional" and "for a reason" claims seem no less true in the first two twists; and in those scenarios, not moving his body is not an action Al performs. Critics should also reflect on the unfortunate negative action theorist who devised, as he saw it, a plan for performing the ultimate negative action. His plan was to demonstrate the existence of negative actions by bringing it about that he performed the negative action of not acting—ever again—from midnight tonight through eternity and to bring this about by taking a pill that would end his life. The pill worked, but the plan did not. There was not after midnight any time at which the theorist was performing an action of not acting. Even so, insofar as the theorist intended to bring it about that he not act after midnight and intentionally brought that about, it was intentional on his part that he did not act after midnight.

Now, for a fourth twist. Al must *continuously* think of the magic word to keep his body paralyzed. He does so, for the purpose of keeping his body limp. Here again, on the same grounds adduced in my discussion of the preceding two twists, I claim that although Al brings it about that he does not move his body and his so doing is an action, his not moving his body is not an action. Critics might encourage me to imagine that Al sometimes *moves* his body by thinking words or that Al is a special agent whose effective plans for moving his body always feature his thinking words. The imagined Al might be put together in such a way that, as he knows, in order to get his arms to rise and to rise in the way he intends, he must think a certain word. His thoughts of words are translated into motor signals, and onlookers believe that Al raises his arms in just the way we normally do. My imagined critics may ask whether, when things go according to plan, Al raises his arms. Other things being equal, I say yes. The normal route from intention to bodily motion in Al is different from the normal route in us, but it is a route and it does involve appropriate trying. Al's trying to raise his arms encompasses thinking a certain word; our trying to raise ours does not. Am I being inconsistent in claiming that Al raises his arms, an action, while also claiming that his not moving his body is not an action, even though he uses magic words in both connections? Not at all. What Al does by thinking the magic word in the alleged "negative action" scenario is to prevent himself from moving his body—that is, from engaging in action of a certain kind—by keeping himself paralyzed. If by "Al performs the negative action of not moving his body" my critics mean no more than that Al performs actions that prevent him from moving his body, I have nothing more to object to than their choice of words.

Here is the final twist. Al knows a mental trick for selectively blocking any motor signal in his body before it can result in bodily motion. The trick is to think a certain magic word. By continuously thinking the word, Al counteracts his urges to move his body in self-protective ways as it is being dragged along. Again, I claim that what Al does is to prevent himself from moving his body by shutting down causal processes necessary for his moving it and that this is not sufficient for his performing the action of not moving his body. Al's preventing himself from moving his body *is* an action, and it is something he *does*.

What about Ann? The question with which this digression began is whether "Ann's not moving her body" describes an action. Given the way Ann's self-control techniques work, she seemingly does more than simply prevent herself from moving her body. Her successful attempt to keep her body limp has a more direct connection to her body's remaining limp. The former is related to the latter in the way that an ordinary agent's successful, ordinary attempt to raise his arms is related to his arms' rising. Ordinarily, agents who try to raise their arms do not so try by trying to prevent their arms from remaining unraised; and Ann, who tries to keep her body limp (which limpness entails her not moving her body), does not so try by trying to prevent herself from moving it. Rather, she tries to prevent herself from moving it—and tries to keep it limp—by trying to keep her muscles relaxed, and she tries to do the latter by employing the cognitive control techniques that send relaxing signals to her muscles. By means of her employment of these techniques, Ann prevents herself from moving her body. Should it be said, then, that "Ann's not moving her body" describes an action? I see no need to say that, for reasons that will become clearer as this section progresses. And there are perfectly fine positive action-descriptions of what she does; for example, Ann keeps her body limp by employing cognitive control techniques that send relaxing signals to muscles, and she keeps herself from moving her body by employing these techniques. The point of this digression has been to mark a relatively direct way of making it the case that one does not move one's body.

I return to this section's main project. Alleged negative actions of another kind require attention. Compare the following case with Ann's. Bob works the midnight shift. On the night before election day he decides not to vote. Because Bob dislikes the candidates, he has been thinking about various modes of protest. He decides on the passive mode of not voting. Bob gets home from work before the polls open. As is his practice, he sets his alarm for 7:00 P.M. and crawls into bed. Since he has decided not to vote, he sees no reason to diverge from his daily routine. When the alarm wakes Bob, the polls are closed.

Plausibly, it is intentional on Bob's part that he does not vote. Suppose that this plausible claim is true. That certainly does not entail that Bob performed the intentional (negative) action of not voting. Bob was sound asleep and not acting at all while the polls were open. So he was not during that time intentionally not voting, if intentionally not voting is supposed to be an action. (Nor was he unintentionally not voting then, if that is supposed to be an action—an unintentional one.) How, then, is it intentional on Bob's part that he does not vote? Well, Bob intentionally prepared himself to fall asleep, owing partly, in a quite ordinary way, to his intention not to vote and in the knowledge that, if things were to go according to plan, he would not vote; and things went according to plan. That may be enough.

The sentence "Bob did not vote for a reason" is ambiguous. On one reading ($R1$), it asserts that it is false that Bob voted for a reason. This itself is ambiguous. Is it being asserted ($R1a$) that it is false that Bob voted, in which case it is false that he voted for a reason; ($R1b$) that Bob voted but not for a reason; or ($R1c$) that either it is false that Bob voted or Bob did vote but not for a reason? On another reading ($R2$), the sentence asserts that it was for a reason that Bob did not vote. Suppose that, on the latter reading, the sentence is true. That supposed truth does not entail that Bob, who was asleep the entire time the polls were open, performed an action of not voting. But then, in virtue of what might the sentence be true on this reading? Suppose that the reason for which Bob did not vote, reason R, is a Davidsonian one constituted by his desire to protest and a belief to the effect that not voting is a fine way of protesting. Obviously, if Bob did not perform an action of not voting, R is not a cause of such an action. But R presumably is a rationalizer of Bob's intention not to vote, which intention plays an important role in the account offered (in the preceding paragraph) of its being intentional on Bob's part that he did not vote. I suggest that the combination of R's rationalizing this intention and the process described in the preceding paragraph that begins with Bob's acquiring this intention and ends when he wakes is sufficient for its being true that, for reason R, Bob did not vote.

The following case differs significantly from both Ann's and Bob's. Like Bob, Cyd has decided to protest against the slate of candidates by not voting in the election. Unlike Bob, she works the morning shift. On election day, she goes about her business as usual. She drives to work, performs various tasks there, eats lunch, and so on. By the time she leaves work, the polls are closed. Although Bob is not acting at all while the polls are open, Cyd is performing all sorts of actions then. Is not voting among her actions?

Consideration of the following pair of cases will shed light on how this question is to be answered. On the evening before the election, Don is worried that he will acquire a compulsive desire to vote tomorrow. He wants to protest by not voting. So he takes a pill that will ensure that he sleeps through the election. Edna is in the same boat; she has a similar worry and a similar desire. However, she has no pills. She locks herself in a cell and throws away the key so that she will not succumb to her anticipated desire to vote. Edna is right about acquiring a powerful desire to vote. While the polls are open, she spends all of her time trying—very hard but unsuccessfully—to break out of her cell.

Don intentionally brings it about that he does not vote. Insofar as this is so, it is intentional on his part that he does not vote. But not voting is not an intentional action that Don performs. Like Bob, he is not acting at all while the polls are open. Edna, too, intentionally brings it about that she does not vote. (Assume that the success of her strategy did not owe too much to luck for this to be so.) Unlike Don and Bob, she is acting while the polls are open. However, not voting is not among the actions that she is intentionally performing then. Indeed, she is doing her best to put herself in a position to vote. The actions that she is intentionally performing are aimed at enabling her to get to the polls in time to vote.

Edna is reminiscent of Odysseus, of course. Wanting to hear the Sirens' song and believing that the normal result of hearing them sing is leaping to one's death, Odysseus has himself tied to his ship's mast. He intentionally brings it about that he does not leap into the sea, and insofar as that is true, it is, in a very real sense, intentional on his part that he does not leap. But *while* he is lashed to the mast, listening to the song and struggling against the ropes so that he can swim toward the Sirens, is it intentional on his part that he does not leap? That is, is it intentional on his part *at this time* that he does not leap. Readers' opinions may diverge. However, neither a yes nor a no answer entails that his not leaping is an action. If the answer is yes, the intentionality derives from an intentional action that Odysseus performed earlier, as in Bob's and Don's cases; and, while the polls were open, they were not performing an action of not voting. If the answer is no, there is little to recommend the thesis that his not leaping is an action. The same is true of Edna's not voting.

Return to Cyd. Unlike Edna, she is not trying to bring it about that she votes. Nor, however, while the polls are open is she trying not to vote or trying to bring it about that she does not vote. She is simply going about her business as usual, as she planned. Her plan was to protest by not voting and to go about her business instead of voting. It is intentional on Cyd's part that she does not vote, and she intentionally makes it true that she does not vote by intentionally going about her business as usual in executing a plan for the day that includes not voting. But none of this entails that not voting is among the actions she performs. I have explained how a not-doing can be intentional on one's part, how one can intentionally make it true that one does not A, and how it can be for a reason that one does not A, without one's performing an action of not A-ing. I have also explained that some things described as not-doings and claimed to be actions are in fact successful tryings and not negative actions at all. These explanations cancel what is supposed to support the intuition that there are not-doings—nonevents whose negative status entails that they do not encompass trying—that are actions while leaving in place another common intuition, namely, that all actions are events.

This cancellation having been accomplished, is it nevertheless "intuitive" that not voting is an action of Cyd's? When going about her business as usual, she performs a variety of actions, and it is appropriate to say that she performs these actions in preference to voting and instead of voting. But that does not imply that not voting is an action Cyd performs. For my own part, it seems intuitive that genuine not-doings are not actions precisely because actions *are* doings.

Consider one last case:

> Peter was placed—face down and head first—on a sled, and pushed from the top of a high, snow-covered hill. The brisk wind and flying snow swiftly awoke him. In moments, he had his wits about him and surmised that this early morning trip down the hill was part of his initiation into the SAE fraternity. Peter quickly surveyed his options. He could put an end to his trip by sliding off the sled, or by turning it sharply. He could grasp the steering handles and guide the sled down the slope. Or, in an effort at oneupmanship, he could pretend to remain asleep the entire time, lying still on the sled without grasping the handles or making any voluntary motions: what a coup it would be to convince his prospective fraternity brothers that he had been utterly unfazed by the prank, indeed, that he was never aware that it had occurred! Peter opted for the devious strategy. He was prepared to take control of the sled should disaster threaten: the rogues might have placed a log in the path of the speeding sled. But, as it happened, he had no need to intervene and simply allowed the sled to take its course. (Mele 1997b, p. 135)

Imagine that although, like Ann, Peter did not move a muscle, unlike her, he did not need to try to keep his body relaxed, and he made no such effort. Peter had a plan for astounding the pranksters. Part of the plan was that he would not move a muscle unless he needed to, and there was no need. Suppose that the pranksters were astounded by what they saw. Then (other things being equal) things went according to plan.

Peter apparently performed the action of monitoring his environment for impending disaster (without moving even an eye muscle). Did he also perform the action of astounding the pranksters or of causing them to be astounded? If so, it may be argued that he performed this action *by* not moving his body and that this not-doing therefore was an action. Again, the fraternity brothers were indeed astounded by what they saw. On the assumption that excessive luck was not involved, it was intentional on Peter's part that they were astounded by this. But it does not follow from this that while he was traveling down the hill, Peter performed an action that caused them to be astounded or an action of causing them to be astounded. I have already explained that *x*'s being intentional on a person's part does not entail that the person performed an action of *x*-ing. It is also worth remarking that the fraternity brothers once were astounded by their dean of students' sleeping at a disciplinary hearing over which he was presiding. What they saw caused them to be astounded, but the dean was not acting then. The dean astounded them by sleeping, and Peter astounded them by lying perfectly still. Part of Peter's plan, one can reasonably say, was *not to act*—beyond monitoring his environment for danger—unless he had to. If the reasonable claim is true, then since things went according to plan, with no threat of danger, Peter performed no action on the sled beyond his monitoring.

To sum up, this admittedly limited survey of various types of alleged negative actions has, in all cases, turned up either nonactions or positive actions misdiagnosed as negative ones. Moreover, I have explained away the main support offered for the thesis that there are truly negative actions—namely, that sometimes it is intentional on a person's part, and "for a reason," that he does not A.[16] I conclude that desires or intentions for so-called negative actions do not pose an evident threat to *T3*.

5. A Refinement and a Worry About Circularity

Two issues about *T3* require some discussion. The first is connected to a worry about the causal relevance of mental states and properties and the second to a worry about circularity. They are the primary business of this section.

In the introduction (section 2), I said that in this book (except where I indicate otherwise), claims about the causal powers and roles of motivation-encompassing attitudes should be read, disjunctively, as claims about the causal powers and roles of the physical realizers of the attitudes or of the attitudes themselves (qua attitudes). One way to reformulate *T3* to express the relevant disjunction is as follows:

> *T3**. In physical beings, a noncompound A-focused attitude x of an agent S essentially encompasses motivation in S to A if and only if
> (1) x and its physical realizer constitute a unit u such that, necessarily, if u were to function nondeviantly and effectively, u would be a cause of x's satisfaction, and not merely of some part of x's satisfaction, and u would contribute to x's satisfaction (a) by inducing S to try to A, or to try to bring it about that he A-s, or (b) by inducing S to try to B, or to try to bring it about that he B-s, where trying to B, or trying to bring it about that he B-s, is the focus of x, and
> (2) either (a) there is some possible scenario in which u functions nondeviantly and effectively in S or (b) there is not such a possible scenario and the only relevant differences between x and A-focused attitudes that are parts of units that satisfy conditions (1) and (2a) are that x's focus is or includes an impossible course of action and any differences entailed by this.

Two thoughts lie behind this reformulation. First, what counts as effectiveness of a unit constituted by an attitude and its physical realizer, n, can be determined (partly) by the attitude even if the attitude itself has no causal clout. Second, what is claimed to be necessary for u's functioning nondeviantly and effectively—namely, that u make a contribution of one of the kinds specified—can happen whether n alone does the causal work, x alone does it, or n and x somehow do it jointly.

I now turn to a worry about circularity. In chapter 2, I pointed out that I favor a causal approach to understanding action and explaining actions according to which an event is an action partly in virtue of its having been suitably produced, in part, by certain mental items or their physical realizations. *EMA* attitudes and events of acquiring those attitudes are mental items of the kind at issue here. So what it is for an event to be an action, on the approach I favor, is partly a matter of items of this kind or their physical realizations being involved in the event's production. And I have characterized *EMA* attitudes partly in terms of actions. Is this viciously or vacuously circular?

Consider an analogy: dictionaries indicate—and I agree—that a necessary condition of something's being a photograph is that a camera be involved in its production and that a necessary condition of something's being a working camera is that it have the capacity to play a certain part in the production of photographs. Assuming that dictionaries are in the business of providing definitions, it can be said that dictionaries define "camera" partly in terms of "photograph" and "photograph" partly in terms of "camera." Is this necessarily a bad thing? Well, if "camera" is properly defined at least partly in terms of the primary function of cameras, as seems to be the case, identifying the function of a camera is utterly appropriate in a definition of "camera"; and if an essential feature of photographs is that cameras figure in their production, a definition's capturing that point is equally appropriate. Of course, if all a dictionary said about cameras and photographs is that cameras are things involved in the production of photographs and photographs are things the production of which requires cameras, the dictionary would be useless to anyone who approached it in total ignorance of the meaning of both terms, except insofar as it indicated that one is indispensable in the production of the other. However, dictionaries do say more. They provide relevant information about how cameras are constructed or how they work, and they say that a photograph is an *image* recorded by a camera and reproduced on a photosensitive surface. (The handy *American Heritage Dictionary* even provides a diagram of a camera. A photograph of a camera might have been more interesting.)

EMA attitudes or "units" constituted by those attitudes and their physical realizations may be related to actions in a way analogous to that in which cameras are related to photographs. *If* they are, one should not be surprised to find roughly the kind of intercharacterizability there that one finds in the case of cameras and photographs. Of course, just as one wants a dictionary to say more about what cameras and photographs are than that cameras are involved in the production of photographs and photographs are things the production of which requires cameras, one wants characterizations of *EMA* attitudes (or units constituted by those attitudes and their physical realizations) and actions to say more about what they are than that the former are things involved in the production of the latter and the latter are things the production of which requires the former. I have said considerably more already. For example, chapter 2 provides a relatively detailed story about how acquisitions of proximal intentions (or their neural realizations) may function in the production of actions and a basis for distinguishing actions from deviantly caused nonactions. There is more to come in subsequent chapters.

A brief comment on a bookkeeping issue is in order. In chapter 1 (section 1), I suggested that readers inclined to use "*X* constitutes motivation to *A*" in a relaxed sense need to distinguish between attitudes that essentially constitute motivation to *A* and attitudes that contingently do so. My own preference is to use the expression in such a way that only attitudes that essentially constitute motivation to *A* in fact *constitute* motivation to *A*. Attitudes that are said, in a looser sense, to constitute motivation to *A*—as my desire to have some cash in my wallet tonight may be said to constitute motivation for me to walk to a nearby cash machine—would instead be said to *provide* motivation to *A*, either actually or potentially (see chapter 1, section 3). However, this is more a matter of bookkeeping than something calling for argumentation.

Working from a perspective on intentional action that accords attitudes an important causal/explanatory bearing on intentional action, I have motivated an account of *EMA* attitudes. *EMA* attitudes have, essentially, a functional connection to intentional action, a connection of an eminently motivational kind; and they differ functionally from "truth-seeking" attitudes. At least some *EMA* attitudes—namely, action-desires and intentions—are *paradigmatic* motivational attitudes in human agents. A proper understanding of such attitudes is a significant plank in a fuller account of human motivation and its place in the lives of human agents.

Notes

1. As I mentioned in chapter 1 (note 2), agents sometimes desire to continue doing something that they are currently doing, and the desired continuation is a prospective course of action.

2. In its simplest version, the view at issue reduces an intention to *A* to a pair of attitudes constituted by a desire to *A* that is stronger than any competing desire and a belief that one will *A*. For criticism of this and of various refined versions, see Brand (1984), Bratman (1987), and Mele (1992e).

3. It is intuitively more obvious that intending to *A* precludes such cognitive states (see Mele 1992e, ch. 8). For a radical position see Ludwig (1992); for a reply, see Adams (1997).

4. For an argument that agents who desire to *A* do not always *explicitly* believe that they can *A*, see Mele (1992e, p. 62).

5. I assume a view of the attitudes according to which every belief that *p* is essentially a belief that *p*, every intention to *A* is essentially an intention to *A*, every desire to *A* is essentially a desire to *A*, and so on. So, for example, *S*'s belief that *p* in *S*'s actual situation is not something other than a belief that *p* in any other possible scenario, and *S*'s desire to *A* in his actual situation is not something other than an desire to *A* in any other possible scenario.

6. Frank Jackson (1985) rejects this. For a reply to Jackson, see Mele (1992e, pp. 48–50).

7. A noncognitivist might urge that to form a belief that I ought to *A* is to issue a command to myself (the command to *A*), or, more prosaically, to form an intention to *A*. If intentions to *A* essentially encompass motivation to *A*, a philosopher who makes a case for the thesis that to form beliefs of certain kinds is to form intentions to *A* will have made a case for the thesis that some beliefs essentially encompass motivation to *A*. However, because they are intentions to *A*, these alleged beliefs cannot falsify *T2*. For a putative connection between assenting to an ought-judgment and assenting to a self-command, see Hare (1963, p. 79). I take Hare's references to self-commands to be metaphorical references to intention formation. For the view that intention is a species of judgment, see Davidson (1980, pp. 99–102; cf. Davidson 1985, p. 206). For criticism of the general idea, see Mele (1995a, ch. 2); and for criticism of the idea, in particular, that *intention* is a species of evaluative judgment or belief, see Bratman (1985) and Mele (1987, pp. 43–44).

8. A desire to order pizza and beer and a belief that Ann and Bob are present are not compound attitudes. They do not have pairs of desires or pairs of beliefs as parts. This desire and this belief are noncompound attitudes with compound content.

9. For some subtleties in this connection see Mele (1994).

10. A theorist may try the alternative tack of maintaining that all action-desires—all desires to *A*—are desires to *A* *intentionally*. If this were true, the professor's desire to gain her students' attention would not have been satisfied (since she did not gain it intentionally). However, because some agents with action-desires lack the conceptual sophistication required for desiring to *A* *intentionally*, this tack fails (Mele 1999a).

11. Basically the same point may be made in response to the suggestion that, necessarily, if Rex's belief, that if he tries to *A*, he will *A*, were to function nondeviantly and effectively, it would contribute to its own satisfaction.

12. On the possibility of scenarios in which an agent who has no motivation to *A* nevertheless has motivation to try to *A*, see Mele (1990b and 1994).

13. On "it was intentional on [*S*'s] part that [*S*] did not [*A*]," see Davidson (1985, p. 219).

14. Readers may be curious to know what advocates of the different positions on action individuation have said about negative actions. Lawrence Davis (1979, p. 82) and Thomson (1977, ch. 15), proponents of componential views, deny that there are negative actions. Ginet, another advocate, says that he "cannot think of a case where . . . a strictly negated action-designator" designates an action (1990, p. 21; cf. p. 1, n. 1), but he holds, for example, that "if by smoking yesterday *S failed* to keep her promise," the expression "*S*'s failing to keep her promise yesterday" designates an action (p. 22). Goldman (1970, pp. 47–48), a proponent of the fine-grained view, says that there are negative actions but that he is not sure what to say about them. Davidson (1985, pp. 217–21), an advocate of a coarse-grained view, countenances negative actions in a reply to Vermazen (1985). Vermazen's project there is to extend Davidson's "theory of action . . . to cover the case of negative action" (p. 93).

15. On control of static postural equilibrium, see Horak and Macpherson (1996; cf. Woollacott and Jensen 1996).

16. One might suggest that considerations of moral responsibility support the thesis that there are truly negative actions, perhaps on the hypothesis that people can be morally responsible only for their actions. However, setting aside skepticism about moral responsibility, either people are morally responsible for some nonactions of the sort I have been discussing (e.g., not voting in an election) or, if this is false, that is because the correct view of moral responsibility is that, in this sphere of cases, people are responsible only for actions (or states of mind) that account, in some specifiable way, for the nonactions for which people *seem* to be responsible but, in fact, are not. I favor the former disjunct, but a defense of it is well beyond the scope of this book.

III

STRENGTH AND CONTROL

7

Motivational Strength

Part III of this book explores a pair of related topics, motivational strength (chapter 7) and agents' control (chapter 8). Although I do not offer an account of motivational strength in general, I do defend a position of the motivational strength of an important species of *EMA* attitude. I also defend a principle relating the motivational strength of these attitudes to intentional action, and I show that—even on the (probably false) assumption that determinism is true—the combination of a causal account of action explanation with a plausible principle linking motivational strength to intentional action does not, as some philosophers have claimed it must, render us helpless victims of our strongest desires. Part III adds to the causal view of the place of motivation in human agency taking shape in this book by clarifying two important elements of that view—strength of motivation and control.

In an article expressing skepticism about the popular idea that our desires vary in motivational strength or power, Irving Thalberg asks what he describes, tongue in cheek, as "a disgracefully naive question" (1985, p. 88): "What do causal and any other theorists mean when they rate the strength of our PAs," that is, our "desires, aversions, preferences, schemes, and so forth?" His "guiding question" in the article seems straightforward (p. 98): "What is it for our motivational states to have some degree of power to generate behavior?" Yet, he argues, "as soon as we endeavor to clarify what philosophers of action and drive theorists in psychology mean by motivational strength, we run across one obscurity after another" (p. 103). This chapter answers a more specific version of Thalberg's question.

The answer to be defended is associated with the causal, motivational perspective on the explanation of intentional action that I called "perspective *P*" in the introduction (section 2). Recall that the following two theses are central to this perspective: (1) all intentional actions are *caused* (but not necessarily deterministically so); (2) in the case of any intentional action, a causal explanation framed partly in terms of *mental* items (events or states), including motivational attitudes, is in principle available. Again (see the introduction, section 2), claims about the causal powers and roles of desires are to be read, disjunctively, as claims about the causal powers and roles of the physical realizers of desires *or* of desires themselves (qua desires).

Because perspective *P* is popular and because motivational strength is an important part of the picture, one may doubt that rebutting criticisms of the idea that action-desires, for example, differ in motivational strength can be worth the time and trouble. Yet this is part of what I propose to do. Simply taking for granted that one's philosophical opponents are mistaken is distinctly unphilosophical. More important, not only will careful attention to familiar criticisms of the notion of motivational strength remove obstacles to a broader acceptance of the perspective at issue, but also it will promote a better understanding of the nature and functions of motivation and motivational strength.

1. Some Background

What does the relative motivational strength of action-desires, in particular, amount to? As I argued in chapter 6, any desire to *A*, by its very nature, is an inclination of the agent to *A*. In being an inclination of the kind it is—a kind that my account in chapter 6 of noncompound *A*-focused attitudes that essentially encompass motivation to *A* (*EMA* attitudes) sheds light on—an action-desire constitutes motivation to act. Given this conception of action-desire, it looks as though the motivational strength of an action-desire is the strength of the inclination just identified. What does that amount to? Three answers that have been discussed by theorists skeptical of the idea that desires differ in motivational strength may quickly be dismissed. As far as I know, none of these answers has been advanced by any recent friend of the idea—*the motivational strength idea*, or *MSI* for short.

First, the strength of an action-desire is not the desire's "felt violence or intensity" (Charlton 1988, p. 127; cf. Thalberg 1985, pp. 89–90). Friends of *MSI* claim that a phenomenologically intense desire may be motivationally weaker than a competing desire with little or no phenomenological intensity. Carol, a morally upright psychiatrist who experiences, to her own consternation, a phenomenologically intense urge for a sexual romp with a seductive patient, may have, in a desire that has little phenomenological kick, a stronger inclination to forego that course of action.

Second, an agent's having a stronger desire to *A* than to *B* is not to be identified with his believing that it would be better to *A* than to *B* (cf. Charlton 1988, pp. 127–28). An agent may have the belief in question and yet be more strongly motivated to *B* than to *A*, as in garden-variety cases of akratic action. So, at least, some friends of *MSI* have argued (see, e.g., Mele 1987).

Third, by the motivationally stronger desire or inclination, friends of *MSI* do not mean "the desire which actually prevails, the desire on which the agent acts" (Charlton 1988, p. 127; cf. Thalberg 1985, pp. 89, 99). A graduate student's desire to write a scholarly book before he dies may be stronger than his desire to take a world cruise before he dies even if an unfortunate accident takes his life before he has time to embark on either project. Friends of *MSI* tend to be realists both about attitudes in general (desires, beliefs, intentions, and the like) and about the motivational strength of such attitudes as action-desires. On a realist view of these things, even if no one—including the unfortunate student himself—has behavioral evidence that one of the two desires is stronger than the other, there is a fact of the matter.

Realism about motivation-encompassing states is evident in a definition of "motivation" offered by psychologist John W. Atkinson: "the term *motivation* is used to designate the activated state of the person which occurs when the cues of a situation arouse the expectancy that performance of an act will lead to an incentive for which he has a motive" (1982, p. 25). By "motive," Atkinson means "the disposition within the person to strive to approach a certain class of positive incentives (goals) or to avoid a certain class of negative incentives (threats). The definition of a particular class of incentives constitutes the general aim of a particular motive" (p. 25). Motivation, as Atkinson understands it, may perhaps be identified with action-desire or a species of action-desire if the activated state that he has in mind is a *representational* state or an aspect of such a state.

In the same article, Atkinson writes:

> If a certain kind of activity has been intrinsically satisfying or rewarded . . . there will be an *instigating force* (*F*) for that activity. This will cause a more or less rapid increase in the strength of an inclination to engage in that activity, an *action tendency* (*T*), depending on the magnitude of the force. If a certain kind of activity has been frustrated or punished in the past, there will be an *inhibitory force* (*I*) and a more or less rapid growth in the strength of a disinclination to act or *negation tendency* (*N*). This is a tendency *not* to do it. The duration of exposure to these forces . . . will determine how strong the action or negation tendency becomes. The latter, the tendency not to do something, will produce *resistance* to the activity. It opposes, blocks, dampens, the action tendency. That is, it subtracts from the action tendency to determine the *resultant action tendency*. . . . The resultant action tendency competes with resultant action tendencies for other incompatible activities. The strongest of them is expressed in behavior. (1982, p. 34)

Although this passage certainly has a deterministic ring, a notion of motivational strength need not presuppose determinism (neither global determinism nor local determinism about the workings of the human brain). This is a source of comfort to any libertarians inclined to believe that some desires have more motivational force than others (see Clarke 1994).[1] Even if Carol's desire to strike an offensive person is more powerful than her desire to walk away instead, it may still be open to her to do the latter. Whether this is open depends on what else is true of her and her world. Perhaps an agent can resist a stronger action-desire and act on a weaker one, and perhaps the connection between action-desires and actions is causally indeterministic in such a way that there is only a probability (less than 1) that one will act on the stronger of two action-desires if one acts on either.

2. *MSI* and Vacuity

A desire to *A*, as I said, is an inclination of the agent to *A*. The action-desire's strength is the strength of this inclination. Atkinson (1982) evidently conceives of such inclinations as causal forces. This idea merits exploration. Depending on their preferred metaphysics of mind, some friends of *MSI* may conceive of the causal force of a desire as the force of the physical condition that realizes the desire, whereas others may view the force as a more intimate feature of the desire. Given my purposes in this book, neutrality on this issue is the most productive course.

A common criticism of principles linking the motivational strength of action-desires to intentional action—and an indirect criticism of *MSI* itself—is that such principles are vacuous because there is no way to gauge the relative forces or strengths of an agent's desire to *A* and his desire to *B* aside from seeing whether he does *A* or *B* (Charlton 1988, p. 127; Gosling 1990, p. 175; Thalberg 1985, pp. 96–99). This objection requires attention. Suppose it is claimed that my arms are stronger than my daughter's arms or that my son's car is faster than mine. We can stage contests to test these claims—relevant weightlifting contests and drag races. But the claims can be tested in other ways, too; for example, we can measure the size of relevant muscles and examine mechanical features of the motionless cars. Since action-desires are inner states and since their strength or force is not to be identified with their phenomenological qualities (e.g., their "felt violence or intensity"; Charlton 1988, p. 127), it may seem that there is, in principle, no possible way to gauge relative strength aside from seeing what the agent does. But is this true?

If one were concerned to measure the force or strength of an action-desire in some other way, how might one proceed? One who holds a certain view about the neurophysiological realization of states of mind might take electrophysiological readings.[2] (Obviously, judgments about what mental phenomena are indicated by the electrical phenomena require a background that includes assumptions about the meanings of mental predicates and past observations of extracranial occurrences statistically correlated with various types of electrical reading.) If action-desires are realized in the brain, this procedure need not be misguided *in principle*, even if current technology is not up to the task. Hypothetical readings might indicate the relative force or strength of contemporaneous action-desires. And what would they be indicating in indicating this? In a properly functioning agent, they would indicate the relative causal capacity of each desire (or its neural realizer) to issue in a corresponding attempt, given how the agent is constituted.[3]

It should also be observed that even if seeing whether an agent does *A* or *B* is, *in fact*, our only way of gauging the relative motivational strengths of his competing desires to *A* and to *B*, this does not entail that motivational strength is an empty notion. Imagine a planet on which there are poisonous plants but no one with even a minimal knowledge of chemistry. Some inhabitants of this planet claim that eating a gram of a plant of kind *x* causes a higher fever than eating a gram of a plant of kind *y* because *x*-s contain a more potent or stronger poison than *y*-s. Their only way of gauging the relative strength of poisons requires seeing how ill poison eaters become. But their claim is not vacuous. As it happens, they are embroiled in a bitter dispute with others who contend that there are no poisonous plants and that the fevers are caused directly by

God, who has issued rules against eating certain plants. God takes different degrees of offense at the eating of different kinds of plant and directly causes proportional illness as punishment. When chemists finally emerge in that world, they provide considerable support for the claim of the former group of inhabitants.

It might be claimed that since there are, in fact, no appropriate physiological tests of motivational strength, it is likely that principles linking motivational strength to intentional action are held on conceptual grounds and that conceptual principles of this kind are useless for explanatory purposes. This claim merits consideration, too.

It is, I think, a conceptual truth that an agent's acting intentionally at a time requires his having some relevant purpose or objective at that time. Suppose it were shown, on conceptual grounds, that desiring or some motivational attitude like desiring is an essential ingredient in having a purpose or objective of the relevant sort. (Barbells and automobiles have purposes of another sort.) Then motivational attitudes would have a firm place in any conceptual scheme that includes intentional actions (cf. Mele 1992e, pp. 17–25, 39–42). Suppose it were also shown, again on conceptual grounds, that proper *explanations* of intentional actions must appeal to or presuppose *causal* roles of motivational attitudes or of the neurophysiological states that realize them, if they are so realized (see chapter 2). For example, it might be shown that we can make sense of an agent's acting *for* a particular reason or purpose only on the assumption that motivational attitudes associated with the agent's having the particular reason or purpose—or the physical realizers of those attitudes, if the attitudes are so realized—make a causal contribution to the pertinent intentional action. Then motivational strength apparently would gain a foothold, too.

It is often observed by opponents of *MSI* that the claim that an agent was most strongly motivated to *A* at the time does not explain why he *A*-ed (see, e.g., Thalberg 1985, p. 97). I agree. And some friends of *MSI* might say that we do not regard the claim as explaining why the agent *A*-ed precisely because we *take it for granted* that agents do, or at least try to do, what they are most strongly motivated to do at the time. Now, imagine that, in light of both the agent's reasons and other features of the case, we learn *why* he was more strongly motivated (i.e., wanted more) at the time to *A* then than to do anything else. For example, we learn why an agent who bought a certain computer at *t* wanted more to do that at *t* than to do anything else at *t*. Would we be satisfied that we understood why he bought that computer? Perhaps so, at least normally. And, as I pointed out elsewhere, "when such information does satisfy us, there is a background presumption at work, namely, that the agent *A*-ed *because* (in some sense) that is what he wanted most to do at the time. If his wanting most to *A* were *irrelevant* to his *A*-ing, the explanation that we have of his wanting most to *A* would also be irrelevant to his *A*-ing, or, at best, tangentially relevant" (Mele 1992e, p. 83). If this is right, principles linking motivational strength to intentional action may have explanatory significance for intentional action. They may articulate background presumptions about intentional action in the context of which people offer explanations of particular intentional actions in terms of such attitudes as desires, beliefs, and intentions. One who presupposes the existence of a tight connection between motivational strength and intentional action would take information about why an agent was most strongly motivated to do what he did to improve one's understanding of why he did it.

3. *MSI* and Associated Principles

Some worries about *MSI* are prompted by particular principles linking motivational strength to action. Donald Davidson has advanced the following principle:

> *P1*. If an agent wants to do *x* more than he wants to do *y* and he believes himself free to do either *x* or *y*, then he will intentionally do *x* if he does either *x* or *y* intentionally. (1980, p. 23)

If wanting to do one thing more than one wants to do another is a matter of relative motivational strength, *P1* is a principle of the kind at issue.

Elsewhere, I showed that *P1* is false on several counts (Mele 1992e, ch. 3). Attention to a certain defect in *P1* will provide background for a replacement. Consider the following case.[4] Mike is psychologically so constituted that the strengths of his action-desires are always in line with his evaluations of the objects of those desires. If he has a desire to *A* and a desire to *B*, and he gives his *A*-ing a higher evaluative rating than his *B*-ing, then his desire to *A* is stronger than his desire to *B*. Mike, a professional basketball player, now has the option of attempting either of two slam-dunks—a "spectacular" dunk and a "fancy" dunk—in a charitable fund-raising event. He is allowed only one attempt. The prizes for successful execution of the dunks are $12,000 for the spectacular one and $10,000 for the fancy one, to be paid to Mike's favorite charity.

Owing to mundane financial considerations, Mike ranks successfully executing the spectacular $12,000 dunk (*D1*) higher than successfully executing the fancy $10,000 dunk (*D2*). He also ranks the former higher than attempting *D1* and than attempting *D2*. Thus, Mike (given the pertinent psychological fact about him) desires successfully executing *D1* more strongly than he desires any of the following: successfully executing *D2*, attempting *D1*, and attempting *D2*.

Mike estimates his chance of successfully executing *D1* (should he attempt *D1*) at 80% and his chance of successfully executing *D2* (should he attempt *D2*) at 99%. He is interested in the two potential dunks only as means of earning money for his favorite charity. Being a good Bayesian, he judges that it would be better to attempt *D2* than to attempt *D1*. Consequently, given the kind of person Mike is, his desire to attempt *D2* is stronger than his desire to attempt *D1*. Accordingly, he attempts *D2*. (To the delight of all concerned, his attempt is successful.)

If this case is coherent, it falsifies *P1*. Mike attempts *D2* even though, by hypothesis, his desire successfully to execute *D1* is stronger than his desire to attempt *D2*. And the scenario is coherent. Mike's rating successfully executing *D1* higher than attempting *D2* is utterly unproblematic. After all, the payoff for the former is $12,000 and the latter merely gains him a chance at $10,000—a 99% chance, in his opinion. And since the strengths of Mike's action-desires always fall in line with his evaluations of the objects of those desires, it should not be puzzling that his desire successfully to execute *D1* is stronger than his desire to attempt *D2*. Furthermore, given that Mike is concerned only with the charitable, financial aspects of his choice and is a reasonable agent, and given his estimates of the likelihood of success regarding the two dunks, we fully expect him to attempt *D2*.

A better formulation of the principle at issue would yield the result that Mike attempts the dunk that he is most strongly motivated to attempt, given that he (intentionally) attempts either.[5] The strengths of his desires successfully to execute *D1* and successfully to execute *D2* are relevant to which dunk he attempts. But, from the perspective that motivates the principle at issue, they are relevant because of their contribution to the strengths of his desires to attempt these dunks. In the present case, the strengths of the latter desires are a consequence of the strengths of Mike's desires for successful execution of the dunks and his estimates of his chances of success, given an attempt.

The desires directly at issue in principles like *P1* are what I term *proximal* action-desires—desires to *A* straightaway, to *A* beginning straightaway, or to continue doing something that one is already doing. If a refined principle along the lines of *P1* is correct, then, other things being equal and given that Mike has a proximal desire to attempt *D2*, whether he successfully executes *D1* straightaway depends on his having a proximal desire to attempt *D1* that is stronger than his competing desire to attempt *D2*. According to a refined principle, if the latter desire is stronger, then, other things being equal, he will not attempt *D1* and therefore will not successfully execute *D1*.

In many cases, as I observed in chapter 1, an agent who *A*-s in order to *B* also *B*-s in order to *C*, *C*-s in order to *D*, and so on. In the example I offered, Sam might flip a switch in order to illuminate the room, in order to make it easier to find his car keys, in order to improve his chances of getting to work on time. Suppose that Sam has a proximal desire to improve his chances of getting to work on time and that his plan for that is the one just sketched. Suppose also that, because he desires not to wake his children, he has a proximal desire not to illuminate his room and, accordingly, a proximal desire not to flip the switch. According to a refined version of *P1*, the strength of any proximal desire Sam may have to flip the switch is directly relevant, other things being equal, to whether he intentionally flips the switch now, and the strength of his proximal desire to improve his chances of getting to work on time is only indirectly relevant to whether he flips the switch.

Some technical terminology will prove useful in formulating a promising successor to *P1*. When and only when the strength of an agent's proximal desire to *A* is less directly relevant to whether he intentionally *A*-s or at least tries to *A* than is the strength of some competing proximal action-desire of his or some competing proximal desire of his for a not-doing of his, his proximal desire to *A* is *trumped* by that competing desire. Thus, Mike's proximal desire successfully to execute *D1*, but not his proximal desire to attempt to execute *D1*, is trumped by his desire to attempt *D2*; and Sam's proximal desire to improve his chances of getting to work on time, but not his proximal desire to flip the switch, is trumped by his proximal desire not to flip the switch. Any proximal action-desire that is not trumped by any pertinent desire is *un-trumped*. A principle relating only agents' strongest *untrumped* proximal action-desires to intentional action (trumped proximal desires being treated as having only an indirect relevance) will avoid the problem encountered in Mike's case.[6]

At the end of this section, I formulate a principle of this kind. Three issues require prior attention: the biasing of mechanisms linking proximal action-desires to associated attempts, desires for not-doings, and a question about the conceptual connection between desiring and intending. I examine each in turn.

Consider scenarios in which an agent's brain, but not the realizer of his untrumped proximal desire to *A*, is tinkered with in such a way as to block or attenuate the connection between that realizer and an attempt appropriate to that desire. I mentioned one such scenario in chapter 6 (section 1). Without altering the neural realization of an agent's desire to raise his arm, a neuroscientist tinkers with the agent's brain in such a way that the desire's neural realization cannot play a role in the production of the agent's trying to raise his arm. In a related scenario, the tinkering results in a greatly reduced chance of an appropriate attempt, rather than no chance at all: a well-placed neural randomizer might turn the trick.

One way to respond to such cases is to refine one's picture of an untrumped proximal action-desire's neural realization in such a way that a neurally realized attitude does not count as a desire of *this* kind in the absence of neural conditions of the kind that the tinkering eliminates. This response has the result that, in fact, the agent under consideration lacks an untrumped proximal action-desire. A theorist who favors this response may claim that what the agent lacks is an action-desire or, instead, may augment the account I offered of what it is for a proximal action-desire to be *untrumped*. The main problem with the claim that the manipulated agent lacks the action-desire is the apparent conceptual possibility of the conjunction of action-desires and blockage of the sort in question. Seemingly, it is conceptually possible that some action-desires are, as it were, analogues of sugar cubes encased in insoluble substances (see chapter 6, section 1). The strategy of augmenting my account of untrumpedness amounts to finding a way to isolate a pertinent subset of untrumped proximal action-desires, but the isolation can be handled in another way.

The capacity of a desire's realizer to play a role in producing an attempt appropriate to that desire depends on intrinsic properties of the realizer and other properties of the agent. The other properties specifically at issue here concern mechanisms linking realizations of untrumped proximal action-desires with attempts. When these mechanisms themselves do not favor attempts appropriate to any of the relevant desires over attempts appropriate to any of the others, the desires may be termed *bias free*.[7] Both bias-freeness and untrumpedness have a place in the successor to Davidson's (1980) *P1* formulated below.

I turn now to desires for not-doings. Such desires, like other desires, can be in the positive or negative motivational bases (see chapter 1, section 3) of bias-free untrumped proximal action-desires. For example, a desire not to *A* can help rationalize—and contribute to the strength of—a desire to do something to ensure that, to make it the case that, or to increase the probability that one does not *A*, including untrumped proximal desires of this kind. A desire not to smoke today may be in the positive motivational base of an untrumped proximal desire to throw one's cigarettes away. Furthermore, desires for not-doings may help motivate decisions or intentions that help produce untrumped proximal action-desires. For example, partly because he wants not to offend his vegan dinner companions, Bob may decide to look for something both tempting and meatless on the menu. In the end, Bob's strongest untrumped proximal desire may be to order a vegetarian pizza, and that fact may be explained in part by the negative desire I have mentioned. None of this is problematic, but a problem looms.

In a long passage quoted in section 1, Atkinson implicitly treats desires not to *A* as "negaction tendencies": a tendency of this kind "opposes, blocks, dampens the [opposed] action tendency" (1982, p. 34). In chapter 6 (section 4), I defended the idea that no genuine not-doing is an action. Atkinson's implicit treatment of desires for not-doings coheres with this. Now, agents' desires not to A would be expected to attenuate any desires to A that they may have, and the stronger the negative desire, the greater one expects the attenuating effect to be. Seemingly, when agents have desires not to A that are stronger than their desires to A, one may reasonably expect the attenuation to be sufficiently great that, normally, some relevant action-desire or other that they have will be stronger than their desires to A.

One may even think that having a stronger desire not to A than to A is impossible, on the grounds that there would be no desire to A in that case; the thought may be that the strength of the desire to A decreases as the strength of the desire not to A increases—by the same amount—and at the point at which the two desires would be equally strong, if they both were to persist, the positive desire must vanish. This thought is problematic. An agent who desires to smoke now, because of modest nicotine deprivation, may also desire not to smoke now, because he desires to please his companions. According to the line of thought just sketched, the desires cannot have the same strength, and the negative desire cannot be stronger than the positive one (for that allegedly entails the nonexistence of the positive one). But if negative desires have the alleged effect on positive desires, it would be extremely difficult to see why positive desires would not have the same effect on negative desires, so that an allegedly stronger positive desire is inconsistent with the existence of a negative counterpart. If an agent cannot simultaneously have a desire to A and a desire not to A that have the same strength or different strengths, the possibility of his having a desire to A while also having a desire not to A is still open, provided that the strengths of the two desires are incommensurable. However, a case for this incommensurability would have to be made.

Just as agents have desires for courses of action that they know are incompatible with one another (e.g., Ann's watching a midnight movie with her daughter tonight at one end of town and her attending a midnight concert with her son tonight at the other end of town), they may desire to A while also desiring not to A. Given this possibility, what should be said about it?

Is a principle asserting that, whenever we act intentionally, we act on our strongest bias-free untrumped proximal action-desire falsified by some cases in which an agent's strongest such desire is to A and he desires even more strongly not to A? Suppose that although Al wants to smoke now more than he wants to do anything else now, he also wants not to smoke now more than he wants to smoke now. From this alone it does not follow that Al does not proceed to smoke. Imagine that, as Al realizes, he will not proceed to smoke only if he immediately takes steps to see to it that he refrains from smoking. He cannot count on his desire not to smoke simply to win out, as he recognizes, and his best method for resisting the urge, as he knows, is a certain self-control technique his therapist has recommended. Now, imagine that, partly because he believes his chance of successfully resisting the urge is slim, although Al has a desire to see to it that he does not smoke, that desire is weaker than his desire to smoke and than his desire not to see to it that he does not smoke. Then, given the details of the case, it is plausible that, if Al proceeds to do something intentionally, he proceeds to smoke, or at least to try to smoke, despite his having a stronger desire not to smoke. The latter desire is an analogue of a trumped proximal action-desire. In the circumstances, its winning out depends on Al's having an instrumental desire to see to it that he does not smoke, and the latter desire—which is more directly relevant to whether Al smokes or not—may be too weak to succeed.

This is not to say that the question with which I opened the preceding paragraph should be answered in the negative. Perhaps a desire for a not-doing that is an analogue of an untrumped proximal action-desire can turn the trick. By analogy with my accounts of trumped and untrumped proximal action-desires, I offer the following accounts. When and only when the strength of an agent's proximal desire not to *A* is less directly relevant to whether he intentionally (or for a reason) does not *A* than is the strength of some competing proximal action-desire of his or some competing proximal desire of his for a not-doing of his, his proximal desire to *A* is *trumped* by that competing desire. Any proximal desire for a relevant not-doing that is not trumped by any pertinent desire is *untrumped*.

Modify the preceding case with the supposition that Al's proximal desire not to smoke is untrumped. Does this yield a counterexample to the assertion that whenever agents act intentionally, they act on their strongest bias-free untrumped proximal action-desire? It is not obvious that the answer is yes. Suppose that Al proceeds to act on his second-strongest proximal action-desire—a desire to sip his coffee, say—and that he does not smoke. *How* did his desire not to smoke succeed? Perhaps partly by helping to produce a proximal intention not to smoke that affected mechanisms linking realizations of untrumped proximal action-desires and attempts in such a way as to "bias" the mechanisms against Al's desire to smoke. For example, Al's acquiring that intention might have effects that block motor processing that would otherwise have activated motoneurons appropriate for a smoking (cf. chapter 8, section 2, on Libet's 1985 position on the "vetoing" of urges). However, there is no need for further speculation about this matter. A successor to Davidson's (1980) *P1* may include a proviso for untrumped desires for not-doings.

The third issue I wish to discuss before offering a successor to *P1* is a question about a conceptual connection between desiring and intending that received some attention in chapter 1 (section 5). In a context in which one is free to define "a desire to *A*" as "any *A*-focused attitude that constitutes motivation to *A*," one may happily treat intentions to *A* as a special, executive kind of desire to *A*, and one may distinguish between "mere" desires to *A*—desires to *A* that are not intentions to *A*—and intentions to *A*. The nature of some of the disputes that I have entered in this book precludes such freedom. My arguments for the irreducibility of intentions to *A* to other attitudes, including compound attitudes having desires to *A* as constituents, are a matter of record (Mele 1992e, chs. 8 and 9), and I do not rehearse them here. Of course, that intentions to *A* are irreducible to complexes of other attitudes is consistent with their having desires to *A* as constituents. Intentions to *A* might encompass desires to *A* and have an irreducible remainder. The apparent oddness of the assertion that someone intends to *A* but does not want or desire to *A*—even instrumentally so—may be offered as support for the claim that intentions to *A* necessarily encompass desires to *A*. Some philosophers certainly do not find the negative assertion at issue at all odd (e.g., Schueler 1995; see chapter 1, section 6 above), owing to their conception of desire. Those who find it extremely odd—in fact, self-contradictory—may understand "does not want to *A*" to mean "has no motivation to *A*" or "has no motivation-encompassing attitude toward *A*-ing" (see W. Davis 1997, pp. 137–38). However, I cannot help myself to this conception of wanting or desiring; if I am right, intentions to *A* necessarily encompass motivation to *A*, but for the purposes of this book, whether they encompass desires to *A* is a substantive question.

Suppose that someone who does not accept the broad reading of "does not want to *A*" just mentioned nevertheless finds the assertion that *S* intends to *A* but does not want to *A* very strange. Such a person may be confusing "does not want to *A*" with "wants not to *A*," but I will suppose that this is not so. How might the person's reaction to the assertion be accounted for? It may normally happen that desires to *A* play a causal role in the production of intentions to *A* and that the desires persist at least as long as the intentions do (see Mele 1992e, pp. 72–77, 143, 168–69, 176–77, 190–91). When this happens, the agent who intends to *A* does desire or want to *A*, even if the intention does not have the desire or want as a constituent. One who is in the business of accounting for the assertion's having a strange ring to my imaginary auditor may point out that, given one's scant information about the auditor, the strangeness may possibly be explained by the auditor's sensitivity to a normal causal connection rather than a constitutive one.

Gilbert Harman argues that "intentions have an inertia that allows them to survive the desires on which they were originally based" (1976, p. 459). Here is a modified version of his example. Because Sam is hungry and likes steak, he desires to order and eat a steak. Because he is hungry and likes ribs, he also desires to order and eat some ribs. He does not want to eat both steak and ribs, so he gives the matter a little thought. Eventually, he decides in favor of steak; that is (see chapter 9), he forms an intention to order and eat a steak. As Harman sees it, after a point Sam may intend to finish his steak even though his desire for steak has been satisfied and it is false that he wants to finish his steak. Is this true? On the very broad interpretation of wanting that I mentioned, the answer is no—at least if intentions to *A* encompass motivation to *A*. But, again, one cannot simply help oneself to that interpretation in the relevant dialectical context (i.e., the context of this book); an argument is required. If desires or wants are real states of mind and, moreover, "a desire to *A*" means something more specific than "any positive motivation-encompassing attitude toward *A*-ing," the answer may be yes. Arguably, although Sam has, in his intention to finish his steak, motivation to finish it, he has no desire or want to finish it. Perhaps, in addition to having no desire to finish it, he even has a weak desire not to finish it because he is beginning to feel a bit bloated, but his intention carries the day.[8]

Another kind of scenario merits attention. Al loves beer, especially dark beer. As he is driving home, he catches sight of a great sale on kegs of Guinness in a shop window. He parks his car and walks into the shop to buy a keg. Al intends to buy a keg of Guinness. Might his psychological makeup be such that his noticing the sale elicited an intention to buy some Guinness without *first* eliciting a desire to do so? I do not see why not. Of course, it may be claimed that although his acquiring the intention need not be preceded by his acquiring the desire at issue, *in* acquiring the intention, he acquires the desire, the desire being a constituent of the intention. As evidence for this, it might be pointed out that it would be absurdly strange to say of a beer lover like Al that he does not desire or want to buy the Guinness. Now, saying this would indeed be strange, but in a formal context the strangeness can perhaps be explained away. One can argue that

Al's attitude toward buying the beer has a settling, executive nature that the term "desire" (or "want") does not capture, that the attitude has an executive function that desires or wants lack, and that if "desire" or "want" is not being used to mean "any motivation-encompassing attitude," it is at least not *absurd* to say that it is true that Al intends to buy the beer and false that he desires to buy it. Intending to A may be to desiring to A roughly as insisting that *p* is to intimating that *p*—more robust without encompassing its less robust counterpart. On my own view, the comparative robustness of intention is a matter, not of its having greater motivational strength than "mere" desire, but of its having a tighter functional connection to action than "mere" desire (Mele 1992e, chs. 9 and 10).

I have no wish to assert that intentions to A do not necessarily encompass desires to A. But I want to leave open the possibility that they do not. In this open-minded spirit and with the idea of untrumped desires in place, I offer the following principle for consideration:

> *Mu.* Assuming bias-free desires and the absence of relevant intentions thus far, if, at a time, an agent has an untrumped proximal desire to A that is stronger than any untrumped proximal desire that he has to do anything else and than any untrumped proximal desire that he has for a relevant not-doing, he proceeds to A or at least to try to A then, provided that he proceeds to do something intentionally then.[9]

In the following section, I discuss the meaning of "stronger" in *Mu.* Readers who find the tone of *Mu* unacceptably deterministic are invited to consider the following variant:

> *Mup.* Assuming bias-free desires and the absence of relevant intentions thus far, an agent's having, at a time, an untrumped proximal desire to A that is stronger than any untrumped proximal desire that he has to do anything else and than any untrumped proximal desire that he has for a relevant not-doing makes it more probable that he proceeds to A or at least to try to A then than that he proceeds to do anything else then, given that he proceeds to do something intentionally then.[10]

4. Action-Desires and Ordinary Dispositions

Action-desires may be instructively compared with familiar dispositions—for example, fragility and elasticity. David Lewis writes, "I take for granted that a disposition requires a certain causal basis: one has the disposition iff one has a property that occupies a certain causal role" (1986, pp. 223–24). (This is not to say that dispositions of the same type must have bases of the same type. To use Lewis's example (p. 224), the basis of one person's immunity to a certain virus might be his having certain antibodies, whereas the basis in someone else is "his possession of dormant antibody makers.") Consider a fragile vase. If its fragility is manifested in a shattering, the basis of its fragility (e.g., its crystalline structure) is a *cause* of this manifestation (p. 224). And even if its fragility is never manifested, the basis of its fragility is still present and capable of playing the pertinent causal role under suitable conditions. Lewis voices neutrality on the question whether the disposition is to be identified with its basis (p. 224).[11] If a disposition is identical with its basis, it occupies whatever causal role its basis occupies; if a disposition is distinct from its basis and the causal role is lodged in the basis, this is not a role that the disposition itself has.

In human beings and other animals with action-desires, such desires are presumably realized physically. But then, just as the fact that one vase is more fragile than another is grounded in differences in the respective physical bases of the fragility of the two vases (e.g., crystalline structures), the fact (if it is a fact) that one member of a pair of contemporaneous action-desires of mine is stronger than another is presumably grounded in differences in the respective physical bases of the strength of the two desires. If there are action-desires, perhaps a future science will uncover the physical bases of their strength and the physical grounds of relative desire-strength. It may be reasonably suggested that we can conceive of the relative strength of a human agent's action-desires at a given time as analogous, in the respect mentioned, to the relative fragility of the vases stored in my son's kitchen and the relative elasticity of the various rubber bands in my desk drawer: there is a physical basis in each case, and comparative truths about the fragility, the elasticity, and the motivational strength of the relevant items are grounded in differences in the physical bases.

To say that vase x is fragile is to say something more like 2 than like 1:

1. If x were struck a hard blow, it would shatter.
2. X is so constituted that 1.

And to say that vase x is more fragile than vase y is to say something more like 4 than like 3:

3. There is some range of forces such that if x and y were struck with the same force in that range, in the same way, and under the same conditions, x would shatter and y would not.
4. X and y are so constituted that 3.

Similarly, to say that my desire to A is stronger than my contemporaneous desire to B is to say something more like 6 than like 5:

5. If I were to act from either desire, I would act from my desire to A.
6. The two desires are so constituted or so realized that 5.[12]

So what might some causal theorist about the explanation of actions have in mind in claiming that, at t, my untrumped proximal desire to A is stronger than any untrumped proximal desire I have to do anything else? Perhaps this:

> *CT.* The physical realizers of the pertinent action-desires have physical properties suitable for playing a certain causal role in me—a role that amounts to contributing to the production of an attempt that is appropriate to the action-desire they realize—and the pertinent realizers differ internally in such a way that, assuming bias-free desires, the absence of relevant intentions thus far, and the absence of any stronger untrumped proximal desire for a relevant not-doing, if, at t, I were to proceed to make an attempt appropriate to any of my pertinent untrumped proximal action-desires because of relevant properties of the desire's realizer, I would proceed to make one appropriate to my desire to A (or it is *more probable* that I would make one appropriate to my desire to A than that I would make any other attempt).

Suggestion *CT* includes the following theses: agents like us have action-desires, including bias-free, untrumped proximal action-desires; these desires are realized in physical states; the realizing states have physical properties suitable for playing an action-causing role; in agents like us, an action-desire's strength is grounded in physical features of the physical state that realizes the desire; differences in the strengths of a human agent's contemporaneous action-desires are grounded in physical differences in the realizing states. And the suggestion links the concepts of desire-strength and intentional action. The relative *strength* of contemporaneous bias-free untrumped proximal action-desires of mine is conceived here partly in terms of what I (probably) would *attempt to do* at the time if I were to make an attempt appropriate to any such desires of mine because of relevant properties of the bases of these desires.

To be sure, the suggestion raises a number of difficult issues, not the least of which is the mind-body problem. But the challenge that Thalberg (1985) and others pose for causal theorists is to say what they mean in asserting that an agent's desires have different motivational strengths, and the suggestion offers a coherent interpretation of the assertion as it applies to untrumped proximal action-desires. Opponents of *MSI*—the idea that desires differ in motivational strength—now have something that they can try to falsify. Complaints about the obscurity of *MSI* can be replaced by arguments for the falsity of this application of *MSI*.

The interpretation that I have offered of the idea that untrumped proximal action-desires vary in motivational strength undermines the charge that motivational strength is an empty notion and the objection that the notion is irremediably obscure. Bias-free desires of this kind are more tightly linked to intentional action than are other desires. They are suited for the role that Atkinson (1982) assigns to resultant action tendencies (see section 1), and they are desires of the kind that any viable version of Davidson's (1980) *P1*, deterministic or otherwise, would call for (see section 2).

5. *MSI* and Agency

Does suggestion *CT* diminish our agency by leaving no room for intentions or practical reasoning in the production of intentional actions? Not at all. I myself favor the view that attempting to *A* requires a relevant intention and that action-desires (or their physical realizers) contribute variously to corresponding intentional actions by contributing to the formation or acquisition of corresponding intentions or by providing enabling conditions of the effectiveness of intentions (Mele 1992e, pp. 72–77 and ch. 10).[13] This idea is plainly consistent with suggestion *CT*. The causal role mentioned there—"a role that amounts to contributing to the production of an attempt that is appropriate to the action-desire"—may include the two roles just identified. Furthermore, the formation or acquisition of an intention may influence the strength of relevant desires (Mele 1992e, p. 190).

Suggestion *CT* is also compatible with the idea that our practical reasoning often plays an important role in generating untrumped action-desires and has a considerable influence on their strength. Untrumped action-desires for means presumably often issue partly from practical means-end reasoning, and as I have already illustrated, the strengths of our untrumped action-desires for means are influenced by our assessments of the chance that we will achieve the end if we attempt the means. Further-more, suggestion *CT* is compatible with its being the case that the strength of our in-trinsic desires (desires for ends) is subject to the influence of critical reflection and self-assessment (see Mele 1995a, pp. 118–21). For the most part, desires—including intrinsic desires—do not come equipped with immutable strengths, or so I have ar-gued elsewhere (Mele 1992e, ch. 4). I return to this point in chapter 8.

The suggestion is also compatible with a libertarian view of agency. Not all liber-tarians reject the idea that free actions are caused, and those who countenance the cau-sation of free actions are not all agent causationists (see Kane 1996).[14] The worry is about deterministic causation, and suggestion *CT* makes no commitment to the thesis that intentional actions are deterministically caused.

My purpose in this chapter has been to give the idea that some of our desires are motivationally stronger than others (*MSI*) a relatively precise content in one major application—its application to bias-free, untrumped proximal action-desires. A thor-ough defense of *MSI* would feature a detailed argument for the thesis that proper explanations of intentional actions are *causal* explanations and that motivation-encompassing attitudes have a significant place in such explanations. Support for *MSI* would also be found in a persuasive defense of a familiar causal view of the *nature* of action (the view that actions are events with a psychocausal history of a certain kind). In chapter 2, I defended causalism in both connections (see also Mele 1992e, 1997a, and 1997b). I have not defended a general account of motivational strength, that is, an account of motivational strength for motivation-constituting attitudes of all kinds. My aims for the present chapter are satisfied if I have refuted the major charges against *MSI* and have given skeptics about *MSI* something concrete to evaluate. Of course, a natural thought about motivation-constituting attitudes of other kinds is, very roughly, that their motivational strength lies in their capacity to combine with subjec-tive probabilities to influence the strengths of pertinent bias-free untrumped proximal action-desires.

Notes

1. For the uninitiated, libertarianism is the conjunction of incompatibilism and the assertion that there are free actions, including decisions. Incompatibilism is the thesis that determinism is incompatible with there being free actions.

2. Physiologist Benjamin Libet (1985) uses such readings to identify the onset of states that he conceives of as intentions of which the agent is not conscious. Producing separate electro-physiological readings for contemporaneous action-desires in an agent would require insight into how desires are realized. It would be presumptuous to insist that this is *conceptually* im-possible. (Readers inclined to regard an electrophysiological approach to the study of our men-tal life as largely a philosophical fantasy should look at the articles in Rugg and Coles 1995.)

3. In a hypothetical agent who, owing to manipulation, cannot try to act as he desires to act, matters are more complicated.

4. For a more detailed version of an objection of this kind, see Mele (1992e, pp. 53–57, 61).

5. Not all successful counterexamples to Davidson's *P1* need feature a divergence between the strength of one's motivation to *A* and the strength of one's motivation to attempt to *A* (see Mele 1992e, pp. 54–57).

6. As I understand trumping, any functional difference between intentions and desires is irrelevant. For example, just as Mike's desire to try *D2* does not trump his desire to try *D1*, his intention to try *D2* also does not trump that desire.

7. For a useful discussion of cases in which pertinent mechanisms are biased in favor of a desire, see Clarke (1994, pp. 6–9).

8. Robert Audi (2001, p. 73) suggests that in a case of the kind at issue the agent desires, irrationally, to continue eating.

9. As I observe elsewhere, "Desires to *A*, where *A* is not a *trying* to do something, need not always be accompanied by a desire to *try* to *A* in order to result in an intentional *A*-ing. Generally, if we are not entertaining doubts about the prospects of our succeeding in *A*-ing (*A* being something that we want to do), we have no desire specifically to try to *A*" (Mele 1992e, p. 61). However, it should be noted that even a desire to perform an action, *A*, that one can perform "at will" can be trumped. Here is an illustration. Sam has been tricked into believing (falsely) that at least one of his arms is temporarily paralyzed and that there is a good chance that they both are: he believes that there is a 90% chance that his right arm is paralyzed and a 70% chance that his left arm is. Sam is offered $100 for raising his right arm when his straitjacket is removed and $50 for raising his left arm then, on the condition that he does not simultaneously try to raise each arm. Wanting $100 more than $50, Sam wants to raise his right arm more than his left. But being a good Bayesian, he raises his left arm. He wants to try to do that more than he wants to try to raise his right arm. In special circumstances of this kind, a desire for an action, *A*, that one can perform at will is trumped by a desire to try to *B*, and if the former desire issues in the agent's intentionally *A*-ing, it does so in a way that depends on his having a distinct instrumental, proximal desire to *try* to *A*.

10. Again, probabilistic causation is an option.

11. For a defense of nonidentity, see Prior (1985).

12. I am not suggesting that the even-numbered statements are proper analyses of the relevant notions but only that they are significantly closer to the mark than their odd-numbered counterparts.

13. For stylistic reasons, I have suppressed references to the physical realizers of intentions. On (action-) desires as dispositions to form or acquire intentions, see Brand (1984, p. 127), Castañeda (1975, p. 284), Harman (1976, p. 437), and Mele (1992e, pp. 72–77, 143, 177).

14. Even an agent causationist may hold that free actions are produced by mental states or events in conjunction with irreducible agent causation (Clarke 1996).

8

Control and Self-Control

___

It is sometimes claimed that theses like *Mu* in chapter 7 entail that we are at the mercy of whatever desire happens to be strongest. I have argued elsewhere that this claim is false (Mele 1987, ch. 5; 1992e, ch. 4; 1995a, ch. 3; 1996b). This chapter provides another route to that conclusion, but my primary aim here is to show how some well-known experiments by physiologist Benjamin Libet bear on this issue. Philosophical discussion of these experiments has focused on Libet's claims about consciousness.[1] The significance of these experiments for the topics of motivation and agential control also merits close attention.

In section 1, I explain the need to modify *Mu* for the purposes of the present chapter and offer a tentative variant for consideration. Partly because of issues about the timing of relevant events made salient by Libet's work (interpreted in section 2), the variant itself requires revision. I address that matter in section 3. In section 4, I venture well beyond the laboratory setting of Libet's experiments and apply the more direct results of my discussion to relatively ordinary cases of self-control.

1. Background

In some cases, exercising self-control in support of one's acting as one judges best is unproblematic. Ted thinks that he spends entirely too much time watching television. At the moment, he is more strongly motivated to bring it about that he does not watch television tomorrow than not to bring this about, and he hits on the following strategy: he drives to a remote cabin that is not wired for television. But consider Ian, who is now more strongly motivated to continue watching a golf tournament on television than he is to do anything else now; and suppose that, nevertheless, he judges it best to turn off the television and get back to work. Can Ian exercise self-control in support of his terminating his television viewing and getting back to work? The question whether a principle *resembling Mu* permits this would be more to the point. *Mu* itself does not bear on cases of this kind. Presumably, Ian intends to be watching television, and *Mu* sets aside cases in which relevant intentions are present.

A variant of *Mu* broad enough to include Ian's case would be useful as a point of departure. Three points about intention help shape a variant. First, intentions to *A* encompass motivation to *A*, as do desires to *A* (see chapter 6). Second, the notion of bias-freeness that I applied to proximal desires is applicable to proximal intentions. Third, as I understand trumping, a proximal intention can be trumped only by another proximal intention. Such trumping is rare. Intending entails settledness on what is intended (see chapter 1, section 5). In any case of proximal intention trumping, therefore, an agent is settled on a proximal course of action or on a proximal not-doing while also being settled on a competing proximal not-doing or course of action. In normal agents, this can happen only when they do not notice the conflict. Possibly, it can also happen in commisurotomized agents.

A technical term will also help in modifying *Mu*. As I have explained, "motivation to *A*" is ambiguous (chapter 1, sections 1 and 3). I need an intuitive classificatory expression that captures a feature of motivation encompassed in desires to *A* and intentions to *A*, attitudes *toward A*-ing. The expression I have chosen is "*A*-focused motivation."

Mu may now be rewritten as follows:

> *Mub*. Assuming bias-free motivation, if, at *t*, an agent's untrumped proximal *A*-focused motivation is stronger than any untrumped proximal motivation he has that is focused on any other course of action and than any such motivation he has for a relevant not-doing, then, at *t*, he *A*-s or at least tries to *A*, provided that he acts intentionally at *t*.

The variable "*t*" should be understood broadly enough that some of its instances are times at which an agent proximally desires to *A* and *proceeds* to act on that desire. Since "bias-free untrumped proximal *A*-focused motivation" is a mouthful, I use the expression "*M*-motivation to *A*" as an abbreviation for it. (The "*M*" stands for "mouthful.")

Does *Mub* permit Ian to exercise self-control in support of his terminating his television viewing and getting back to work? This question is associated with what I elsewhere dubbed "the paradox of uphill self-control" (Mele 1987, p. 64). I distinguished two versions, a weaker and a stronger one (pp. 64–67). The basic worry is that, initially at least, "it is difficult to understand how someone who is more motivated at *t* to *A* at *t** than not to *A* at *t** can be sufficiently motivated at *t* to exercise self-control in defense of his not *A*-ing at *t**" (p. 64). (I mentioned that "*t** may or may not be identical with *t*" [p. 63].)

Among the planks in an argument that I have offered elsewhere for a resolution of the puzzle and for an affirmative answer to the questions about Ian is the idea that even jointly satisfiable contemporaneous desires need not agglomerate (Mele 1987, ch. 5; 1995a, ch. 3). As my sister is watching television tonight, she might simultaneously munch on a sandwich and reach for her beer. She might have desires or intentions to do each of these things without having a single compound desire or intention to do all of them. At least, that seems to be a plausible assumption on a realistic view of desires and intentions. If desires and intentions are actual states of mind, my sister might have a desire or intention to watch television now, another desire or intention to chew gum now, and a third desire or intention to scratch her itchy knee now, without having a desire or intention for the combination of these three activities. And, seemingly, the three intentional actions can be sufficiently independent of one another that no compound desire or intention need be posited to explain them. My thought, in part, is that if jointly satisfiable contemporaneous motivation-encompassing attitudes do not always agglomerate, then *Mub* leaves open the possibility that agents sometimes act on two or more distinct desires or intentions at a time, and one of those desires or intentions might issue, appropriately, in an exercise of self-control. For example, even if Ian's strongest *M*-motivation is to continue watching the tournament on television, he might also have a proximal desire to try a self-control technique that his therapist has prescribed for just this sort of situation that is stronger than any desire he has not to try the technique. *While* he is watching television (as he is most strongly motivated to do), he might, consistently with *Mub*, try the technique. And the technique might work: Ian's attempt at self-control might bring it about that his strongest *M*-motivation is no longer to continue watching television and that he gets back to work.[2]

Elsewhere, I have fleshed out the general line of thought I just described (Mele 1995a, ch. 3; cf. 1987, ch. 5), and I return to it shortly. More recently (Mele 1998c, 1999b), in response to a pair of articles on self-control by Jeanette Kennett and Michael Smith (1996, 1997), I defended the background idea that jointly satisfiable desires do not always agglomerate.[3] That idea does not need further defense here, but a certain point of contact between it and *Mub* requires brief discussion.

Assuming that my sister's desire to watch television now is her strongest relevant motivation at the time, *Mub* applies to that desire and her television viewing. But what about my sister's other intentional actions at the time? Here one might appeal to a companion principle, some of the central terms of which are defined as follows (Mele 1992e, p. 66):

> *Subjective openness*: A course of action *A* is *subjectively open* at *t* for an agent *S* if and only if, at *t*, *S* takes himself to be able to *A* then.[4]
>
> *Mutual independence*: *S*'s intentional *A*-ing and *S*'s intentional *B*-ing are *mutually independent actions* if and only if they are not parts of the same intentional action, neither is identical with or part of the other, and neither is performed as a means to the other.
>
> *Action competition*: *S*'s intentionally *A*-ing at *t* *competes* with *S*'s intentionally *B*-ing at *t* if and only if either he takes himself to be unable to do both *A* and *B* or his doing either would make his doing the other sufficiently unattractive that he would neither intentionally do nor try to do each.[5]

The companion principle reads as follows:

> *Mubc.* Assuming bias-free motivation, if, at *t*, (1) *S*'s untrumped proximal *A*-focused motivation is stronger than any untrumped proximal motivation he has that is focused on any other course of action and than any such motivation he has for a relevant not-doing; (2) *S* has untrumped proximal *B*-motivation that is stronger than any untrumped proximal motivation he has that is focused on any other course of action, with the exception of *A*, and than any such motivation he has for a relevant not-doing; and (3) *B* is subjectively

open to S at the time, does not compete with S's A-ing at the time, and is independent of S's A-ing at the time, then S B-s then, or at least tries to B then, if, in addition to intentionally A-ing or trying to A, S performs an independent intentional action at the time.

The pair, $Mub + Mubc$, can be similarly augmented to handle additional intentional actions of S's at a time that are independent of his A-ing, his B-ing, and their conjunction. Indeed, Mub itself is applicable to any number of independent intentional actions performed by S at a time, provided that in each successive application one does two things: (1) exclude from the relevant domain of subjectively open actions the actions identified in the consequents of the preceding applications and all actions with which they compete and (2) suitably augment, à la $Mubc$, the proviso with which Mub concludes.[6]

The idea that an agent's jointly satisfiable contemporaneous action-desires do not always agglomerate is not an obstacle to action explanation. More specifically, it is consistent with there being true explanation-backgrounding principles of the sort at issue here. The various intentional actions that my sister is performing at the same time can be explained in a principled way without our having to suppose that she is acting on just one complex agglomerated action-desire or intention.

2. Libet's Studies

I turn to Libet's studies. Because Libet apparently uses such terms as "intention," "decision," "desire," and "urge" interchangeably, some conceptual spadework is in order in interpreting his work. In the present section, I develop an interpretation of his relevant studies that is sensitive to important conceptual distinctions. In section 3, I display the bearing of Libet's studies, as interpreted here, on our prospects for agential control, given a principle like Mub. In section 4, I branch out, moving beyond Libet's laboratory setting.

In some of Libet's studies, subjects are instructed to flex their right wrists or the fingers of their right hands whenever they wish. Electrical readings from the scalp (averaged over at least forty flexings for each subject) show a "negative shift" in "readiness potentials" (RPs) beginning at about 550 milliseconds (ms) prior to the time at which an electromyogram shows relevant muscular motion to begin (1985, pp. 529–30).[7] Subjects are also instructed to "recall . . . the spatial clock position of a revolving spot at the time of [their] initial awareness" (p. 529) of something, x, that Libet variously describes as an "intention," "urge," "desire," "decision," "will," or "wish" to move. On the average, "RP onset" preceded what the subjects identified as the time of their initial awareness of x (time W) by 350 ms. Time W, then, preceded the beginning of muscle motion by about 200 ms. Thus, we have the following:

−550 ms	−200 ms	0 ms
RP onset	time W	muscle begins to move

Libet finds independent evidence of a slight error in subjects' recall of the times at which they first became aware of sensations (pp. 531, 534). Correcting for that error, time W is −150 ms.

When does the *action* begin in all this—that is, the agent's flexing his wrist or fingers? This is a conceptual question, of course; how one answers it depends on one's answer to the question "What is an action?"[8] Following Brand (1984), Frederick Adams and I have defended the thesis that overt intentional action begins in the brain, just after the acquisition of a proximal intention; the action is initiated by the acquisition of the intention (Adams and Mele 1992). To simplify exposition, I assume here that this thesis is true.[9] The relevant intention may be understood, in Libet's words, as an intention "to act now" (1989, p. 183; 1999, p. 54). (Of course, for Libet, as for me, "now" need not mean "this millisecond.") If I form an intention on Sunday night to mow my lawn Friday morning and act accordingly on Friday, my action of mowing the lawn does not start on Sunday. But if I form the intention now to start mowing "now," the action that is my mowing may begin just after the intention is formed, even though the relevant muscular motions do not begin until milliseconds later.

At what point, if any, does the proximal intention to flex one's wrist arise in Libet's subjects? Libet writes that "the brain 'decides' to initiate or, at least, to prepare to initiate the act before there is any reportable subjective awareness that such a decision has taken place" (1985, p. 536).[10] If we ignore the second disjunct in this quotation, Libet's apparent answer is that the intention to flex appears on the scene with "RP onset," about 550 ms before relevant muscular motion and about 350 ms before the agent becomes aware of the intention, for to decide to initiate an act is to form an intention to initiate it (see chapter 9). *If* this is right, then assuming a view like mine about action, the subject's action of flexing his wrist starts about half a second before the relevant muscles move. But are decision and intention the most suitable mental items to associate with RP onset? Again, Libet describes the relevant occurrence of which the agent later becomes aware not only as an "intention," a "decision," and a "will" to move but also as an "urge," a "desire," and a "wish" to move. This leaves open the possibility that at −550 ms, rather than acquiring an intention or making a decision of which he is not conscious, the agent instead acquires a *desire* or *urge* of which he is not conscious—and perhaps, more precisely, a desire or urge that is stronger than any competing desire or urge at the time.

Recall that desiring to do something is distinguishable from intending to do it (see chapter 1, section 5). One can have a desire to *A* without being at all settled on *A*-ing. An hour ago, at noon, I had a desire to take my daughter to the midnight dance tonight and a competing desire to take my son to the midnight movie. I needed to make up my mind about what to do. Currently, having just formed an intention to take my daughter to the dance and to make it up to my son tomorrow, my mind is made up. To intend to do something is, at least in part, to be settled (but not necessarily irrevocably) on doing it (chapter 1, section 5; Mele 1992e, chs. 9 and 10). Desiring to do something is compatible with being unsettled about whether to do it.

Admittedly, my practical question was about what to do several hours later, not about what to do then. However, given that there is a conceptual difference between intentions and desires (including urges), it is conceptually open that what emerges at −550 ms in Libet's studies is not an intention to flex one's wrist but rather, as he often puts it, an "urge" to do so, and perhaps an urge that is stronger than any competing urge, desire, or intention—a *preponderant* urge. I believe that if Libet himself were to distinguish between intentions and desires (including urges) along the lines sketched here, he would associate the readiness potentials with the latter rather than the former. To explain why, I turn to another experiment reported in Libet (1985).

Libet proposes that "conscious volitional control may operate not to initiate the volitional process but to select and control it, either by permitting or triggering the final motor outcome of the unconsciously initiated process or by vetoing the progression to actual motor activation" (1985, p. 529; cf. 1999, p. 54). "In a veto, the later phase of cerebral motor processing would be blocked, so that actual activation of the motoneurons to the muscles would not occur" (1985, p. 537). Libet offers two kinds of evidence to support the suggestion about vetoing. One kind is generated by an experiment in which subjects are instructed both to prepare to flex their fingers at a prearranged time (as indicated by a revolving spot on a clock face) and "to veto the developing intention/preparation to act . . . about 100 to 200 ms before the prearranged clock time" (p. 538). Subjects receive both instructions at the same time. Libet states that:

> a ramplike pre-event potential was still recorded . . . resembl[ing] the RP of self-initiated acts when preplanning is present. . . . The form of the "veto" RP differed (in most but not all cases) from those "preset" RPs that were followed by actual movements [in another experiment]; the main negative potential tended to alter in direction (flattening or reversing) at about 150–250 ms before the preset time. . . . This difference suggests that the conscious veto interfered with the final development of RP processes leading to action. . . . The preparatory cerebral processes associated with an RP can and do develop even when intended motor action is vetoed at approximately the time that conscious intention would normally appear before a voluntary act. (p. 538)[11]

Keep in mind that the subjects were instructed in advance *not* to flex their fingers but to prepare to flex them at the prearranged time and to "veto" this. The subjects complied with the request, presumably intentionally. They intended from the beginning not to flex their fingers at the appointed time. So what is indicated by the RP that resembles "the RP of self-initiated acts when preplanning is present"?[12] Not the acquisition or presence of an *intention* to flex; for then, at some time, the subjects would have both an intention to flex at the prearranged time and an intention not to flex at that time (and how can a normal agent simultaneously be settled on *A*-ing at *t* and settled on not *A*-ing at *t*?).[13] But this observation does not preclude the emergence of an *urge* to flex (or a desire to prepare to flex).[14] Perhaps a subject's desire to comply with the instructions—including the instruction to prepare to flex at the appointed time—in conjunction with his recognition that the time is approaching produces a growing urge to flex. And the "flattening or reversing" of the RP "at about 150–250 ms before the preset time" might indicate a motivational consequence or constituent of the subject's "vetoing" this urge. (This vetoing might be construed as the formation or acquisition of an intention not to act on this urge.[15])

If, in the "veto" experiment, the RP prior to its reversing or flattening is not indicative of an intention to flex, even though it does resemble RP readings in some cases in which subjects do flex, then perhaps the RPs present in the latter cases also do not indicate intentions. Even so, they might be indicative of *urges* to flex (or to prepare to flex), urges that agents become conscious of later. Once again, Libet (1985) describes in a variety of ways the mental item that is indicated by RPs. If "intention" and "decision" (to flex) are not apt choices, that still leaves "urge" and "desire" in the running.

Elsewhere, I have suggested that *one* route to the acquisition of a proximal intention is a relatively simple causal default procedure that takes a proximal action-desire of a certain kind as input and yields a corresponding intention as output: if an agent proximally wants to A more than he proximally wants to perform any competing action "and nothing preempts the immediate acquisition of a corresponding proximal intention, the intention is formed or acquired at once" (Mele 1992e, p. 190). (Intention formation is a species of intention acquisition; as I argue in chapter 9, although forming an intention is a mental action, not every instance of intention acquisition is an action.) In a context featuring milliseconds, "immediate" and "at once" should be read loosely.[16] Perhaps the relevant input is the *persistence* of a preponderant proximal action-desire for a certain amount of time rather than the emergence of such a desire, and the operation of the default procedure itself will not be instantaneous.

The existence of the suggested default procedure is consistent with Libet's results. "RP onset" in cases of "spontaneous" flexing might indicate the emergence of the agent's strongest proximal (or roughly proximal) desire for overt action; and that desire (which emerges without the agent's being conscious of it, if Libet is right), or its persisting for n ms, may issue by default in a proximal intention to flex. The intention itself may emerge at some point between RP onset and time W or *at* time W; alternatively, at time W the agent may be aware only of an urge that has not yet issued in an intention. Again, Libet writes, "In a veto, the later phase of cerebral motor processing would be blocked, so that actual activation of the motoneurons to the muscles would not occur" (1985, p. 537). Perhaps, in nonveto cases, activation of these motoneurons is the direct result of the acquisition of a proximal intention (or the neural realizer of this acquisition).[17] Libet suggests that this activation event occurs between 10 and 90 ms before the muscle begins moving and apparently favors an answer in the 10–50 ms range (p. 537).[18]

Although I do not make much of the following point, it is worth mentioning that the desires that may be correlated with RP onset (at −550 ms) might not be *proximal* desires, strictly speaking. Possibly, they are desires to flex *very soon*, as opposed to desires to flex straightaway. And perhaps they either evolve into or produce proximal desires. Another possibility is that desires to flex very soon give rise to proximal intentions to flex without first evolving into or producing proximal desires to flex. Some disambiguation is in order. A smoker who is rushing toward a smoking section in an airport with the intention of lighting up as soon as he enters it desires to smoke soon. His desire has a specific temporal target—the time at which he enters the smoking section. A smoker walking outside the airport may desire to smoke soon without having a specific time in mind. My suggestion here is that Libet's (1985) subjects, like the latter smoker, might at times have desires to flex that lack a specific temporal target. Action-desires to A very soon or to A beginning very soon, in this sense of "very soon," are *roughly proximal* action-desires.

For my own purposes here, the time at which an agent becomes *conscious* of an "urge," "desire," "wish," "decision," "intention," or "will" to flex his fingers is not the central issue. Libet's (1985) experimental design promotes consciousness of the pertinent state or event since his subjects are instructed in advance to be prepared to report on this later, using the rapidly revolving spot on the clock to pinpoint the time. I myself have no ax to grind against the hypothesis that agents have and act on some proximal intentions of which they are never conscious. For my purposes, what is of special interest are the relative times of the emergence of a (roughly) proximal desire or urge to flex, the emergence of a proximal *intention* to do so, and the beginning of muscle motion. If the RPs indicate the emergence of (strongest) proximal or roughly proximal desires for overt action, and if acquisitions of corresponding intentions (or the neural realizers of these acquisitions) directly activate the motoneurons to the relevant muscles, we have the following picture in the straightforward cases in which subjects comply with the instruction to flex "spontaneously":

    a. −550 ms: (strongest) proximal or roughly proximal desire emerges.
    b. −90 to −10 ms: corresponding proximal intention is aquired.
    c. 0 ms: muscle begins to move.

Given a conception of action like mine, the relevant actions would begin in these cases with the activation of the motoneurons, just after the proximal intentions are acquired (Adams and Mele 1992).

As I mentioned, Libet offered a second kind of evidence for "veto control." Subjects instructed to flex "spontaneously" (in nonveto experiments) "reported that during some of the trials a recallable conscious urge to act appeared but was 'aborted' or somehow suppressed before any actual movement occurred; in such cases the subject simply waited for another urge to appear, which, when consummated, constituted the actual event whose RP was recorded" (1985, p. 538). RPs were not recorded for the suppressed urges.[19] But if these urges fit the pattern of the unsuppressed ones, they appeared on the scene about 550 ms before the relevant muscles would have moved if the subjects had not "suppressed" the urges, and subjects did not become conscious of them for about another 350 ms. If these (roughly) proximal urges or desires are stronger than any competing desires the agent has at the time, then apparently an agent can "veto" or "suppress" the strongest of his competing desires at a time. Shortly, I ask whether this is compatible with *Mub*.

3. Urges, Intentions, and Actions

When a subject in Libet's studies becomes aware of what may be construed as a preponderant (roughly) proximal desire to flex his fingers, Libet contends that he still has about 150 ms to "'veto' motor performance" (1985, p. 529). This veto may be construed as encompassing the formation or acquisition of a proximal intention not to flex (or not to act on this desire). Proponents of *Mub* face two questions: (1) if, at the time of first awareness of the (roughly) proximal desire to flex (time W), that desire is stronger than any competing motivation, how can a proximal intention not to flex fail to be violated? (2) If at time W the (roughly) proximal desire to flex is stronger than any competing motivation, how can the agent acquire or form a proximal intention not to flex?

Regarding question (1), two points should be made. First, *Mub* is consistent with inaction, given its final clause: "provided that [the agent] acts intentionally at *t*." However, this point has little significance in the present context since a subject who does not flex is doing something intentionally, for example, watching the revolving spot on the clock. Second, if the rapid acquisition or formation of a proximal intention not to flex (or the physical realizer of that event) can rapidly result in a significant decrease in the agent's motivation to flex, his doing something other than flexing may be consistent with *Mub*. After all, there is a significant gap between time W and the beginning of the time of action. Because of a significant decrease in the strength of his motivation to flex, the agent's strongest *M*-motivation now may be, for example, to continue watching the clock. (*M-motivation to A*, again, is bias-free untrumped proximal *A*-focused motivation.) His acquisition of the intention not to flex may even eradicate the urge to flex.

Question (2) is more challenging. Suppose that, as Libet (1985) claims, subjects who were not instructed to veto (roughly) proximal urges to flex nevertheless did veto them occasionally. Suppose also that, in some cases at least, the vetoed urges were stronger than any competing motivation at the time of the veto. Suppose, finally, that vetoing a (roughly) proximal urge to flex encompasses acquiring or forming a proximal intention not to flex that somehow defeats the urge. Then not all proximal intentions issue from corresponding preponderant proximal or roughly proximal desires. But this is not surprising. When I see a dog dart in front of my car and I intentionally depress the brake pedal, why should we suppose that *first* I acquire a relevant proximal desire to hit the brake and *then* I acquire an intention to do so? I might be psychologically so constituted at the time that the sight of the dog elicits an intention to hit the brake without first eliciting a desire to do so.

Of course, even someone who grants that some proximal intentions do not issue from (roughly) proximal desires may doubt that an agent can acquire or form a proximal intention that is at odds with his strongest (roughly) proximal motivation at the moment. It may be thought that having a (roughly) proximal desire to *A* that is stronger than any competing motivation precludes acquiring a proximal intention not to *A*. This thought is associated with the paradox of uphill self-control. It requires attention. Two questions require discussion: can a proximal intention not to *A* be *nonactionally* acquired in the circumstances? Can an agent *decide* not to *A* in these circumstances?

Recall that in the primary experiment reported in Libet (1985), subjects are instructed to flex whenever they wish and to be prepared to report later at what time the wish or desire emerged, and each session with an individual subject involved at least forty different flexings. Under these conditions, it would not be surprising if subjects were occasionally to desire (consciously or otherwise) to know what it would feel like to suppress an urge to flex or to learn whether they can resist an urge to flex. Such a desire is not an *action*-desire; rather, it is a desire for information on a certain topic. The hypothesis that a desire of this kind might contribute to the agent's nonactionally acquiring an intention not to flex even though, prior to his acquiring that intention and at the time of intention acquisition, his (roughly) proximal desire to flex is stronger than any competing motivation of his is consistent with *Mub*—unless the conjunction of *Mub* and the details of the case entails that the agent performs an action that is inconsistent with his nonactionally acquiring this intention. For *Mub* is a claim about what we intentionally do under certain conditions, not about the nonactional acquisition of desires or intentions.

Libet contends that at the time at which subjects first become conscious of the urge to flex, "there remains 100–150 ms in which the conscious function could 'evaluate' and decide on whether to veto" that urge before relevant motoneurons are activated (1985, p. 563). Elsewhere I have argued that, in many cases (admittedly in a very different context, featuring deliberation), intentions are acquired primarily on the basis of an agent's *evaluation* of the objects of his desires rather than the *motivational strength* of his desires (Mele 1987, pp. 36–45; cf. 1992e, ch. 12). If intention acquisition is often more sensitive to evaluative states of mind than to the motivational strength of desires, it is conceivable that Libet's subjects sometimes do acquire *intentions* not to flex, even though their proximal desire to flex is their strongest proximal motivation at the time of intention acquisition. And the acquisition of such intentions may function as I have suggested intention acquisition sometimes does in my answer to question (1): the acquisition of a proximal intention not to flex (or the physical realizer of that event) can rapidly result in a significant decrease in—and even eradicate—the agent's motivation to flex.

What about *forming* a proximal intention—that is, *deciding*—not to flex, as opposed to merely acquiring such an intention? Suppose that what the agent is aware of at −200 ms (time W) is a proximal urge to flex. And imagine that, after having spontaneously flexed on a dozen or so occasions without giving the matter much thought, he began to entertain the prospect of resisting one of his impulses as a test of his own powers of agency—a prospect he entertained for some time during the experiment. Aware of his current urge to flex, curious about his control over urges of this kind, and thinking that it would be interesting to "veto" the urge, the subject may acquire a proximal desire not to flex that significantly diminishes his urge to flex and provides motivation for deciding not to flex. If he desires more strongly to decide at the time not to flex than to do anything else then, he may decide not to flex.

It may be replied that if this is what happens, then whether this person decides not to flex is not subject to his control, for whether he so decides hinges on whether he happens to acquire a proximal desire not to flex. But notice that the acquisition of a proximal desire not to flex is not mere happenstance, and it is not "mindless," as the acquisition of the "spontaneous" urge to flex apparently is. The desire arises partly as a consequence of the person's reflection on his own agency, and the desire is reasonable partly in light of that reflection. Furthermore, his acquiring the desire may be explained partly by a rapid evaluation of the relative merits of flexing and not flexing that is informed by his earlier reflections on his agency.

Another worry requires attention. Principles like Davidson's (1980) *P1* and *Mub* are designed for a theoretical context that is more relaxed about temporal considerations than the present one. Indeed, *P1* does not even mention time. Again, *Mub* reads as follows:

> *Mub.* Assuming bias-free motivation, if, at *t*, an agent's untrumped proximal *A*-focused motivation is stronger than any untrumped proximal motivation he has that is focused on any other course of action and than any such motivation he has for a relevant not-doing, then, at *t*, he *A*-s or at least tries to *A*, provided that he acts intentionally at *t*.

As I have mentioned, "*t*" here is not a variable only for "instants"; the thought, in part, is that proximal desires play a role in producing overt actions, and of course, that takes time. A proponent of *Mub* means to allow sufficient time for the initiation of overt actions after the acquisition of untrumped proximal action-desires. On my view, action-desires help to initiate actions by helping to produce pertinent proximal intentions the formation or acquisition of which directly initiates actions. If my view is correct, if "enough time for the [indirect] initiation of" a flexing is also more than enough time for an agent to decide not to flex even though his strongest motivation of the relevant sort at, say, −200 ms is to flex, and if some such decisions are made and not violated, principles like *Mub* face a problem. There are situations in which *Mub* and details of the case jointly entail that the agent begins to *A*, even though he does not. Suppose that *Mub* applies to a temporal span of at least 200 ms and that at the beginning of that period an agent has *M*-motivation to flex that is stronger than any bias-free untrumped proximal motivation he has that is focused on any other course of action and than any such motivation he has for a relevant not-doing. Suppose also that 150 ms later, he decides not to flex. Since deciding is an intentional action, he acts intentionally at the time. So *Mub* implies that he flexes or at least tries to flex at *t*. (A more careful version would imply that he begins trying to flex at *t*.) And in cases in which a decision blocks the agent's even beginning to try to flex, this implication of *Mub* is false. *Mub* requires refinement.

One solution is to rewrite *Mub* as follows (for ease of exposition, I separate *M*-motivation for *A*-ings already in progress from *M*-motivation of which this is not the case):

Mub*. Assuming bias-free motivation, (1) if, at *t*, an agent who is *A*-ing intentionally has untrumped proximal motivation focused on continuing to *A* that is stronger than any such motivation he has that is focused on any other course of action and than any such motivation he has for a relevant not-doing, he continues *A*-ing (possibly only for a very short time), provided that he continues acting intentionally, and (2) if, at *t*, an agent who is not already *A*-ing has untrumped proximal *A*-focused motivation that is stronger than any such motivation he has that is focused on any other course of action and than any such motivation he has for a relevant not-doing, he intentionally begins to *A* shortly, provided that he intentionally begins to do something shortly and no stronger competing untrumped proximal motivation emerges in time to preempt his intentionally beginning to *A*.[20]

In an earlier scenario, an agent's strongest relevant motivation at a time is to decide not to flex. Might it happen, consistently with *Mub**, that at −100 ms, say, although an agent's strongest relevant motivation is to flex, he decides not to flex? Might such an agent, Al, have a desire to *decide* not to flex that is strong enough to issue in such a decision? A theorist may claim that if Al is more strongly motivated to flex than not to flex, he must also be more strongly motivated to decide to flex than to decide not to flex, on the grounds that the strength of the decision-regarding motivation must derive solely from the strength of the flexing-regarding motivation. However, the grounds offered are mistaken. Al may have motivation to decide not to flex that is not itself also motivation not to flex. For example, he may desire to enable himself to feel or understand what it is like to *decide* not to act on an urge to flex, and the desire would naturally enter into the positive motivational base of his desire to *decide* not to flex, even if it does not strengthen or has not yet strengthened his desire not to flex. Here there is a special incentive for *deciding* not to flex that is not itself an incentive not to flex.[21] Even if at −100 ms Al's proximal desire to flex is stronger than any proximal desire he may have not to flex, he may simultaneously be more strongly proximally motivated to decide not to flex than he is to decide to flex (or not to make the former decision).

Mub* is consistent with Al's deciding not to flex while his strongest relevant motivation is to flex. The principle does not entail that someone who, at a time, has relevant motivation to flex that is stronger than his relevant motivation to decide not to flex will begin flexing shortly, if he acts on either desire. *Mub** leaves open the possibility that the decision may occur and preempt the beginning of a flexing. Moreover, Libet's (1985) data suggest that such preemption occurs.

It may be objected that if Al's deciding not to flex hinges on his being more strongly motivated so to decide at the relevant time than not so to decide, then his decision is not subject to his control.[22] But suppose that Al's motivational condition at the time is partly explained by his own uncompelled reflection (during earlier parts of the experiment) about how it would be best, or most interesting, to respond to some spontaneous urges to flex, and if he had come to a different judgment on this matter his motivational condition would not have favored deciding not to flex this time. Would that soften the blow? Alternatively, does the truth of the claim that the decision an agent made to *A* was subject to his control entail that in some other possible world that has exactly the same laws as the actual world and exactly the same past, right up to the moment at which he makes his decision, the agent does not decide to *A* (or decides to do something else)?[23]

We have run headlong into the issue of free will. The primary worry that some theorists would have about *Mub** may be explained by the principle's deterministic tone and a libertarian abhorrence of deterministic connections between action and its antecedents (see McCann 1995). This worry is a topic for another occasion, as is the potential attractiveness of a probabilistic version of *Mub** (see Clarke 1994).[24] Given a compatibilist conception of agents' control over their actions, Libet's (1985) work helps us understand why *Mub** need not place agents at the mercy of their strongest (roughly) proximal motivation for overt action even in cases in which there is no longer time for present deliberation.[25] It takes time to act. And, in the case of an agent who has not yet made the transition from proximally desiring to perform some overt action to proximally intending to perform it, forming or acquiring a proximal intention requires less time than beginning to move his body does, on the assumption that such beginnings are initiated by acquisitions of intentions.[26] Intentions may be formed or acquired for not-doings and courses of action that are at odds with the courses of action at which the agents' strongest proximal action-desires at the time are directed. And the effectiveness of such intention formation or acquisition is compatible with the truth of *Mub**, which leaves open the possibility that forming or acquiring such an intention (or the physical realizer of that event) can change one's motivational condition and prevent an *A*-ing or issue in intended overt conduct. There are grounds for maintaining that this is what happens when Libet's subjects veto "spontaneous" urges to flex. But even a theorist who finds these grounds less than compelling can find in Libet's work a basis for skepticism about the assumption that *Mub** places us at the mercy of our strongest proximal motivation (assuming a compatibilist conception of control).

It is an empirical question whether all intentional actions are deterministically linked with action-desires. Although principles like *P1* and *Mu* have a deterministic ring, I am open to probabilistic variants, as I indicated in chapter 7. Of course, an explicitly probabilistic version of *Mub** would take the sting out of the puzzle about uphill self-control, for example, since the question is about the *possibility* of exercising self-control against one's strongest desire at the time. In any case, the resolution that I have been sketching is compatible both with determinism and with indeterminism.

Libertarians contend that at least some of our actions are free and that freedom is incompatible with determinism. If the resolution I have been sketching to the puzzle about uphill self-control is correct, perhaps libertarians need not be particularly concerned to find the indeterminism they prize in the connection between proximal motivation and action. If I am right, *Mub** is consistent with scenarios in which an agent who is proximally most strongly motivated to *A*, or to continue *A*-ing, exercises self-control in bringing it about that his motivational condition changes and that he does not *A* or stops *A*-ing very soon. *Mub** does not preclude self-control. Libertarians may find that indeterminism elsewhere in action-producing processes is more valuable to them. However, that is a long, complicated story, and I have spun it at some length elsewhere (see Mele 1995a, chs. 11–13; 1996e; 1999d).

4. Branching Out

Given the relatively trivial nature of most finger and wrist flexings, we should not expect Libet's (1985) experimental subjects to shape the strength of their desires for or against these activities in remarkable ways. Even so, they apparently do exhibit some control in this sphere. To get a less limited picture of the control that agents are capable of exercising over proximal and roughly proximal desires, one needs to branch out.

Sam has resolved not to eat between meals until he loses ten pounds, and he knows that he has lost only five. He opens his refrigerator to get a diet soft drink to sip while watching a late movie on television and spies a large piece of chocolate pie. The sight of the pie elicits a roughly proximal desire to eat the dessert, and this is Sam's strongest relevant motivation at the moment. If *Mub** is true, does it follow that Sam will eat (or try to eat) the pie? ("Proximal motivation" in *Mub** can be read to include roughly proximal motivation.)

Not at all. It takes time to act, and, in principle, there is time for Sam to come to desire more strongly to see to it that he does not eat the pie than to eat it. Other things being equal, if it is consistent with *Mub** that Libet's (1985) subjects occasionally veto a preponderant, proximal, "spontaneous" urge to flex by acquiring or forming a proximal intention not to flex that contributes to their no longer being preponderantly proximally motivated to flex, then, in principle, *Mub** is consistent with Sam's acquiring or forming an intention not to eat the pie tonight (despite the relative strength of his urge to eat it), with the result that he is no longer preponderantly motivated to eat it.[27]

A related point should also be made. Even if Sam's psychological constitution is such that, at the moment, he is not in a position simply and directly to intend not to eat the pie, there may be time for a successful exercise of self-control. Consider a version of the case in which Sam consulted a behavioral therapist about losing weight. The therapist taught him a technique for situations like the present one. Sam was told that when he feels an urge for a snack, he should remind himself of his resolution, slowly and silently count to ten, and then concentrate on the primary reasons for his resolution before making up his mind about whether to eat. Suppose that in the present case, when he feels the urge to eat, Sam recalls the therapist's advice and soon starts counting. His counting is an intentional action and something he is motivated to do. Now, from the conjunction of *Mub** and Sam's intentionally counting, it does not follow that Sam is more strongly motivated to count than to eat the pie. *Mub** (like *Mub*) does not assert that the *only* thing we do intentionally at a time is what we are most strongly motivated to do at that time; it is consistent with *Mub** that Sam simultaneously starts counting and starts reaching for the pie (even if he is not equally strongly motivated to do each). But a version of the case is imaginable in which, once Sam comes to want to count to ten, that desire is his strongest proximal motivation; and Sam's desire to eat the pie now or very soon may become or be replaced by a desire to eat it within the next few minutes.[28]

Motionless in front of the refrigerator, Sam starts counting to ten. It is consistent with this and *Mub** that, at the time, his (roughly) proximal desire to eat the pie is stronger than his desire not to eat it. Indeed, Sam may recognize that the former desire is stronger than the latter, and his counting may be motivated by a higher-order desire to bring about a reversal of the strength of these two desires. His therapist may have told him that the technique works (when it does) precisely by sufficiently diminishing the strength of one's desire for a snack while increasing the strength of one's desire not to eat and, consequently, of one's desire to see to it that one does not eat. Even after he has counted to five, say, Sam may still desire more strongly to eat the pie (soon) than to see to it that he does not eat it tonight. But, as yet, he may neither intend to eat it nor intend not to eat it. He may be unsettled about what to do. A moment later, he may be mentally prepared to decide not to eat the pie tonight. Even if Sam was in no position to make this decision immediately upon feeling the urge to eat the pie, he may be in a position to do this a little later, with the help of his technique for self-control. He may decide not to eat the pie tonight and do something other than eat it.

One may object that if Sam is more strongly motivated to eat the pie than not to eat it, then he is more strongly motivated not to try to reverse this balance of motivational strength than to try to reverse it. This objection fails, as I have argued elsewhere (Mele 1987, pp. 69–72; 1995a, pp. 41–55; 1996b, pp. 57–62). Consideration of the following case will help to make a long story considerably shorter.

> Wilma, who suffers from agoraphobia, has been invited to her son's wedding in a church several weeks hence. Her long-standing fear of leaving her home is so strong that were the wedding to be held today, she would remain indoors and forego attending. Wilma is rightly convinced that unless she attenuates her fear, she will not attend the wedding. And there is a clear sense in which she is now more strongly motivated to remain at home on the wedding day and miss the wedding than to attend it: her current motivational condition is such that, unless it changes in a certain direction, she will [stay home]. (A nice conceptual test of what one is now most motivated to do at a later time is, roughly, what one would do at that later time if one were then in the motivational condition that one is in now.) Further, Wilma believes that, owing to her motivation to remain in her house indefinitely, she probably will miss the wedding. (Mele 1996b, pp. 55–56)

If, as I believe, intending to A is incompatible with believing that one probably will not A (Mele 1992e, ch. 8), Wilma is not yet in a position to intend to attend the wedding. Even so, it certainly is conceivable that, under the conditions described, she does not have an intention to miss the wedding and, indeed, intends to do her best to reduce her fear so that she will be in a position to attend. Furthermore, there is no good reason to hold that because Wilma is now more strongly motivated (in the sense identified) to stay home on the wedding day than to attend the wedding, she is also more strongly motivated not to try to attenuate her fear than to try to do this. She sees her fear as an obstacle to something she values doing, and the strength of any desire she may have not to try to attenuate her fear may be far exceeded by the motivational strength of her fear itself and exceeded, as well, by the strength of her desire to try to bring it about that she is in a position to leave her house on the wedding day and attend the wedding.[29]

To be sure, Wilma has a few weeks to adjust her motivational condition whereas Sam may have only a few moments. One of the virtues of Libet's (1985) work is that it spreads out before us for reflection what may happen between the time at which a preponderant proximal urge for overt action is acquired and the earliest time at which the urge may be acted on. It takes time to act, and Libet's data indicate that there is time enough for the vetoing of preponderant proximal urges. Just as Wilma may desire more strongly to try to change her motivational condition than to allow it to persist, so may Sam. And just as Wilma may desire more strongly to try to attenuate her fear with a view to bringing it about that she attends the wedding than not to try this, even though her fear currently is stronger than her desire to attend, Sam may desire more strongly to try his therapist's technique with a view to bringing it about that he abides by his resolution than not to try this, even though his proximal desire to eat the pie is currently stronger than his desire not to eat it tonight. An agent's desiring more strongly to A than to B (or not to A) is consistent with his judging it better to B (or not to A) than to A, and sometimes agents have the motivational capacity to attempt to bring it about that the strength of their desires falls in line with their evaluative judgments.[30] As I observed earlier, desires—even proximal desires—do not, by and large, come to us equipped with immutable strengths; and unless a desire is irresistible, it is up to us (at least in a compatibilist sense of "up to us") whether we act on it (chapter 7, section 5; cf. Mele 1992e, p. 79).[31]

I cannot vouch for the accuracy of Libet's (1985) interpretations of his data. Indeed, I have challenged Libet's association of RPs with intentions. But this chapter is not an exercise in neuroscience. Elsewhere, I have appealed to the truism that it takes time to act in defending the thesis that a principle like *Mub* is consistent with our having significant control over what we do even when faced with preponderant proximal temptation and in exploring related issues (Mele 1987, pp. 18–20, 43–44; 1995a, pp. 47–49). Libet's work gives us a sense of how much time might elapse between the acquisition of a (roughly) proximal desire and the beginning of an overt action motivated by that desire. More important, it gives us a sense of possibilities for practically relevant motivational change during that span and adds to the extant case for the view that principles like *Mub* do not entail that we are at the mercy of our strongest desires.

Notes

1. See, for example, Dennett (1991, pp. 154–66) and Flanagan (1996, pp. 59–62).

2. Consistently with *Mub*, Ian might try the self-control technique while watching television, even if he has an agglomerated desire for the conjunction of watching television and trying the technique and even if that desire is weaker than his desire to watch television. Scenarios of this kind lack the psychological realism of the kind of scenario to be explored in this chapter.

3. Incidentally, Kennett (2000, pp. 145–46) seems to have come around to this view.

4. I have motivated and explained my notion of taking oneself to be able to *A* as follows:

> The supposition that whenever we *A* intentionally we occurrently believe that we are able to *A* is psychologically unrealistic. Often, when we intentionally perform an action *A*, nothing prompts the occurrent thought we are able to *A*: the issue simply does not arise. I have been intentionally typing this section for some time now; but I acquired the occurrent belief that this is something that I am able to do only a couple of minutes ago, when a philosophical question prompted a thought about my ability to do what I was doing. It is not as though I made a remarkable *discovery*, of course. I knew all along, we might loosely say, that I was able to type this section. But, it seems, I had no occurrent belief to that effect until just recently. As I . . . understand the expression, at a particular time *t* an agent "takes himself to be able" to *A* then if and only if, at *t*, he both possesses a representation of his (current or prospective) *A*-ing then and does not believe that he cannot (owing to external or internal circumstances, or both) *A* then. Since this account of taking oneself to be able does not require that the agent *occurrently assent* to a proposition to the effect that he is able to *A* at *t*, *taking* oneself, at *t*, to be able to *A* then is weaker than *believing* oneself, at *t*, to be able to *A* then—on one common construal of belief." (Mele 1992e, p. 62)

5. I understand taking oneself to be unable to *A* as follows: "At a time *t*, an agent 'takes himself to be unable' to *A* then if and only if, at *t*, he believes that he cannot (owing to external or internal circumstances, or both) *A* then" (Mele 1992e, p. 78, note 9). "Thus if, at *t*, an agent possesses a representation of his (prospective) *A*-ing then, he takes himself (at *t*) to be able to *A* then, unless he believes (at *t*) that he cannot *A* then. Taking oneself, at *t*, to be able to *A* at the time is . . . the default condition of possessing such a representation" (p. 78, note 9).

6. Here I borrow from earlier work (Mele 1992e, p. 67).

7. For background on the generation, analysis, and use of electroencephalograms (EEGs) and "event-related brain potentials," including readiness potentials, see Coles and Rugg (1995).

8. Libet identifies "the actual time of the voluntary motor act" with the time "indicated by EMG recorded from the appropriate muscle" (1985, p. 532).

9. Little hangs on this assumption for the purposes of this chapter. Its primary role here is to simplify exposition. For a discussion of the central issues of this chapter that is noncommittal about when an overt action begins, see Mele (1997c).

10. In a later article, Libet states that "the brain has begun the specific preparatory processes for the voluntary act well before the subject is even aware of any wish or intention to act" (1992, p. 263).

11. For a more thorough discussion of the experiment, see Libet, Wright, and Curtis (1983).

12. In invited instances of preplanning, subjects are instructed in advance to flex when the revolving spot reaches a certain position (see Libet, Wright, and Curtis 1983). The RPs in cases of preplanning differ from those in cases of "spontaneous" flexings (see Libet 1985, p. 531).

13. I do not wish to exclude the possibility of such settledness in commissurotomy cases.

14. It also does not preclude the development of an intention to prepare to flex, if *preparing* is understood in such a way that so intending does not entail intending to flex.

15. On the assumption that RP readings are associated specifically with preparation to move, the vetoing intention would not be associated with an RP reading of its own.

16. A default procedure of this kind that works in a less than strictly immediate way need not preclude there being more sudden intentional actions. As I explain later, a proximal intention to A may be acquired without there being any prior proximal desire to A.

17. Here again I forego discussion of the metaphysical nuts and bolts of mental causation (but see Mele 1992e, ch. 2).

18. The following is from Daniel Dennett's description of a lecture given by neurosurgeon R. Grey Walter at Oxford in 1963:

> He arranged for each patient to look at slides from a carousel projector. The patient [thought he] could advance the carousel at will, by pressing the button on the controller. . . . Unbeknownst to the patient, however, the controller button was . . . not attached to the slide projector at all! What actually advanced the slides was the amplified signal from the electrode implanted in the patient's motor cortex. . . . [The patients] were startled by the effect, because it seemed to them as though the slide projector were anticipating their decisions. They reported that just as they were "about to" push the button, but before they had actually decided to do so, the projector would advance the slide— and they would find themselves pressing the button with the worry that it was going to advance the slide twice! (1991, p. 167)

Perhaps the signal from the electrode is associated with a conscious desire to advance the slide that had not yet issued in an intention to advance it. If so, the patients' surprise should be unsurprising to us.

19. Recall that RP figures are produced by averaging the electrical readings for a subject over many trials. The phenomenon presently at issue was relatively infrequent, but it is measurable in principle.

20. "S begins to A" does not entail "SA-s." A baseball player may begin to swing at a pitch without swinging at the pitch, and a contractor may begin to remodel my kitchen without remodeling my kitchen. Incidentally, I leave the task of modifying $Mubc$ (section 1) to fit Mub^* as an exercise for the reader.

21. There are well-known cases of this general kind, for example, Kavka's (1983) toxin puzzle (see Mele 1992b, 1995b, 1996c).

22. This objection parallels the one considered five paragraphs earlier.

23. R. Jay Wallace (1999, pp. 237–38, 241–42), for one, recently answered affirmatively. For the worry that an agent who satisfies the allegedly entailed condition lacks a kind of control over his decision required for his deciding freely and being morally responsible for that decision, see Mele (1999d).

24. Elsewhere (Mele 1995a), I have offered a pair of overlapping sets of sufficient conditions for free action—one for compatibilists and one for libertarians—and I argue that both are satisfiable by real human agents, for all we know. I am officially agnostic about the main metaphysical issue that divides compatibilists and libertarians. My remarks about libertarianism here should not be taken as dismissive; rather, specifically libertarian worries about principles like Mub raise issues that would require a separate, extensive discussion.

25. For a compatibilist conception of agential control, see Mele (1995a, chs. 9 and 10).

26. Notice that in addition to "vetoing" urges for actions that are not yet in progress, agents can abort attempts, including attempts at relatively short lived actions. When batting, baseball players often successfully halt the motion of their arms while a swing is in progress. Presumably, they acquire or form an intention to stop swinging while they are in the process of executing an intention to swing.

27. I am not suggesting that the formation of an intention always has this result. Sometimes, having formed an intention not to A now, an agent is more strongly motivated to A, and the in-

tention is replaced by an intention for the course of action that the agent proximally desires most. The same is true of positive intentions, intentions to *A* (see Mele 1987, pp. 38–44; 1992e, pp. 163–66, 191).

28. I forego discussion of identity conditions for desires over time.

29. For support, see Mele (1996b, pp. 58–62).

30. For support for the claim about consistency, see Mele (1987, chs. 3 and 6).

31. I offer an analysis of irresistible desire in Mele (1992e, ch. 5). (Compatibilism about what is up to us is the thesis that determinism does not preclude its being true that some of what we do is up to us.) I continue to be puzzled by the claim that on views like mine, agents are "passive" with respect to their desires (see, e.g., Wallace 1999, p. 232, n. 2, and 233–38). My diagnosis is that philosophers who make this claim understand "activity" with respect to an attitude as requiring forming or shedding that attitude *at will*.

IV

DECISION, AGENCY, AND BELIEF

9

Deciding

The topic of decision has emerged in the preceding chapter and arises again in chapter 10. If, as is plausible, practical decisions are motivated and play an important role in the etiology of a significant range of motivated behavior, decision requires attention in a book on motivation. I open part IV with a chapter on that topic. In chapter 10, I explore a phenomenon in which deciding has been claimed to have a central place, human action par excellence. Chapter 11 completes part IV—and this book—with a discussion of motivationally biased belief and of what different kinds of motivational explanation have in common.

Deciding seems to be part of our daily lives. But what is it to decide to do something? It may be true, as some philosophers have claimed, that to decide to A is to perform a mental action of a certain kind—specifically, an action of *forming* an intention to A.[1] (The verb "form" in this context is henceforth to be understood as an action verb.) Even if this is so, there are pressing questions. Do we form all of our intentions? If not, how does forming an intention differ from other ways of acquiring one? Do we ever form intentions, or do we rather merely acquire them in something like the way we acquire beliefs or desires? If we do form intentions, what explains our forming the ones we form? These are among the focal questions of this chapter. My aim is to clarify the nature of deciding to act, to make a case for the occurrence of genuine acts of intention formation, and to shed some light on how decisions are to be explained.

1. Background: Four Views of Practical Decision

We speak not only of deciding to act but also of deciding that something is the case, as an economist, on the basis of careful research, might decide that oil prices are likely to rise dramatically in the next few months. For stylistic purposes, it is useful to have labels for the two kinds of deciding. Following Arnold Kaufman (1966, p. 25), I call deciding to act *practical* deciding and deciding that something is the case *cognitive* deciding. I also count decisions *not* to A—for example, not to vote in the upcoming election—as practical decisions. My focus, however, is on deciding to act.

Are instances of practical deciding *actions*, or is action the wrong category for them? A brief sketch of a familiar nonactional conception of cognitive deciding will help to explain why someone may take practical deciding to be nonactional. On one possible view, to decide that *p* is the case is simply to acquire a belief that *p* is the case on the basis of reflection. For example, the economist's deciding that oil prices are likely to rise soon is a matter of his acquiring the belief that this is likely on the basis of reflection on considerations that he takes to be relevant. The economist's belief is a product of his reflective activity, but it is not as though his acquiring that belief is itself an action. It is not as though, on the basis of his reflection, he performs an action of belief formation. In some spheres, acquiring an *x* may have both an actional and a nonactional mode. The economist's acquiring a car, say, may or may not be an action of his. In buying my car, he performs an action of car acquisition; if, instead, I give him my car, his acquiring it is not an action of his. According to a nonactional view of cognitive deciding, acquiring a belief on the basis of reflection is never an action.

View 1: practical deciding as nonactional. An analogous view of *practical* deciding is possible. According to this view, to decide to A is simply to acquire an intention to A on the basis of practical reflection, and acquiring an intention—in this way or any other—is never an action. To be sure, many intentions are products of reflective activity, but that is not to say that there are any acts of intention acquisition. Buying a car is an act of car acquisition, as is stealing a car. But there are no analogues of these activities in the realm of intention acquisition.[2]

View 2: practical deciding as extended action. A variant of this view that represents practical deciding as actional is imaginable. The view just sketched highlights a process that culminates in intention acquisition. The process centrally involves practical reflection, a mental activity. It may be suggested that "practical deciding" is a name for the whole process. In any case in which an agent (nondeviantly) acquires an intention on the basis of practical reflection, there is a process of practical deciding that begins when the reflection begins and ends with the acquisition of the intention. Since much of that process is actional and since the process is a unified whole, it is claimed that the process itself is properly counted as an action—specifically, an action of deciding to do (or not to do) something.

View 3: practical deciding as mythical. A skeptical variant of view 1 is also conceivable. Practical deciding, it may be insisted, is essentially actional, but not in the way claimed by view 2. Deciding to A, by definition, is a momentary mental action of intention formation. Practical reflection is not part of any act of deciding, although such reflection may typically precede instances of practical deciding. However, there is no such thing as practical deciding, for as view 1 asserts, no instance of acquiring an intention is an action. In this respect, intention acquisition is like belief acquisition, on a plausible, nonactional conception of the latter.

View 4: practical deciding as a momentary mental action of intention formation. A fourth view is view 3 without the skepticism.

I now comment on each of these views in turn. A proponent of view 1 owes us an account of how intentions are, or might be, acquired on the basis of practical reflection, reflection about what to do. No consensus has been reached about the form such reflection takes. As I understand practical reflection or reasoning, it is, roughly, reflection about what to do that is sustained by motivation to answer a practical question (chapter 4, section 1; Mele 1992e, ch. 12; 1995a, ch. 2). Again, reflection about what to do sometimes takes the form of reasoning about what it would be best to do. It takes other forms as well, as I have observed. For example, an agent who is inclined to A may reflect about whether to A, and that reflection may take the form of reasoning about whether A-ing is acceptable, or good enough (chapter 4, section 1). And someone who intends to A may reflect practically on acceptable means to A-ing.

Practical reflection, as I understand it, often issues in evaluative beliefs about action: for example, the belief that it would be best to A, the belief that A-ing would be acceptable, and the belief that A-ing is a satisfactory means to a desired end (chapter 4, section 1; Mele 1992e, ch. 12; 1995a, ch. 2). Such beliefs, based as they are on reflection, are cognitive decisions. One might argue that cognitive decisions of the kinds just mentioned often issue directly in corresponding intentions, without any act of intention formation, and that acquiring an intention on the basis of practical reflection is just a matter of an intention's being directly produced by the acquisition of a reflective evaluative belief. That, it may be alleged, is how intentions are acquired on the basis of reflection. Accordingly, it may be claimed that instances of practical deciding are really not *acts* of deciding at all; rather, they are the nonactional production of intentions by instances of cognitive deciding that are based on practical reflection. It may be claimed, for example, that if an agent judges that it would be best to A, that judgment's issuing, without any *act* of practical deciding, in an intention to A is an instance of deciding to A.

There may be an element of truth in this. In some cases, having judged or decided on the basis of practical reflection that it would be best to A, one seemingly need not proceed to do anything to bring it about that one intends to A. The judgment may issue straightaway and by default in the intention. So, at least, I have argued elsewhere (Mele 1992e, ch. 12). However, things are not always so simple. Consider Joe, a smoker. On New Year's Eve, he is contemplating kicking the habit. Faced with the practical question what to do about his smoking, Joe is deliberating about what it would be best to do about this. It is clear to him that it would be best to quit smoking at some point, but as yet he is unsure whether it would be best to quit soon. Joe is under a lot of stress, and he worries that quitting smoking might drive him over the edge. Eventually, he decides that it would be best to quit—permanently, of course—by midnight. Joe's cognitive decision settles an evaluative question. But Joe is not yet settled on quitting. He tells his partner, Jill, that it is now clear to him that it would be best to stop smoking, beginning tonight. She asks, "So is that your New Year's resolution?" Joe sincerely replies, "Not yet; the next hurdle is to *decide* to quit. If I can do that, I'll have a decent chance of kicking the habit."

This little story is coherent. In some instances of akratic action, one intends to act as one judges best and then backslides (Mele 1987, chs. 3 and 6). In others, one does not progress from judging something best to intending to do it.[3] Seemingly, having decided that it would be best to quit smoking, Joe may or may not form the intention to quit. His *forming* the intention, as opposed to his nonactionally acquiring it, apparently would be a momentary mental action of the sort highlighted in views 3 and 4. (Recall my convention of using the verb "form" in "form an intention" as an action verb.) Whether there are such actions remains to be seen.

I turn to view 2, "practical deciding as extended action." It is best construed as a reformative view, as opposed to an explication of a commonsense notion of deciding. A student who says, "I was up all night deciding to major in English" lacks a firm grip on the language. Seemingly, what he means is that he was up all night deliberating about what major to declare or about whether to major in English, and he eventually decided (or acquired an intention) to declare English as a major on the basis of his deliberation.[4] However, on view 2, claims of the sort this student made are often true on a literal interpretation; according to this view, an instance of deciding, an extended action, begins when relevant practical reflection begins and ends when the agent (nondeviantly) acquires an intention on the basis of that reflection.

If there are events that conform to a commonsense notion of deciding, view 2 loses much of its kick. Where there is no need for conceptual reform, there should be little interest in pursuing it. Whether further discussion of view 2 is in order depends on what the ensuing discussion of views 3 and 4 uncovers.

According to view 3, practical deciding is a momentary mental action of intention formation and there are no such actions. Return to Joe. Although he decided that it would be best to quit smoking, he does not yet have an intention to quit. Can he proceed to *form* an intention to quit? Conventional wisdom suggests that he can. But it is difficult to be confident that conventional wisdom is correct about this independently of a good grasp of what it is to form an intention. Intentions themselves are relatively well understood (see Brand 1984; Bratman 1987; Mele 1992e); in chapter 1 (section 5), I sketched my own understanding of their constitution. The question now is what it is to *form* an intention as opposed to nonactionally acquiring one.

Does one want to understand the *means* by which agents form intentions? No. Assume that there are *basic actions*—roughly, actions that an agent performs, but not by means of doing something else. If there are momentary actions of intention formation, they fall into this group. Perhaps the best way to get a handle on what forming an intention might be is to catalogue ways in which intentions are arguably nonactionally acquired and to see what conceptual space might remain for the actional acquisition of intentions.

I have already commented on one way in which an agent arguably may acquire an intention without forming it: perhaps a cognitive decision of a certain kind may issue directly in a corresponding intention. There may be other ways, as well. Consider the following claim: "When I intentionally unlocked my office door this morning, I intended to unlock it. But since I am in the habit of unlocking my door in the morning, and conditions this morning were normal, nothing called for a *decision* to unlock it" (Mele 1992e, p. 231). It seems that some intentions arise as part of a routine without having to be actively formed. If I had heard a terrible ruckus in my office, I might have paused to consider whether to unlock the door or call the campus police, and I might have decided to unlock the door. But given the routine nature of my conduct, I see no need to postulate an act of intention formation in this case. Moreover, if an act of intention formation must occur in a simple case of this kind to account for my act of unlocking the door, why not suppose that the former act must be the product of another one—a decision to form the intention to unlock the door? An infinite regress threatens.

Arguably, some intentions may nonactionally arise out of desires (Audi 1993, p. 64). Suppose that an agent acquires a proximal desire to A. Perhaps, if the agent has no (significant) competing desires and no reservations about A-ing, the acquisition of that desire may straightaway give rise to the nonactional acquisition of an intention to A. Walking home from work, Helen notices her favorite brand of beer on display in a store window. The sight of the beer prompts a desire to buy some, and her acquiring that desire issues straightaway in an intention to buy some. This seems conceivable.

It also seems conceivable that, given Helen's psychological profile, the sight of the beer in the window issues *directly* in an intention to buy some, in which case there is no intervening desire to buy the beer (cf. chapter 7, section 2). Perhaps in some emergencies, too, a perceptual event, given the agent's psychological profile, straightaway prompts an intention to A. Seeing a dog dart into the path of his car, an experienced driver who is attending to traffic conditions may immediately acquire an intention to swerve. This seems conceivable, too (cf. chapter 8, section 3).

Brian O'Shaughnessy, a proponent of view 1 ("practical deciding as nonactional"), claims that decidings are "those comings-to-intend events that resolve a state of uncertainty over what to do" (1980, vol. 2, p. 297). This claim may be divorced from his commitment to view 1. If the basic point about resolving practical uncertainty is correct, it may be correct even if practical decidings are momentary mental actions. Notice also that if the point is correct, it helps to account for common intuitions about scenarios of the kind discussed in the preceding three paragraphs. In the cases I described, there is no uncertainty that intention acquisition resolves. I was not uncertain about whether to unlock my door, Helen was not uncertain about whether to buy the beer, and the driver was not uncertain about what course of action to take. At no time were any of us uncertain about the matters at issue. Furthermore, if there are cases in which a cognitive decision based on practical reflection issues directly (and therefore without the assistance of an act of intention formation) in a corresponding intention, the agent's reaching his cognitive conclusion resolves his uncertainty about what to do. Reaching the conclusion directly results in settledness on a course of action (or, sometimes, in settledness on *not* doing something). In Joe's case, of course, matters are different; even though he has decided that it would be best to quit smoking, he continues to be uncertain or unsettled about what to do.[5]

If one has some sense of various ways in which intentions might arise without being formed, why should one think that we sometimes form intentions? As a proponent of view 3 or 4 might put the question, why should one think that we *decide* to do (or not to do) things?

It is natural to consider ordinary experiences of agency in this connection. Many people insist that they have robust experiences of deciding to act, of making up their minds to do things. A proponent of view 1 or 3 may argue that what these people in fact experience is cognitive deciding about action, for example, arriving at the belief that it would be best to A on the basis of practical reflection. It may also be suggested that people sometimes experience the sort of intention acquisition that occurs in the beer scenario or in some emergencies and mistakenly take themselves to have *formed* those intentions in an act of practical decision making. However, the experience claims cannot safely be quickly dismissed.

I now report on some common experiences of mine and then try to ascertain whether they might be veridical. Sometimes I find myself with an odd hour or less at the office between scheduled tasks or at the end of the day. Typically, I briefly reflect on what to do then. I find that I do not try to ascertain what it would be *best* to do at those times; this is fortunate since settling that issue might often take more time than it is worth. Rather, I look at a list that I keep on my desk of short tasks that need to be performed sooner or later—reply to an e-mail message, write a letter of recommendation, and the like—and decide which to do. So, at least, it seems to me. Sometimes I have the experience not only of settling on a specific task or two but also, in the case of two or more tasks, of settling on a particular order of execution.

I have an e-mail system that plays a few notes when a message arrives. Occasionally, when I hear the notes, I pause briefly to consider whether to stop what I am doing and check the message. Sometimes I have the experience of deciding to check it or the experience of deciding not to check it. Sometimes I do not even consider checking the new message.

In situations of both of the kinds under consideration (the odd hour and incoming e-mail), I sometimes have the experience of having an urge to do one thing but deciding to do another instead. For example, when I hear that a new e-mail message has arrived, I may have an urge to check it straightaway but decide to finish what I am doing first. (When I am grading tests, these urges tend to be particularly strong.) When I am looking at my list of short tasks at the beginning of an odd hour, I may feel more inclined to perform one of the more pleasant tasks on my list but opt for a less pleasant one that is more pressing.

That I lead an exciting life is obvious. The question now is whether my reported experiences ever match reality. Sometimes, it seems, practical uncertainty is resolved by our arriving, on the basis of practical reflection, at cognitive decisions that issue directly in corresponding intentions. Do we also resolve practical uncertainty by deciding—in the momentary mental action sense—what to do? If my utterly mundane experiences in my office can be trusted, the answer is yes. But can they? A persuasive response to this last question requires a careful look at some sources of skepticism about the existence of practical decisions, construed as momentary mental actions.

2. Intentions in Practical Deciding

In this section and the next, I assume that practical decidings are momentary mental actions of intention formation, and I investigate a pair of problems for the thesis that practical deciding, so understood, is a genuine phenomenon. That there are mental actions should be uncontroversial. If you feel inclined to demur, please take a break from this chapter and solve the following multiplication problem in your head: $157 \times 15 = ?$ Unless you are uncommonly talented in this sphere, it will take you at least a few seconds to succeed. If you persist, you will perform the mental action of solving the problem in your head; and even if you give up too soon, you will have performed mental actions in trying to solve the problem in your head. That practical deciding is a mental action is not a mark against it. But some other aspects of it might be.

One potential source of skepticism about the existence of practical decisions is a worry about their etiology. To decide to A, according to the working assumption of this section, is to form an intention to A. Does deciding to A require an intention in addition to the intention to A formed in so deciding? Donald Davidson (1980, ch. 3) has claimed that every action is intentional under some description or other. According to another popular thesis, in every case of overt intentional action, some intention or other plays an action-producing role (Mele 1992e, ch. 10; cf. Brand 1984, ch. 2; Bratman 1987, pp. 119–27). Assuming that practical decidings are actions, Davidson's thesis entails that they are intentional under some description. In that case, a counterpart of the second thesis would imply that in every case of deciding to A, some intention or other plays a productive role. If it is plausible that our best account of overt intentional action places intentions in causal roles and that practical decisions are mental analogues of some overt intentional actions, we should expect intentions to play a role in the production of practical decisions. If it should turn out that there are no plausible candidates for intentions that play such a role in garden-variety practical decision making, there may be grounds for skepticism about the existence of practical decisions, construed as actions.

Hugh McCann (1986a) has defended the view that practical decisions are intentional actions. He also contends that to say that an agent's decision to A "is intentional cannot mean that he made it out of a prior intention so to decide, for if he already intended to decide that way then he had already decided" (p. 266).[6] Although this is not quite right, McCann is on to something. Seeing where he goes wrong will prove useful.

Can someone intend to decide to A without already having decided to A? Consider the following story. Brian is deliberating about whether to A or to B. A demon has manipulated Brian's brain in such a way that he temporarily cannot decide to A, decide to B, or nonactionally acquire either intention (i.e., the intention to A or the intention to B). The demon informs Brian that if he is to decide to A he must first press a certain green button that will enable him to decide to A in just the way he decides to do other things and that pressing a certain blue button will enable him to decide to B in the normal way. Brian continues deliberating and eventually comes to the conclusion that it would be best to A. In other circumstances, his so judging might have issued straightaway in an intention to A, but the demon has prevented that from happening. Judging it best to A and believing that it is very unlikely that he will A without intending to, Brian wants to form the intention—that is, to decide—to A. In fact, he intends to decide to A. Believing, correctly, that he must press the button in order to enable himself to decide to A, he presses the button. And then he decides to A.

Is this story coherent? Is there a hidden contradiction or perhaps a contradiction that is evident to everyone but me? One might claim (1) that intending to decide to A is conceptually sufficient for being settled on A-ing and (2) that being settled on A-ing is conceptually sufficient for intending to A. If claims (1) and (2) are true, the story has a large hole in it. According to the story, Brian cannot intend to A until he presses the green button. But claims (1) and (2) and the detail that Brian intends to decide to A

before he presses the button jointly entail that Brian has the intention to A before he presses the button.

The culprit here is claim (1), not the story. Claim (1) is part of what the story is designed to test. Grant that the demon's machinations will prevent Brian from being settled on A-ing unless and until he presses the green button. Does it follow from this that Brian cannot intend to decide to A? Does it follow that he cannot intend to bring it about that he is settled on A-ing? I do not see how. Being settled on A-ing is one thing, and being settled on bringing it about that one is settled on A-ing is another. If being in the latter, higher-order condition were to entail being in the former, lower-order condition, only confused agents could be in the higher-order condition. Plainly, an agent who is settled on bringing it about that he is settled on A-ing is under the impression that he is not yet settled on A-ing. It is difficult to see why it should be thought that his impression *must* be mistaken. McCann (1986a, p. 251) urges, reasonably, that a psychological commitment to A-ing is central to intending to A.[7] That the demon has set up an obstacle to Brian's being psychologically committed to A-ing is compatible with Brian's being psychologically committed to removing the obstacle and to bringing it about that he is psychologically committed to A-ing.

Although this is, to be sure, a highly contrived case, it undermines McCann's (1986a) claim. More important, it helps set the stage for a useful positive observation. The idea that decisions to A are normally produced in part by intentions to decide to A is indeed odd and unacceptable, as I explain shortly. Another bit of stage setting is in order first.

If an agent acquires an intention to decide to A, either he acquires it nonactionally or he decides to decide to A. The latter disjunct points the way to an impossible regress that can be cut short by supposing that at some point the agent nonactionally acquires a pertinent decisional intention—say, the intention to decide to decide to A. Since we wind up with a nonactionally acquired decisional intention in either case, we do better to consider the former disjunct.

Now, why might it happen that an agent nonactionally acquires an intention to *decide* to A rather than nonactionally acquiring an intention to A? In a normal scenario, in which there is no special payoff specifically for deciding to A or for intending so to decide, an agent's nonactionally acquiring an intention to decide to A when he could just as easily have nonactionally acquired an intention to A would be notably inefficient.[8] For example, having acquired a *proximal* intention to A, he would proceed to A straightaway, if all goes smoothly, whereas having acquired a proximal intention to *decide* to A straightaway, he would, if all goes smoothly, make the decision before he A-s. Similarly, acquiring at t a distal intention to A (an intention to A later, as opposed to straightaway) is an instance of becoming settled at t on A-ing later, whereas acquiring at t an intention to decide (straightaway or later) to A later is the sort of thing that would lead to settledness on A-ing by way of an additional step—decision making. Setting aside the above-mentioned special payoff scenarios, I conjecture that an agent would nonactionally acquire an intention to decide to A only if there were some obstacle to his nonactionally acquiring an intention to A that is not also an obstacle (or not as great an obstacle or not accompanied by as great an obstacle) to his nonactionally acquiring an intention to decide to A. There is such an obstacle in my demon story. Other scenarios featuring an obstacle of the kind at issue would, I believe, also be highly unusual. In normal cases, there would be no purpose in nonactionally acquiring an intention to decide to A that would not be more efficiently served by a nonactional acquisition of an intention to A. In the absence of a reason to suppose that our nonactional mental life normally is inefficiently complicated in this way, the assumption of greater efficiency and simplicity is very plausible.

If intentions to decide to A do not normally play a role in producing our decisions to A, should we abandon the idea that we perform actions of practical decision making? Might intentions of another kind be useful in this connection? Arguably, there are a great many things that we do intentionally without having intentions specifically to do them. When I walk to work, for example, my individual steps are intentional actions, but there is no need to suppose that each step requires its own distinct intention. In a typical case, a single, more general intention—an intention to walk to work along my normal route—is intention enough. Similarly, when a man intentionally runs a mile, he runs its various parts (e.g., the first quarter-mile and the seventh eighty-yard segment), and his runnings of those segments are intentional actions; but there is no need to suppose that he has distinct intentions for each of these segments.[9]

If one can A intentionally without having an intention specifically to A, perhaps one can decide to B without having an intention to decide to B. If a certain kind of intention is normally at work in the production of decisions, it might be an intention to decide what to do (Mele 1997a, p. 243; cf. Kane 1996, pp. 138–39). In a normal agent who decides to B while lacking an intention to decide to B, an intention to decide what to do may make an important contribution to the production of that decision. The idea that in every instance of practical deciding some intention or other plays a productive role does not have the unfortunate implication that decisions to B always or normally are produced (in part) by intentions to decide to B.

This section's topic has been a specific challenge to the view that there are momentary mental actions of practical decision making. The challenge rests on two assumptions: $(A1)$ practical decidings are intentional actions; $(A2)$ intentions play a role in the production of all intentional actions. The worry was that there are no plausible candidates for intentions that play a productive role in garden-variety practical decision making. I endorse $A1$. Why have I not explicitly endorsed $A2$? The answer is partly pragmatic. Although I am inclined to accept $A2$ (partly for reasons of simplicity), a proper defense of $A2$ would require a chapter of its own; given space constraints, such a chapter is dispensable. More important, the adequacy of my response to the worry addressed in this section does not depend on the truth of $A2$; rather, the worry itself derives largely from $A2$. If $A2$ is false, the worry may be dismissed on the grounds that it rests on a falsehood. So suppose that $A2$ is true. In that event, I have suggested, there is a kind of intention that is plausibly involved in the production of garden-variety practical decisions—an intention to decide what to do.[10]

3. Are Practical Decisions Inexplicable?

I turn to a worry about the explicability of practical decisions. If we were to discover that the concept of deciding to act entails that practical decisions are uniformly inexplicable, that itself would be a reason to doubt that agents ever decide to do anything.

As in the preceding section, I assume that practical decisions are momentary mental actions of intention formation. The issue is whether, on this construal, there *are* any practical decisions.

When we are asked to explain our own practical decisions, we often appeal to reasons. Typically, we attempt to explain our deciding to *A* at least partly by appealing to reasons we had for *A*-ing.[11] If a friend tells us that he has decided to leave his position at university X for a position at university Y and we ask why, we would not be at all surprised to hear a list of reasons for making the move. "I have no idea" and "For no reason at all" would be surprising responses. Again, Davidson's (1980) challenge to anticausalists about reasons-explanations (see chapter 2, section 1) applies straightforwardly to *deciding* for reasons. In the illustration I offered, Al has a pair of reasons for mowing his lawn this morning—a vengeful one and an innocuous one—and he mows his lawn this morning for only one of those reasons. Suppose that the reason for which Al mowed his lawn this morning was the vengeful one and that Al *decided* to mow his lawn this morning (as opposed to nonactionally acquiring an intention to do so). Then it is a good bet that the vengeful reason was the reason for which Al decided to mow his lawn this morning. In that case, on a causal view of acting for reasons, that reason (or a relevant neural realizer) was a cause of his decision. (This is not to say that Al's decision was causally *determined*. Again, probabilistic causation is an option.)

Given the suppositions just made, Al's decision to mow his lawn this morning seems to be explained, in part, by Al's desire to repay his neighbor for his recent rude awakening and his belief that his mowing his lawn this morning would constitute suitable repayment. But why, one might ask, did Al decide for this reason rather than for his benign one? And why did he decide to mow his lawn this morning rather than deciding to mow it at some other time?

Martha Klein has offered a detailed position on the explanation of practical decisions. Her position provides a recipe for generating ostensible answers to questions of these kinds. Klein contends that a decision to "fulfil a certain desire . . . is caused by (*a*) the desire to resolve uncertainty which prompts the attempt to decide; (*b*) the desire to do what will yield the most satisfactory result; and (*c*) the belief that this (whichever desire it is decided to fulfil) will fulfil (*b*)" (1990, p. 121). According to a popular view, which Klein accepts (ch. 5), reasons are belief-desire pairs. Against this background, Klein's remarks suggest the following sort of reasons-explanation of practical decisions: *S* decided to (fulfill his desire to) *A* because he desired to do whatever would yield the most satisfactory result and believed that his *A*-ing would do that.[12]

Klein's (1990) position is problematic. Two problems merit mention. First, it is far from clear that in all or even most instances of practical decision making, what we decide is to fulfill a desire to *A*, as opposed to deciding, more simply, to *A*. Does Al decide to fulfill his desire to mow his lawn this morning (or his desire to avenge his rude awakening or his desire to avenge his rude awakening by mowing his lawn this morning)? Or does he instead decide to mow his lawn this morning (or to avenge his rude awakening or to avenge his rude awakening by mowing his lawn this morning)? Can a being who does not represent his options in terms of desire-fulfillment make practical decisions? As it happens, Al is an eliminativist about desires. It would be at best misleading to attribute to him the belief that by mowing his lawn this morning he can fulfill his desire to do what will yield the most satisfactory result, for he is convinced that desires are mythical. It would also be misleading to say that what he decided was to fulfill his desire to mow his lawn this morning. However, Al's eliminativist convictions need not prevent him from making practical decisions. Perhaps, believing that mowing his lawn this morning would yield the most satisfactory result, he decided to do that.

Second, and much more important, it is doubtful that all practical decisions are produced in part by a desire to do what will yield the most satisfactory result and a corresponding instrumental belief. On a popular view of akratic action, it sometimes happens that an agent believes that A-ing (or not B-ing) would produce the most satisfactory result and a more satisfactory result than B-ing, but nevertheless decides to B and does not decide to A. In one version of Joe's case, for example, Joe decides to continue smoking into the new year, even though he believes that, all things considered, quitting smoking tonight and forever would produce a more satisfactory result than continuing to smoke. In the absence of a telling argument against the possibility of such decisions, one's position on decision making should leave that possibility open.

Again, some theorists have claimed, roughly, that in any case of intentional action, we do, or at least try to do, what we have the strongest motivation to do at the time. A similar thesis specifically for practical decisions may be formulated as follows:

DEC. If, at t, S has stronger motivation to decide at t to A than to decide at t in favor of anything else, then he decides at t to A, if he makes any practical decision at all at t.[13]

With this thesis in hand, one may attempt to explain practical decisions by explaining how relevant motivational facts about the agents came to obtain. Even setting aside predictable worries from some quarters about *DEC*'s deterministic tone, this strategy is worrisome.[14] Notice that *DEC* does not assert that (1) having stronger motivation to decide at t to A than one has to decide at t in favor of anything else is a sufficient condition for (2) deciding at t to A. An agent who satisfies condition (1) may still be uncertain about what to do, and he may, for example, continue to deliberate for some time before he makes a decision. An hour before midnight, Joe may have stronger motivation to decide to keep smoking than to decide in favor of anything else. Even so, he may remain undecided about what to do and continue to mull the matter over. If *DEC* is true, then (setting aside any alleged possibility of making two or more decisions at a time) if an agent decides at t to A, he has stronger motivation at the time to make that decision than to make any other, but that does not explain why he made that decision at t rather than remaining undecided then.

Constructing an explanatory scheme for practical decision making, as Klein (1990) attempted to do and as a proponent of *DEC* may try to do, is an enormously challenging task. Partly in light of the distinct possibility of akratic decisions and of the point that continued reflection on a practical issue does not require a decision to continue to reflect, I doubt that any simple formula for explaining all practical decisions will work. Sometimes what we decide to do is what we deem it best (or "most satisfactory") to do, but only *sometimes*. Sometimes we make the decision that we have the strongest motivation to make at the time, but someone who has stronger motivation to decide to A than to decide on anything else may simply continue deliberating about what to do.

Consider a more sophisticated version of *DEC*, an instance of *Mub* (chapter 8, section 1):

> *DECm*. Assuming bias-free motivation, if, at *t*, an agent's untrumped proximal motivation to decide to *A* is stronger than any untrumped proximal motivation he has that is focused on any other course of action (including prospective decidings) and than any such motivation he has for a relevant not-doing, then, at *t*, he decides to *A*, provided that he acts intentionally at *t*.

Given that deliberating is intentional activity, *DECm* differs significantly from *DEC* in one salient respect: *DECm* would be falsified by *S*'s continuing to deliberate at *t* about whether to *A* and not deciding at *t* to *A*, if *S* satisfies the principle's antecedent. However, if I am right (chapter 7, section 2), an agent's being most strongly motivated at *t* to do what he does at *t* does not explain why he does it and the explanatory significance of principles like *Mu* and *Mub* (and, by extension, *DECm*) lies in their articulating background presumptions about intentional action in the context of which explanations of particular intentional actions in terms of the attitudes are offered. On this view of things, *DECm* would point us to something to investigate in attempting to explain an agent's deciding at *t* to *A*. Accounting for an agent's motivational condition at the time might account for his decision. However, developing a general scheme for accounting for agents' motivational conditions is a challenging project, a point to which I return shortly.

The question now is whether, in light of the complexity of the task of constructing an explanatory scheme for practical decision making, there is good reason to believe that practical decisions are in principle inexplicable. The news that they are would be welcomed by proponents of view 3 ("practical deciding as mythical").

If we do make explicable practical decisions, factors of a variety of kinds seemingly enter into the explanatory mix. This may be true even of the *proximate* explanatory mix, the explanatory items present at the time of decision making. The factors may include cognitive decisions of various kinds—judgments about what it is best to do, about satisfactory means to desired ends, about whether there are good reasons for not acting as one is currently inclined to act, and so on. They may also include the relative motivational strengths of competing trumped desires at the time the decision is made, the relative salience of competing considerations at the point of decision, and more. Now, suppose you and I were to discover that our world is deterministic. Would we infer that no one has ever made a practical decision? I doubt it. But if, as I should think, practical decisions may be made in deterministic worlds, then decisions are not in principle inexplicable. Presumably, no matter how complex the etiology of a particular decision is, that decision would be explicable at least in terms of relevant laws and antecedent conditions in a deterministic world. Complexity itself should not worry us in this connection.

A skeptic may reply (1) that an event counts as a practical decision only if it has a *reasons*-explanation, rather than an explanation of just any kind, and (2) that in a deterministic world, no alleged practical decision is explicable in terms of reasons.[15] I do not reopen the debate about whether reasons can be causes. Instead, I start with the observation that it is very unlikely that we would conclude that we have never performed an intentional action if we were to discover that our world is deterministic.

Surely, we would continue to believe that we have sent e-mail messages, read books, watched sporting events, and the like; and we would be justified in so believing. Now, except in very unusual cases, an agent who is acting intentionally is acting for some reason or other (Mele 1992b). If, as I have argued (chapter 2; Mele 1992e, chs. 2 and 13), part of what it is to act for a reason is for that reason to play a role in explaining the agent's action, we would also be justified in believing that reasons played a role in explaining our ordinary intentional actions, even if we were to discover that determinism is true. The same line of reasoning applies to *deciding* for reasons.

My claim here is *not* that, on the basis of a proper analysis of determinism itself, determinists should favor the view that intentional actions have reasons-explanations. Rather, I claim (1) that a proper account of intentional action will reveal that, setting aside truly exceptional cases, intentional actions are done for reasons, (2) that a proper analysis of acting for a reason will reveal that so acting requires that the relevant reason play a role in explaining the action, and (3) that both points are consistent with causal determinism. [Claims (1) and (2) are defended in the work just cited. For a defense of a broader view that implies (3), see Mele (1995a, chs. 8–10).] Even if we were to discover that determinism is true, we would—and *should*—continue to believe that we have performed intentional actions. So if I am right about the nature of intentional action and acting for reasons, then even if we were to discover that determinism is true, we should also believe that reasons played a role in explaining our commonplace intentional actions. And the same is true of intentional actions that are practical decisions.

My primary reason for bringing determinism into the discussion is to show that the complexity of the task of constructing an explanatory scheme for practical decision making is consistent with the explicability of practical decisions. In a deterministic world, with the possible exception of chaotic events, *all* events are explicable, at least in terms of laws and antecedent conditions. The point now is that some of these explicable events can be intentional actions, including practical decidings, and that given the nature of intentional actions, reasons play a role in explaining the unexceptional ones.

The assumption that decision making always or sometimes is causally *undetermined* would seem to add another layer of complexity. But if one's pessimism about one's prospects of constructing a successful, simple formula for explaining all practical decisions does not support the thesis that causally determined decisions are inexplicable, it is difficult to see why this pessimism should lead one to hold that causally undetermined decisions are inexplicable. To be sure, if a decision made for a reason is causally undetermined, the reason for which it is made will not be part of something that deterministically causes the decision. But that is consistent with the reason's entering into a causal explanation of the decision.

4. Practical Deciding

In an attempt to resolve a particular practical uncertainty—about whether to *A* or *B*, for example—we may do a variety of things. We may gather relevant data or hire someone to gather data, we may assess data or pay someone for a professional assessment, and so on. However, even an agent who is convinced both that all the relevant information is in and that further assessment or deliberation would prove fruitless may be unsettled about what to do. Such an agent might consider attempting to resolve his practical uncertainty by deciding to abide by the toss of a coin and then tossing it. But if a roundabout attempt of this kind at resolving uncertainty is open to him, what is to prevent him from making a direct attempt? (It might even occur to the agent that if he can decide to abide by the result of a coin toss, he can, in the same way, decide to A or decide to B.) Well, what would the directness of an attempt to resolve uncertainty amount to in a situation of the imagined kind? A philosopher who cannot answer this question is in no position to treat the preceding one as rhetorical.

This brings me back to my original question. What is it to decide to do something? In sections 2 and 3, I argued that view 4 ("practical deciding as a momentary mental action of intention formation") survives the most pressing worries about it. In this section, I articulate the view more fully and tie together the main strands of argument in earlier sections.

Assume that intentions to act are executive attitudes toward plans (chapter 1, section 5). As I have argued, one can distinguish between *merely acquiring* such an attitude and *actively settling* on a course of action. Given the assumption just made, deciding to A is the latter. Deciding to act—actively settling on a course of action—may be understood as a mental act of executive assent to a first-person plan of action. If you tell me that Mike is an excellent basketball player and I express complete agreement, I thereby assent to your claim. This is overt *cognitive* assent. If you propose that we watch Mike play tonight at the arena and I express complete acceptance of your proposal, I thereby assent to your proposal. This is overt *executive* assent: I have agreed to join you in executing your proposal for joint action. Now, perhaps my overt act of assenting to your proposal was a matter of my giving voice to a nonactionally acquired intention to join you in watching Mike play. For example, upon hearing your proposal, I might not have been at all uncertain about what to do; straightaway, I nonactionally acquired an intention to join you, and I voiced that intention in an overt act of assenting to your proposal. (In that case, what happens in me is like what happens in Helen in one of the beer scenarios discussed earlier.) Or I might have weighed the pros and cons, decided that it would be best to join you, and on the basis of that cognitive decision, nonactionally acquired an intention to join you. However, there seems also to be a distinctly different possibility. Perhaps, because I already had plans and because your offer was attractive, I was uncertain about what to do. Perhaps, upon reflection, I judged that I could revise my plans without much inconvenience but was still uncertain about what to do since my prior plans were attractive as well. And perhaps I performed a mental action of assenting to your proposal and then expressed that inner assent to you. Surely, in performing that mental action, if that is what occurred, I *decided* to join you: my mentally assenting to your proposal was an act of intention formation, an act of settling on joining you to watch Mike play tonight.

My own theoretical proposal about deciding to act is that it is a mental act of executive assent to a first-person plan of action (on the representational conception of action-plans that I sketched in chapter 1, section 5). In deciding to act, one forms an intention to act, and in so doing one brings it about that one has an intention that incorporates the plan to which one assents. In some cases, the plan is very schematic; details need to be filled in. For example, without having given any thought to the details, Ann may decide now to vacation in Hawaii for the first time two summers from now. She can settle the details later, at her leisure. In other cases, the details have been worked out, and one has finally resolved one's uncertainty about whether to execute the detailed plan. (Ann may have formulated a specific plan for proposing marriage to Bob while being uncertain about whether to propose marriage.) There is, of course, a range of degrees of specificity in between.

In the case of a decision *not* to *A*, where not *A*-ing is represented by the agent as a genuine not-doing, the plan associated with the intention formed is simply *not to A*. Such an intention is not, in my view, an intention to act (see chapter 6, section 4). Intentions to see to it that one does not *A*, however, are intentions to act. And an intention not to *A* may help rationalize an intention to see to it that one does not *A* when, for example, one believes that one is in danger of succumbing to temptation to *A*.

My proposal requires that there be some plan that one assents to in making a practical decision (the limiting case for decisions to act, again, being an action-plan with a single node). That is as it should be. If we decide for reasons, notice that at least minimal representations of a relevant sort are present in reasons for which we decide, on a Davidsonian (1980) view of reasons.[16] If Al decided to mow his lawn this morning because he wanted to repay his neighbor for rudely awakening him and believed that his mowing his lawn this morning would constitute suitable repayment, his belief includes a representation of his mowing his lawn this morning—what he decided to do. In deciding to mow his lawn this morning, Al brings it about that he has an intention that incorporates that representation. However, that representation need not exhaust the representational content of the intention that Al forms. A first-person lawn-mowing schema may be stored in Al's memory, and that schema may be part of the content of the intention he forms in deciding to mow his lawn this morning. Some practical decisions to *A* may integrate (some of) the representational content of the reason or reasons for which one decides to *A* with other representational content.[17]

Practical deciding is a direct way of resolving practical uncertainty. Of course, someone's deciding to *A* may generate new practical uncertainties. Now that Ann has decided to spend some time in Hawaii two years from now, she is uncertain about how she will get there, where she will stay, and so on. These matters may be settled eventually by future practical decisions. Similarly, in some circumstances, agents who decide not to *A* subsequently decide what to do instead.

Again, if there are basic actions, practical decidings on the present construal are among them. Practical decidings, then, are relatively simple structurally; their complexity is in the content of the intention formed, not in the structure of the act of decision making itself. Deciding to *A* is more like raising one's arm than like signaling that one wants to ask a question by raising one's arm. The proposal that practical deciding is a momentary mental action of executive assent to a first-person plan of action (or, in some cases, a momentary act of settling on not *A*-ing) coheres with this relative simplicity.

Early in this chapter, I asked how practical deciding differs from nonactionally acquiring an intention. If what I have said about practical deciding is correct, there is a correct answer. Practical deciding is a mental act of the sort I have been discussing, and nonactionally acquiring an intention plainly is not an act of any kind.

We make practical decisions only when we are uncertain or unsettled about what to do.[18] It is also true that, normally, at least, when we reason about what it would be best, good enough, or permissible to do, we do so in situations involving practical uncertainty. Again, our practical decisions may accord with cognitive decisions that we have reached, or conflict with them, as in some cases of akratic action. If an agent who judges it best to A, *decides* to A or *decides* not to A, his practical decision resolves practical uncertainty that his cognitive conclusion left unresolved. I have suggested that some cognitive decisions resolve practical uncertainties, in a sense: if an agent is uncertain about whether to A, his acquiring the belief that it would be best to A may straightaway result in his acquiring an intention to A, and in acquiring that intention he becomes settled on A-ing (thereby removing the relevant practical uncertainty).[19] But I have also suggested that some practical uncertainties—including some uncertainties that any cognitive decision one reaches fails to resolve—are resolved instead by practical decisions. Practical deciding is an important mode of uncertainty resolution, and it is a straightforwardly actional mode—the mode being momentary mental action of intention formation, as opposed, for example, to the extended process featured in view 2. That we sometimes decide, in this actional sense, to do things is a pronouncement of ordinary experience, as I explained in section 1; and I take sections 2 and 3 to have resolved the strongest worries about the truth of that pronouncement.

My aim in this chapter has been threefold: to clarify what practical deciding is; to defend the idea that there are genuine instances of practical deciding, on the actional account of the phenomenon that I have advanced; and to shed some light on how practical decisions are to be explained. In connection with the second aim, I have been willing to be very receptive to claims that what we find in a variety of cases is nonactional intention acquisition rather than acts of practical decision making. (Again, I made and defended such claims myself in Mele 1992e, ch. 12, but my concern now is the dialectical situation in this chapter.) My contention is that, even on the assumption that nonactional intention acquisition is very common, there is good reason to believe that not all intentions are nonactionally acquired and that there are acts of practical decision making. Should it turn out that I have been *overly* receptive to nonactional intention acquisition—should it be true, for example, that whenever cognitive decisions that it is best to A issue smoothly in intentions to A, they in fact do so by prompting a mental act of deciding to A, or that seeing something one likes in fact leads one to try to acquire it only if it leads one to perform the mental action of deciding to acquire it— that is not a problem for the view advanced here.[20] The upshot would be that practical deciding, on the view of it that I have advanced, is more pervasive than I have been willing to claim it is. That obviously is consistent with my having achieved the aims I identified.

The power to make practical decisions lies at the heart of much of the literature on freedom of the will and freedom of action—incompatibilist and compatibilist literature alike. Agents who act intentionally but lack this power are conceivable (Frankfurt 1988, p. 176). Perhaps cats and dogs are like that. They may have beliefs and desires, nonactionally acquire relatively short-term intentions on the basis of their beliefs and desires, and execute those intentions in intentional actions. This is consistent with their never *forming* an intention. We would like to believe that we do form intentions, that we make up our minds—or decide—to do certain things and not to do others. If I am right, it is reasonable to believe this. Setting aside practical decisions for not-doings, it is reasonable, as well, to understand practical decisions as mental acts of executive assent to first-person plans of action. Again, in the case of bare not-A-ings, the plan assented to in deciding not to A is *not to A*.

Notes

1. See, for example, Frankfurt (1988, pp. 174–76), Kane (1996, p. 24), Kaufman (1966, p. 34), McCann (1986a, pp. 254–55), Mele (1992e, p. 156), Pink (1996, p. 3), and Searle (2001, p. 94).

2. Brian O'Shaughnessy (1980, vol. 2, pp. 300–1) defends a view of this kind. Cf. Williams (1993, p. 36).

3. On akratic failures to intend, see Audi (1979, p. 191), Davidson (1980, ch. 2; 1985, pp. 205–6), Mele (1992e, pp. 228–34), and Rorty (1980).

4. Incidentally, to say that one was up all night deciding *whether* to major in English—or deciding what major to declare—is to speak loosely. What one means is that one was up all night deliberating about whether to major in English—or deliberating about what major to declare.

5. Being uncertain about what to do should not be confused with not being certain about what to do. Rocks are neither certain nor uncertain about anything.

6. McCann's positive view is that intending to decide to A is a constituent of deciding to A. For criticism, see Mele (1997a, pp. 242–43).

7. On this, McCann and I agree. Again, intending to A, as I understand intentions, encompasses being settled on A-ing (Mele 1992e, ch. 9), and this settledness is a psychological commitment to A-ing. Intentions not to A encompass settledness on not A-ing. (Like Bratman 1987, p. 5, and others, I take this kind of commitment to be revocable. Acquiring an intention does not irrevocably stick one with it. We can change our minds.)

8. In Gregory Kavka's (1983) well-known toxin puzzle, there is a payoff specifically for *intending* to drink a certain toxin—a reward for intending to drink it that is not contingent on one's drinking it. The payoff might just as well have been for *deciding* to drink the toxin.

9. What I say here is at odds with what Michael Bratman (1984) has dubbed "the simple view"—the thesis that S A-ed intentionally only if S intended to A (see Adams 1986; McCann 1986b, 1991). For detailed criticism of the simple view, see Bratman (1987, ch. 8; cf. Mele 1992e, ch. 8).

10. Since practical decisions include decisions *not* to A, the intention may be described more fully as an intention to decide what to do or not to do.

11. In section 2, I mentioned cases in which there are reasons for deciding to A that are not also reasons for A-ing, as in Kavka's (1983) toxin puzzle. Elsewhere, I have argued that in some such cases, an agent can decide on the basis of a reason of this kind (Mele 1995b; cf. 1992b).

12. Read literally, the quoted claim asserts, in part, that beliefs that certain *desires* will fulfill "the desire to do what will yield the most satisfactory result" play a systematic causal role in producing decisions. But such beliefs are plainly false. Although successfully acting on a certain desire—or doing A, A being something that one desires to do—may fulfill a desire to do whatever will yield the most satisfactory result, a desire itself will not fulfill this desire. I assume that the beliefs Klein mentions in (c) are meant to be beliefs about prospective courses of action.

13. Two points should be made about this formulation. First, the expression "at t S has motivation to decide at t to A" is not redundant. After all, at t S might have motivation to decide at or by some much later time to A. Second, deciding at t to A should be distinguished from deciding to A at t. Today, at noon, Ann decided to play racquetball at 5:00 P.M.

14. Those who object to *DEC*'s deterministic ring may prefer the following probabilistic variant: (*DEC**) an agent's having stronger motivation at t to decide at t to A than to decide at t in favor of anything else makes it more probable that he decides at t to A than that he makes an alternative decision at t, given that he makes a practical decision at t. Again, probabilistic causation is an option. David Lewis writes that "causes make their effects more probable" and "if distinct events c and e both occur, and if the actual chance of e (at a time t immediately after c) is sufficiently greater than the counterfactual chance of e without c, that implies outright that c is a cause of e" (1986, pp. 178, 180).

15. I am grateful to Randy Clarke for motivating me to address this worry.

16. Cf. McCann (1998, ch. 8). On some other views of reasons, representations of the sort I identify are not present in the reasons for which we decide.

17. On the representational content of intentions, see Mele (1992e, ch. 11). Obviously, I am not suggesting that all reasons for which we decide are represented in the contents of our decisions. See chapter 2, section 1.

18. There are very special cases in which an agent who is offered a reward for deciding to A is convinced that he will A whether or not he intends (or decides) to A (Mele 1992b). Perhaps such an agent may decide to A. An agent offered Kavka's (1983) toxin deal may be convinced that someone will cause him to drink the toxin unintentionally if he does not intentionally drink it. On being offered a prize for deciding to drink the toxin, he may be uncertain about whether to make this decision. He may be uncertain about that even though—being convinced that if he does not drink the toxin intentionally, he will drink it unintentionally—he is not uncertain about whether he will drink the toxin.

19. In Mele (1995a, pp. 25–30), I attempt to explain why best judgments sometimes result in corresponding intentions and sometimes fail to do so.

20. A theorist who holds that cognitive and perceptual events of these kinds can issue in intentions or actions only by way of practical decisions regards such cognitive and perceptual events as incapable of resolving practical uncertainty.

10

Human Agency par Excellence

It is sometimes claimed that a standard causal approach to understanding and explaining actions leaves agents out of the picture, that theorists attracted to this approach face the problem of disappearing agents. A. I. Melden writes, "It is futile to attempt to explain conduct through the causal efficacy of desire—all *that* can explain is further happenings, not actions performed by agents. . . . There is no place in this picture . . . even for the conduct that was to have been explained" (1961, pp. 128–29). Thomas Nagel voices a similar worry: "The essential source of the problem is a view of persons and their actions as part of the order of nature, causally determined or not. That conception, if pressed, leads to the feeling that we are not agents at all. . . . *my doing* of an act—or the doing of an act by someone else—seems to disappear when we think of the world objectively. There seems no room for agency in [such] a world . . . there is only what happens" (1986, pp. 110–11).

It is generally agreed that elephants, tigers, and dogs are part of the natural order and that such animals act. Setting aside the mind-body problem and radical skeptical hypotheses (it is all a dream, the only biological entities are brains in vats, and the like), the commonsense judgment that such animals act is difficult to reject. Apparently, elephants, tigers, and dogs train their young, fight, run, and so on. If they do these things, they act. Seemingly, we human beings do these things, too. If we do them, we act, even if we are of the natural order. One suspects, then, that when Nagel says that we never do anything—never act—if we are "part of the order of nature," he either has a specific kind of action in mind or has extraordinarily high standards for action. Some philosophers hold that we never act *freely* if we are part of the natural order.[1] But Nagel says that the problem of disappearing agents is not "the problem of free will" (1986, pp. 110–11). If the agency that allegedly disappears on the assumption that we are part of the natural order is not just free agency and any kind of agency that depends on it, what is it?

In an influential article on the problem of disappearing agents, David Velleman contends that standard causal accounts of action and its explanation do not capture what "distinguishes human action from other animal behavior" and do not accommodate "human action *par excellence*" (1992, p. 462). Although, as I explain, Velleman does not make it clear what action of the latter kind is supposed to be, he does point his readers in a general direction. My aim in this chapter is to display the resources of my causal conception of human motivation and agency in the sphere of human action to which Velleman points. Unfortunately, I cannot begin with a useful description of human action par excellence. Ascertaining what such action is supposed to be is a significant task.

Some theorists worry about how states of mind (qua states of mind) can be causally relevant to bodily motions. This is a part of the mind-body problem that I have attempted to resolve elsewhere (Mele 1992e, ch. 2). The worry can motivate skepticism about there being any actions—hence, any agents—in the natural order. For example, if the occurrence of actions (including actions of nonhuman animals) is conceptually dependent on there being causally efficacious desires and there are no such desires, there are no actions. However, Velleman (1992, pp. 468–69) says that the problem of disappearing agents would remain even if the mind-body problem were solved. And, like Nagel, he regards the former problem as "distinct from the problem of free-will" (p. 465, n. 13). Since I am taking my lead from Velleman, the problem to be examined in this chapter is distinct from both of these more familiar problems.

One reason for locating my problem in Velleman (1992) rather than Nagel (1986) is that Nagel's worry is too easily read as groundless. What is it *not* to be part of the natural order, after all? Supernatural beings, if there are any, are not part of the natural order. That a being needs to be supernatural in order to act is an interesting proposition, but it is difficult to muster the motivation to try to falsify it in the absence of an argument for it. There is a tradition of thinking that acting *freely* requires being supernatural, but, again, Nagel says that his worry is about all action, not just free action. Another way not to be part of the natural order is to be abstract in the way that numbers and propositions are. However, human beings are not abstract in that way.

1. Human Agents

What is it to be a human agent? There are fancier and less fancy answers in the literature. My preferred answer is far from fancy: to be a human agent is to be a human being who acts. Human agents are not always acting. When they are not, they are not functioning as agents.

Consider the following cases:

Case 1. By means of direct electrical stimulation, a neuroscientist uses Sam's brain as a calculator to do multiplication problems. Sam has no desire to do mental arithmetic, and he does not try to do multiplication problems in his head. Sam is conscious of various results of the manipulation. He has conscious thoughts like the following: "Problem: 17 × 11. Answer: 187." Sam has no idea that he is being manipulated. These thoughts occur with great frequency. Sam thinks he is going crazy.

Case 2. The calculations occur spontaneously in Sam's brain, but everything else is the same, including Sam's lacking a desire to do mental multiplication. Again, he thinks he is going crazy.

Case 3. Uma has practiced and learned a useful method for solving multiplication problems in her head. Just now, in utterly ordinary circumstances, she used the method to solve 113 × 15 in order to calculate the gratuity on a dinner bill.

Case 4. This case differs from the preceding one in that Uma has compulsive desires to solve multiplication problems in her head and she was motivated by such a desire to solve 113 × 15. Uma does not like having those desires. She regards them as alien forces.

In cases 1 and 2, Sam, in Nagel's words, is "merely . . . the scene" of the pertinent events (1986, p. 113). He is not solving multiplication problems; he is not playing an agent's role in their being solved. Uma, in case 3, does solve a multiplication problem; she plays an agent's role.[2] Uma solves the same problem in case 4. In that case, as in case 3, she performs the mental action of solving that problem, and insofar as she does this, she plays an agent's role. The difference between the two cases is not that she acts in one but not in the other. Rather, the difference is that her action is not compulsive in one and is compulsive in the other.

This may be disputed. It may be claimed that it is not Uma who acts in case 4 but something else. I disagree. Uma has the psychological problem, and that problem of hers manifests itself in the compulsive desire that motivates her solving the multiplication problem. If it is something other than Uma that acts in case 4, what is it? Certainly neither her desire to solve the problem nor her compulsion. Desires and compulsions are simply not capable of performing the pertinent action since they have no idea how to solve multiplication problems, or how to do anything at all, for that matter.[3]

Velleman reports, "The cases of defective action that occupy [Harry] Frankfurt's attention are cases in which the agent fails to participate because he is 'alienated' from the motives that actuate him . . ." (1992, p. 470). Here, a distinction is in order between failing to participate in an action and participating defectively in an action. The task of accommodating human action par excellence arises whether one conceives of human agents as human beings who act or as something fancier. On the less fancy view, one can safely say that Uma, a human agent, acts defectively in case 4, and one may also say that the defect is such that her action is not a human action par excellence. On a fancier view, one can say that Uma qua agent and Uma qua human being are different things and that the agent does not act, in which case neither the agent nor the human being engages in human action par excellence. I myself have never felt the need to use the expression "human agent" to mean something fancier than "human being who acts."

Frankfurt also calls attention to another kind of behavior that might be regarded as defective action: "To drum one's fingers on the table, altogether idly and inattentively, is surely not a case of passivity: the movements in question do not occur without one's making them. Neither is it an instance of action, however, but only of being active. . . . We should not find it unnatural that we are capable, without lapsing into mere passivity, of behaving as mindlessly as [an active] spider" (1988, p. 58; cf. Velleman 2000, pp. 1–2). Arguably, the drumming Frankfurt describes *is* an instance of action, a relatively "mindless" instance. But there is no need to argue about that here, for, presumably, it is not an instance of human action par excellence. One can search for action of the latter kind without struggling to locate the lower boundary of human action.

2. Velleman's Objection to the "Standard Story"

Velleman reports that his objection to what he calls the "standard story of human action" (1992, p. 461), a causal story, "is not that it mentions mental occurrences in the agent instead of the agent himself [but] that the occurrences it mentions in the agent are no more than occurrences in him, because their involvement in an action does not add up to the agent's being involved" (p. 463). The objection is motivated by a pair of considerations: the phenomenon of alienation from a desire and the difference between passively acquiring an intention and deciding to act. Velleman proposes to solve the problem of disappearing agents by finding "mental events and states that are functionally identical to the agent, in the sense that they play the causal role that ordinary parlance attributes to him" (p. 475). He claims that this causal role—that is, "the functional role of agent"—"is that of a single party prepared to reflect on, and take sides with, potential determinants of behaviour at any level in the hierarchy of attitudes" (p. 477). What plays this role, he argues, is "a desire that drives practical thought"— "a desire to act in accordance with reasons" (p. 478).

Velleman introduces his objection with an interesting description of a case of "action from which the distinctively human feature is missing" (1992, p. 462). I quote at length:

> I have a long-anticipated meeting with an old friend for the purpose of resolving some minor difference; but . . . as we talk, his offhand comments provoke me to raise my voice in progressively sharper replies, until we part in anger. Later reflection leads me to realize that accumulated grievances had crystallized in my mind, during the weeks before our meeting, into a resolution to sever our friendship over the matter at hand, and that this resolution is what gave the hurtful edge to my remarks. In short, I may conclude that desires of mine caused the decision, which in turn caused the corresponding behaviour; and I may acknowledge that these mental states were thereby exerting their normal motivational force, unabetted by any strange perturbation or compulsion. But do I necessarily think that I made the decision or that I executed it? Surely, I can believe that the decision, though genuinely motivated by my desires, was thereby induced in me but not formed by me; and I can believe that it was genuinely executed in my behaviour but executed, again, without my help. Indeed, viewing the decision as directly motivated by my desires, and my behaviour as directly governed by the decision, is precisely what leads to the thought that as my words became more shrill, it was my resentment speaking, not I. (pp. 464–65)

The protagonist here—I call him Ed—thinks that it was his resentment speaking, not he. Obviously, this thought is not literally true. What Ed may be thinking is that his real or true self was not speaking and that the desires that drove his behavior were alien to that self. It is open to a theorist who regards this, too, as metaphorical to contend that actions partly explained by desires that lack certain credentials are not human actions par excellence. It may be claimed, for example, that human action of this kind requires, among other things, that the agent want to be moved by the desires that move him, realize that he is being moved by these desires, and make a relevant decision partly on the basis of his evaluation of the objects of these desires.

Although it is not obvious that a difference between deciding to act and nonactionally acquiring an intention is at work in this passage, the distinction is playing a role. Velleman says that Ed "can believe that the *decision*" to sever his friendship with the other party was "induced in [him] but not formed by [him]" (1992, p. 464, my emphasis). But in a note on this passage, he describes Ed's behavior as "springing directly from intentions that have simply come over [him]" (p. 465, n. 12). This suggests that, in fact, there was no decision to sever the friendship and that instead Ed passively acquired an intention to do this.

In chapter 9, I developed the idea that to decide to do something is to perform a mental action of intention formation and that not all of our intentions come about in this way. The illustrations I offered of nonactional intention acquisition included a mundane scenario featuring habitual intentional action, the acquisition of an intention to buy an inexpensive item one notices in a store window, and the sudden acquisition of an intention to avoid hitting a wayward dog with one's car. Similarly, in Ed's case, the intention to sever the friendship may have come over him, as Velleman (1992) says, without any decision's having been made to sever it. In my simple illustrations, we do not see behavior worthy of the designation "human action par excellence," as will become clear later, and Ed's conduct may fall short of action that merits this description in virtue of his not having made a relevant decision. It may also fall short in virtue of his alienation from his guiding desires.

3. Human Action par Excellence and a Special Desire

Can the problem of disappearing agents be solved by isolating a species of action that involves the execution of a decision and the absence of alienation and then providing a causal account of it? That depends, among other things, on what human action par excellence is. After all, the problem of disappearing agents, as Velleman (1992) presents it, is supposed to be that causal theorists lack an account of agency that is adequate to such action. So what is human action par excellence? Is it action on one extreme of a continuum that has the simplest (intentional) animal action on the other extreme? Or can one find human action par excellence short of the extreme? How high are the standards for human action par excellence?

The term is Velleman's. Where does *he* draw the line? According to Velleman, in human action par excellence,

> What really produces the bodily movements that you are said to produce . . . is a part of you that performs the characteristic functions of agency. That part . . . is your desire to act in accordance with reasons, a desire that produces behaviour, in your name, by adding its motivational force to that of whichever motives appear to provide the strongest reasons for acting, just as you are said to throw your weight behind them. (1992, p. 479)

This, of course, is part of Velleman's answer to the problem of disappearing agents. At the moment, my concern is what the passage shows about the height of the bar he sets for human action par excellence, not the merits of his answer.

The passage at issue implies that human action par excellence does not include ordinary akratic actions—uncompelled intentional actions that are contrary to what one judges best. In human action par excellence, according to Velleman, one acts in accordance with what one takes to be the "strongest" (i.e., best) reasons for action (1992, p. 479). One's "desire to act in accordance with reasons" produces one's action "by adding its motivational force" to the force of those reasons or the associated motives. That ordinary akratic actions are not among human actions par excellence is an acceptable result. Ordinary akratic action is commonly deemed irrational, and it is plausible that there is no place for irrationality in human action par excellence.[4]

Incidentally, this is a nice indication that the project of providing an account of human agency par excellence, as it manifests itself in Velleman (1992), is distinct from the project of providing an account of what it is to be a free agent or a morally responsible agent. Agents can act freely and morally responsibly when they are not at or near peak levels of performance, as when they act akratically. To be sure, this point is consistent with its being true that unless one's behavior sometimes satisfies certain high standards of agency, one can never act freely or morally responsibly, even if acting freely or morally responsibly at a time does not depend on satisfaction of those standards at that time. But if the bar for human agency par excellence is not set with an eye to identifying standards for free and morally responsible action, it is unlikely that the notch one settles on will mark such standards. That one's objective in searching for a characterization of human action par excellence is not specific to the domain of freedom or moral responsibility, however, does not deprive one of a target. There is still the sphere of self-control, for example.[5]

The observation that ordinary akratic actions are not instances of human action par excellence suggests two further points that merit comment. First, the problem Velleman (1992) attempts to solve is not really the problem of disappearing agents. Obviously, akratic actions are actions, but they do not fall into Velleman's net.[6] What attracts his attention is, rather, what may be termed the problem of *shrinking agents*. "The standard story of human action," in his telling, does not say what goes on in robust human action of a sort that he, I, and others regard as important and interesting— a sort that exhibits self-control, as I explain.

The second point is that the problem of disappearing—or, actually, shrinking— agents cannot be solved in the way I asked about, that is, simply by isolating a species of action that involves the execution of a decision and the absence of alienation and then providing a causal account of it. An akratic action can be the execution of a decision, and akratic agents need not be alienated from the desires that move them when they act akratically, at least in any robust sense of "alienated" (Schroeder and Arpaly 1999). This leaves open, of course, the possibility that the problem can be solved by adding something further to executing a decision and the absence of alienation—perhaps, in Velleman's (1992) words, a "desire to act in accordance with reasons," which desire makes a special contribution to the agent's deciding and acting as he does.

Why would a desire to act in accordance with reasons add its motivational force to the force of what one takes to be one's better reasons at the time rather than to the force of the competing reasons? If the content of the desire is "that I act in accordance with reasons," the desire would be satisfied even if one were to act in accordance with one's lower-ranked reasons. Now, Velleman says that his expression "a desire to act in accordance with reasons" is not meant to pick out "a particular desire" and that his preferred candidate for the desire that plays the role of the agent is "a desire to do what makes sense, or what's intelligible to [me], in the sense that [I] could explain it" (1992, p. 478; cf. Velleman 2000, pp. 26–29).[7] However, this desire can be satisfied by an akratic action. We can explain our akratic actions, and they make sense, or are intelligible to us, in that sense.[8]

The following desire is not satisfiable by a garden-variety akratic action: a desire to act in accordance with whatever reasons one takes to be superior.[9] Perhaps it is a desire of this kind that Velleman needs in his picture. In an agent who takes himself to have superior reasons for A-ing, a desire of this kind can enter, along with desires associated with his reasons for A-ing, into the positive motivational base of his desire to A (see chapter 4, section 4). It can play the motivational role that Velleman gestures at in this connection. Whether something of this kind should be seen as, "functionally speaking, the agent's contribution to the causal order" (Velleman 1992, p. 479) is a question I take up shortly.

I have argued elsewhere (Mele 1990a), that an appeal to a disposition to have desires of roughly this kind is needed in an account of what it is to be a self-controlled person, a person whose *traits of character* include self-control (understood as the contrary of *akrasia*). A significant capacity for self-control is plausibly regarded as a crucial ingredient in the sort of agency exhibited in what Velleman calls "human action par excellence." In cases of such action, as Velleman sees it, "the agent's concern in reflecting on his motives [is] to see which ones provide stronger reasons for acting, and then to ensure that they prevail over those whose rational force is weaker" (1992, p. 478). Indeed, an important virtue of his position, he contends, is that it accounts for the truth of the plausible idea that "a person sometimes intervenes among his motives because the best reason for acting is associated with the intrinsically weaker motive, and he must therefore intervene in order to ensure that the weaker motive prevails" (p. 480). One wonders how the weaker motive can prevail: the puzzle about "uphill" self-control discussed in chapter 8 emerges (cf. Mele 1987, ch. 5; 1995a, ch. 3). Velleman's proposed solution is that the agent intervenes by throwing "his weight behind" this weaker motive (motive W) and this consists of the weaker motive's "being reinforced by" the agent's desire to act in accordance with reasons (desire R); "the two [i.e., W and R] now form the strongest combination of motives" (p. 480).

Velleman's formulation of his solution is awkward. On his view, one prominent role for an agent's desire to act in accordance with reasons (desire R) in human action par excellence is to motivate the agent to reflect "on his motives" (1992, p. 478). So R is present even before the agent throws his weight on the side of the weaker motive (motive W), and perhaps the strength of R plus the strength of W was already greater than that of the motive that opposes W. If so, then, even before the agent throws his weight around, there is a sense in which R and W "form the strongest combination of motives." In that sense, however, the two motives are combined only artificially, in somewhat the way that the coins in my pockets and those in yours combine—add up—to 90 cents. What is needed is a *relevant* combination, if one wants to speak in terms of combinations. On my view, the relevant "combining" would be a matter of R, or a similar desire, entering into the positive motivational base of W, increasing W's strength.

In any case, Velleman's (1992) position on agency par excellence clearly places such agency in the sphere of self-control.[10] I turn to the argument (from Mele 1990a) that I have mentioned. My reason for reproducing the relatively brief argument here is partly that, without appealing to a fancy conception of human agency, it makes a case for the claim that being a human agent of a certain kind—one who has self-control as a trait of character—requires having something that might reasonably be called a desire to act for superior reasons.[11]

A person who has developed remarkable powers of self-control may, because of a personal tragedy, lose all motivation to exercise them. A man who recently lost his family in a fatal plane crash may no longer care how he conducts himself, even if, out of habit, he continues to make better judgments; he may suffer from acedia. As a partial consequence, he may cease, for a time, to make any effort at self-control, even when he recognizes that his preponderant motivation is at odds with his better judgments. He may simply act in accordance with whatever happens to be his strongest motivation, without being at all motivated to exert an influence over how his motivations stack up. If, as seems plain, we are unwilling to describe such an agent at the time in question as a self-controlled person, we must include a motivational element in an account of what it is to be a self-controlled agent. A self-controlled person cares how he conducts himself—he is a practically concerned individual—and he is appropriately motivated to exercise self-control.

Exercise it in support of what? Notice that although normal (and, hence, largely rational) human agents do care how they conduct themselves, they do not care *equally* about all of their projects or the objects of all of their hopes and desires. Practical concern is not egalitarian in this way. What one cares most about, if one is largely rational, are the things one deems most important. In a largely rational individual, this variegated system of concerns is reflected in the agent's decisive better judgments. This reflection may be collective rather than individual. An occasional better judgment may miss the mark; but, on the whole, what an agent judges best indicates what he cares most about. And if it is his lack of practical concern that leads us to withhold the epithet "self-controlled person" from our unfortunate man, we should expect the presence of such concern in the same man to manifest itself partly in motivation to attempt to make things go as he judges they should go and to exercise his powers of self-control in support of his decisive better judgments when they are challenged by competing motivation. Given the discriminativeness of practical concern, the self-controlled individual's motivation to exercise self-control will typically be aimed at the support of his decisive better judgments.[12] A largely rational person who does not care equally about the objects of all of his desires will not be uniformly motivated to exercise self-control in support of each of them. Because he is for the most part internally coherent, his motivation to exercise self-control will generally fall in line with his *better judgments*.

The self-controlled person's motivation to exercise self-control, as I am understanding it, is associated with his practical concern—that is, with his caring how he conducts himself, with his not being a victim of acedia. *Because* he cares how he conducts himself and because practical concern is discriminative in the way explained, he is disposed to see to it that his behavior fits his better judgments and to intervene into his own motivational condition when competing motivation threatens to render his better judgments ineffective. This disposition's manifestations include desires for specific exercises of self-control on particular occasions. Such a disposition, I should think, is present to some degree in all normal adult human agents.

That is the argument (from Mele 1990a). What does it suggest about human agency par excellence, on the assumption that a significant capacity for self-control is central to such agency? If the argument is on target, being a self-controlled person—that is, having self-control as a trait of character—entails caring how one's life goes, the caring being manifested partly in motivation to do what it takes to bring one's conduct into line with one's better judgments. Such motivation can take the form of something describable as "a desire to act for superior reasons." Now, largely rational, mature human beings are very likely to have learned—and hence to believe, at least tacitly— that things tend to go better for them if, when faced with relatively important practical issues, they give the matter some thought and then act in accordance with the reasons they deem superior. Rational agents who believe this and care how their lives go are very likely to be disposed to desire, when facing relatively important practical issues, that they reflect on what it would be best, or at least good enough, to do and then act in accordance with their conclusions about this. On a traditional conception of standing desires, the disposition to desire this is a standing desire (see chapter 1, section 7), and it may be dubbed "a standing desire to act for superior reasons." I have no need to count so-called standing desires as desires. The point to emphasize for present purposes concerns desires that are manifestations of the disposition in which the so-called standing desire consists. These desires include desires of a sort that I suggested in chapter 4 play an important role in accounting for practical reasoning that takes the form of reasoning about what it is best to do or about what it is good enough to do— namely, desires to do whatever is best in the circumstances and desires for acceptable courses of action. These desires themselves may reasonably be described as desires to act for superior reasons.

The desires just identified—manifestations of a disposition to desire to act for superior reasons—can play the causal roles Velleman highlights. They can help explain why an agent assesses his reasons for action, and they can contribute to the motivational strength of desires for particular courses of action (Velleman 1992, pp. 478–79; cf. Velleman 2000, pp. 11–12), courses of action that one takes oneself to have superior reasons to pursue, by entering into the positive motivational base of those desires. The argument reproduced from Mele (1990a) focuses on motivation to bring it about that one acts as one has judged best, and Velleman instructively calls attention to the point that a desire that plays an important motivational role in this connection can also motivate practical reflection that issues in such a judgment (cf. chapter 4).

Velleman motivates the problem of disappearing (or shrinking) agents in such a way that it is important to him to attribute a specific role to human agents in the production of actions that is not found in the lower animals and to identify it with the agent's role. Anticausalists are not likely to be impressed by his solution to the problem since his account of action is a causal one. What he has done is to gesture toward a causal account that he takes to capture an important missing element in standard accounts. For reasons advanced in chapter 2, I believe that anticausalists are mistaken. But I also see no reason to hold that a properly functioning desire to act for superior reasons "play[s] the role of the agent and consequently *is* the agent, functionally speaking" (Velleman 1992, p. 480). Human agents are human beings who act. What philosophers of action want is a proper account of the nature and explanation of intentional action, including what might be termed, with Velleman, "human action par excellence." A human agent—a human being who acts—can only metaphorically be identified, functionally speaking or otherwise, with a desire. I return to this point shortly.

I close this section by voicing some simple reservations about the project of locating human action par excellence by searching for "that which distinguishes human action from other animal behavior" (Velleman 1992, p. 462). Such a project can easily go astray; the distinction between human action and other animal behavior can be taken too seriously in the present connection. For example, human beings may be the only animals that act akratically, as Aristotle said (*Nicomachean Ethics* 1147b3–5). If so, that is part of what distinguishes human action from the behavior of other animals, but akratic action is not part of human action par excellence. A related point may be made about *alienation* from a desire on which one acts if human beings are the only animals that sometimes are alienated from their desires. And should it turn out that there are nonhuman animals in the universe that have the full action-repertoire of human beings, human action par excellence could not be located by finding "that which distinguishes human action from other animal behavior."[13]

4. Deciding and Reduction

An agent who judges it best to *A* may come to intend to *A* nonactionally or, instead, by way of deciding to *A*. Elsewhere, I have observed that in an agent who has "a generic want to act as he judges best"—that is, a desire to do whatever he judges best or, as one might say, a desire to act for superior reasons—"a decisive better judgment in favor of his *A*-ing may increase his motivation to *A* by injecting the generic want into the positive motivational base of his desire to [*A*]" (Mele 1987, p. 101). Perhaps in some cases, the resultant motivation to *A* is sufficiently strong relative to competing motivation that there is no need in the circumstances for the agent to perform a mental action of intention formation, and he nonactionally acquires an intention to *A*, as he might if he had no competing motivation at all. If, as Velleman (1992) claims, deciding is necessary for human action par excellence, these cases are not instances of such action.

A desire to act for superior reasons can also play a role in motivating an agent who decisively judges it best to *A* to decide to *A*. In a version of Joe's case (chapter 9) in which he decides to quit smoking, this desire might be part of what motivates him so to decide. Velleman says that his "reduction of agent-causation enables us to say both that the agent makes the weaker motive prevail and that the contest always goes to the strongest combination of motives" (1992, p. 480). Recall that the agent makes this motive prevail by throwing "his weight behind" it, and "this consists in [the weaker motive's] being reinforced by" the agent's desire to act in accordance with reasons; "the two now form the strongest combination of motives" (p. 480). In what sense is this a *reduction* of agent causation?

Some agent causationists may be willing to grant that if a desire to act for superior reasons plays a causal, motivational role in producing an intention to A that does not involve deciding to A, A being what one judges it best to do, what they mean by "agent causation" is not involved in the production of that intention. After all, the intention was acquired without being actively formed. However, agent causationists who can accept that a desire to act for superior reasons plays a causal, motivational role in the production of a *decision* to A will say that what they mean by agent causation *is* involved there. A decision might be produced by mental states or events in conjunction with irreducible agent causation (Clarke 1996).

Velleman aims to advance "a reductionist account of agent causation" that places it in the natural order, where causes are events and states. That is why he looks for "events and states to play the role of the agent" (1992, p. 475). For obvious reasons, he steers clear of events that are *actions* in his search for something to play the agent's role. If all actions are caused by their agents, an action that is supposed to play the role of the agent would itself have an agent as its cause, and Velleman therefore would have another instance of agent causation to reduce. If, alternatively, an action is the causing of an event or state by an agent (Bishop 1989, p. 68; cf. O'Connor 1995, pp. 181–82), an action that plays the role of the agent would be an instance of agent causation, which instance Velleman would need to reduce.

I believe that his project is misguided. Apparently, what human agents—human beings who act—do in instances of human action par excellence, at least in significant part, is to deliberate and to decide and act on the basis of the reasons they judge superior, all of this being motivated by a desire to act for superior reasons. The agent's role in human action par excellence lies here. A desire cannot play this role because no desire can deliberate and decide, for example. And even if deliberating and deciding are irreducibly actional, that fact does not entail that instances of deliberation and particular decidings cannot be caused solely by events and states, including desires to act for superior reasons. An agent's causing something that is irreducibly an action, if one chooses to speak of agents—human beings who act—as causes, may be a matter of the action's being caused by relevant states and events. If, alternatively, "actions consist in the causing by their agents of certain events or states of affairs" (Bishop 1989, p. 68), an agent's suitably causing a pertinent event or state may be a matter of that effect's being caused by relevant states and events. Chapter 2 shows how this can be.

5. Alienation and the Elusive Location of Human Agency par Excellence

My primary concern in this chapter thus far has been the identification of a kind of *master desire* that might make a special contribution to human action par excellence by way of its contribution to practical reasoning, decision making, and subsequent action. I have suggested that desires that are manifestations of a disposition to desire to act for superior reasons may make a contribution of this kind. I have had relatively little to say about alienation, a phenomenon featured along with the passive acquisition of intentions in Velleman's (1992) presentation of the problem of disappearing (or shrinking) agents.

Consider the hypothesis that desires to act for superior reasons play a central role in human agency par excellence. Might the hypothesis be undermined by the truth of the claim that some people are alienated from these desires? Would the possibility of alienation from desires suitable for the purposes of a causal account of human agency par excellence—or alienation from a disposition to have such desires—pose a problem for that account? I doubt it, but for reasons other than Velleman's (1992). (His reasons are discussed shortly.)

My doubt rests on a simple point. It is plausible that although being alienated from, say, one's disposition to desire to act for superior reasons is compatible with being a human agent, it is not compatible with being a human agent par excellence. Seemingly, if human action par excellence is the sort of thing Velleman says it is, alienation from this disposition would tend to hinder one's engaging in such action and stand in the way of human agency par excellence. Recall Velleman's statement that in human action par excellence, the agent reflects on his motives, and his concern in so doing is "to see which ones provide stronger reasons for acting, and then to ensure that they prevail over those whose rational force is weaker" (1992, p. 478). Alienation from a psychological state is supposed to involve such things as regarding the state as foreign to who one is and wishing to be rid of it. So alienation from one's disposition to desire to act for superior reasons, or from an associated desire, would be expected to have an attenuating effect on it and, therefore, to attenuate attempts that may be made to identify superior reasons for acting and to ensure that they prevail. But even if there were no such attenuation in a particular case and a relevant desire were to play its role despite one's alienation from it, the possibility of such a case would in no way show that a causal account of human agency par excellence that appeals to desires to act for superior reasons is doomed to failure. The height of the bar for human agency par excellence is not fixed independently of theoretical discoveries, and, plausibly, a proper location for the bar includes the absence of alienation from the disposition at issue and from desires that manifest it. Alienation from a desire to act for superior reasons at least entails a kind of psychological fragmentation or disunity for which a highly desirable form of agency would seem to have no place. Why settle for saying that human agency par excellence is manifested in every action motivated by a desire to act for superior reasons when one can reserve the label for a more desirable kind of agency that is manifested in action motivated by the desire in the absence of alienation from the desire and from the disposition the desire manifests?

An example may prove useful. Bob judges that, all things considered, it would be best to attend his father's birthday party, but he feels alienated from that judgment. He feels that his real self is a rebellious, unconventional agent and that his judgment about the party does not represent his real self's point of view. Bob realizes that he currently has a desire to act for superior reasons, and he believes that that desire motivated his reasoning about what to do, but he feels alienated from that desire and from his reasoning. Bob believes that his attraction to acting for superior reasons was imposed on him by his strict upbringing, and he sees his real self as an agent who yearns to be free from that attraction's shackles. In the end, Bob decides to attend the party and he acts accordingly, but he is upset with himself for so doing; he feels that he has betrayed his real self. Bob's unhappy state of mind is reflected in his boorish behavior at the party.

If the other guests had thought that Bob had a real self that wanted not to attend, they would have wished that it had had its way.

Bob certainly seems not to be exhibiting human agency par excellence in this story. He is much too conflicted, troubled, and confused for that. One need not agree with Bob that a real self lies within him in order to take his feelings and beliefs seriously; and in light of the pertinent feelings and beliefs, Bob evidently lacks a kind of psychic integration or unity that is required for the kind of agency at issue.

In pursuing the question where the bar should be set for human agency par excellence, at least two kinds of consideration are involved: desirability and psychological richness. Instead of simple absence of alienation from one's desires to act for superior reasons and one's disposition to have such desires, a philosopher can push for *identification* with them.[14] Perhaps a case can be made for the claim that agency involving this kind of identification is more desirable than agency that has a mere absence of alienation from the disposition and associated desires in its place. It may be argued, for example, that identification with one's disposition to desire to act for superior reasons and with associated desires is more likely to sustain the useful disposition and desires than is mere absence of alienation from them and that, other things being equal, agency that involves such identification is preferable on these grounds to agency that does not. Turning to the second consideration, one notices that identification with these things certainly *sounds* psychologically richer or more robust than the mere absence of alienation from them. Theorists disposed to measure levels of human agency partly in terms of psychological richness may, on these grounds, be disposed to include identification with the disposition and associated desires as a requirement for human agency par excellence.

On a relatively thin account of identification, to identify with a desire one has is, roughly, a matter of desiring to continue to have that desire and believing that one's having it is a good thing (Mele 1995a, p. 177).[15] Of course, there are psychologically richer views of identification in the literature, and a theorist may want to require for human agency par excellence a richer kind of identification with one's disposition to desire to act for superior reasons and with manifesting desires, or at least a more robust attitude or stance toward them. Michael Bratman (1996) has argued for an account of identification with a desire that requires that an agent *decide* to treat the desire in a certain way, and one might contend that human agency par excellence requires that one have *decided* on the policy of, for example, being guided by one's desires to act for superior reasons and that one continue to possess the general intention formed in so deciding.[16] A theorist may wish to raise the bar higher still, contending that we should add to what has already been mentioned that the person currently endorses or values *being the sort of person* who has this general intention.[17] Here there is another layer of psychological richness, and if it does not come at the cost of significantly decreased desirability, it is in the running for a place in human agency par excellence.

Pursuing the bar-raising issue threatens to induce philosophical vertigo. However, it is not for that reason to be shunned. Provided that the bar is not placed so high that no actual human being reaches it, the exercise can prove useful in constructing an inventory of psychological items that are sometimes involved in producing human actions and of the roles they can play in producing actions. The upper range of human action is an interesting range, and exploring it can give us a fuller and deeper appreciation of that portion of human psychology that bears on action explanation.

Even so, some philosophical self-control is in order. One can imagine a philosophical contest in which the prize goes to the theorist who identifies the psychologically richest kind of agency open to human beings that ranks no lower on a desirability scale than, say, the kind of agency Velleman (1992) gestures at. One measure of richness is the number of kinds of higher-order attitudes involved in an agent's production of an action. In this chapter, I have already mentioned intentions regarding desires, identification with a desire, second-order desires, beliefs about desires, decisions about desires, and valuing being the sort of person who has an intention of a certain kind. Of course, the contest's judges will not award points for items that are reducible to other items on one's list. And only fractions of points will be awarded for cogent arguments that a specific type of attitude (e.g., desire about one's desires or belief about one's intentions) located at a level higher than the highest level at which it had previously been shown to be potentially effective can, in fact, play a role in producing action. Although such a contest sounds like fun, I do not take part in it here.

Velleman claims that "the desire to act in accordance with reasons cannot be disowned by an agent, although it can be disowned by the person in whom the agency is embodied" and that "the sense in which an agent cannot disown his desire to act in accordance with reasons is that he cannot disown it while remaining an agent" (1992, p. 479; cf. Velleman 2000, p. 30). If a human agent is simply a human being who acts, these claims are false and Velleman has neither discovered a truth about what it is to be a human agent nor uncovered a desire that no human agent can disown. However, it is plausible, as I have explained, that human agency par excellence depends on the efficacy of desires to act for superior reasons.

On a fancy conception of what it is to be a human agent, one faces the task of finding the human agent within the human being, perhaps largely by attending to psychic integration of suitable attitudes. If the line for human agency is drawn at whatever is required for human action par excellence, this gives the project of setting the bar for such action a very serious air; the task of identifying human action par excellence becomes central to the task of identifying *what it is to be a human agent*. On my simple conception, matters sound less deep and serious: human agents are human beings who act; they may exercise their practical powers more and less impressively; and theorists can perhaps be more relaxed about exactly what does and does not count as human action par excellence.

One issue about which a relaxed attitude may be in order is whether actively exercising self-control in support of a practical decision that one has made is consistent or inconsistent with human action par excellence. Jeanette Kennett and Michael Smith defend the thesis that synchronic self-control is always nonactional: it is a matter of passively having "thoughts which prevent [a relevant] desire from having its characteristic effect" (1997, p. 128).[18] Human agency par excellence, on Velleman's account, can be exhibited in scenarios involving nonactional synchronic self-control. Typical cases of self-control include, among other things, the agent's judging it best to A (or better to A than to B), his being tempted to B instead, and his intentionally A-ing. Fred, a married man, is having a pleasant and somewhat intimate conversation with a charming woman he met this evening. They are sitting in a bar, and some of Fred's friends are present. He has an urge to kiss the woman, but on the basis of brief reflection on salient considerations, he judges that this would be a mistake. He decides not to kiss her and he acts accordingly. The urge passes. Here, "a desire to act in accordance with reasons" may "produce [Fred's] behavior . . . by adding its motivational force" to the motives associated with what Fred took to be the better reasons (Velleman 1992, p. 479). If this is what happens, Fred exemplifies what Velleman counts as human agency par excellence. Notice that what happens does not require that Fred actively exercise self-control in the service of his decision. Motive addition might have turned the trick on its own.

Suppose that this is in fact what happened, and consider a variant of the case. After Fred decides not to kiss the woman and after a desire to act for reasons enters into the positive motivational base of his desire to refrain from kissing her, Fred needs to struggle to protect his decision against his amorous desire. He actively exercises self-control and masters his temptation. In neither case is Fred alienated from his judgment or decision. Is this a clearer instance of human action par excellence than the preceding one? Some may claim that it is since Fred is more active in it. But others may contend, on grounds of desirability, that the first case provides a clearer instance of such action. It may be claimed that the need to struggle in the second case points to an agential defect—or, more fully, a defective form of agency—that is absent in the first case. In a superior (more rational, more fully integrated) agent, it may be said, the very insertion of a desire to act for reasons into the positive motivational base of a desire to A, without the assistance of any subsequent effort at self-control, is enough to ensure that the agent will not akratically B. It is hard to take sides in this dispute, for it is unclear precisely what one's objective should be in attempting to characterize human action par excellence.

A related dispute may arise about the importance of deciding to A, as opposed to nonactionally acquiring an intention to A. An agent whose judgment that it would be best to A issues straightaway and nonactionally in an intention to A and injects a desire to act for superior reasons into the positive motivational base of that intention enjoys more psychic integration at the time, other things being equal, than an agent who, after having judged that it would be best to A, continues to be uncertain about what to do and resolves his uncertainty by deciding to A. The latter agent, for a time, is torn in a way that the former is not. Then again, the latter agent is active in a way that the former is not. Only the latter agent performs the action of forming an intention to A. Is activity significantly more important to human agency par excellence in this connection than it is in connection with the issue about self-control that I just raised?

Velleman (1992) uses the expressions "human action *par excellence*" and "full-blooded action" interchangeably. In a later article, he asserts that "full-blooded human action occurs only when the subject's capacity to make things happen is exercised to its fullest extent" (2000, p. 4). Arguably, agents exercise that capacity more fully the more actively involved they are in the production of their actions (other things being equal), and agents seemingly are more actively involved in the production of an action when they decide to perform an action of that kind and actively exercise self-control in support of so acting than when they do not. Indeed, it seems that the more vigorously one exercises self-control, the more active one is in the production of the action in the service of which the exercise is performed; and conflicted agents who are very strongly tempted to do things that they are very confident they should avoid doing may need to pull out all the stops. Then again, one may take a very different perspective on this. It may be argued that the capacity at issue is at its acme only when the agent is thoroughly psychologically integrated, and there consequently is no call for decisions and exercises of self-control; the agent works hard to figure out what it would be best to do, and his evaluative judgment carries the day by producing a corresponding intention that he proceeds to execute without any need to exercise self-control. It may be argued further that exercising the capacity to its fullest extent is a matter of exercising it nondefectively at its acme. Again, in the absence of clear instructions about the proper goal of a characterization of human action par excellence, taking sides in this disagreement would be rash.

A somewhat relaxed attitude is also appropriate regarding how impressive a person's practical reasoning must be to be part of an episode of human action par excellence. People can use their reflective energy irrationally or inefficiently. Presumably, the more impressive one's reflection is—the more rational, efficient, and perceptive; the broader and deeper, where breadth and depth are in order—the better claim it has to being part of an episode of human action par excellence. Some practical reasoning is impressively broad and deep. In relatively simple cases, a person who has a simple, well-defined end reasons about acceptable means. Some complex cases feature considerable soul searching. Sometimes, for example, in an attempt to assess the value of certain things that one strongly desires, one thinks long and hard about what accounts for one's desires for those things and about what one would and should be willing to sacrifice to achieve the objects of those desires. The same episode of practical reasoning may feature sustained deliberation about how to combine the pursuit of distinct goals that one reflectively deems worthy of pursuit and finds to be in some tension with one another, as well as sophisticated reflection about the relative value of these goals. All of this, and much more, can be driven in part by a desire to act for superior reasons. The project of identifying a precise point of demarcation between deliberation that is sufficiently impressive to be part of an instance of human action par excellence and deliberation that is not seems absurd. The same is true of the project of finding a point at which one's deliberative capacity—that aspect of one's "capacity to make things happen"—has been "exercised to its fullest extent."

6. Causalism, Real Selves, and Human Agents

Certain claims about free action and about the causal relevance of the mental constitute significant challenges to a traditional causal approach to understanding and explaining human action. I have attempted to meet both challenges elsewhere.[19] The challenge posed by human action par excellence—or, at least, the challenge that Velleman (1992) poses in terms of such action—is comparatively modest. It is, roughly, a challenge to the causalist to produce a useful framework for explaining a range of actions within the sphere of self-control.

Some causalists may complain that Velleman's (1992) own response to the challenge—his proposed solution to the problem of shrinking agents—shows that he has been unfair to them. In his description of "the standard story," he apparently has in mind the sort of thing one finds in the work of causalists who are looking for what is common to all (overt) intentional actions, or all (overt) actions done for reasons, and for what distinguishes actions of these broad kinds from everything else. Conceptually sufficient conditions for actions that exhibit self-control, for example, should not be expected to show up in a story with this topic, for not all intentional actions, or actions done for reasons, exhibit self-control. Some are ordinary akratic actions, and some may be a lot like the actions of tigers. Human action par excellence may be intentional action, or action done for a reason, in virtue of its having the properties identified in a causal analysis of these things. That the analysis does not provide sufficient conditions for, or a story about, human action par excellence is not a "flaw" in the analysis. If Velleman were to believe that causalism lacks the resources for accommodating human action par excellence, he might attack "the standard story" on that front; he might argue that it is impossible to extend it to handle such action. But Velleman himself is a causalist. Moreover, causalists have offered accounts of kinds of action— for example, free action, autonomous action, and action exhibiting self-control—that exceed minimal requirements for intentional action or action done for a reason. It is not as though their story about minimally sufficient conditions for action of the latter kinds is their entire story about human actions. Nevertheless, Velleman properly calls attention to a kind of action that merits examination in its own right, even if the kind of action at issue is not precisely specified.[20]

The most detailed discussions of identification and alienation tend to be associated with *real-self* conceptions of autonomy, freedom, moral responsibility, or human agency. Harry Frankfurt claims that "when someone identifies himself with one rather than with another of his own [conflicting] desires, the result is . . . to alter" the nature of the conflict. "The conflict between the *desires* is in this way transformed into a conflict between *one* of them and the *person* who has identified himself with its rival" (1988, p. 172). Galen Strawson, in a discussion of the kind of psychic integration required for freedom and moral responsibility, suggests that an agent satisfies this condition in virtue of having "a sense of himself as a thinking 'mental someone' who has and acts upon pro-attitudes or desires he feels to be his in a way that one can characterize by saying that, for him, their being involved in the determination of the action (citable in true rational explanations of it) *just is* his being so involved" (1986, p. 245). John Christman, commenting on this passage, remarks, "This amounts to simply acknowledging the desire as *me*" (1989, p. 7).[21]

I have criticized real-self accounts of autonomy, freedom, and moral responsibility elsewhere (Mele 1995a), as have others, and there are competing accounts of these phenomena in the literature that, by my lights, are much more promising (Fischer 1994; Fischer and Ravizza 1998; Mele 1995a). Obviously, I cannot argue for the competing accounts here, but if the move from a conception of human agents as human beings who act to a conception of human agents as real selves lying within human beings is a dead end in the spheres just identified, there is little to motivate it. Some human beings do, in some sense, identify with—or feel alienated from—some of their desires. But saying what that amounts to does not require endorsing a conception of a human agent as something narrower than a human being who acts. In some discussions of real selves, what may seem to be an exploration of the metaphysics of human agency may rather be an exploration of potentially misleading metaphors about such agency.

If to be a human agent is to be a human being who acts, attention to human action par excellence will not yield an analysis of what it is to be a human agent. Even so, an examination of the topic can yield discoveries about the springs of some human actions in the sphere of self-control. Again, according to Velleman, in cases of human action par excellence, an agent has two concerns "in reflecting on his motives": "to see which ones provide stronger reasons for acting, and "to ensure that they prevail over those whose rational force is weaker" (1992, p. 478). For him, this ensuring involves deciding in accordance with the reasons deemed stronger and executing that decision. So human action par excellence, as Velleman conceives of it, involves activity on at least three fronts: practical reflection, decision, and action executing a decision. I have explained that desires to act for superior reasons have a significant role to play in each of these connections and that absence of alienation from those desires is a plausible requirement for human agency par excellence. Such desires are not required for intentional action. But, as I argued a decade ago, they are required for being a person who has self-control as a trait of character and exercises that trait (Mele 1990a). If human agency par excellence clearly belongs to any special group, it belongs to highly rational, highly and effectively reflective, self-controlled human beings who are not alienated from their desires to act for superior reasons.[22] The conception of human motivation and action that I have been developing in this book accommodates such agency.

Notes

1. For discussion and some references, see Kane (1996, pp. 117–19).

2. Saying this does not beg the question against Nagel since I have not stipulated that Uma is part of "the order of nature."

3. It may be replied that electronic calculators solve multiplication problems even though they have no idea how to do so. However, electronic calculators do not act.

4. In a later article (2000, ch. 1), Velleman places akratic actions in the sphere of something similar to human action par excellence. He argues there that action is behavior regulated by a certain aim (pp. 14–20)—the aim of knowing what one is doing (pp. 20–31)—and that akratic actions are regulated by this aim (p. 28, n. 34). Velleman's standards for action in this later article, as he indicates (p. 2, n. 3), are stricter than those he had in mind in 1992; but, evidently, they are not identical with the standards he offered for human action par excellence in the earlier work.

5. The conceptual road from self-control to freedom and moral responsibility is, I believe, a long, hard one. At least, I devoted considerable effort in a previous book (Mele 1995a, chs. 8–13) to hacking out a path—or, rather, two paths, one for compatibilists and one for libertarians. Even setting incompatibilism aside, owing to the possibility of certain kinds of manipulation, being a self-controlled agent is not sufficient for being a free or morally responsible agent, nor is a self-controlled agent's exemplifying his self-control in action sufficient for his acting freely or morally responsibly (see Mele 1995a, p. 122 and ch. 9).

6. Velleman (1992, p. 462) allows, as he should, that human beings perform actions that are not instances of human action par excellence.

7. Notice the connection between the content of this desire and a Davidsonian rationalization of an action (see chapter 3).

8. For an explanation of akratic action, see Mele (1987).

9. On a desire of this kind, see Velleman (2000, pp. 14–15).

10. One may understand the sphere of self-control broadly, to include behavior of hypothetical agents who have become so good that they are no longer in danger of acting akratically. Aristotle's temperate agents are like this regarding bodily appetites (see *Nicomachean Ethics* 1151b34–1152a3). (Discussion with Karin Boxer suggested that this note will help forestall confusion.)

11. The next three paragraphs are reproduced with some minor stylistic changes from Mele (1990a, pp. 55–56).

12. I say "typically," not "always," because there are unorthodox exercises of self-control—for example, exercises in support of practical decisions that are at odds with what the person judges best (see Mele 1990a; 1995a, pp. 60–64).

13. Of course, one might say that human action par excellence is action of a kind *K* in which, as it happens, some nonhuman beings engage, the difference being that human action par excellence is performed by human beings. But *K* would be the topic of philosophical interest. For an account of what is "special about human agency" that features "our conception of our agency as temporally extended," see Bratman (2000).

14. Harry Frankfurt's work on identification has been very influential. Many of the articles in his 1988 book, and several in his 1999 book, are relevant.

15. This modest account of identification is available both to real-self theorists and to their opponents, for it does not take a stand on who *one* is—that is, on how persons, "selves," or agents are to be conceived.

16. How one analyzes identification will depend partly on the theoretical work one wants it to do. Velleman suggests that one intended role for identification is to assist in advancing "a reductionist account of agent causation" that places it in the natural order, where causes are events and states (1992, pp. 474–75). Bratman's analysis of identification does not help with *this* project. If, as I have argued, deciding to do something is a mental action, he has analyzed identification partly in terms of something that a typical agent-causationist would insist is irreducibly agent-caused.

17. On endorsing of roughly this kind, see Korsgaard (1996). Bratman (1999, pp. 267–68) identifies what Korsgaard is after as "human action 'par excellence'." For a distinct but related account of endorsing a desire, see Bratman (2000).

18. For criticism of this idea, see Mele (1997d and 1998c).

19. On the former, see Mele (1995a, chs. 8–13); on the latter, see (1992e, ch. 2).

20. In a later article, Velleman writes, "The claim made for the standard model is that it is a model of action, in which my capacity to make things happen is exercised to its fullest extent" (2000, p. 4). I have just explained that this misrepresents the standard model.

21. This is not an endorsement of Christman's interpretation.

22. For a detailed account of self-control and its practical significance, see Mele (1995a, chs. 1–7).

11

Motivated Belief and Motivational Explanations

My original plan for this book included a detailed investigation of the roles of motivation in the production, sustaining, and revision of beliefs. While this book was in progress, I decided to tackle that topic instead in a book on self-deception (Mele 2001). My initial thought was that motivated belief merits discussion in a book on motivation not only for the obvious reason but also because an exploration of the topic would foster a fuller and deeper understanding of motivation than any account guided solely by a concern with intentional action and agency—or, more specifically, by concerns to understand intentional action and agency, to explain intentional actions, and perhaps to evaluate intentional actions or their agents. That thought was a good one, I believe. In the present chapter, I pick up one of its threads—the bearing of motivationally biased belief on the project of producing an account of motivational explanation. (I do my best to avoid unnecessary repetition of material from Mele 2001.)

1. Motivationally Biased Belief and a Theory

In chapter 1, I quoted William Alston's remark that "the concept of motivation is an abstraction from the concept of a motivational explanation, and the task of specifying the nature of motivation is the task of bringing out the salient features of this kind of explanation" (1967, p. 400; emphasis eliminated). In what sense is motivational explanation a *kind* of explanation? Do all motivational explanations have the same general form? Is the common element significantly less robust than this? I have already argued, in effect, that some, but not all, motivational explanations are or include instrumental rationalizations (chapter 1, section 3). Some are or include noninstrumental rationalizations instead. Ann's hope that the Pistons won last night figures in a non-instrumental rationalization of her desire to learn that they won, which rationalization is a motivational explanation of that desire.

A related moral may be gleaned from attention to motivationally biased belief, as I explain.[1] Thomas Gilovich reports:

> A survey of one million highschool seniors found that 70% thought they were above average in leadership ability, and only 2% thought they were below average. In terms of ability to get along with others, *all* students thought they were above average, 60% thought they were in the top 10%, and 25% thought they were in the top 1%! ... A survey of university professors found that 94% thought they were better at their jobs than their average colleague. (1991, p. 77)

Such data suggest that motivation sometimes biases beliefs. The aggregated self-assessments are wildly out of line with the facts (e.g., only 1% can be in the top 1%), and the qualities asked about are desirable. There is powerful evidence that people have a tendency to believe propositions that they want to be true even when an impartial investigation of readily available data would indicate that they probably are false. A plausible hypothesis about that tendency is that wanting something to be true sometimes biases what one believes.

Controlled experiments provide confirmation for this hypothesis.[2] In one persuasive study, undergraduate subjects (seventy-five women and eight-six men) read an article asserting that "women were endangered by caffeine and were strongly advised to avoid caffeine in any form"; that the major danger was fibrocystic disease, "associated in its advanced stages with breast cancer"; and that "caffeine induced the disease by increasing the concentration of a substance called cAMP in the breast" (Kunda 1987, p. 642). (Because the article did not personally threaten men, they were used as a control group.) Subjects were then asked to indicate, among other things, "how convinced they were of the connection between caffeine and fibrocystic disease and of the connection between caffeine and ... cAMP on a 6-point scale" (pp. 643–44). In the female group, "heavy consumers" of caffeine were significantly less convinced of the connections than "low consumers." The males were considerably more convinced than the female "heavy consumers," and there was a much smaller difference in conviction between "heavy" and "low" male caffeine consumers (the heavy consumers were slightly more convinced of the connections).

Given that all subjects were exposed to the same information and assuming that only the female heavy consumers were personally threatened by it, a plausible hypothesis is that a desire that their coffee drinking has not significantly endangered their health helps to account for their lower level of conviction (cf. Kunda 1987, p. 644). Indeed, in a study in which the reported hazards of caffeine use were relatively modest, "female heavy consumers were no less convinced by the evidence than were female low consumers." Along with the lesser threat, there is less motivation for skepticism about the evidence.

Attention to some phenomena that have been argued to be sources of *unmotivated* or "cold" biased belief sheds light on motivationally biased belief. A number of such sources have been identified in the psychological literature, including the following two:[3]

1. *Vividness of information.* A datum's vividness for a person is often a function of the person's interests, the concreteness of the datum, its "imagery-provoking" power, or its sensory, temporal, or spatial proximity (Nisbett and Ross 1980, p. 45). Vivid data are more likely to be recognized, attended to, and recalled than pallid data. Consequently, vivid data tend to have a disproportional influence on the formation and retention of beliefs.
2. *The confirmation bias.* People testing a hypothesis tend to search (in memory and in the world) more often for confirming than for disconfirming instances and to recognize the former more readily (Baron 1988, pp. 259–65; Klayman and Ha 1987; Nisbett and Ross, 1980, pp. 181–82). This is true even when the hypothesis is only a tentative one (as opposed, e.g., to a belief one has). People also tend to interpret relatively neutral data as supporting a hypothesis they are testing (Trope, Gervey, and Liberman, 1997, p. 115).

Although sources of biased belief apparently can function independently of motivation, they may also be triggered and sustained by motivation in the production of particular *motivationally* biased beliefs.[4] For example, motivation can enhance the vividness or salience of data. Data that count in favor of the truth of a proposition that one hopes is true may be rendered more vivid or salient by one's recognition that they so count. Similarly, motivation can influence which hypotheses occur to one and affect the salience of available hypotheses, thereby setting the stage for the confirmation bias.[5] Because of a desire that *p*, one may test the hypothesis that *p* is true rather than the contrary hypothesis. In these ways and others, a desire that *p* may help to explain the acquisition of an unwarranted belief that *p*.

Sometimes people generate their own hypotheses, and sometimes hypotheses—including extremely unpleasant ones—are suggested to them by others. If people were consistently to concentrate primarily on confirmatory instances of hypotheses they are testing, independently of what is at stake, that would indicate the presence of a cognitive tendency or disposition that uniformly operates independently of motivation. For example, it would indicate that motivation never plays a role in influencing the proportion of attention people give to evidence for the falsity of a hypothesis. However, there is powerful evidence that the confirmation bias is much less rigid than this. For example, in one study (Gigerenzer and Hug 1992), two groups of subjects were asked to test "social-contract rules such as 'If someone stays overnight in the cabin, then that person must bring along a bundle of firewood . . . '" (Friedrich 1993, p. 313). The group asked to adopt "the perspective of a cabin guard monitoring compliance" showed an "extremely high frequency" of testing for disconfirming instances (i.e., for visitors who stay in the cabin overnight but bring no wood). The other group, asked to "take the perspective of a visitor trying to determine" whether firewood was supplied by visitors themselves or by a local club, displayed the common confirmation bias.

An interesting recent theory of lay hypothesis testing is designed, in part, to accommodate data of the sort I have been describing. Elsewhere (Mele 2001), I offered grounds for caution about and moderation of it and argued that a qualified version is plausible.[6] I named it the "FTL theory," after the authors of the two articles on which I primarily drew, Friedrich (1993) and Trope and Liberman (1996). A thumbnail sketch of the theory is in order.

The basic idea of the FTL theory is that lay hypothesis testing is driven by a concern to minimize making costly errors. The *errors* on which the theory focuses are false beliefs. The *cost* of a false belief is the cost, including missed opportunities for gains, that it would be reasonable for the person to expect the belief—if false—to have, given his desires and beliefs, if he were to have expectations about such things. A central element of the FTL theory is the notion of a "confidence threshold," or "threshold," for short. The lower the threshold, the thinner the evidence sufficient for reaching it. Two thresholds are relevant to each hypothesis: "The acceptance threshold is the minimum confidence in the truth of a hypothesis," p, sufficient for acquiring a belief that p "rather than continuing to test [the hypothesis], and the rejection threshold is the minimum confidence in the untruth of a hypothesis," p, sufficient for acquiring a belief that $\sim p$ "and discontinuing the test" (Trope and Liberman 1996, p. 253). The two thresholds are often not equally demanding, and the acceptance and rejection thresholds, respectively, depend "primarily" on "the cost of false acceptance relative to the cost of information" and "the cost of false rejection relative to the cost of information." The "cost of information" is simply the "resources and effort" required for gathering and processing "hypothesis-relevant information" (p. 252).

Confidence thresholds are determined by the strength of aversions to specific costly errors together with information costs. Setting aside the latter costs, the stronger one's aversion to falsely believing that p, the higher one's threshold for belief that p. These aversions influence belief in a pair of related ways. First, because, other things being equal, lower thresholds are easier to reach than higher ones, belief that $\sim p$ is a more likely outcome than belief that p, other things being equal, in a hypothesis tester who has a higher acceptance threshold for p than for $\sim p$. Second, the aversions at issue influence *how* we test hypotheses, not just *when we stop* testing them (because we have reached a relevant threshold). Recall the study in which subjects asked to adopt "the perspective of a cabin guard" showed an "extremely high frequency" of testing for disconfirming instances, whereas subjects asked to "take the perspective of a visitor" showed the common confirmation bias.

It might be claimed that if aversions of the kind under discussion function in the second way, they function in conjunction with beliefs to the effect that testing-behavior of a specific kind will tend to help one avoid making the costly errors at issue. It might be claimed, accordingly, that the pertinent testing-behavior is performed for a (Davidsonian) reason constituted by the aversion and an instrumental belief of the kind just mentioned and that this behavior is therefore performed with the intention of avoiding, or of trying to avoid, the pertinent error. The thrust of these claims is that the FTL theory accommodates the confirmation bias, for example, by invoking a model of intentional action.

This is not a feature of the FTL model, as its proponents understand it. Friedrich, for example, claims that desires to avoid specific errors can trigger and sustain "automatic test strategies" (1993, p. 313); the triggering and sustaining supposedly occur in roughly the nonintentional way in which a desire that p results in the enhanced vividness of evidence for p. A person's being more strongly averse to falsely believing that $\sim p$ than to falsely believing that p may have the effect that he primarily seeks evidence for p, is more attentive to such evidence than to evidence that $\sim p$, and interprets relatively neutral data as supporting p, without this effect's being mediated by a belief that such behavior is conducive to avoiding the former error. The stronger aversion may simply frame the topic in such a way as to trigger and sustain these manifestations of the confirmation bias without the assistance of a belief that behavior of this kind is a means of avoiding certain errors. Similarly, having a stronger aversion that runs in the opposite direction may result in a skeptical approach to hypothesis testing that in no way depends on a belief to the effect that an approach of this kind will increase the probability of avoiding the costlier error. Given the aversion, skeptical testing is predictable independently of the agent's believing that a particular testing style will decrease the probability of making a certain error. So at least I have argued elsewhere (Mele 2001, pp. 41–49, 61–67).

I do not defend this thesis again here, nor am I claiming that the FTL theory should be accepted without qualification. The theory may accurately describe what happens in some or many cases of lay hypothesis testing that results in belief. My concern is the theoretical implications for the nature of motivational explanation, even if the theory should be rejected. The nature of motivational explanation hinges on what sorts of motivational explanation are *possible*.

2. Motivated Belief and Motivational Explanations

It is often supposed that, as Jeffrey Foss has put it, "desires have no explanatory force without associated beliefs" that identify means, or apparent means, to the desires' satisfaction, and this is part of "the very logic of belief-desire explanation" (1997, p. 112). Recall the survey of a million high school seniors that found, among other things, that "25% thought they were in the top 1%" in ability to get along with others (Gilovich 1991, p. 77). A likely hypothesis about this striking figure includes the idea that desires that p can contribute to biased beliefs that p. If Foss's claim were true, a student's wanting it to be the case that he is superior in this area would help to explain his believing that he is superior only in combination with an instrumental belief (or a collection thereof) that links his believing that he is superior to the satisfaction of his desire to be superior. But one searches in vain for instrumental beliefs that are plausibly regarded as turning the trick frequently enough to accommodate the data. Perhaps believing that one is exceptionally affable can help to bring it about that one is in fact superior in this sphere, and some high school students may believe that this is so. But it is highly unlikely that most people who have a motivationally biased belief that they are exceptionally affable have that belief, in part, *because* they want it to be true that they are superior in this area *and* believe that believing that they are superior can make it so. No other instrumental beliefs look more promising. Should one infer, then, that wanting it to be true that one is superior in this area plays a role in explaining only relatively few instances of false and unwarranted belief that one is superior? No. There is powerful empirical evidence (see Mele 2001) that desiring that p makes a broad causal contribution to the acquisition and retention of unwarranted beliefs that p.[7] Desires that do this enter into causal *explanations* of the pertinent biased beliefs. Given the place of desires in these explanations, the explanations are naturally counted as *motivational* ones.

Consider an example of motivationally biased belief that I have discussed elsewhere (Mele 2001, pp. 18–19). Beth's father died some months ago as she approached her twelfth birthday. She hopes that he loved her deeply. Beth finds it comforting to reflect on pleasant memories of playing happily with her father, to look at family photographs of such scenes, and so on, and she finds it unpleasant to reflect on memories of her father's leaving her behind to play ball with her brothers, as he often did. Sometimes, she intentionally focuses her attention on the pleasant memories, intentionally lingers over the pictures, and intentionally averts her attention from memories of being left behind and from pictures of her father playing only with her brothers. As a partial consequence of such activities, Beth acquires the unwarranted belief that her father cared more deeply for her than for anyone else. By hypothesis, although the intentional activities I mentioned are caused, in part, by Beth's desire that her father loved her deeply, those activities are not also caused by a desire (or an intention or an attempt) to deceive herself into believing this proposition, to cause herself to believe it, or to make it easier for herself to believe it.[8] Beth's activities are explicable on the hypothesis that she was seeking pleasant experiences and avoiding painful ones without in any way trying to influence what she believed.

It is relatively easy to construct a Davidsonian instrumental rationalization of, for example, Beth's looking at certain pictures in her family photo albums, and this rationalization may be, or be encompassed in, a motivational explanation of her so doing. Perhaps Beth desires to cheer herself up and believes that looking at these pictures will accomplish that. Her looking at the pictures in turn contributes to her coming to believe that her father loved her most (belief B). But a promising motivational explanation of her acquiring B features another desire—Beth's desire that her father loved her deeply (desire D). By hypothesis, it is owing significantly to D that she finds it so pleasant to attend to certain pictures and memories and so unpleasant to attend to others. Moreover, it is plausible that D triggers and sustains biased hypothesis testing of the sort the FTL theory predicts. A plausible motivational explanation of Beth's acquiring B traces a causal path *from* conditions that include D, *through* (among other things) D's effects on her relevant confidence thresholds and hypothesis testing and on her relevant intentional overt and mental activities, *to* her acquiring the belief. A D-featuring explanation of this kind is not an instrumental rationalization, for D does not function in it as a *goal*-representing attitude.

In chapter 1 (section 3), I argued that, if there are rationalizing causes, Ann's hope that the Pistons won noninstrumentally rationalizes her desire to learn that they won in virtue of making a causal contribution to the occurrence of the desire that helps to explain that occurrence partly by revealing an agreeable feature of learning that they won, namely, its pleasantness. Ann's hope reveals this agreeable feature to us in light of our awareness that people are pleased by "good news"—news that current hopes or desires of theirs are satisfied. And the rationalization is not an instrumental one because neither Ann's desire to learn that the Pistons won nor her learning that they won, as she knows, can influence whether they won.[9] Does Beth's desire that her father deeply loved her noninstrumentally rationalize her belief that he loved her most in virtue of making a causal contribution to the occurrence of the belief that helps to explain that occurrence partly by revealing an agreeable feature of her believing that he loved her most—pleasantness again (see Mele 1998b, pp. 242–48)?[10] If so, is the non-instrumental rationalization (part of) an adequate motivational explanation of her acquiring this belief?

The FTL theory has the resources for explaining, in the same general way, agreeable motivationally biased beliefs like Beth's and distinctly *disagreeable* counterparts. "Twisted" self-deception (Mele 1999c; 2001, ch. 5), exemplified by an insecure, jealous husband who believes that his wife is having an affair despite possessing only very weak evidence for that proposition and despite unambivalently wanting it to be false that she is so engaged, is accommodated by the FTL theory. Whereas many people may have a lower threshold for belief that their spouses are faithful than for belief that they are unfaithful, the converse may well be true of some insecure, jealous people. The belief that one's spouse is unfaithful tends to cause significant psychological discomfort; it tends to be extremely disagreeable. Even so, the aversion to falsely believing that their spouses are faithful may be so strong in some people that they test relevant hypotheses in ways that are less likely, other things being equal, to lead to a false belief in their spouses' fidelity than to a false belief in their spouses' infidelity. Suppose that the FTL theory is on the right track. It may be argued that because it applies in the same way both to Beth's agreeable belief that her father loved her most and to the jealous husband's disagreeable belief that his wife is having an affair, and because the explanation in the latter case does not include a noninstrumental rationalization that reveals an agreeable feature of the belief, the same is true of the explanation of Beth's belief. What are the merits of this line of argument?

It is true that whereas Beth's desire that her father loved her deeply is alleged to play an important role in producing her belief that he loved her most, the hypothetical jealous husband, Jeff, lacks a parallel desire—for example, a desire that his wife is having an affair. Even so, a putative noninstrumental rationalization of Beth's belief along the lines at issue can contribute to an explanation of that belief. On the FTL model, Beth's relevant desires, including the one just mentioned, and Jeff's relevant desires function in the same general way in fixing confidence thresholds. Beth's desires contribute to a lower threshold for belief that her father loved her most than for belief that he did not, and Jeff's desires contribute to a lower threshold for belief that his wife is having an affair than for belief that she is not. The putative noninstrumental rationalization in Beth's case tells part of the explanatory story while leaving out the explanatory machinery. It helps to explain her belief that her father loved her most partly by revealing an agreeable feature of her believing that, its pleasantness. But it omits to mention that her desire that her father loved her deeply—which accounts, in significant part, for the pleasantness—plays its role at least partly by way of its contribution to Beth's balance of error costs (if the FTL theory is roughly right).

Standard instrumental rationalizations of actions are incomplete in a similar way. We say that Sal crossed the street because he wanted a newspaper and believed he could buy one there, thereby offering an instrumental rationalization of the crossing. That rationalization omits to mention that his desire for a newspaper played its role partly by way of its contribution to Sal's strongest untrumped proximal motivation at the time, or to his acquiring an intention to cross the street, or the like. When what one's audience wants answered is the question for what reason an agent *A*-ed, a correct instrumental rationalization should satisfy them.[11] When the audience's question runs deeper—for example, when they want to know not only the reason for which an agent A-ed but also why he acted for that reason rather than acting for another—satisfying them requires a richer story.

I have mentioned motivational explanations of two kinds in this chapter: motivational explanations of intentional actions that feature Davidsonian instrumental rationalizations of the actions, and motivational explanations of states of mind that feature noninstrumental rationalizations of the mental states (e.g., Ann's desire to learn that the Pistons won and Beth's belief that her father loved her most). Both kinds of explanation were discussed in chapter 1 (section 3), along with a third kind: motivational explanations of action-desires and intentions that feature Davidsonian instrumental rationalizations of their objects (i.e., of what the agent desires or intends to do). In each case, motivation-constituting items make a causal contribution to the explanandum that (1) helps to explain the explanandum at least partly by revealing (sometimes in conjunction with an instrumental belief) an agreeable feature, from the perspective of the agent's desires, either of the explanandum itself or of its object and (2) is of such a kind that our learning of contributions of that kind tends to improve our "folk-psychological" understanding—that is, the understanding we have in, roughly, commonsense psychological terms—of why the explanandum came to be. This compound feature is the core of ordinary motivational explanations. We speak, in ordinary conversation, of a mental state's motivating an action or another mental state. For example, we say such things as "John's desire for fame motivated him to work hard on that book," "Paul's desire to drink some paint motivated him to pry the lid off that can," "Beth's belief that her father loved her most was motivated by her desire that he loved her deeply," "John's desire to write a great book was motivated by his desire for fame," and "Ann's desire to learn that the Pistons won was motivated by her desire that they won." If these claims are true, then in each case, if I am right, the identified motivator makes a causal contribution to the identified product of which (1) and (2) are true.

The remainder of this section is pretty much an appendix. "Rationalizing" is a term of art in Davidson's work. I, too, have been using it as a term of art, but with a broader application. Motivational explanation is my concern in this section, not rationalization per se. Even so, a claim in an argument about rationalizing that I rejected in this section merits further attention. This is the claim that if the FTL theory is on the right track, Jeff's motivationally biased belief that his wife is having an affair does not include a noninstrumental rationalization that reveals an agreeable feature of the belief, given his desires (including aversions).

Even though Jeff does not desire that his wife is having an affair, his belief that she is so engaged does have an agreeable feature, assuming that the FTL theory is roughly right; and Beth's belief that her father loved her most has the same feature. In light of Jeff's strong aversion to believing falsely that his wife is not having an affair, an agreeable feature of his believing that she is having an affair is that, barring obviously contradictory beliefs (i.e., beliefs whose contents are obviously contradictory), so believing precludes his falsely believing at the time that she is not having an affair (by precluding his believing the latter proposition then). Similarly, in light of Beth's strong aversion to believing falsely that her father did not love her most (which is partially accounted for by the strength of her desire that her father loved her deeply), an agreeable feature of her believing that he did love her most is that, again barring obviously contradictory beliefs, so believing precludes her falsely believing at the time that he did not love her most (by precluding her believing the latter proposition then).

It may be argued that even if these beliefs do have this agreeable feature, that they do is not revealed by the aversions in a way appropriate to rationalizations. It may be claimed that appropriateness in this connection is constrained by commonsense psychology and that the latter does not include any platitudes that provide a context in which the aversions would reveal the agreeable feature. However, it certainly is part of commonsense psychology that avoiding discomfort is agreeable and that people tend to suffer discomfort when something to which they are averse comes to be and they are aware of its existence. Furthermore, the truth that, barring obviously contradictory beliefs, believing that p precludes one's simultaneously falsely believing that $\sim p$ is not a stretch for commonsense psychology. In light of these truths, the aversions do reveal the agreeable feature at issue.[12]

3. Reasons-Explanations and Motivational Explanations

Davidsonian reasons-explanations of intentional actions are motivational explanations. They are not, however, *complete* explanations, nor are they meant to be.[13] The same is generally true of ordinary motivational explanations of intentional actions. The Davidsonian explanations are answers to questions of the form "For what reason(s) did S A?" or "Why did S A?" in a reasons-requesting sense of "why" (see note 11). Correct Davidsonian explanations offer correct answers to questions of that form. Sometimes, however, when we ask why someone did something, we want to know more than the reason(s) for which he did it.

This broader curiosity naturally arises in discussions of akratic action. Joe sneaked outside and smoked because he wanted to have a cigarette without anyone seeing him and believed that he could do that outside. He was convinced that it would be best not to smoke. Indeed, it is partly because of that conviction that Joe wanted to smoke undetected; he did not want his children to see him doing something they know he knows he should not do. Given this information, curious minds wonder why Joe sneaked outside and smoked even though he judged it best not to do so or why he acted for the reasons he did rather than for his reasons for not smoking. These questions take the discussion beyond ordinary reasons-explanations of actions—that is, beyond motivational explanations of this kind—into more deeply theoretical territory (cf. Mele 1987, pp. 39–41). Someone who assents to a theoretical principle like *Mub** (chapter 8) may want to know how it came to be that Joe's untrumped proximal motivation to sneak outside and smoke was stronger than any relevant competing motivation.

A similar question arises when agents successfully resist temptation, as I have observed elsewhere (Mele 1987, pp. 84, 98). Suppose that a day later, around the same time, Joe is in a very similar position, with reasons pro and con of the same kind and a powerful urge to smoke. This time, he resists the urge to sneak outside for a smoke and chews some gum inside instead. Why did Joe act for the reasons he did rather than for his reasons for sneaking outside and smoking, as he did yesterday? The answer that he judged it better to act for the former reasons (or judged those reasons better or judged it better not to smoke) is not satisfying. After all, part of the story may be that Joe judged the same thing yesterday and smoked anyway.

Two observations are in order. First, a theory of motivation should provide some guidance in answering deeper questions of this kind. I have tried to provide such guidance both in earlier work (especially Mele 1987 and 1995a) and in this book. Second, the fact that warranted questions such as these arise even after ordinary reasons-explanations—ordinary motivational explanations—have been given of the actions at issue does not undermine those explanations. Again, explanations of that kind are meant to answer questions of the form "For what reason did S A?" It should not be thought that true answers to questions of that form always tell us everything we want to know about why the agent A-ed.

Motivational explanations differ in the kinds of explananda explained, in the kinds of rationalizations involved (when rationalizations are involved), and in the depth and breadth of the explanantia. Relevant explananda include not only actions but also desires, intentions, and beliefs, and not only tokens in this sphere but also patterns of actions and attitudes both within and across individuals. Relevant rationalizations include the kinds identified in section 2. Relevant explanantia range from simple reasons-explanations of particular intentional actions and simple noninstrumental rationalizations of particular desires to attempts to explain general patterns of human behavior.

4. Conclusion

My aim in this book has been to develop plausible answers to a web of important and challenging questions about motivation and human agency and to do this in a way that is sensitive to the theoretical concerns both of philosophers of mind and action and of moral philosophers and is informed by relevant empirical work. My hope is that the web of answers I have offered can eventually be combined with future work and refined in light of that work—work of mine and others, and work both in philosophy and in allied disciplines—to produce a robust, general theory, in a refined and enriched commonsense psychological vocabulary, of the explanation of human behavior.

A brief review of some of the major elements in my web of answers is in order. The main thesis defended in part I is that proper motivational explanations of goal-directed actions are causal explanations. Part II took up the place of motivation in practical reasoning (chapter 4) and in moral conduct (chapter 5) and offered an account of what it is for an attitude that is focused on A-ing essentially to constitute motivation to A (chapter 6). In part II, I defended a version of the antecedent motivation theory about practical reasoning and argued that no plausible cognitivist moral theory will require that moral ought-beliefs essentially encompass motivation to act accordingly or even, more modestly, that some of them are intrinsically motivating. This latter argument cleared some ground for the account offered in chapter 6 of essentially motivation-constituting attitudes of the kind mentioned. At least some such attitudes—namely, action-desires and action-intentions—are *paradigmatic* motivational attitudes in human agents. Another ground-clearing enterprise in part II, which began in chapter 3, concerned two competing approaches to understanding reasons for action, one emphasizing their role in explaining intentional actions and the other highlighting their place in the evaluation of intentional actions or their agents. My aim in that project was to leave conceptual space for theories consonant with the latter approach while preserving the integrity of the project of explaining intentional human action, including moral conduct, in terms of states of mind, including motivational states.

In part III, I refuted the major arguments in the literature against the idea that desires differ in motivational strength (*MSI*) while giving skeptics a concrete proposal to evaluate (chapter 7), and I argued that a plausible principle relating motivational strength to intentional action does not entail that we are at the mercy of our strongest desires (chapter 8). Both *MSI* and the principle leave ample room for self-control. In part IV, I defended an account of practical decisions as mental acts of executive assent to first-person plans of action (chapter 9); argued for the existence of practical decisions so understood (chapter 9); defended a conception of human agency that accommodates the impressive practical reasoning, decision making, and exercises of self-control that may be involved in the upper range of human action while fitting nicely with my general causal approach to action explanation (chapter 10); sketched a view of the role of motivation in explaining motivationally biased beliefs (chapter 11); and outlined the core of ordinary motivational explanations (chapter 11).

As I observed in a previous book (Mele 1992e, p. 3), even if our current understanding of human behavior is far from perfect, we understand the behavior of others and ourselves well enough to coordinate and sustain the wealth of complicated, cooperative activities integral to normal human life, and the understanding we have achieved is expressed largely in our commonsense psychological vocabulary—that is, in terms of belief, desire, intention, decision, emotion, reasoning, and the like. This is significant evidence that that vocabulary is, at least, very useful. Moreover, if it were not useful, it is unlikely that it would still have the prominence it does today. Philosophers of mind and action and moral philosophers, who have traditionally used and refined this vocabulary in their attempts to understand and explain human conduct, should also be emboldened by the fact that this vocabulary is flourishing in, for example, social, motivational, and developmental psychology. This philosophical tradition has a firm basis of support in the human sciences, and the potential for mutual intellectual benefit is enormous.

Notes

1. Parts of the remainder of this section and the first paragraph of section 2 derive from Mele (2001, pp. 11, 23–24, 28–30, 33–35, 42–44).
    2. This paragraph and the next derive from Mele (1995a, p. 88).
    3. On an additional source, the availability heuristic, see Mele (2001, pp. 28–29).
    4. I developed this idea in 1987 (ch. 10) and again in 2001. Kunda (1990) develops the same theme, paying particular attention to evidence that motivation sometimes primes the confirmation bias (see also Kunda 1999, ch. 6).
    5. For motivational interpretations of the confirmation bias, see Frey (1986, pp. 70–74), Friedrich (1993), and Trope and Liberman (1996, pp. 252–65).

6. See Mele (2001, pp. 31–49, 63–70, 90–91, 96–98, 112–18).

7. Recall my practice (announced in the introduction, section 2) of understanding claims about the causal roles and powers of attitudes disjunctively, as claims about the causal roles and powers of the physical realizers of the attitudes *or* of the attitudes themselves (qua attitudes).

8. I have defended the coherence of this hypothesis (Mele 2001, pp. 17–19, 58–59).

9. This is a sufficient condition of a rationalization's not being an instrumental one, not a necessary condition.

10. A salient difference between the suggestion embedded in this question and my claim about Ann is that what this suggestion asserts to be agreeable is some feature of the rationalized attitude itself, whereas my claim about Ann specifies the *object* of the rationalized attitude (i.e., learning that the Pistons won) in this connection.

11. Here I assume an audience of normal people. I take it that normal people are often very happy to be given action explanations in terms of broadly Davidsonian reasons. Theorists who deny that broadly Davidsonian reasons are reasons should read "reason" in this chapter as "reason*" (see chapter 3, section 5).

12. If Beth's and Jeff's aversions help to explain their beliefs that are at issue by revealing an agreeable feature of these beliefs, they may be said to rationalize these beliefs. If I am right (Mele 2001), the aversions do their work without the assistance of instrumental beliefs (e.g., beliefs to the effect that believing that *p*—or getting oneself to believe that *p*—would preclude one's falsely believing that ~*p*).

13. In chapter 3, section 2, I cited Davidson (1980, p. 42; 1982a; 1999, p. 639) in this connection.

References

Adams, Frederick. 1997. "Cognitive Trying." In G. Holmström-Hintikka and R. Tuomela, eds., *Contemporary Action Theory*. Dordrecht: Kluwer.

———. 1986. "Intention and Intentional Action: The Simple View." *Mind and Language* 1: 281–301.

Adams, Frederick, and A. Mele. 1992. "The Intention/Volition Debate." *Canadian Journal of Philosophy* 22: 323–38.

Alston, William. 1967. "Motives and Motivation." In P. Edwards, ed., *The Encyclopedia of Philosophy*. New York: Macmillan.

Altham, James. 1986. "The Legacy of Emotivism." In G. Macdonald and C. Wright, eds., *Fact, Science and Morality*. Oxford: Blackwell.

Anscombe, G. E. M. 1963. *Intention*. 2nd ed. Ithaca, N.Y.: Cornell University Press.

Aristotle. 1915. *De Anima*. Vol. 3 of W. Ross, ed., *The Works of Aristotle*. London: Oxford University Press.

———. *Nicomachean Ethics*. 1915. Vol. 9 of W. Ross, ed., *The Works of Aristotle*. London: Oxford University Press.

Armstrong, David. 1980. *The Nature of Mind*. Ithaca, N.Y.: Cornell University Press.

Atkinson, John. 1982. "Old and New Conceptions of How Expected Consequences Influence Actions." In N. Feather, ed., *Expectations and Actions*. Hillsdale, N.J.: Lawrence Erlbaum.

———. 1957. "Motivational Determinants of Risk-Taking Behavior." *Psychological Review* 64: 359–72.

Audi, Robert. 2001. *The Architecture of Reason*. New York: Oxford University Press.

———. 1997. *Moral Knowledge and Ethical Character*. New York: Oxford University Press.

———. 1994. "Dispositional Beliefs and Dispositions to Believe." *Noûs* 28: 419–34.

———. 1993. *Action, Intention, and Reason*. Ithaca, N.Y.: Cornell University Press.

———. 1979. "Weakness of Will and Practical Judgment." *Noûs* 13: 173–96.

———. 1973. "Intending." *Journal of Philosophy* 70: 387–402.

Baron, Jonathan. 1988. *Thinking and Deciding*. Cambridge: Cambridge University Press.

Bishop, John. 1989. *Natural Agency*. Cambridge: Cambridge University Press.

Bond, Edward. 1983. *Reason and Value*. Cambridge: Cambridge University Press.

Brand, Myles. 1984. *Intending and Acting*. Cambridge, Mass.: MIT Press.

Bratman, Michael. 2000. "Reflection, Planning, and Temporally Extended Agency." *Philosophical Review* 109: 35–61.

———. 1999. *Faces of Intention*. New York: Cambridge University Press.

———. 1996. "Identification, Decision, and Treating as a Reason." *Philosophical Topics* 24: 1–18.

———. 1987. *Intention, Plans, and Practical Reason*. Cambridge, Mass.: Harvard University Press.

———. 1985. "Davidson's Theory of Intention." In E. LePore and B. McLaughlin, eds., *Actions and Events*. Oxford: Blackwell.

———. 1984. "Two Faces of Intention." *Philosophical Review* 93: 375–405.

Brink, David. 1989. *Moral Realism and the Foundations of Ethics*. Cambridge: Cambridge University Press.

Castañeda, Hector. 1975. *Thinking and Doing*. Dordrecht: Reidel.

Charlton, William. 1988. *Weakness of Will*. Oxford: Blackwell.

Christman, John. 1989. "Introduction." In J. Christman, ed., *The Inner Citadel*. New York: Oxford University Press.

Clarke, Randolph. 1996. "Agent Causation and Event Causation in the Production of Free Action." *Philosophical Topics* 24: 19–48.

———. 1994. "Doing What One Wants Less: A Reappraisal of the Law of Desire." *Pacific Philosophical Quarterly* 75: 1–10.

Cohon, Rachel. 2000. "The Roots of Reasons." *Philosophical Review* 109: 63–85.

———. 1993. "Internalism About Reasons for Action." *Pacific Philosophical Quarterly* 74: 265–88.

———. 1986. "Are External Reasons Impossible?" *Ethics* 96: 545–56.

Coles, Michael, and M. Rugg. 1995. "Event-Related Brain Potentials: An Introduction." In M. Rugg and M. Coles, eds., *Electrophysiology of Mind*. Oxford: Oxford University Press.

Collins, John. 1988. "Belief, Desire, and Revision." *Mind* 97: 333–42.

Dancy, Jonathan. 2000. *Practical Reality*. Oxford: Oxford University Press.

———. 1995. "Why There Is Really No Such Thing as the Theory of Motivation." *Proceedings of the Aristotelian Society* 95: 1–18.

———. 1993. *Moral Reasons*. Oxford: Blackwell.

Darwall, Stephen. 1992. "Internalism and Agency." *Philosophical Perspectives* 6: 155–74.

———. 1983. *Impartial Reason*. Ithaca, N.Y.: Cornell University Press.

Davidson, Donald. 1999. "Reply to Jennifer Hornsby." In L. Hahn, ed., *The Philosophy of Donald Davidson*. Chicago: Open Court.

———. 1987. "Problems in the Explanation of Action." In P. Pettit, R. Sylvan, and J. Norman, eds. *Metaphysics and Morality: Essays in Honour of J. J. C. Smart*. Oxford: Blackwell.

———. 1985. "Replies to Essays I–IX." In B. Vermazen and M. Hintikka, eds., *Essays on Davidson*. Oxford: Clarendon.

———. 1982a. "Paradoxes of Irrationality." In R. Wollheim and J. Hopkins, eds., *Philosophical Essays on Freud*. Cambridge: Cambridge University Press.

———. 1982b. "Rational Animals." *Dialectica* 36: 318–27.

———. 1980. *Essays on Actions and Events*. Oxford: Clarendon.

———. 1963. "Actions, Reasons, and Causes." *Journal of Philosophy* 60: 685–700. Reprinted in Davidson 1980.

Davis, Lawrence. 1979. *Theory of Action*. Upper Saddle River, N.J.: Prentice Hall.

Davis, Wayne. 1997. "A Causal Theory of Intending." In A. Mele, ed., *The Philosophy of Action*. New York: Oxford University Press.

Deci, Edward, and R. Ryan. 1985. *Intrinsic Motivation and Self-Determination in Human Behavior*. New York: Plenum.

Dennett, Daniel. 1991. *Consciousness Explained*. Boston: Little, Brown.

Dreier, James. 1990. "Internalism and Speaker Relativism." *Ethics* 101: 6–26.

Dretske, Fred. 1988. *Explaining Behavior: Reasons in a World of Causes*. Cambridge, Mass.: MIT Press.

Dum, Richard, and P. Strick. 1996. "The Corticospinal System: A Structural Framework for the Central Control of Movement." In L. Rowell and J. Shepherd, eds., *Handbook of Physiology*. New York: Oxford University Press.

Falk, W. D. 1948. "'Ought' and Motivation." *Proceedings of the Aristotelian Society* 48: 111–38.

Fischer, John. 1994. *The Metaphysics of Free Will*. Cambridge, Mass.: Blackwell.

Fischer, John, and M. Ravizza. 1998. *Responsibility and Control: A Theory of Moral Responsibility*. New York: Cambridge University Press.

Flanagan, Owen. 1996. *Self-Expressions*. New York: Oxford University Press.

Foot, Philippa. 1978. *Virtues and Vices*. Los Angeles: University of California Press.

Foss, Jeffrey. 1997. "How Many Beliefs Can Dance in the Head of the Self-Deceived?" *Behavioral and Brain Sciences* 20: 111–12.

Frankena, William. 1958. "Obligation and Motivation in Recent Moral Philosophy." In A. Melden, ed., *Essays in Moral Philosophy*. Seattle: University of Washington Press.

Frankfurt, Harry. 1999. *Necessity, Volition, and Love*. New York: Cambridge University Press.

———. 1988. *The Importance of What We Care About*. Cambridge: Cambridge University Press.

Frey, Deiter. 1986. "Recent Research on Selective Exposure to Information." In L. Berkowitz, ed., *Advances in Experimental Social Psychology*. New York: Academic Press.

Friedrich, James. 1993. "Primary Error Detection and Minimization (PEDMIN) Strategies in Social Cognition: A Reinterpretation of Confirmation Bias Phenomena." *Psychological Review* 100: 298–319.

Gallistel, Charles. 1980. *The Organization of Action: A New Synthesis*. Hillsdale, N.J.: Lawrence Erlbaum.

Garrard, Eve, and D. McNaughton. 1998. "Mapping Moral Motivation." *Ethical Theory and Moral Practice* 1: 45–59.

Georgopoulos, A. 1995. "Motor Cortex and Cognitive Processing." In M. Gazzaniga, ed., *The Cognitive Neurosciences*. Cambridge, Mass.: MIT Press.

Gert, Joshua. 2000. "Practical Rationality, Morality, and Purely Justificatory Reasons." *American Philosophical Quarterly* 37: 227–43.

Ghez, Claude, J. Krakauer, R. Sainburg, and M. Ghilardi. 2000. "Spatial Representations and Internal Models of Limb Dynamics in Motor Learning." In M. Gazzaniga, ed., *The New Cognitive Neurosciences*. Cambridge, Mass.: MIT Press.

Gigerenzer, Gerd, and K. Hug. 1992. "Domain-Specific Reasoning: Social Contracts, Cheating, and Perspective Change." *Cognition* 43: 127–71.

Gilovich, Thomas. 1991. *How We Know What Isn't So*. New York: Macmillan.

Ginet, Carl. 1990. *On Action*. New York: Cambridge University Press.

Goldman, Alvin. 1970. *A Theory of Human Action*. Upper Saddle River, N.J.: Prentice Hall.

Gopnik, Alison. 1993. "How We Know Our Minds—The Illusion of 1st-Person Knowledge of Intentionality." *Behavioral and Brain Sciences* 16: 1–14.

Gosling, Justin. 1990. *Weakness of the Will*. London: Routledge.

Hampton, Jean. 1998. *The Authority of Reason*. Cambridge: Cambridge University Press.

Hare, R. M. 1972. *Practical Inferences*. Berkeley: University of California Press.

———. 1963. *Freedom and Reason*. Oxford: Oxford University Press.

Harman, Gilbert. 1993. "Desired Desires." In R. Frey and C. Morris, eds., *Value, Welfare, and Morality*. Cambridge: Cambridge University Press.

———. 1986. *Change in View*. Cambridge, Mass.: MIT Press.

———. 1976. "Practical Reasoning." *Review of Metaphysics* 79: 431–63.

Heckhausen, Heinz. 1991. *Motivation and Action*. Berlin: Springer-Verlag.

Heil, John, and A. Mele, eds. 1993. *Mental Causation*. Oxford: Clarendon.

Hollis, Martin. 1987. *The Cunning of Reason*. Cambridge: Cambridge University Press.

Hooker, Brad. 1987. "Williams' Argument Against External Reasons." *Analysis* 47: 42–44.

Horak, Fay, and J. Macpherson. 1996. "Postural Orientation and Equilibrium." In L. Rowell and J. Shepherd, eds., *Handbook of Physiology*. New York: Oxford University Press.

Hornsby, Jennifer. 1980. *Actions*. Boston : Routledge and Kegan Paul.

Humberstone, I. Loyd. 1992. "Direction of Fit." *Mind* 101: 59–83.

Hume, David. [1739] 1975. *A Treatise of Human Nature*. Ed. L. Selby-Bigge. Oxford: Clarendon Press.

Hursthouse, Rosalind. 1991. "Arational Actions." *Journal of Philosophy* 87: 57–68.

Hutcheson, Francis. 1897. "Illustrations on the Moral Sense." In L. Selby-Bigge, ed., *British Moralists*. Oxford: Clarendon.

Jackson, Frank. 2000. "Psychological Explanation and Implicit Theory." *Philosophical Explorations* 3: 83–95.

———. 1985. "Internal Conflicts in Desires and Morals." *American Philosophical Quarterly* 22: 105–14.

Jackson, Frank, and P. Pettit. 1990. "Program Explanation: A General Perspective." *Analysis* 50: 107–17.

———. 1988. "Functionalism and Broad Content." *Mind* 97: 381–400.

James, William. 1981. *The Principles of Psychology*, vol. 2. Cambridge, Mass.: Harvard University Press.

Jeffrey, Richard. 1985. "Animal Interpretation." In E. LePore and B. McLaughlin, eds., *Actions and Events*. Oxford: Blackwell.

Jordan, Michael. 1996. "Computational Aspects of Motor Control and Motor Learning." In H. Heuer and S. Keele, eds., *Handbook of Perception and Action*, vol 2. London: Academic Press.

Kane, Robert. 1996. *The Significance of Free Will*. New York: Oxford University Press.

Kaufman, Arnold. 1966. "Practical Decision." *Mind* 75: 25–44.

Kavka, Gregory. 1983. "The Toxin Puzzle." *Analysis* 43: 33–36.

Kennett, Jeanette. 2000. *Agency and Responsibility*. Oxford: Oxford University Press.

Kennett, Jeanette, and M. Smith. 1997. "Synchronic Self-Control Is Always Non-action." *Analysis* 57: 123–31.

———. 1996. "Frog and Toad Lose Control." *Analysis* 56: 63–73.

Kenny, Anthony. 1989. *The Metaphysics of Mind*. Oxford: Oxford University Press.

Klayman, Joshua, and Y.-W. Ha. 1987. "Confirmation, Disconfirmation, and Information in Hypothesis Testing." *Psychological Review* 94: 211–28.

Klein, Martha. 1990. *Determinism, Blameworthiness, and Deprivation*. Oxford: Clarendon.

Korsgaard, Christine. 1996. *Sources of Normativity*. New York: Cambridge University Press.

———. 1986. "Skepticism About Practical Reason." *Journal of Philosophy* 83: 5–25.

Kunda, Ziva. 1999. *Social Cognition*. Cambridge, Mass.: MIT Press.

———. 1990. "The Case for Motivated Reasoning." *Psychological Bulletin* 108: 480–98.

———. 1987. "Motivated Inference: Self-Serving Generation and Evaluation of Causal Theories." *Journal of Personality and Social Psychology* 53: 636–47.

Lewis, David. 1988. "Desire as Belief." *Mind* 97: 323–32.

———. 1986. *Philosophical Papers*, vol. 2. New York: Oxford University Press.

———. 1973. *Counterfactuals*. Cambridge, Mass.: Harvard University Press.

Libet, Benjamin. 1999. "Do We Have Free Will?" *Journal of Consciousness Studies* 6: 47–57.

———. 1992. "The Neural Time-Factor in Perception, Volition and Free Will." *Revue de Métaphysique et de Morale* 2: 255–72.

———. 1989. "The Timing of a Subjective Experience." *Behavioral and Brain Sciences* 12: 183–84.

———. 1985. "Unconscious Cerebral Initiative and the Role of Conscious Will in Voluntary Action." *Behavioral and Brain Sciences* 8: 529–66.

Libet, Benjamin, E. Wright, and A. Curtis. 1983. "Preparation- or Intention-to-Act, in Relation to Pre-Event Potentials Recorded at the Vertex." *Electroencephalography and Clinical Neurophysiology* 56: 367–72.

Locke, Don. 1974. "Reasons, Wants, and Causes." *American Philosophical Quarterly* 11: 169–79.

Ludwig, Kirk. 1992. "Impossible Doings." *Philosophical Studies* 65: 257–81.

MacKay, Donald. 1981. "Behavioral Plasticity, Serial Order, and the Motor Program." *Behavioral and Brain Sciences* 4: 630–31.

Mackie, John. 1977. *Ethics: Inventing Right and Wrong*. Harmondsworth: Penguin.

McCann, Hugh. 1998. *The Works of Agency*. Ithaca, N.Y.: Cornell University Press.

———. 1995. "Intention and Motivational Strength." *Journal of Philosophical Research* 20: 283–96.

———. 1991. "Settled Objectives and Rational Constraints." *American Philosophical Quarterly* 28: 24–36.

———. 1986a. "Intrinsic Intentionality." *Theory and Decision* 20: 247–73.

———. 1986b. "Rationality and the Range of Intention." *Midwest Studies in Philosophy* 10: 191–211.

———. 1975. "Trying, Paralysis, and Volition." *Review of Metaphysics* 28: 423–42.

———. 1974. "Volition and Basic Action." *Philosophical Review* 83: 451–73.

McDowell, John. 1995. "Might There Be External Reasons?" In J. Altham, ed., *World, Mind, and Ethics*. New York: Cambridge University Press.

———. 1985. "Values and Secondary Qualities." In T. Honderich, ed., *Morality and Objectivity*. Boston: Routledge and Kegan Paul.

———. 1982. "Reason and Action." *Philosophical Investigations* 5: 301–305.

———. 1979. "Virtue and Reason." *Monist* 62: 331–50.

———. 1978. "Are Moral Requirements Hypothetical Imperatives?" *Proceeding of the Aristotelian Society*. 52 (suppl.): 13–29.

McGinn, Colin. 1982. *The Character of Mind*. Oxford: Oxford University Press.

McNaughton, David. 1988. *Moral Vision*. Oxford: Blackwell.

Melden, Abraham. 1961. *Free Action*. London: Routledge and Kegan Paul.

Mele, Alfred. 2001. *Self-Deception Unmasked*. Princeton, N.J.: Princeton University Press.

———. 2000a. "Deciding to Act." *Philosophical Studies* 100: 81–108.

———. 2000b. "Goal-Directed Action: Teleological Explanations, Causal Theories, and Deviance." *Philosophical Perspectives* 14: 279–300.

———. 1999a. "Is There a Place for Intention in an Analysis of Intentional Action?" *Philosophia* 27: 419–32.

———. 1999b. "Motivation, Self-Control, and the Agglomeration of Desires." *Facta Philosophica* 1: 77–86.

———. 1999c. "Twisted Self-Deception." *Philosophical Psychology* 12: 117–37.

———. 1999d. "Ultimate Responsibility and Dumb Luck." *Social Philosophy & Policy* 16: 274–93.

———. 1998a. "Motivational Strength." *Noûs* 32: 23–36.

———. 1998b. "Noninstrumental Rationalizing." *Pacific Philosophical Quarterly* 79: 236–50.

———. 1998c. "Synchronic Self-Control Revisited: Frog and Toad Shape Up." *Analysis* 58: 305–10.

———. 1997a. "Agency and Mental Action." *Philosophical Perspectives* 11: 231–49.

———. 1997b. "Passive Action." In G. Holmström-Hintikka and R. Tuomela, eds., *Contemporary Action Theory*. Dordrecht: Kluwer.

———. 1997c. "Strength of Motivation and Being in Control: Learning from Libet." *American Philosophical Quarterly* 34: 319–33.

———. 1997d. "Underestimating Self-Control: Kennett and Smith on Frog and Toad." *Analysis* 57: 119–23.

———. 1996a. "Internalist Moral Cognitivism and Listlessness." *Ethics* 106: 727–53.

———. 1996b. "Motivation and Intention." *Journal of Philosophical Research* 21: 51–67.

———. 1996c. "Rational Intentions and the Toxin Puzzle." *Proto Sociology* 8/9: 39–52

———. 1996d. Review of G. F. Schueler, *Desire*. *Minds and Machines* 6: 253–56.

———. 1996e. "Soft Libertarianism and Frankfurt-Style Scenarios." *Philosophical Topics* 24: 123–41.

———. 1995a. *Autonomous Agents*. New York: Oxford University Press.

———. 1995b. "Effective Deliberation About What to Intend: Or Striking It Rich in a Toxin-Free Environment." *Philosophical Studies* 79: 85–93.

———. 1995c. "Motivation: Essentially Motivation-Constituting Attitudes." *Philosophical Review* 104: 387–423.

———. 1994. "Desiring to Try: Reply to Adams." *Canadian Journal of Philosophy* 24: 627–36.

———. 1992a. "Acting for Reasons and Acting Intentionally." *Pacific Philosophical Quarterly* 73: 355–74.

———. 1992b. "Intentions, Reasons, and Beliefs: Morals of the Toxin Puzzle." *Philosophical Studies* 68: 171–94.

———. 1992c. "Recent Work on Intentional Action." *American Philosophical Quarterly* 29: 199–217.

———. 1992d. Review of Carl Ginet, *On Action*. *Philosophy and Phenomenological Research* 52: 488–91.

———. 1992e. *Springs of Action: Understanding Intentional Behavior*. New York: Oxford University Press.

———. 1991. "Dretske's Intricate Behavior." *Philosophical Papers* 20: 1–10.

———. 1990a. "Errant Self-Control and the Self-Controlled Person." *Pacific Philosophical Quarterly* 71: 47–59.

———. 1990b. "He Wants to Try." *Analysis* 50: 251–53.

———. 1989. "Motivational Internalism: The Powers and Limits of Practical Reasoning." *Philosophia* 19: 417–36.

———. 1988. "Effective Reasons and Intrinsically Motivated Actions." *Philosophy and Phenomenological Research* 48: 723–31.

———. 1987. *Irrationality: An Essay on Akrasia, Self-Deception, and Self-Control*. New York: Oxford University Press.

———. 1984a. "Aristotle on the Roles of Reason in Motivation and Justification." *Archiv für Geschichte der Philosophie* 66: 124–47.

———. 1984b. "Aristotle's Wish." *Journal of the History of Philosophy* 22: 139–56.

Mele, Alfred, and P. Moser. 1994. "Intentional Action." *Noûs* 28: 39–68.

Mele, Alfred, and S. Sverdlik. 1996. "Intention, Intentional Action, and Moral Responsibility." *Philosophical Studies* 82: 265–87.

Millgram, Elijah. 1996. "Williams' Argument against External Reasons." *Noûs* 30: 197–220.

Milo, Ronald. 1984. *Immorality*. Princeton, N.J.: Princeton University Press.

Mook, Douglas. 1987. *Motivation: The Organization of Action*. New York: Norton.

Nagel, Thomas. 1986. *The View from Nowhere*. New York: Oxford University Press.

———. 1970. *The Possibility of Altruism*. Oxford: Oxford University Press.

Narveson, Jan. 1984. "Reason, Value and Desire." *Dialogue* 23: 327–35.

O'Connor, Timothy. 1995. "Agent Causation." In T. O'Connor, ed., *Agents, Causes, and Events*. New York: Oxford University Press.

Nisbett, Richard, and L. Ross. 1980. *Human Inference: Strategies and Shortcomings of Social Judgment*. Upper Saddle River, N.J.: Prentice Hall.

O'Shaughnessy, Brian. 1980. *The Will*, vol. 2. Cambridge: Cambridge University Press.

Parfit, Derek. 1997. "Reasons and Motivation." *Proceedings of the Aristotelian Society* 71 (suppl.): 99–130.

Penfield, Wilder. 1975. *The Mystery of the Mind*. Princeton, N.J.: Princeton University Press.

Peters, Richard. 1958. *The Concept of Motivation*. London: Routledge and Kegan Paul.

Pettit, Philip. 1987. "Humeans, Anti-Humeans, and Motivation." *Mind* 96: 530–33.

Pettit, Philip, and H. Price. 1989. "Bare Functional Desire." *Analysis* 49: 162–69.

Pettit, Philip, and M. Smith. 1990. "Backgrounding Desire." *Philosophical Review* 99: 565–92.

Pigden, Charles. n.d. "Hume, Motivation and the Moral Problem" (unpublished).

Pink, Thomas. 1996. *The Psychology of Freedom*. Cambridge: Cambridge University Press.

Plato. *Phaedrus*. 1953. In B. Jowett, trans., *The Dialogues of Plato*. Oxford: Clarendon Press.

Porter, Robert, and R. Lemon. 1993. *Corticospinal Function and Voluntary Movement*. Oxford: Clarendon.

Price, Huw. 1989. "Defending Desire-as-Belief." *Mind* 98: 119–27.

Price, Richard. 1969. "A Review of the Principal Questions in Morals." In D. Raphael, ed., *The British Moralists*. New York: Oxford University Press.

Prior, Elizabeth. 1985. *Dispositions*. Aberdeen: Aberdeen University Press.

Quinn, Warren. 1993. *Morality and Action*. New York: Cambridge University Press.

Reid, Thomas. 1788. *Essays on the Active Powers of Man*. Edinburgh: J. Bell.

Robertson, John. 1986. "Internalism About Moral Reasons." *Pacific Philosophical Quarterly* 67: 124–35.

Rorty, Amelie. 1980. "Where Does the Akratic Break Take Place?" *Australasian Journal of Philosophy* 58: 333–46.

Rosenbaum, David, and H. Krist. 1996. "Antecedents of Action." In H. Heuer and S. Keele, eds., *Handbook of Perception and Action*, vol 2. London: Academic Press.

Roth, Abraham. 1999. "Reasons Explanations of Actions: Causal, Singular, and Situational." *Philosophy and Phenomenological Research* 49: 839–74.

Rugg, Michael, and M. Coles. 1995. *Electrophysiology of Mind*. Oxford: Oxford University Press.

Scanlon, Thomas. 1998. *What We Owe to Each Other*. Cambridge, Mass: Harvard University Press.

Schroeder, Timothy, and N. Arpaly. 1999. "Alienation and Externality." *Canadian Journal of Philosophy* 29: 371–87.

Schueler, George F. 1995. *Desire: Its Role in Practical Reason and the Explanation of Action*. Cambridge, Mass.: MIT Press.

Searle, John. 2001. *Rationality in Action*. Cambridge, Mass.: MIT Press.

———. 1983. *Intentionality*. Cambridge: Cambridge University Press.

Sehon, Scott. 1997. "Deviant Causal Chains and the Irreducibility of Teleological Explana-
tion." *Pacific Philosophical Quarterly* 78: 195–213.
———. 1994. "Teleology and the Nature of Mental States." *American Philosophical Quarterly*
31: 63–72.
Sheridan, Martin. 1984. "Planning and Controlling Simple Movements." In M. Smyth and A.
Wing, eds., *The Psychology of Human Movement*. London: Academic Press.
Simpson, Evan. 1999. "Between Internalism and Externalism in Ethics." *Philosophical Quarterly* 49: 201–14.
Skinner, B. F. 1953. *Science and Human Behavior*. New York: Macmillan.
Smith, Michael. 1996. "The Argument for Internalism: Reply to Miller." *Analysis* 56: 175–84.
———. 1994. *The Moral Problem*. Oxford: Blackwell.
———. 1992. "Valuing: Desiring or Believing?" In D. Charles and K. Lennon, eds., *Reduction,
Explanation, and Realism*. Oxford: Clarendon.
———. 1988. "On Humeans, Anti-Humeans, and Motivation: A Reply to Pettit." *Mind* 97:
589–95.
———. 1987. "The Humean Theory of Motivation." *Mind* 96: 36–61.
Stocker, Michael. 1979. "Desiring the Bad." *Journal of Philosophy* 76: 738–53.
Strawson, Galen. 1986. *Freedom and Belief*. Oxford: Clarendon.
Taylor, Richard. 1966. *Action and Purpose*. Upper Saddle River, N.J.: Prentice Hall.
Teitelbaum, Philip. 1977. "Levels of Integration of the Operant." In W. Honig and J. Staddon,
eds., *Handbook of Operant Behavior*. Upper Saddle River, N.J.: Prentice Hall.
Thalberg, Irving. 1985. "Questions About Motivational Strength." In E. LePore and B.
McLaughlin, eds., *Actions and Events*. Oxford: Blackwell.
———. 1984. "Do Our Intentions Cause Our Intentional Actions?" *American Philosophical
Quarterly* 21: 249–60.
———. 1977. *Perception, Emotion, and Action*. New Haven, Conn.: Yale University Press.
Thomson, Judith. 1977. *Acts and Other Events*. Ithaca, N.Y.: Cornell University Press.
Toates, Frederick. 1986. *Motivational Systems*. Cambridge: Cambridge University Press.
Trope, Yaacov, B. Gervey, and N. Liberman. 1997. "Wishful Thinking from a Pragmatic
Hypothesis-Testing Perspective." In M. Myslobodsky, ed., *The Mythomanias: The Nature
of Deception and Self-Deception*. Mahwah, N.J.: Lawrence Erlbaum.
Trope, Yaacov, and A. Liberman. 1996. "Social Hypothesis Testing: Cognitive and Motiva-
tional Mechanisms." In E. T. Higgins and A. Kruglanski, eds., *Social Psychology: Hand-
book of Basic Principles*. New York: Guilford.
van Inwagen, Peter. 1983. *An Essay on Free Will*. Oxford: Clarendon.
Velleman, J. David. 2000. *The Possibility of Practical Reason*. Oxford: Oxford University
Press.
———. 1992. "What Happens When Someone Acts?" *Mind* 101: 461–81.
Vermazen, Bruce. 1985. "Negative Acts." In B. Vermazen and M. Hintikka, eds., *Essays on
Davidson*. Oxford: Clarendon.
Vollmer, Fred. 1993. "Intentional Action and Unconscious Reasons." *Journal for the Theory of
Social Behavior* 23: 315–26.
Wallace, R. Jay. 1999. "Three Conceptions of Rational Agency." *Ethical Theory and Moral
Practice* 2: 217–42.
———. 1990. "How to Argue About Practical Reason?" *Mind* 99: 355–85.
Wiggins, David. 1991. "Moral Cognitivism, Moral Relativism and Motivating Moral Beliefs."
Proceedings of the Aristotelian Society 91: 61–85.
Williams, Bernard. 1993. *Shame and Necessity*. Berkeley: University of California Press.
———. 1979. "Internal and External Reasons." In R. Harrison, ed., *Rational Action: Studies in
Philosophy and Social Science*. Cambridge: Cambridge University Press.

———. 1973. *Problems of the Self*. Cambridge: Cambridge University Press.

Wilson, George. 1997. "Reasons as Causes *for* Action." In G. Holmström-Hintikka and R. Tuomela, eds., *Contemporary Action Theory*. Dordrecht: Kluwer.

———. 1989. *The Intentionality of Human Action*. Stanford, Calif.: Stanford University Press.

Wittgenstein, Ludwig. 1953. *Philosophical Investigations*. G. Anscombe, trans. New York: Macmillan.

Woods, Michael. 1972. "Reasons for Action and Desires." *Proceedings of the Aristotelian Society* 46: 189–201.

Wooldridge, Dean. 1963. *The Machinery of the Brain*. New York: McGraw-Hill.

Woollacott, Marjorie, and J. Jensen. 1996. "Posture and Locomotion." In H. Heuer and S. Keele, eds., *Handbook of Perception and Action*, vol. 2. London: Academic Press.

Index